New Deal Art
in Alabama

New Deal Art in Alabama

The Murals, Sculptures and Other Works, and Their Creators

Anita Price Davis *and*
Jimmy S. Emerson

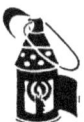

McFarland & Company, Inc., Publishers
Jefferson, North Carolina

LIBRARY OF CONGRESS CATALOGUING-IN-PUBLICATION DATA

Davis, Anita Price.
 New Deal art in Alabama : the murals, sculptures and other works, and their creators / Anita Price Davis and Jimmy S. Emerson.
  p. cm.
 Includes bibliographical references and index.

 ISBN 978-0-7864-9829-1 (softcover : acid free paper) ∞
 ISBN 978-1-4766-2114-2 (ebook)

 1. Art, American—Alabama—20th century. 2. New Deal art—Alabama. 3. Federal Art Project. I. Emerson, Jimmy S., 1976– II. Title.

 N6530.A2D38 2015
 709.761'0904—dc23   2015023120

BRITISH LIBRARY CATALOGUING DATA ARE AVAILABLE

Front cover: *top* detail of Constance Ortmayer bas-relief sculpture *Alabama Agriculture* is installed over the postmaster's door in Scottsboro; *bottom* Conrad Alfred Albrizio's *Shipment of First Iron Produced in Russellville* in the Russellville Post Office; illustration of a camelia, Alabama's state flower © 2015 iStock/Thinkstock

Printed in the United States of America

McFarland & Company, Inc., Publishers
 Box 611, Jefferson, North Carolina 28640
 www.mcfarlandpub.com

To those of you who remember the New Deal era,
may this volume revive only good memories.

To those of you who have learned of the era
vicariously, may *New Deal Art in Alabama*
further enhance your knowledge of and
appreciation of that important time.

To those of you who are exploring the 1920s,
the 1930s and early 1940s for the first time, may
this work bring you a new appreciation for the
period, the state, the artists, and the art.

May all of us work to preserve and
publicize the New Deal art that remains.

Table of Contents

Preface

This volume, *New Deal Art in Alabama*, has many reasons to be. It encourages readers to consider the features of the 24 Alabama cities and towns that the federal agencies selected for the location of public art during the 1930s and 1940s. Readers can examine the photographs of and consider the details of the public buildings that the governmental agencies constructed to house New Deal art and/or the current locations of the art. Many of the images are new and were taken by Jimmy S. Emerson. Readers can also review details of the images of the New Deal artwork placed in the public buildings of Alabama, study biographical sketches of the artists who prepared the 24 New Deal artworks for the state of Alabama, analyze the information related to New Deal art in Alabama, develop an appreciation of the importance of New Deal art, and promote the conservation and restoration of those artworks and facilities developed during the Great Depression.

The authors present this book in order to preserve this part of Alabama's history, educate the public, and encourage the appreciation and conservation of the images and structures that are a part of our heritage. The volume assembles all the pertinent information about New Deal art in Alabama in one place and includes images of artwork (even some now missing or relocated), pictures of federal buildings that house or once housed the federal art, and biographies and photographs of these federal artists, who are all now deceased.

Introduction

The Beginning of the Great Depression

For much of the nation, the 1920s had come to symbolize the New Woman, the Jazz Age, and unprecedented economic expansion. The general public did not expect an economic depression. By the closing months of the Twenties there were a few signals of the coming economic downturn that would eventually affect many Americans.

Despite the revelry of the Roaring Twenties for many Americans, some laborers had long been miring in debt and fighting bank foreclosures on their land and assets. Many Alabamians, in particular, had long been experiencing hard times and were acutely aware of the maldistribution of wealth that McElvaine attributes to being the leading cause of the Great Depression. Alabamians were aware of some of the problems long before the rest of the nation acknowledged the troubles.[1]

The morning of Thursday, October 24, 1929, brought immediate panic to most of the nation. Traders exchanged more than 12 million shares in a single day. The crash of the stock market followed on Tuesday, October 29, 1929; Black Tuesday was a sixteen-million-share day. The nation's losses quickly reached more than $30 billion.[2]

At the time, however, the federal government of the United States was hesitant to offer financial assistance to America's citizens. President Herbert Hoover, in particular, opposed direct federal relief funds—*the dole*—for Americans.

A Quaker, President Hoover believed the care of the less fortunate was the responsibility of churches, families, friends, and the local communities. He urged voluntary charity, local aid, and state relief; he committed the care of the less fortunate to socially responsible individuals. The President's Organization on Unemployment Relief (POUR) and the Committee on the Mobilization of Relief Resources placed in the *Farm Journal* of December of 1931 an ad urging individuals to "lend a hand." Some Americans, however, continued to beg the issue.[3]

Two dramatic occurrences served to amplify the arrival of hard times.

The Bonus Army. The first of these significant events was a Washington assembly of eleven thousand people: the Bonus Expeditionary Force. The purpose of this congregation in the summer of 1932 was to request from Congress additional government payments for veterans. Some of these ex-servicemen brought their families and camped in vacant buildings for shelter; others set up shacks outside of Washington.[4]

Observers called these cardboard-and-scrap villages *Hoovervilles*. The Washington Hoovervilles were like those that countless homeless people were setting up in vacant lots across the country; for many, it was a bleak period in American history.[5]

Congress refused to pay additional funds to the Bonus Army. President Hoover attempted to settle the issue by finally offering $100,000 to help the 11,000 veterans make the return trip to their homes. Six thousand troops accepted the travel money, but the remaining 5,000 veterans refused to leave Washington. To force the eviction of the remaining Bonus Army members, President Hoover called up the troops.[6]

Tanks, infantry and cavalry troops, led by General Douglas MacArthur and Major Dwight Eisenhower, marched to Pennsylvania Avenue on July 28, 1932. Their orders were to evict the Bonus Army from the buildings and encampments and to usher them out of the city.

Disaster resulted. One baby succumbed to the tear gas. Two veterans died. Two people suffered serious wounds. A storm of protest followed. Many Americans seemed to be losing faith rapidly in Washington. When President Hoover and General MacArthur attempted to defend their actions, many citizens became even more concerned.[7]

The collapse of the bank system. A second dramatic occurrence—on the morning of March 4, 1933—proclaimed loudly that hard times had arrived. Herbert Hoover and the nation awoke to the collapse of the banking system. Hoover remarked, "We are at the end of our string."[8] Caught with no money in their pockets and with foreclosures imminent, many Americans had to agree.

Further calamities of the Thirties. The decade of the Thirties brought further calamities. Stocks dropped. Banks closed. Industries failed. Lenders foreclosed. Jobs decreased. Workloads increased, but salaries declined. Farmers borrowed, accumulated debts, went without, took out mortgages, and sold land and family possessions. Even the well-to-do knew of pain and suffering about them. Many citizens felt fear.

Nature itself seemed to turn on the people. Droughts and floods ravaged the land. Disease and malnutrition escalated. Despair prevailed. Hard times had come.

By 1932 one-fourth of all Americans were without work.[9] In Franklin

Delano Roosevelt's campaign for president, he promised the people a "New Deal."

Art, Artists and the Great Depression

By March 4, 1933, when Roosevelt came to office, the unemployed in this country included 10,000 out-of-work artists. Works of art, to many Americans, had become an expendable luxury as budgets tightened. With fifteen million jobless Americans, the number of unemployed artists—to some people—seemed insignificant and just a minor percentage of the total of needy people across the country.[10] Artists, therefore, became both "unemployed and unemployable."[11]

On May 9, 1933, George Biddle (1885–1973) wrote to President Franklin Delano Roosevelt about the plight of these unemployed American artists—victims of the Great Depression. Roosevelt and Biddle had been fellow classmates at Groton School in Massachusetts and at Harvard; Roosevelt read with concern Biddle's words describing the plight of artists in America.

Biddle had received his law degree but had immediately turned to art. He had worked in stone, clay, paint, wood, and block printing. Being an artist of great versatility, Biddle observed in a letter to Roosevelt how Mexican artists were producing murals through a national program of painting. These painters—including Diego Rivera—were displaying their frescoes on the walls of Mexican government buildings and expressing the social ideals of their country.

Biddle reminded the president that American artists, too, were aware of the social revolution within their country and that they would be eager to express national ideals through a permanent art form. Biddle called this proposed vital national experience the first in America's art history.[12]

On May 9, 1933 (the same day that Biddle wrote to President Roosevelt praising the Mexican artists and Diego Rivera, in particular), Nelson Rockefeller ordered the covering and expunging of the mural that Diego Rivera had painted in the new Rockefeller Center. In Rockefeller's view, the painting—like some other paintings on the walls of public buildings in the nation—carried symbols of Communism.[13]

Ten days later—May 19, 1933—Roosevelt responded to the letter from his friend Biddle. He expressed interest in Biddle's suggestion of the "expression of modern art through mural paintings." Roosevelt suggested that Biddle might talk "some day with Assistant Secretary of the Treasury [L.W.] Robert [Jr.], who is in charge of the Public Buildings Work."[14] (In 1933–1934, Robert and others would serve on the staff of the Public Works Art Project, designed to assist artists and promote art.)

Secretary of the Treasury Henry Morgenthau, Jr., and his wife Elinor expressed interest in Biddle's proposal to the Treasury. Along with Eleanor Roosevelt and others they began to explore the proposal.[15] Elinor Morgenthau and Eleanor Roosevelt, in particular, would work closely together on many projects in the days to come.

From these beginnings, the Public Works of Art Project (PWAP) developed; through its program 300 artists found employment. Furthermore, Biddle recognized the beginning of an art revolution within the nation. Art was beginning to move to the core of national life.[16]

President Roosevelt signed the Federal Emergency Relief Act (FERA) on May 12, 1933, and appointed Harry Lloyd Hopkins to direct the administration of its work; Ellen Sullivan Woodward joined FERA in 1933 also. Hopkins took over the massive federal relief efforts, which culminated in the creation of the WPA in 1935. (Later, during World War II, Hopkins would serve as chair of the Combined Munitions Assignment Board.)

FERA provided matching funds and grants to relief agencies in individual states. Its final effect, however, was generally direct relief: the dole. Hopkins viewed these handouts as degrading and self-defeating. He advocated work-relief to dignify the recipients, to preserve whatever skills they might possess, and to prime the economy.[17]

Heretofore, artists had not necessarily been a part of mainstream American society. Painters and sculptors often worked apart from other people. Easel painting was the typical type of art in the nation up until this time. Hopkins, however, was aware of the needs of the artists and was quick to note "artists had to eat, too."

Biddle recognized in the nation what he considered to be a universal conviction: life could be more beautiful, but it was not. He advocated art for the public to improve their lives. Murals, sculptures, paintings, and reliefs in public buildings could enhance the emotional range of the viewers.

The government in the 1930s began accepting increased responsibility for indigent plumbers, bricklayers, agricultural workers, the elderly, and other people who were "up against it." For the first time in history, the federal government in the United States recognized that art in society was a necessity—not a luxury—and that art and the government were particularly important during times of depression.

Biddle noted a division among the artists: those whose focus was primarily the expression of social ideas and those whose focus was primarily still life, including—in Biddle's view—models, flowers, nudes, etc. Biddle emphasized that mural paintings could be both social and collective.

L.W. Robert, Jr., Assistant Secretary of the Treasury, was in charge of the public buildings work. He issued on November 29, 1933, a statement that had significance for the nation:

... it is obvious such provisions [for encouraging the fine arts] should be enlarged in times of depression. The work of artists and craftsmen greatly aids everyone by preserving and increasing our capacity for enjoyment and is particularly valuable in times of stress. Hitherto this field has not been adequately developed. As the Treasury is the Department concerned with Federal buildings, a movement to aid the fine arts and artists and craftsmen is its particular concern.

We consider it a great pleasure and privilege to encourage this movement and hope that it will promote the appreciation of art in our country. It will be the purpose of the committee to find merit wherever it exists and the search will not be dominated by any particular school or group. We plan to find opportunities for this work in the embellishment of Federal buildings, with murals, sculpture and craftsmanship, in similar work on state and municipal buildings financed by the Federal Government, and in other directions where the opportunity develops. We hope that private enterprise will follow our lead and realize that the encouragement of art is a vital factor in our civilization and culture and should be continuously supported in depressed as well as in boom periods.[18]

Biddle's 1934 article in *Scribner's Magazine* calls Robert's remark and his attitude "the beginning of an epoch." The accomplishment of involving the government in art and in the lives of artists was a result of correspondence among such people as President and Mrs. Eleanor Roosevelt; Secretary of the Treasury Morgenthau; Assistant Secretary of the Treasury Robert; FERA Commissioner Hopkins; Secretary of Agriculture Rexford Tugwell; and others.[19]

In the years to come, the government would spend $83,500,000 on art projects.[20] Some of these projects would directly affect the state of Alabama and would provide art for the public in its public buildings.

Twenty-four towns in Alabama would benefit directly from the expenditures that the federal government allocated for public art. These projects encompassed the entire state of Alabama.

Alexander City

Franc Dorothy Epping, an artist specializing in sculpture, prepared three federally commissioned, terracotta bas-reliefs. Epping's *Tobacco, Wheat,* and *Cotton* went on display in 1941 in the Alexander City Post Office in Alexander City, Alabama.

Epping (June 27, 1910–February 20, 1983) also executed the terracotta artworks for the post office in Oakmont, Pennsylvania (1942). Federal commissions enabled her to prepare these sculptures.[1]

Federal Art Programs. The funds for many New Deal artworks came originally from a federal program that started in 1934 and was titled the Treasury Section of Painting and Sculpture. In 1938 some of the details of the federal program changed. The name of the revised program became the Treasury Section of Fine Arts to distinguish this new program from the earlier Treasury Section of Painting and Sculpture.

More change was yet to come. When the federal government funded the construction of public buildings, a designated portion of the allocated money was often for artwork. In 1940, therefore, the Section of Fine Arts of the Public Buildings Administration of the Federal Works Agency became responsible for much of the artwork in public buildings.[2]

It was this section that awarded Franc Epping her commissions. Her art reliefs for both Oakmont, Pennsylvania, and Alexander City, Alabama, are still on display in public buildings. Her terracotta sculptures for Oakmont remain in the Oakmont Post Office, a public building funded through the federal government and the site of their original display.

Franc Eppings's Alexander City terracotta bas-reliefs, however, are no longer in the original post office building nor in the Alexander City Hall, which stored them during their refurbishment. Instead, the reliefs are on display in a glass case in the Adelia Russell Public Library in Alexander City.

The Alexander City area is in east central Alabama and has enticed visitors and residents for years. The city is 70 miles southeast of Birmingham (the largest city in the state) and 50 miles northeast of Montgomery (the state capital).[3] The name of the state—Alabama—had probably come from a Choc-taw word that means "thicket clearers."[4]

The incorporation of Alexander City dates from 1872. The town's name was originally Youngsville in honor of its founder, James Young. Young had bought 372 acres of land in the area and had set up a trading post.

In the following year, however, the name changed when the Savannah and Memphis Railroad came to Youngsville. To recognize Edward Porter Alexander, the president of the railroad and a Confederate hero during the Battle of Gettysburg, Youngsville became Alexander City in 1873.[5]

An important feature of Alexander City is Lake Martin, with its 44,000 acres of water and its 750 miles of shoreline. Lake Martin has attracted visitors and residents to the area for recreation, business, and industry for more than seventy-five years. The Martin Dam, completed in 1926, created the reservoir Lake Martin, the largest man-made lake in the world at the time. Lake Martin is important in the production of power for the area. Alexander City in Talla-poosa County carries the nickname "The Gateway to Lake Martin."[6]

"Alex City," as the residents endearingly call it, faced much hardship on June 13, 1902, and shortly thereafter. At 1 p.m. a fire erupted in the Alexander City Machine Shop. In the absence of a water system to fight the fire, the conflagration quickly spread. The inferno destroyed much of the town. Among other facilities, the town lost its telegraph office, its post office, and three banks. Yet the majority of the people did not move; they rebuilt their lives in Alexander City.[7]

The city employs a mayor-council system of government. The six dis-tricts elect the mayor in at-large election. There are six city council members; each of the six districts elects its own representative.

Mayor Charles R. Shaw, Sr., the current mayor of Alexander City (2014), uses his website *Welcome Home* to invite new industries, new businesses, vis-itors, and new residents to town. He emphasizes that U.S. Highway 280 pro-vides quick access from Alexander City to Birmingham, Montgomery, and to Atlanta, Georgia. Shaw reminds readers that an airport—the T.C. Russell Field Airport—helps to make Alexander City "a progressive city with positive prospects." Its total land area is 39.0 square miles, and its total water area is 0.2 square miles. Its population in 2000 was 15,008.[8]

Terracotta reliefs for Alexander City. The sculptor Franc Epping pre-pared terracotta bas-reliefs appropriate for Alexander City. Even though Epping was from Massachusetts and not the South, she recognized that the areas around Tallapoosa County, Alabama, and Alexander City were suitable for farming. The region has a mild climate that is ideal for agriculture, espe-cially tobacco, wheat, and cotton. The short winters with an average temper-ature of 51.4°, the long summers with an average temperature of 80°, and the annual precipitation of 53.87" provide a lengthy growing season. The increase in cotton mills in the state intensified the need for cotton. Franc Epping noted these facts in selecting the topics for her works.[9]

The terracotta works of art that Epping sculpted represented three agricultural products. Epping selected tobacco, wheat, and cotton for her subjects. Although Epping was not living in Alabama at the time she prepared the reliefs, her research and her experience enabled her to complete the assignment successfully. These three reliefs originally hung in the Alexander City Post Office in 1941. The display order of the artworks was (left-to-right) *Tobacco*, *Wheat*, and *Cotton*. The photograph shows the 1941 display in the Alexander City Post Office.

The first relief on the left was *Tobacco*. This terracotta artwork hung over a bulletin board outside the postmaster's door in the Alexander City Post Office. The clay piece uses large leaves to represent the tobacco crop. Two persons—who seem to be harvesting the crop—hold the tobacco leaves.

The second terracotta relief hung directly over the postmaster's door in the lobby. The large artwork is in two parts and represents the cutting of the wheat. The mule pulling the harvester is one piece of the work; the farmer guiding the animal is the second part of the sculpture. The two parts hung together as one display.

The third relief that originally hung on the far right on the post office wall represents the cotton crops in the Alexander City area. This terracotta figure hung directly over a second bulletin board beside the postmaster's door in the photo. A man and woman seem to be harvesting the cotton, which was important to the textile mills that started in Alexander City in 1900. The fact that the couple appears to be working together suggests that the cultivation of a cotton crop was often a family business.

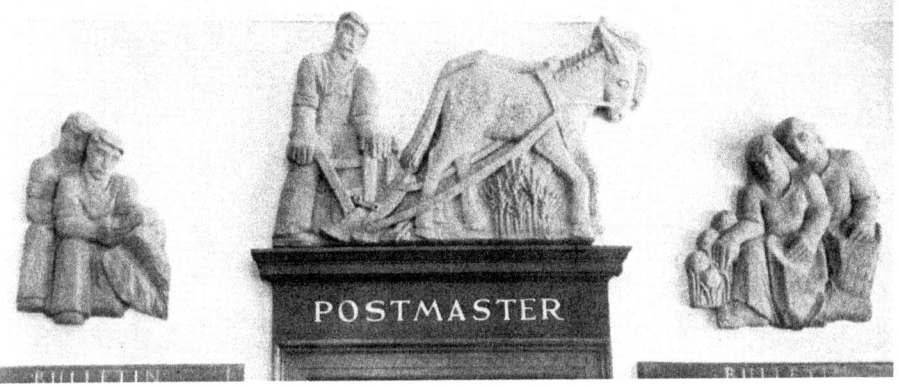

The original installation of the three reliefs prepared by Franc Epping was in the Alexander City Post Office lobby in 1941. The reliefs are now in the Adelia Russell Library (National Archives).

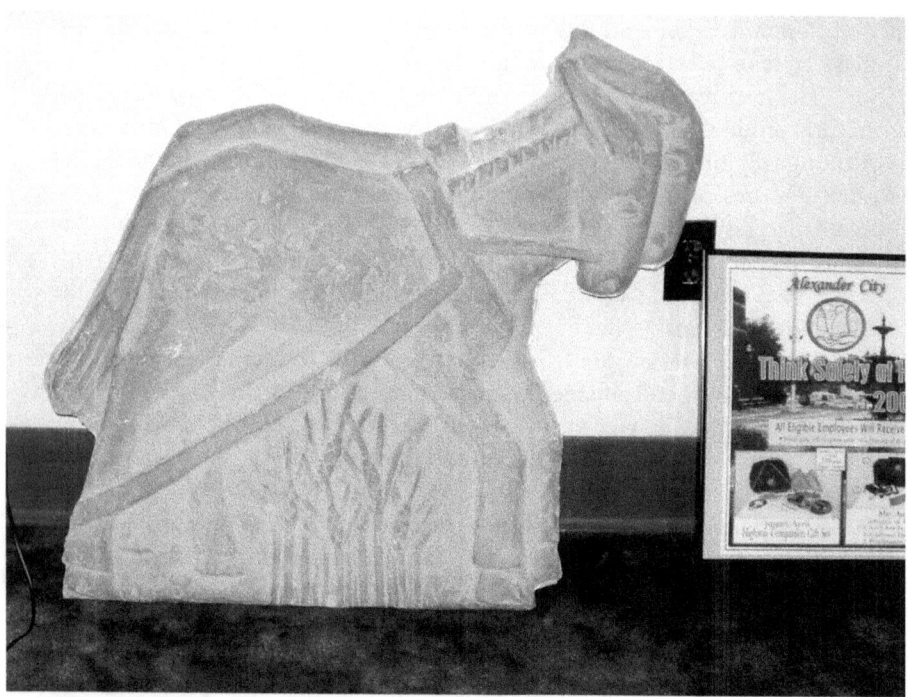

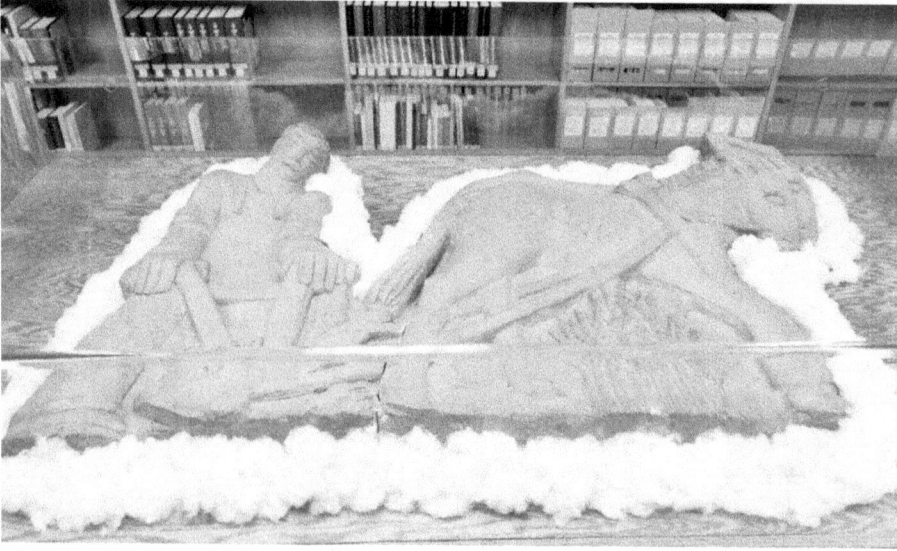

Top: This part of the terracotta section called *Wheat* shows the mule that pulled the plow. Franc Epping created this second terracotta in two pieces. *Bottom:* This image of the bas-reliefs of Franc Epping shows both the farmer and the mule in the agriculture exhibit.

Locations of Epping's terracotta reliefs in Alexander City. The three terracotta reliefs that Epping prepared for Alexander City have changed venues several times over the years. The facility originally built as the city post office is now the Charles T. Porch Center and serves as a city community center. The one-story building is in the Colonial Revival style. The brick structure has a hip roof, a basement, and a central entrance. The center took its name from Charles T. Porch (November 24, 1911–October 6, 1993), who was a resident of Tallapoosa County. Porch is buried in the City Cemetery (once called the "Laurel Park Cemetery") in Tallapoosa County.[10]

In 2006, however, the Alexander City hall took the reliefs that had hung in the Alexander City Post Office. The purpose of the relocation to the city hall was to refurbish and store the reliefs. In 2008 the reliefs found a new home and display area: the Adelia M. Russell Library in Alexander City.[11]

The Adelia M. Russell Library. Alexander City has long been committed to education. The Tuesday Study Club founded the first community library in the area near Alexander City in June 1921; the location of this first library was the local Masonic Building.

The city organized the Alexander City public library in 1942; the library occupied a room in the brick courthouse, built in 1939. As the library holdings increased, the public library expanded to a second—and later a third—room.

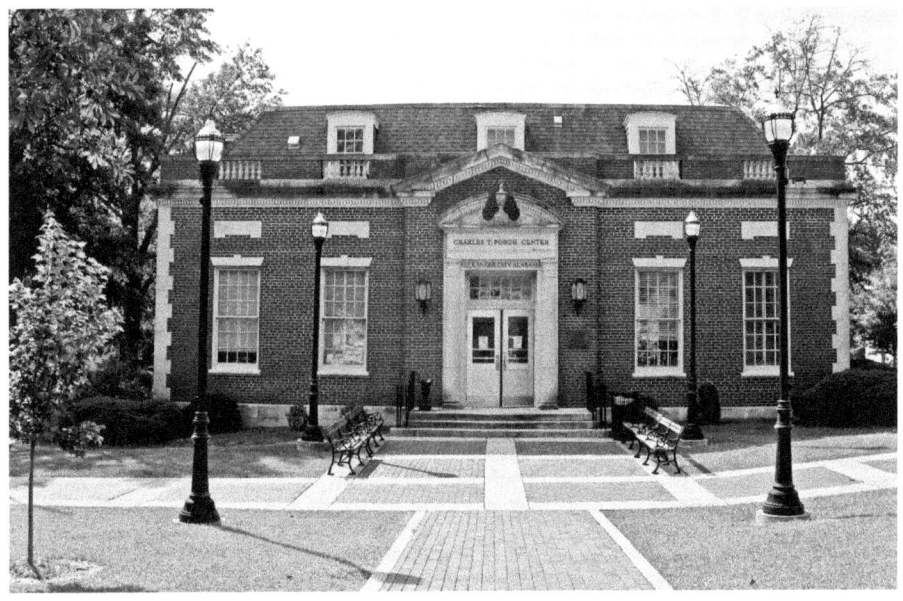

The Charles T. Porch Center housed the Alexander City Post Office and other offices. Franc Epping's reliefs hung in the lobby of the post office until 2006, when the City Hall stored the objects until their 2008 refurbishment.

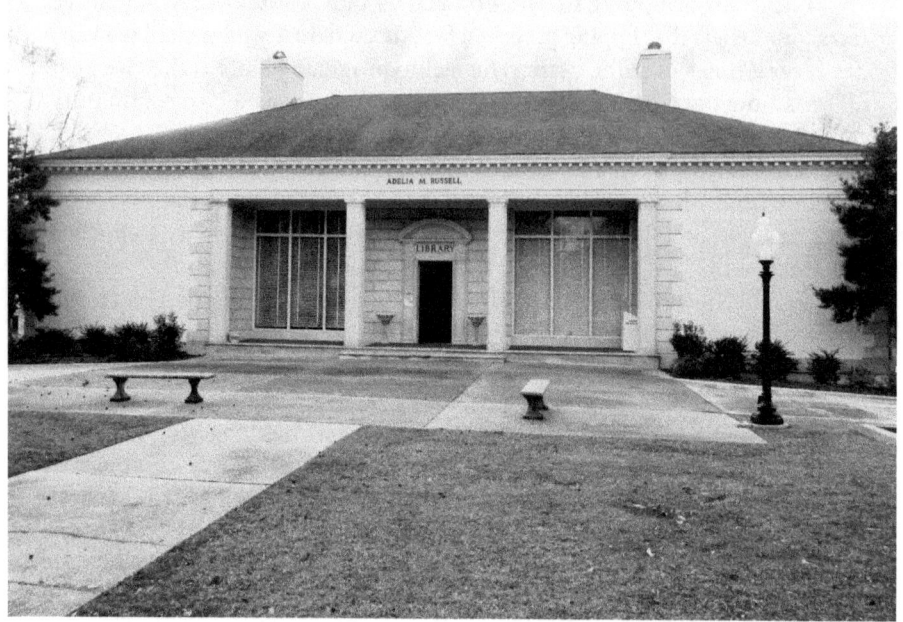

The Adelia Russell Library took Epping's reliefs for display in 2008 after their refurbishment. This photograph shows the current Adelia Russell Library that houses the federal art (courtesy Amy Huff, Adelia M. Russell Library, Alexander City, Alabama).

The citizens of the area began to contemplate building a dedicated library structure for Alexander City. Plans and fundraising began in 1959. Six years later (June 2, 1965) a three-level facility opened, named the Adelia McConnell Russell Library in honor of a benefactor to the community and the library.[12]

The brick building is one block from the main downtown business district; ample parking is available for patrons. The library holds in a display case the terracotta reliefs prepared by Franc Epping.

Originally, only one floor served as a library. By 2014 all three floors were operational and fully automated for adult patrons. Genealogy materials and reference materials currently occupy the main floor. The third floor holds the fiction and nonfiction collections. The ground floor houses all media materials and patron-use computers.

The building, which now houses Epping's artwork, provides a quiet atmosphere amenable to those studying and working within its walls. Its website encourages visitors.[13]

Franc Dorothy Epping: Her Life and Work. Franc Epping was born Christine Roselyn Mutchler on June 27, 1910, in Alhambra, California. In

1913 John C. Epping, a successful motion picture executive who had hired the child's mother as a housemaid, adopted the little girl; on her legal papers he changed the place of her birth to Providence, Rhode Island. He shuffled her around from home to home in the Catskills, in Germany, and in an Alhambra convent. She finished her secondary education in Los Angeles and was finally reunited with her original family.

Franc Dorothy Epping's elite art education was varied. Her education included the Otis Art Institute, established in 1918 in Los Angeles; the Corcoran School of the Arts, established in Washington, D.C., in 1875; and the Royal Bavarian Academy in Munich. Because she was a woman, she sometimes listened to the lectures in Germany in the hall.[14]

Epping belonged to such highly regarded organizations as the Sculptors Guild and the Federation of Modern Painters and Sculptors. The latter was a "non-political alternative to the declining American Artists Congress"; the organization promoted *avant-garde* art, which is art that departs from the existing norm.[15]

As a trained sculptor, Epping was able to create three-dimensional forms in three basic ways: assembling, carving, and modeling. Assembling—joining prefabricated parts—was not the sculpting method that Epping most often used, however. She employed carving and modeling for her usual works.

With carving, she removed unwanted material to reveal the form "imprisoned in the mass." Hard materials like stone and wood were frequently her preferred materials. Epping did prepare carvings, but not for her two federal commissions.

The other art form that Epping sometimes employed was modeling. For modeling, Epping created a form by building it up from a lump of malleable material. Epping used clay from the earth for the modeling of her displays in Oakmont, Pennsylvania, and in Alexander City, Alabama.[16]

Any work which projects from a background is a relief; a relief is different from three-dimensional works, or sculpture in the round. With the three-dimensional sculpture in the round, the artwork has form on all sides; one can view sculpture in the round from any angle. One cannot view the artwork in Alexander City from any angle, however; the back of the artwork is unfinished. Epping's works both in Pennsylvania and in Alexander City illustrate the use of relief.

There are two main types of reliefs. In high relief, the figures project "at least half of their natural circumference from the background."[17] By contrast, in low relief (*basso-relievo, bas-relief*) the figures project only slightly from the background; no part of the artwork is detached from the background. Crushed relief is the lowest degree of relief. The figures barely exceed the background. Another type of low relief is hollow relief. With hollow relief the carving lies within a hollowed-out area below the surface. Epping's work in Alexander City is bas-relief. Her medium was terracotta (sometimes called *terra cotta* or *terra-cotta*).[18]

The word *terracotta* means "cooked earth." The resulting terracotta work is often brownish red or even buff in color. Typically the clay is unglazed. Terracotta has been in use since prehistoric times; the technique reached its peak in ancient Greece. The Etruscans in Renaissance Italy employed terracotta for large-scale art.[19]

Epping's artwork for Alexander City uses natural clay. She did not use a plastic or manufactured clay. She did not paint or glaze the clay for her terracotta bas-relief for Alexander City. Rather her clay was "native earth consisting mainly of decomposed feldspathic rock containing kaolin and other hydrous aluminous minerals." She left the clay in its natural, reddish color.[20]

Franc Dorothy Epping: Her Career. Epping taught art at Berea College in Berea, Kentucky. Berea was somewhat unusual in that it offered a work-study program. Students did not pay tuition; instead, they worked at least ten hours a week. This work experience helped students pay for their expenses and enabled those with limited economic resources to pursue an education. The work experience also taught enrollees that both mental work and menial labor have worth.[21]

Berea College had opened in 1869 as a democratic, racially integrated community for women and men. This was a time when integration was not generally accepted. In 1904 the policies of Berea College changed when the Kentucky Legislature passed the Day Law, which prohibited integration in education.

Berea provided funds to establish the Lincoln Institute for the education of African-American students. Berea contributed to Knoxville College, Hampton Institute, Tuskegee, and Wilberforce. With the amendment in 1950 of the Day Law, colleges could integrate. Berea again became the first college in Kentucky to integrate its programs.

Berea served the Appalachian area primarily through its services and education. Its mission statement through the years has reflected the value of work, service, and study.[22] Art was a part of the Berea curriculum. Epping taught in the art program at Berea.

Epping also conducted classes also at the Lenox School in Massachusetts.[23]

Franc Dorothy Epping's Achievements. Epping's awards for and exhibits of her artworks were numerous. Epping received awards from the Connecticut Academy of Fine Arts (1954) and the Silvermine Guild (1955).[24]

The results of her displays included—among others—a prize from the Munich Academy of Fine Arts in 1933 and a prize from the Los Angeles Museum of History, Science, and the Arts in 1929. The Smithsonian Institution (1937), Berea College, Washington College, the High Museum of Art in

Atlanta, the Metropolitan Museum of Art, and the Riverside Museum (1941) were some of the highly recognized institutions that exhibited artworks of Franc Epping. The federal government also noted her talent and commissioned her for artwork in Alexander City, Alabama, and in Oakmont, Pennsylvania. Epping died on February 20, 1983, in Lenox, Massachusetts, but her art still remains.[25]

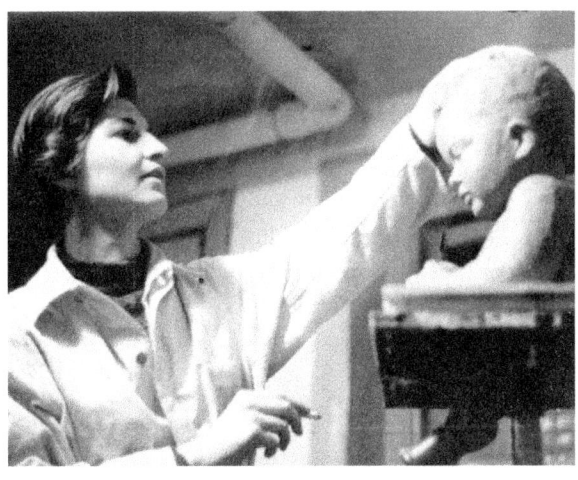

This photograph of Franc Dorothy Epping and one of her sculptures was provided by her nephew Michael Shermer, editor of *Skeptic* magazine (courtesy Michael Shermer, Skeptic.com).

Epping's bas-relief for the post office in Oakmont, Pennsylvania, was possible through a commission from the Treasury Department's Section of Fine Arts. Epping prepared the bas-relief titled *Alleghany River* in 1942.

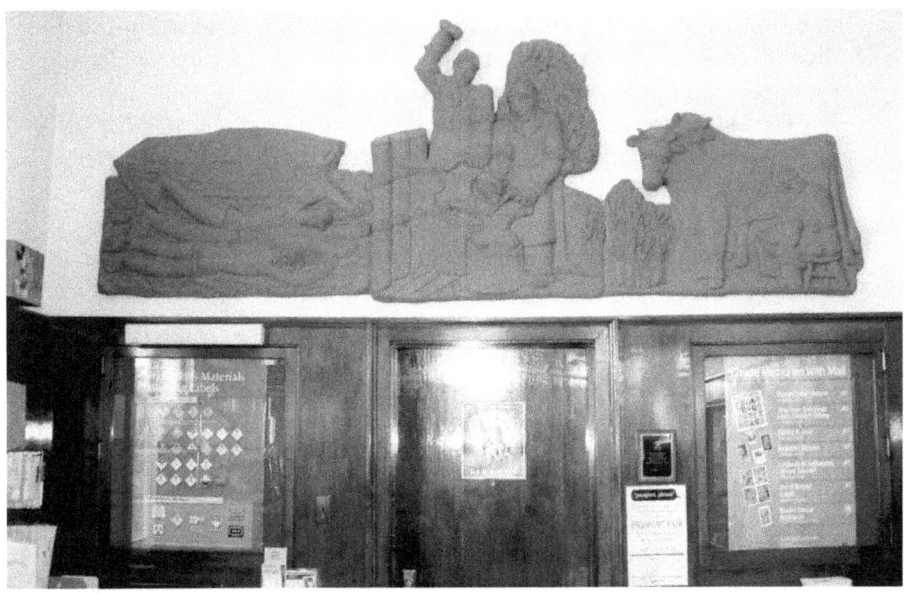

Epping prepared a terracotta relief for Oakmont, Pennsylvania. She titled the artwork *Allegheny River*.

Often mistaken for WPA art, post office murals were actually executed by artists working for the Section of Fine Arts. Commonly known as "the Section," it was established in 1934 and administered by the Procurement Division of the Treasury Department. Headed by Edward Bruce, a former lawyer, businessman, and artist, the Section's main function was to select art of high quality to decorate public buildings if the funding was available. By providing decoration in public buildings, the art was made accessible to all people.[26]

Eppings's work is, therefore, still accessible to the people who visit the Oakmont, Pennsylvania, post office and the Adelia M. Russell Library in Alexander City, Alabama.

Atmore

Anne Wilson Goldthwaite's federally commissioned mural *The Letter Box* (1938) is on display in the Atmore, Alabama, Post Office (constructed in 1935).

Anne Wilson Goldthwaite (June 28, 1869–January 29, 1944) was the only woman to receive two federal commissions for artwork in the state of Alabama. Goldthwaite's first federally commissioned artwork in Alabama was her oil-on-canvas mural *The Road to Tuskegee* (1937), installed in the post office in Tuskegee, Alabama. The good reviews of *The Road to Tuskegee* encouraged Goldthwaite to continue her work.

The Letter Box (1938). A year after the installation of *The Road to Tuskegee*, Goldthwaite completed a second federal commission: *The Letter Box* (1938). This oil-on-canvas mural still occupies a prominent position over the postmaster's door inside the Atmore Post Office in Atmore, Alabama.

Goldthwaite generally preferred painting rural Southern scenes rather than depicting urban settings. Having been born in Montgomery, Alabama, she had many opportunities to associate with and paint both African Americans and Caucasians; these experiences with others and with the rural South are evident in much of her work. Her depiction of human figures and scenes are as they appear in nature; she did not often use stylization or distortion in her works.[1] Dunford remarks that Goldthwaite's works "convey the sense of heat and the characteristics of life in the south."[2]

When the Treasury Section of Fine Arts suggested that artists who were applying for federal commissions for Alabama art in 1938 include postal history in their work, Goldthwaite was able to do so from her own experiences.[3] Her oil-on-canvas painting features six young children—both African American and Caucasian—in a rural setting; their eager faces as they open the

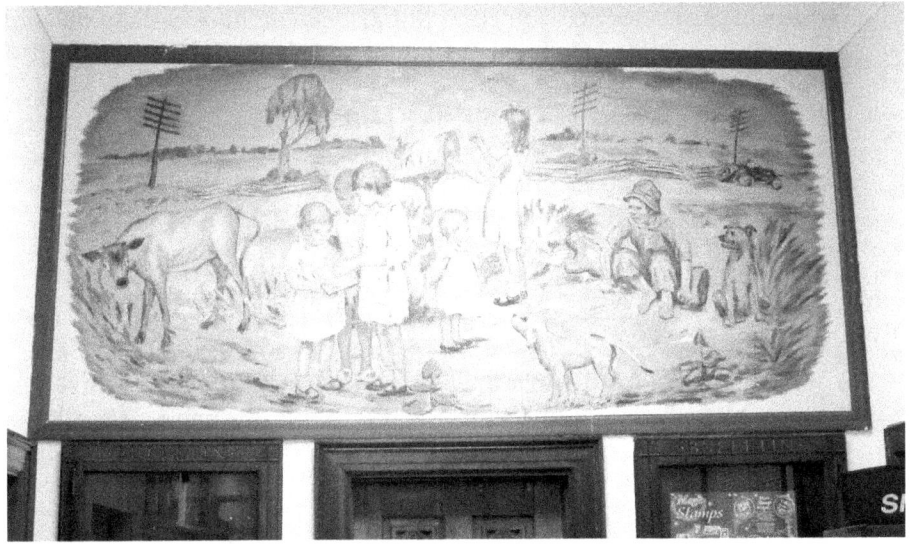

The 1938 oil-on-canvas mural *The Letter* by Anne Wilson Goldthwaite includes two of Goldthwaite's favorite subjects for painting: African-Americans and the South. She also included references to postal history and communication, as suggested by the announcement of the Arlington, New Jersey, Post Office competition of 1936.

newly delivered mail indicate the importance of the postal system and of the mail in their lives, in their communication, and in Southern history. The mural conveys the warmth of the summer day in rural Alabama and illustrates a daily routine: checking the mailbox.

It was not unusual for African-American and Caucasian children in the rural South to associate with each other; this association was not as common, however, in the urban areas of the South. In the rural areas, African American and Caucasian children often worked side-by-side in the fields and played with each other after the workday was over; in the sparsely settled rural areas, children did not usually have a lot of other children with whom they could play. The two racial groups at the time did not, however, attend school together, worship together, or eat together in a public restaurant.

In the urban areas, such social contacts were less frequent. The fact that Anne Wilson Goldthwaite's depiction of this socialization in the rural area is an example of Social Realism, or depicting social relations as they existed at the time in and around Atmore, Alabama.

Atmore, Alabama. Atmore—the location of *The Letter Box* (1938)—is in the southwestern part of Alabama and is the largest city in Escambia County. Escambia County in Alabama and Escambia County in Florida border each other across their state lines. They are two of only 22 counties or parishes in the United States to claim this distinction. At places, the city of Atmore is less than a mile from the Florida state line. The Alabama State Prison (Holman) is nine miles outside of Atmore.[4]

The first recorded geographic use of the name *Atmore* came from Charles Pawson Atmore, who worked with the railroads—especially in the area of Escambia County, Alabama. C.P. Atmore (1834–1900) worked with both the Mobile and the Great Northern Railroad and with the Louisville and Nashville Railroad; these railroads were vital to the vicinity because of the transporting of agricultural and timber products.

C.P. Atmore served as a general passenger agent and ticket seller for the Louisville and Nashville Railroad. To recognize Atmore, the Mobile and the Great Northern Railroad named a significant stop on its line for him. In 1897 the town—like the train stop—took its name from C.P. Atmore.[5] A marker that the Alabama Tourism Department, the Atmore Area Chamber of Commerce, and the City of Atmore erected in 2010 states, "There is no record that he ever visited the little town named for him."[6]

The blogger "Jen" recorded the writing on Charles P. Atmore's marker in Cave Hill Cemetery in Louisville, Kentucky. The inscription was short and to the point: "He was a man." This dedication was from "His employes" [*sic*].[7]

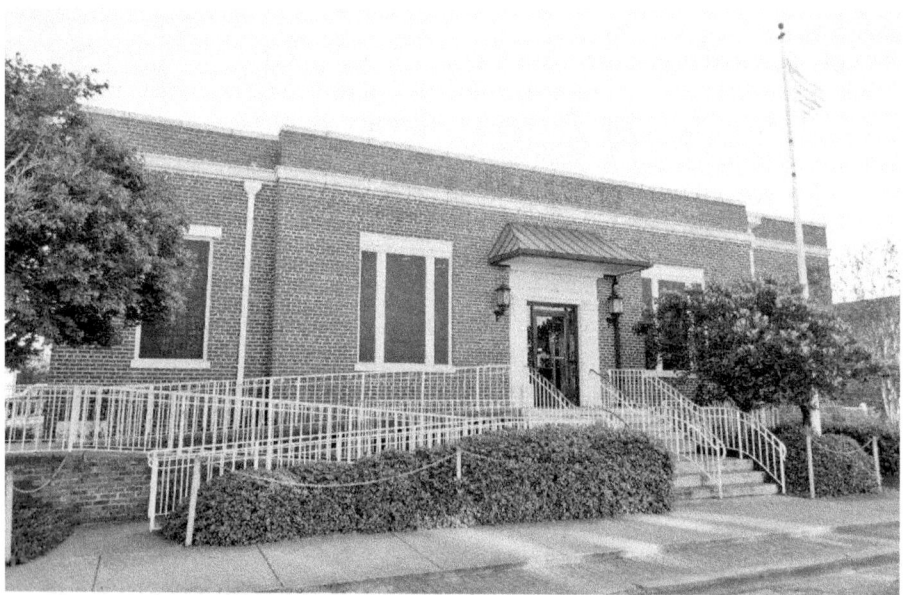

The Atmore Post Office on Main Street in Atmore, Alabama, dates from 1935. This image shows the federal building after accommodations to make the building more accessible to those with disabilities.

The Atmore Post Office. The Atmore Post Office is at 114 North Main Street in Atmore, Alabama. The post office lies almost midway between two other New Deal post offices: Bay Minette and Brewton. The cornerstone on the side of the Atmore Post Office building credits the 1935 structure to Henry Morgenthau, who was secretary of the treasury at the time; James A. Farley, who was postmaster general; and Neal A. Melick, who was supervising engineer at the time.

The name of only one architect—Louis A. Simon—is on the stone. The Treasury Department had found that using numerous private architects for its many small architectural projects was neither economical nor efficient. Using only one supervising architect was most efficient.

Architect Louis A. Simon (1867–1958) had started work with the federal government as an architect in 1896. In 1933 he began serving as the federal supervising architect in the Treasury Department. He designed federal buildings, including post offices, across the nation until 1939. In that year the office of the supervising architect moved from the Public Works Administration to the Works Progress Administration. Simon was 72 years old when he retired from his federal office.[8]

The Atmore Post Office was one of twenty-four structures in Alabama to receive art decoration through the Treasury Section of Fine Arts. One courthouse received an artwork; the other twenty-three Alabama artworks at the time went to post offices.

The Atmore Post Office is a flat-topped red brick building. No cupola, dome, or turret decorates the rooftop. On each side of the front of the post office is a recessed brick section measuring about half the size of the front of the brick post office; these sections increase the size of the structure. Each of the two recessed sections holds a white-trimmed window.

Three centered outside cement steps lead visitors to a concrete landing. Five more steps from the flat platform take the patron to the front door with its white trim and bas-relief. The front of the Atmore Post Office displays a centered front door and a window with three vertical divisions on each side of the door. Currently a metal awning protects the doorway. The symmetrical front of the Atmore Post Office provides patrons with a pleasant view.

This attractive entrance, however, was not easily accessible to those with disabilities. Because the first occupation of the Atmore Post Office came before January 26, 1993, under Title III the building did not have to meet the full construction requirements of the Americans with Disabilities Act (ADA).[9]

To enhance the safety of customers and to increase accessibility to the Atmore Post Office, however, visitors now have access to ramps with wrought-iron handrails. These white handrails are easily visible, useful, and attractive. The recently installed ramps provide both access and decoration. The ramps provide 1" of rise for every 12" of length and allow those in wheelchairs or with other physical and mobility problems to enter the front entrance of the Atmore Post Office with ease.[10]

Anne Wilson Goldthwaite. Alabama artist Anne Goldthwaite was born in Montgomery, Alabama, on June 28, 1869, to Lucy Boyd Armistead Goldthwaite and former Confederate Captain Richard Wallach Goldthwaite. Captain Goldthwaite practiced law after his military service. Anne's mother was a housewife.

Anne was the oldest of four children. When she was twelve, her father died; shortly thereafter her mother died. Loving relatives took the four children into their homes.[11]

In 1887 Anne Wilson Goldthwaite officially "came out in Southern society."[12] Anne's aunt[13] sent her to New York City to study art.[14] Anne studied from 1898 to 1904 with Charles Frederick William Mielatz (1864–1919) at the National Academy of Design in New York City. Mielatz had a reputation as a prominent etcher of archi-tectural subjects.[15] In 1915 Anne was able to claim the bronze medal for etching at the Panama-Pacific Interna-tional Exposition in San Francisco.[16]

Goldthwaite also had lessons in New York City under the Scottish artist Walter Shirlaw (1838–1909), a founder of the Society of American Artists and its first president (1874). Such edu-cational opportunities were unusual for women at the time.[17] Anne was able also to travel abroad and continue her studies.

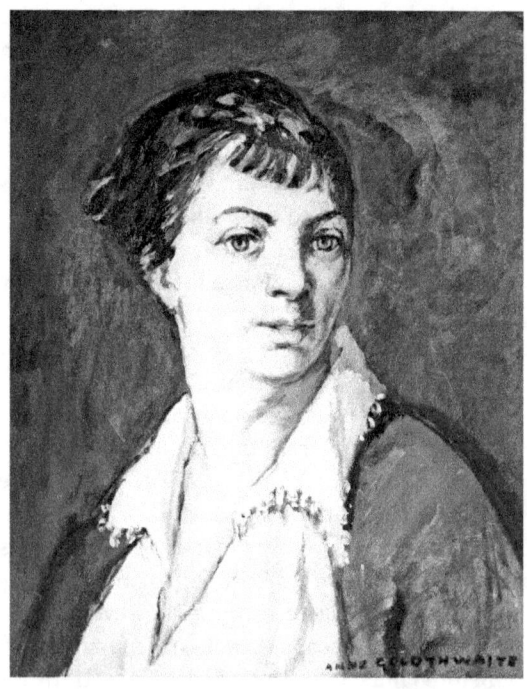

Anne Goldthwaite, American, 1869–1944, *Self-Portrait*, ca. 1920, oil on canvas, 46 × 37.8 cm. Gift of Mrs. Gustav Radeke 20.395, Museum of Art, Rhode Island School of Design Museum (photography by Erik Gould; courtesy Museum of Art, Rhode Island School of Design, Providence).

In the early twentieth cen-tury the Americans Anne Goldthwaite (1869–1944) and Jane Peterson (1876–1965) traveled to Paris to study Modernism, and interpreted the new man-ners very differently. Goldthwaite's Paris years

(1906–13) were an extraordinary opportunity for this artist open to change—she collaborated with other students in founding a new académie dedicated to modernist art. Upon her return to New York in 1913, Goldthwaite exhibited in the watershed Armory Show, which introduced Modernism to America, and shocked artists, critics, and collectors alike into heeding this sea of change. Although Goldthwaite lived and taught in New York, she spent part of each year back home in Alabama; her paintings and etchings convey the slow, easy rhythms of Southern life, as well as debilitating heat and poverty. She primarily painted figures, and frequently African American subjects such as *The Coffeur* (n.d.), a brisk, insightful watercolor of women engaged in an everyday activity.[18]

The fact that Anne was able to study abroad also indicated her talent and the privilege her adopted family provided. When Anne Wilson Goldthwaite went to Paris in 1907, she joined with other art students to study art. Anne Goldthwaite visited with Gertrude Stein while she was in France; Stein introduced her to Henri Matisse and Pablo Picasso. Goldthwaite's studies included work at the Académie Moderne in Paris.[19]

During her travels she met the dancer Isadora Duncan. Duncan's sister introduced Goldthwaite to many dancers; Goldthwaite drew and painted several of them.

Before World War I began, Goldthwaite returned to the United States and brought with her many of the prints she had created abroad. Goldthwaite set up her residence in New York and taught at the Art Students' League (1922–1944).[20] One of her students in a high school watercolorist class and also in a Saturday morning class in February of 1943 at the Art Students' League was Stanley Kubrick (1928–1999), the director, producer, screenwriter, editor, and cinematographer, perhaps best-known for the film *The Shining*.[21] "Goldthwaite taught her students to portray their subjects respectfully and she worked as an advocate for both women's and minorities' rights."[22]

Goldthwaite took commissions from her home in New York. One of her commissions was for a print of Woodrow Wilson. Goldthwaite returned to Montgomery every summer. She became well-known for her pictures featuring African-Americans.[23]

Goldthwaite's Career in Art. Anne Goldthwaite was very active as an artist. She was a member of the National Association of Women Artists, Painters, and Sculptors; the New York Watercolor Club; the California Printmakers; the Society of American Engravers; and the Society of Printmakers of New York.

Anne Goldthwaite exhibited her work with the National Association of Women Painters and Sculptors; she took their prize in 1915. Goldthwaite exhibited in the Panama-Pacific International Exposition in San Francisco and took a medal. She exhibited also at the 1939 New York World's Fair.

Goldthwaite's work is at the Library of Congress, the Metropolitan Museum of Art, the New York Public Library, the Art Institute of Chicago, the Baltimore Museum of Art, and the Cleveland Museum of Art.

The information about Anne Wilson Goldthwaite's displays, memberships, and prizes indicates her influence on others. The fact that she taught students at the New York Art Students' League for many years suggests her ability to relate to others and to convey her expertise in depicting scenes of the South, portraits, still life drawings, and landscapes.[24]

Anne Wilson Goldthwaite (June 28, 1869–January 29, 1944) died in New York City. Her burial was in the Oakwood Cemetery in Montgomery, Montgomery County, Alabama.[25]

It seems fitting that Anne Wilson Goldthwaite's body lies in the state of Alabama, where she was born. Her burial site is near that of her father, Confederate Captain Richard Wallach Goldthwaite (February 3, 1839–March 11, 1881)[26] and her mother, Lucy Boyd Armistead Goldthwaite (March 9, 1842–March 21, 1884).[27]

Anne Wilson Goldthwaite's grave marker and her parents' markers help the public remember this artist. It is her artwork, however, that remains a lasting memorial to her for years to come.

> As the United States plotted a path forward in the aftermath of the Civil War, painter and printmaker Anne Goldthwaite (1869–1944) blazed her own trail, albeit at odds with accepted roles for American women. Whether sketching home folk in the South, or chronicling Continental scenes when living abroad, she would imbue her observations with a sunny spirit reflecting the élan of her own interesting life.[28]

The last chapter of this book tells more about Anne Wilson Goldthwaite and her first federal mural, *The Road to Tuskegee*, for Tuskegee, Alabama.

Bay Minette

The 1939 federally commissioned mural *Removal of the County Seat from Daphne to Bay Minette, 1901* by Hilton Leech is on display in the current Bay Minette, Alabama, Post Office.

The artist Hilton Leech (October 13, 1906–October 18, 1969) accepted two federal commissions during the 1930s. These two assignments were for murals for two public buildings: one in Chattanooga, Tennessee (1937), and one in Bay Minette, Alabama (1939). Both artworks are still on display.[1]

The first of Leech's federal contracts was for the Joel W. Solomon Federal Building and the United States Courthouse in Chattanooga, Tennessee; this building is on the National Register of Historic Places. The lobby of the building has marble walls; an inlaid seal of justice on the terrazzo floor in the lobby reminds visitors of the purpose of the structure. Curving behind the judge's bench in the courtroom is Hilton Leech's mural *Allegory in Chattanooga* (1937).[2]

Leech painted this mural in Tennessee under the auspices of the Section of Painting and Sculpture of the Treasury Department. The 17' × 5' painting traces the history of the city through the Great Depression and the New Deal. The chosen mural was one of three studies that Hilton Leech submitted to the U.S. Treasury Department for consideration.

The mural depicts familiar scenes: a dam, tobacco fields, mountains, a cabin. Familiar objects—a train, a musket, a rifle, a cross, bags of cotton and vegetables, and a Bible—are identifiable in the painting. Although the study is of the land and its people, the work is able to "conjure a feeling of movement" to its viewers.

Marling states that the painted figures are "so fine that each could be a significant portrait." The figures include soldiers, the Cherokee, pioneers, railroad workers, a slave, a pastor, and nurses.

The $493,000 building itself was a design of Chattanooga architect R.H. Hunt. In 1938 Hunt won the award from the American Institute of Architects as one of the outstanding buildings of two decades.[3]

In 2010 one of the three studies that Leech had submitted for the Joel W. Solomon Federal Building and U.S. Courthouse surfaced for sale on eBay. An art dealer in Sarasota, Florida, had listed the remaining Leech art collection for Leech's daughter, Jayre Leech. Jayre Leech was living on a ranch in Virginia City, Montana, the town where her father is buried.

The federal court in Chattanooga and the Court Historical Society purchased the rare artwork. The unveiling of the 6' × 2' study was in April of 2010 at the Chattanooga Theatre Center.[4]

Leech contracted with the Section of Painting and Sculpture of the Treasury Department for a second commission: the Bay Minette Post Office in Alabama. Hilton completed his mural for display in 1939. The public received Hilton Leech's artwork at 25 Hand Avenue in Bay Minette favorably.

Hilton Leech's mural is still on display, but it is currently in a newer (1987) post office building at 601 McMeans Avenue in Bay Minette. The mural reminds viewers of the history of the county seat of Baldwin County.

Bay Minette, Alabama. Bay Minette is currently the county seat of Baldwin County in Alabama. The town is about 20 miles southeast of Atmore in Escambia County. (See Chapter Two on Atmore, Alabama, in *New Deal Art in Alabama*.) The two counties—Baldwin County and Escambia County—adjoin each other. Baldwin County is one of the largest and oldest counties east of the Mississippi River.

The occupation of Baldwin County and the Bay Minette area dates back 10,000 years. The Native American cultures that lived in the area were "mound builders." Some of their residential, burial, and festive mounds remain. A few of these mounds are just north of Bay Minette at Stockton. Baldwin County was the site of Spanish, French, and English settlements. It was also the site of many battles in the Indian wars, in the War of 1812, and in the Civil War.[5] Bay Minette took its name from Minette Bay, which received its name from a French surveyor named *Minet*.

At the turn of the twentieth century, the county seat of Baldwin County was the town of Daphne, which had served in this capacity since 1868. Through an election, however, the people voted to move the county seat to Bay Minette. Such a move of the county seat of Baldwin County to Bay Minette would be the third change of the Baldwin county seat: McIntosh Bluff (1803), Blakeley (1810), and Daphne (1868) had previously held the distinction. Daphne public officials, however, would not recognize the results of the election.[6]

Some of the irate citizens of Bay Minette devised a scheme after the election to move the county seat from Daphne to Bay Minette. In the dark of night, Bay Minette residents took their oxen to Daphne, which was 30 miles away to the south. The men loaded the records of Baldwin County and the contents of the jail (prisoners and furniture included) on their oxen-drawn wagons. They delivered the items—including the records—to Bay Minette. The records remain in Bay Minette to this day.[7]

The 1938 Bay Minette Post Office and the North Baldwin Utilities Facility (2014). In 1937 Louis A. Simon, the federal supervising architect in the Treasury Department, designed the Bay Minette Post Office. The cost of the structure he designed was $66,000. The building began serving the public in 1938 and continued its service as a postal facility until 1987—almost half a century.

The Bay Minette structure that Simon planned still sits on the corner of Hand Avenue and First Street. The Alabama Historical Commission has recognized the edifice as a member since 1985. The building is now (2014) in use by the North Baldwin Utilities.

The brick North Baldwin Utilities Building—once used as the Bay Minette Post Office—has a full portico that measures 37' × 7'. The application for the Alabama Register of Historic Places describes the building as having "four Doric columns and two engaged pilasters with full entablature and pediments."[8]

The building is largely unaltered from the time of its construction in the 1930s. The tympanum still has the round vent in the center. The gable roof still runs the length of the original building. Ribbon windows run along the side eaves of the gable roof to provide ventilation. A loading dock

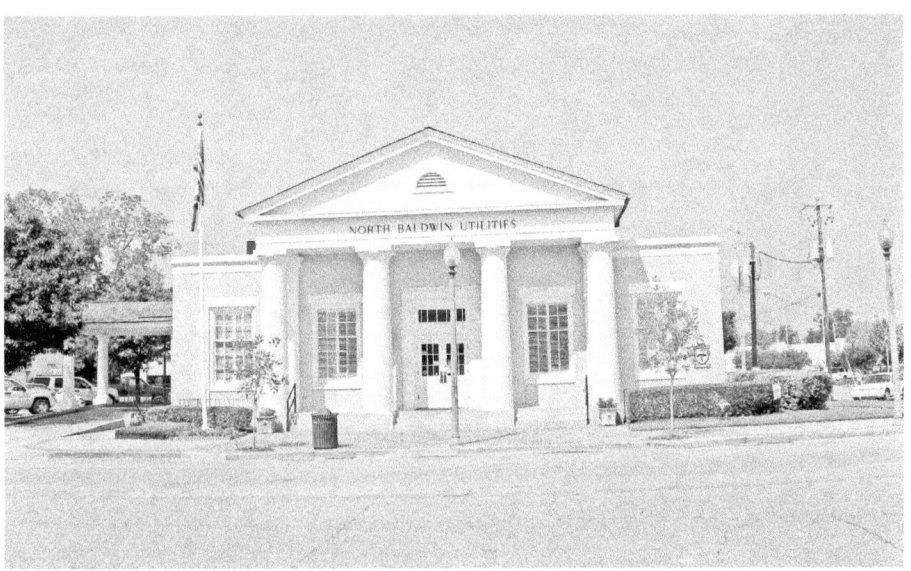

The brick Bay Minette Post Office—now North Baldwin Utilities—remains a prominent building in Baldwin County and the nation. It has been a part of the Alabama Register of Historic Places since the 1980s.

was added to the rear during the years that the building served as a post office.[9]

The Fine Arts Program (1936–1941) of the United States Treasury Department sometimes installed murals and sculptures as decoration in certain public buildings. The department set aside six hundred and sixty dollars—one hundredth of the $66,000 cost of the building—for artistic decorations for the lobby of the Bay Minette Post Office.

The Treasury Department invited the artist Hilton Leech to submit three designs for a painting for the Bay Minette Post Office lobby. Leech had designed an appropriate mural (1937) for the courthouse in Chattanooga, Tennessee; the department administrators thought he might be able to prepare a suitable work for Alabama. Leech submitted his sketches. The department selected Leech's painting *The Removal of the County Seat from Daphne to Bay Minette, 1901* for display in the recently constructed Bay Minette Post Office.

The Removal of the County Seat from Daphne to Bay Minette, 1901. The 12' × 5' mural by Hilton Leech decorated the lobby of the Bay Minette Post Office from May of 1939 until 1987. The work occupied a position over the postmaster's door. The postmaster wrote to the Section of Fine Arts that the mural had brought "a great deal of comment—pro and con."[10] Bay Minette residents speculated that the negative comments came from residents of Daphne.

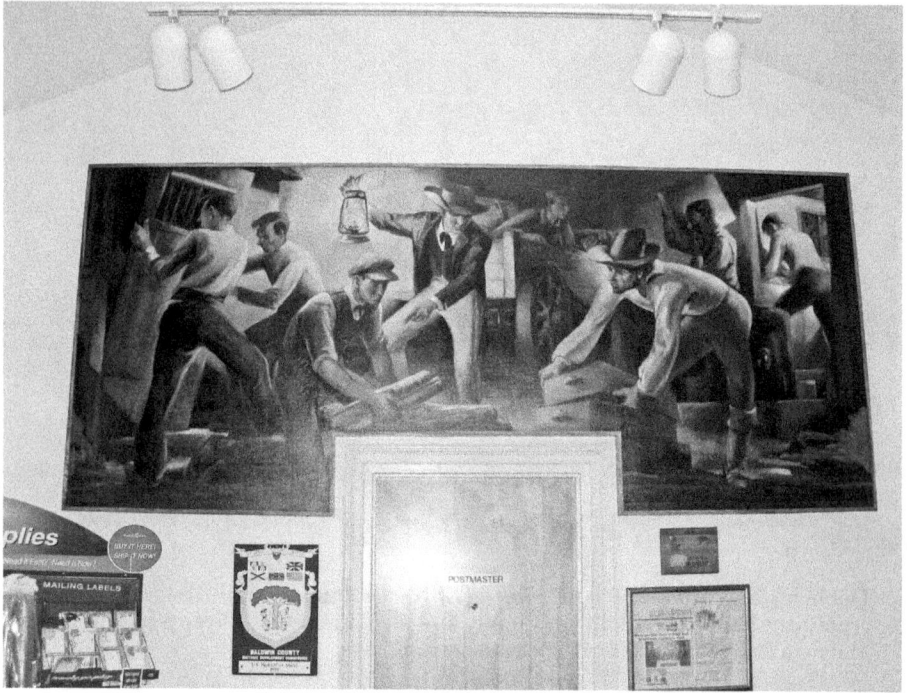

Hilton Leech painted the mural *Removal of the County Seat from Daphne to Bay Minette, 1901* for the lobby of the Bay Minette Post Office. Leech used dark colors to suggest the darkness surrounding the activity.

Leech had illustrated a local scene from Bay Minette history for his 1939 panel. The actual event had taken place on October 1, 1901, when a group of citizens from Bay Minette had gone to Daphne, under the cover of darkness, and gathered all the records of Baldwin County to take to Bay Minette. For years before 1901, Daphne had served as the county seat, but the election and the actions of Bay Minette citizens changed things.

The Removal of the Baldwin County Seat from Daphne to Bay Minette, 1901 is one of the two Alabama murals that has been moved from the original post office site to a new post office location. The other relocated mural is in Tuskegee. Before the workers moved the Hilton Leech painting in 1987 to the newer post office at McMeans Avenue, professionals cleaned and restored it.[11]

Hilton Leech. The artist Hilton Leech (1906–1969) had been born in Bridgeport, Connecticut. At an early age Leech liked to draw and paint and even won a few local art contests, but he did not decide to pursue art as a career until he was 20. With his love of art, he enrolled in the Grand Central Art School in New York. He studied watercolors, used stencils, and tried mix-

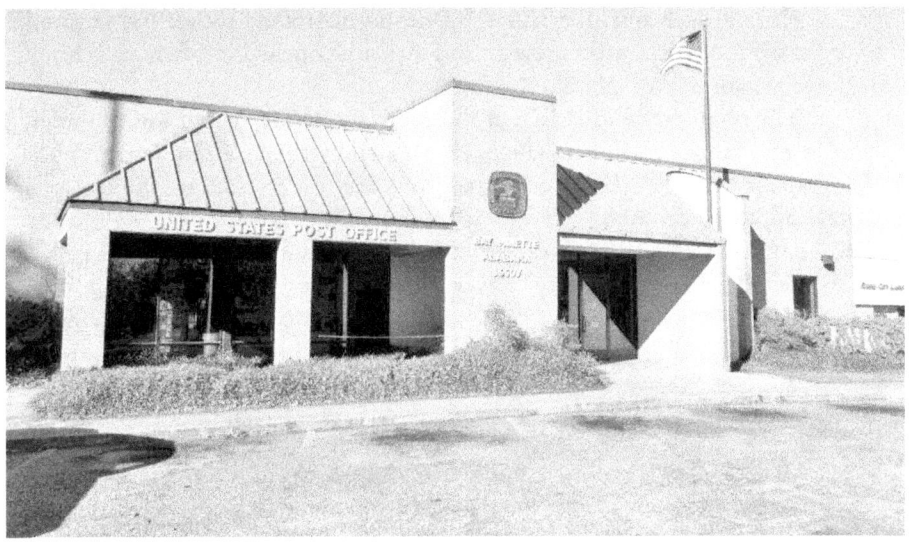

The mural *Removal of the County Seat from Daphne to Bay Minette, 1901* by Hilton Leech received a new display building in 1987. When the new Bay Minette Post Office opened in 1987, the mural that Leech painted was restored and relocated to the new facility.

ing liquid plastics with his media to give various textures. Leech also studied lithography at the Art Students' League in New York.[12]

Leech's instructors at the Grand Central Art School included the artist George Pearce Ennis (July 21, 1884–August 1936). Ennis was an American artist known best for his watercolors and for his stained glass windows. Ennis hired Leech as his assistant, and the two went to the new Ringling School of Art and Design in Sarasota, Florida, as instructors in 1931.[13]

Although Ennis returned to New York, Leech continued to teach during the winters of 1931–1936 and 1939–1945 at the Ringling School. Leech spent his summers teaching at his own school in Amagansett, Long Island.[14]

In the summer of 1941 the Amagansett summer school moved to North Carolina. The retreat was in a rustic mountain setting near Little Switzerland. The retreat carried the name *Wildacres*. The public regarded it highly. Wildacres is still in operation with a different owner.[15]

During World War II, Hilton Leech contributed to the war effort in a unique way. At the age of 35 when the war started, Leech was not of the usual age for the military draft. As an artist, however, he was able to contribute to the war effort in his own way. He created illustrated directions for aircraft construction. Leech performed these military responsibilities in Buffalo, New York. He produced these illustrated directions—as needed—during most of the war.[16]

Hilton Leech and his artist-wife Dorothy Sherman Leech (1913-) moved to Sarasota, Florida, after the war. In Florida he opened his own art school: the Amagansett Art School.

The photograph of Hilton at the Amagansett Art School was the work of Joseph Janney Steinmetz (1905–1965). Steinmetz was a commercial photographer whose work was popular throughout the world. His photographs have appeared through the years in *Saturday Evening Post*, *Life*, *Look*, *Time*, *Holiday*, *Collier's*, and *Town & Country*. Steinmetz's work is sometimes called "An American Social History." His work captures diverse scenes and people from many social classes: affluent northeasterners to middle-class Floridians. In 1941 Steinmetz moved to Sarasota from Philadelphia.[17]

The Leeches worked together to create large paintings of circus side-shows and their people; their commissions came from the Ringling Brothers, Barnum & Bailey Circus. John Ringling (1866–1936) and his brothers had originally founded the Ringling Brothers Circus, which merged with the Barnum and Bailey Circus in later years. Under the name of the American Circus Corporation, the company became the largest circus organization in the world. Ringling had established a museum and an art school in Sarasota before his death in 1936. A circus tent fire in Hartford, Connecticut, in 1944 destroyed the priceless work of the Leeches and other artists. John was not alive to mourn the loss.[18]

Here Hilton Leech is speaking to his Amagansett Art School class of adult painters on the grounds of the Ringling Mansion in Sarasota, Florida, on February 25, 1950. Joseph Janney Steinmetz, a world-renowned photographer, captured this image. Steinmetz had moved from Philadelphia to Sarasota in 1941 (State Archives of Florida, Florida Memory).

Hilton and Dorothy went to Virginia City, Montana, in 1957. The two set up an art school in their Montana basement.

Hilton enjoyed the rich colors of the western landscape. His interest in nature and science enticed him to remain in the west and to travel with Dorothy in the region. The two enjoyed fishing in Canada and exploring Central America. With experimentation, Leech was able to render watercolor paintings with texture and with both opaque and translucent areas in the painting. Leech produced watercolor paintings with rich, vibrant colors—not the traditional watercolor rendering with light colors and translucent areas.

Leech died unexpectedly in Virginia City, Montana, in 1969. He had just turned 63.[19] His daughter Jayre Leech remained on the family farm in Virginia City.[20]

Hilton Leech had begun writing the book *The Joys of Watercolor* before his death. His student Emily Holmes, a watercolorist, completed the book in 1970. Van Nostrand Reinhold Company published the book on January 1, 1973.[21]

Leech encouraged others to paint. He wrote:

> Anyone who has the desire to paint will find the ways, the means and the time to do it. How you feel when you start working—rushed, tired, bored or enthusiastic—are all factors in how you work. To be inspired or "moved by the spirit" is terrific, but don't sit around and wait for that to happen. Inspiration and the creative spirit are more apt to take hold of you after you get started. The important thing is to start.[22]

During the course of his art career, Hilton Leech took many prestigious awards. He won the Audubon Society of Artists Casein Award and both the Knickerbocker Artists Medal of Honor and its Gold Medal of Honor. As a member of the American Watercolor Society, he won its purchase prize. His work is on display in such well-known museums as the Metropolitan Museum of Art and the High Museum in Atlanta.[23]

In 1993, Sarasota assigned a new name to the Hilton Leech House and the Amagansett Art School; the two would be the Hillview Art Colony. In 1995, the National Register of Historic Places designated the colony as listing number 95000732 in the list of the nation's historic places.[24]

Leech's work, his school, his Sarasota home, and his writing remain.

Brewton

John G.F. Von Wicht's federally commissioned mural *Logging* (1939) was originally on display in the Brewton, Alabama, Post Office.

The city of Brewton is in Escambia County, as is Atmore, the subject of an earlier section. Escambia County is the only county in Alabama to have two federal murals: Brewton and Atmore. Brewton, only 28 miles east of Atmore, is on the Escambia River. This waterway was especially important in the transporting of logs during the Great Depression and in the early history of Brewton.[1]

The Brewton area was originally a part of the Creek Nation. After the Creek War of 1813–1814, General Andrew Jackson ordered the construction of Fort Crawford in the Brewton area. Thomas Mendenhall, a settler in the area, constructed a sawmill near the Conecuh River and Escambia River. When settlers began arriving in the area, the area took the name Newport.[2] The name came from the barges that traveled to Pensacola, Florida, by the way of the Murder Creek and the Burnt Corn Creek. Eventually, train tracks came to the area, and Brewton's establishment began. Brewton dates from May of 1861. The name of *Brewton* came from Edmund Troupe Brewton, who managed the railway station.

By the time of the Civil War, the town had a population of 500 and hosted several mercantile businesses. The Brewton area suffered during the Civil War. Severed train lines and damaged and destroyed local lumber mills marked the period of conflict. When peace came at last, however, the people returned to Brewton to start anew.

After the end of the war, small business began to thrive. The economy improved. When the overseas market began to demand lumber in the 1870s, timber and lumber companies in the area stepped up to meet the need. Their main way of transporting the timber and lumber products for shipment abroad was the Conecuh-Escambia waterway and delta; this system flows all the way down to the Gulf of Mexico. It seems appropriate that *Logging* was the topic for the Brewton Post Office; the mural showed the water, the logs on the waterway and delta, and the men with hooks controlling the path of the logs.[3]

Brewton's economy remains tied to forest products. Its major town newspaper remains the *Brewton Standard*, which dates from 1906. The Brewton Historic Commercial District is listed on the National Register of Historic Places. Brewton, Alabama, still serves as the county seat of Escambia County, Alabama. The population of Brewton at the time of the 2000 Census was 5,498.

Although Pollard was originally the county seat of Escambia County, Brewton became the new county seat in 1883. In 1886, fire devastated much of Brewton, but the residents soon rebuilt—as they did after several later fires. Brewton did not become a town officially until February 13, 1885. It had, however, hosted many people for decades. A mayor and a five-member city council today comprise the city government of Brewton.[4]

In his books *The 100 Best Small Towns in America*, Norman Crampton has twice recognized Brewton and East Brewton, Alabama. The two towns are just north of the Florida panhandle in the extreme south central part of Alabama. The beaches of the Gulf of Mexico are just an hour away to the south; the state capital—Montgomery—is about two hours away to the north. Brewton is about an hour and a half away from Mobile—one of the most historic cities in the South. The Chamber of Commerce is quick to note that Brewton and East Brewton provide residents "one of the most advanced telecommunications infrastructures anywhere in the world."[5]

Brewton and East Brewton form the "Blueberry Capital of Alabama." On the third Saturday in June each year, Burnt Corn Creek Park holds the annual Alabama Blueberry Festival. This event is an enjoyment for all ages. The celebration includes blueberry dishes of all types and arts and crafts booths, live entertainment, an antique car show, motorcycle and car shows, and a food court with fresh blueberries and ice cream.[6]

The Brewton Post Office, the Initial Site of the Mural by John G.F.

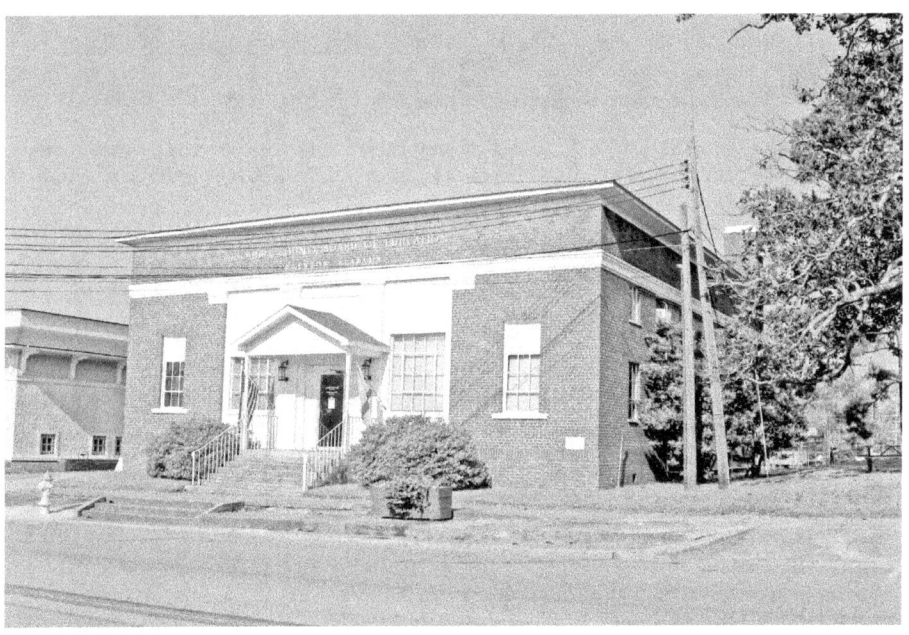

The exterior of the Escambia County Board of Education, a building that originally housed the Brewton Post Office. Access to the front door requires climbing eight steps—a problem for those with disabilities; the physical makeup of the facility indicates that the 1935–1936 construction of the post office was before the passage of the Americans with Disabilities Act. The red-brick building has a centered front door with two windows on each side. A covered porch protects patrons from the elements as they open the door.

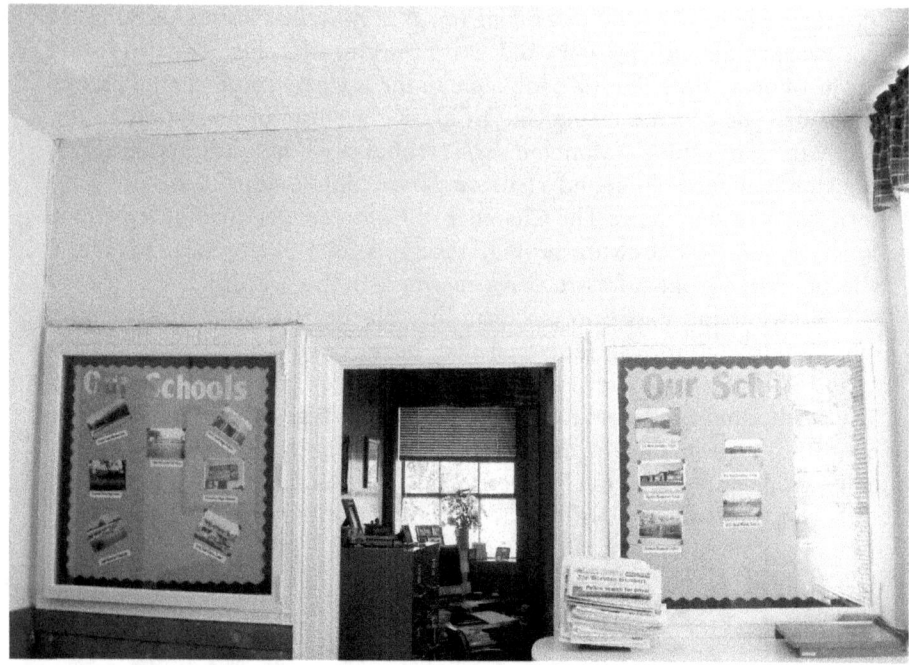

The lobby of the Escambia County Board of Education, which occupies the former Brewton Post Office. The mural *Logging* by John G.F. Von Wicht hung in the lobby of the Brewton Post Office.

Von Wicht. As the photograph shows, the initial installation of the mural *Logging* was over the postmaster's door in the Brewton Post Office. The red brick federal building at 301 Belleville Avenue in Brewton has a centered front door with two windows on each side of the entrance. A covered entryway protects patrons after they climb the seven steps from the sidewalk. Of course the construction indicates that the building of the post office might have been before the passage of the Americans with Disabilities Act.

The building no longer serves as a post office and no longer houses *Logging*. The building now serves as the administration building of the Escambia County Board of Education. The wall where the mural once hung is bare. It has since received a coat of paint.

The United States Postal Service did not begin keeping official records of locations of the federal art projects until 1971; there was no inventory of the artworks before this date. Many federal artworks disappeared in the 1950s and 1960s. There is some question, therefore, as to where *Logging* resides now or even if has been destroyed. Many locals believe that it had been painted over at some time; others suggest that someone removed the work before the re-painting of the wall.

Co-author Jimmy Emerson received a letter from Dallan C. Wordekemper, the federal preservation officer. Wordekemper knew that the removal of the mural occurred in 1965, but he himself was not sure of the location of John G.F. Von Wicht's mural. It is certain, however, where the original location of the mural was.[7]

The 1935 Brewton Post Office was the original location of *Logging*. When the post office was moved in 1965, the mural must not have accompanied the transition.

Logging (1939). The theme of *Logging* was an appropriate topic for the mural John G.F. Von Wicht designed to decorate the post office in Brewton, Alabama. Logging and lumber mills have long been important to the history of Brewton:

> ... [T]here were several men who took the chance to go into the lumber business. By the late 1800s, there were several lumber mills in the immediate area. These included the Cedar Creek Lumber Mill, the Lovelace Lumber Mill, and the one that still remains a large part of the community, the T.R. Miller Mill Company. Many men became rich in the business, and they were often called "lumber barons."[8]

Logging remained a main industry in Brewton during the Great Depression. The American city of Brewton still has the fourth largest percentage of its men employed in the logging industry.[9]

Because of its location on major railroads, the town became a commercial and manufacturing center, with mills and warehouses in abundance. Its longleaf pines made it a hub for exporting lumber and timber; the town and the forest products remain heavily tied together. The T.R. Miller Mill, which dates from 1848, still operates today and remains one of the oldest private companies in the state.[10] The Brewton sawmills employed more than one thousand workers at the time John G.F. Von Wicht prepared the mural; the lumber and timber business was the chief business of the town.[11]

Von Wicht pictured a river running through a forest of pine in the Brewton mural. In the scene, loggers are riding the logs carried by the river and are preventing a jam on the Escambia River with their use of long hooks. This image of the John G.F. Von Wicht mural over the postmaster's door in Brewton comes from the National Archives and the files of Jimmy S. Emerson; the mural is no longer available for viewing in the old Brewton Post Office.[12]

John G.F. Von Wicht (1888–1970). The artist who created *Logging*, John G.F. Von Wicht, was born in Malente-Holstein, Germany, on February 3, 1888.[13] When John was in elementary school, his mother moved the family to Oldenburg. John began visiting Gerar Bakenhaus, an artist in town; Bakenhaus guided Von Wicht in nature studies and in recognizing the old masters. John's mother next arranged for him to serve as an apprentice to painter

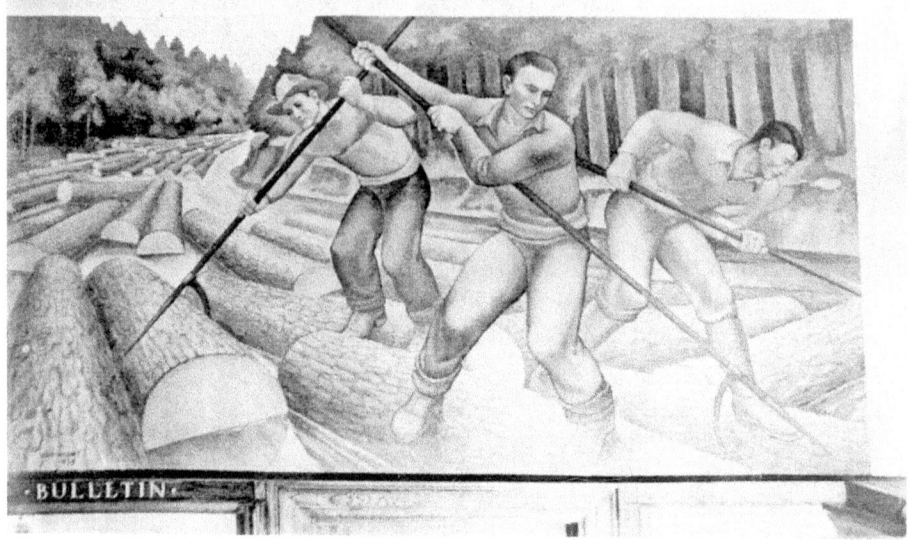

This image is of the mural *Logging* by John G.F. Von Wicht. The mural is no longer extant (courtesy National Archives).

F. W. Adels; John learned to mix linseed oil into his paints. John was 19 before he completed his first painting.

The Grand Duke of Hesse accepted Von Wicht to his private art school in Darmstadt. Next came a three-year scholarship to a prestigious Berlin school, the Royal School of Fine and Applied Arts. The Free Berlin Secession Exhibition included Von Wicht's work in 1911. Von Wicht served in World War I. Unfortunately, he was wounded, which resulted in his being partially paralyzed. He worked on designing and illustrating books during his recovery. He left Berlin and economic hardships to immigrate to the United States in 1923.

In America, Von Wicht studied at the Ardsley Art Academy in Brooklyn. He worked at the United States Printing and Lithography Company and later at Ravenna Mosaic. Before long, he became an independent mosaic contractor with an office on Park Avenue; in 1936 Von Wicht became an American citizen.

Von Wicht earned the federal commission for artwork in Brewton in the state of Alabama as a result of his receiving an Honorable Mention in a Section of Fine Arts national competition.[14] The financing for the mural came from the Section of Fine Arts, which had as its aim to secure quality artwork to embellish federal buildings; the cost for such decorative artwork was normally about 1 percent of the cost of the building. To select the artwork, jury members with experiences in and knowledge of art and not connected to the

Section judged the entries in each competition. These competitions could be local, state, region, or national. All citizen artists were eligible to enter the competition. The judges were to consider both (1) the quality of the work and (2) the relationship of the art to the intended display setting in selecting the artwork.

Von Wicht and others began experimenting with abstract expressionism as early as 1937. In that year Von Wicht used watercolor to create his "Force" series. This group of paintings was in honor of "the first director of the Whitney Museum of American Art."

Von Wicht's initial experimentation with the new style of abstract expressionism, therefore, began even before he created the mural *Logging* (1939), but the Brewton mural did not reflect abstract expressionism. The abstract expressionism style became more important later in John G.F. Von Wicht's career. It "developed in New York City in the mid–1940s, [and] became fully established during the 1950s...."[15]

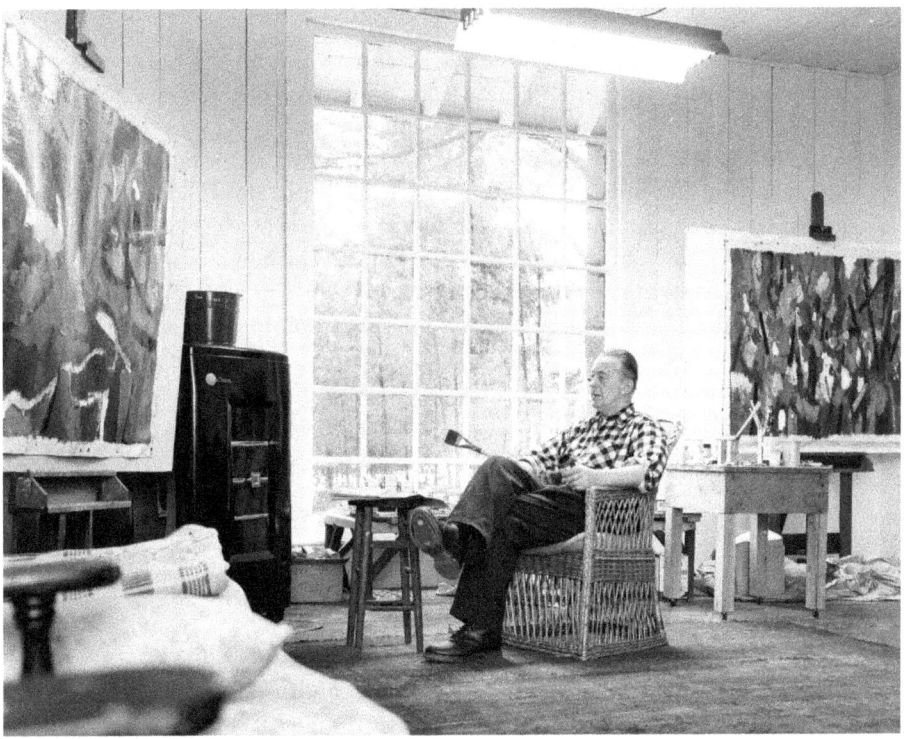

John G.F. Von Wicht is seated in front of one of his paintings in 1959. The photograph was the work of Gordon N. Converse and is a part of the MacDowell Colony Records in the Library of Congress (courtesy Library of Congress Prints and Photographs Division).

With abstract expressionism the typical paintings are bold, large, and forceful; the results often include accidental effects, like the flow of paint. The colors are often bright and even discordant. *Logging* does not demonstrate the bold colors of abstract expressionism.[16]

In the 1940s Von Wicht had additional concerns: making a living. He began serving as captain of a supply barge. He ferried food to army transport ships in New York harbor; his work began to reflect harbor themes.[17]

In 1954 John Von Wicht completed his first of twelve annual residencies at the MacDowell Colony in New Hampshire. He began spending his winters in New Hampshire and his summers in Majorca, New York.

Von Wicht held his first European art show in Paris in 1959. Shows in Brussels and Liege followed. During this time, Von Wicht began experimenting with vertical canvases and using the four seasons as themes.

In the 1960s Von Wicht began taking older canvases and reworking them, a technique known as over-painting. The resulting canvases were heavier; the surface had a deeper texture. Many times the content of the canvas changed entirely.

During the late 1960s Von Wicht's themes changed. He began to focus on the spiritual realms and on nature; he employed color to reach the emotions of viewers.[18]

During this decade, John G.F. Von Wicht also began making arrangements for the placement of his works after his death. He gifted the Syracuse University Art Collection with the majority of his art.[19]

Von Wicht's death came on January 20, 1970, when he succumbed to a bout with pneumonia. Before that date he was able to hold 13 solo exhibitions and to participate in 15 group exhibitions. He took the Brooklyn Museum Exhibition Prize (1950 and 1955), the Audubon Artists Exhibition Medal (1958), the Boston Art Festival Prize (1958), and the Ford Foundation Purchase Prize (1960).

John G.F. Von Wicht exhibited at the Metropolitan Museum of Art, the Brooklyn Institute of Art and Science, and numerous galleries. He taught at the Art Students' League of New York (1951–1952) and at the John Herron Art Institute in Indianapolis, Indiana (1953). Zelaya observed that those who knew John G.F. Von Wicht remember him as "'an artist's artist.'"[20]

In 1971, Kunigunde von Wicht—John's widow, about whom little has been published—donated some of the John G.F. Von Wicht papers (1950–1970) to the Archives of American Art at the Smithsonian. The rest of the papers there came from Alfred Nordtveldt through Mr. Keller of the Bertha Schaefer Gallery in 1973. The papers take up 27 linear feet.[21]

John G.F. Von Wicht's work is still on display in many prominent places. His murals are in Carville, Louisiana; the old Federal Court House in Knoxville, Tennessee; both the Court Room Building and the Department of Health in New York City; radio station WNYC in New York; and the Trenton Railroad Station.[22] This work ensures his memory for some time to come.

Carrollton

Stuart R. Purser's federally commissioned mural *Farm Scene with Senator Bankhead* (1943) is on display in the Carrollton, Alabama, Post Office and Agriculture Building.

The artist Stuart R. Purser was much in demand by the Section of Fine Arts of the United States Treasury Department. Not only did Purser prepare the mural for Carrollton, Alabama, but he prepared three other murals that received funding through the Treasury Department. Purser's four artworks enhanced public buildings in Gretna, Louisiana; Leland, Mississippi; Ferriday, Louisiana; and Carrollton, Alabama.

The website for Purser Studios noted that Purser completed the four murals during the Great Depression and that all four murals had local themes as their focus. The Gretna mural shows New Orleans and its river traffic; called *Steamboats on the Mississippi,* the mural dates from 1938. Purser completed the mural in Leland in 1939; it illustrates wagons carrying cotton to the local gin and has the title *Ginnin' Cotton.* The Ferriday work dates from 1940 and has the title *Southern Pattern*; the painting shows workers in the cotton gin. The Carrollton mural, dated 1943, concentrates on agriculture and legislation in Carrollton, Alabama.[1]

Carrollton is about 130 miles south of the Tennessee state line and about fifteen miles east of the Mississippi state line. The Gulf of Mexico and the state of Florida form the southern boundary of the state of Alabama; 200 miles lie between Carrollton and the state's southernmost peripheries. Carrollton is the county seat of Pickens County. In 2012 Carrollton was still categorized as a rural area; its population was 1,006.[2]

The old Pickens County Courthouse is, of course, located in Carrollton, the county seat. A marker indicates the courthouse and the legend associated with it:

Pickens County Courthouse: Erected 1877–78

Pickens County, named for General Andrew Pickens of South Carolina, was established December 19, 1820. First County Site was Pickensville. On March 5, 1830, the government awarded 80 acres of land at Carrollton for the County Site. The first courthouse erected at Carrollton was burned on April 5, 1865, by troops of Union General John T. Croxton. A freedman, Henry Wells, was accused of burning the second on November 16, 1876. He was arrested in

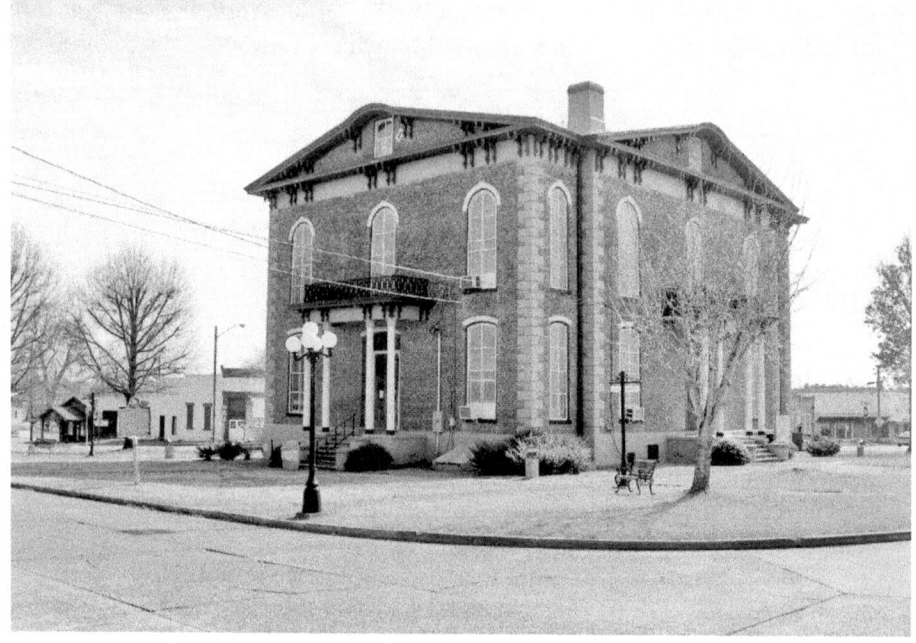

The old Pickens County Courthouse in Carrollton, Alabama.

January, 1878, and held in the garret of this building. Legend holds that as Wells peered out of the North window at a mob gathering below, lightning struck nearby, indelibly etching his image on the pane.[3]

Visitors to the courthouse can look up and see an arrow pointing to the window where the likeness of Henry Wells is supposedly still visible. The marker reminds the onlookers of the details of the legend.

The Carrollton, Alabama, Post Office and Agriculture Building dates from 1940. Accessibility to the front door of the building by patrons did not meet the 1990 requirements of the ADA (Americans with Disability Act) at the time of the passage of ADA. To ease access to the front door of the building for individuals with disabilities, a ramp makes it easier to navigate the seven steps to the main entrance of the multi-floored building. An awning provides some protection from the elements to visitors using the front entrance, which is on the left side of the front of the building.

Inside the structure is a federally-sponsored mural titled *Farm Scene with Senator Bankhead*. Stuart R. Purser prepared the work, which has political overtones. The tempera mural on Masonite board is still present over the patrons' post office boxes in the Carrollton Post Office. The 10'10" × 5'11" mural shows United States Senator John Hollis Bankhead II (July 8, 1872– June 12, 1946) talking with a farmer in the barnyard.

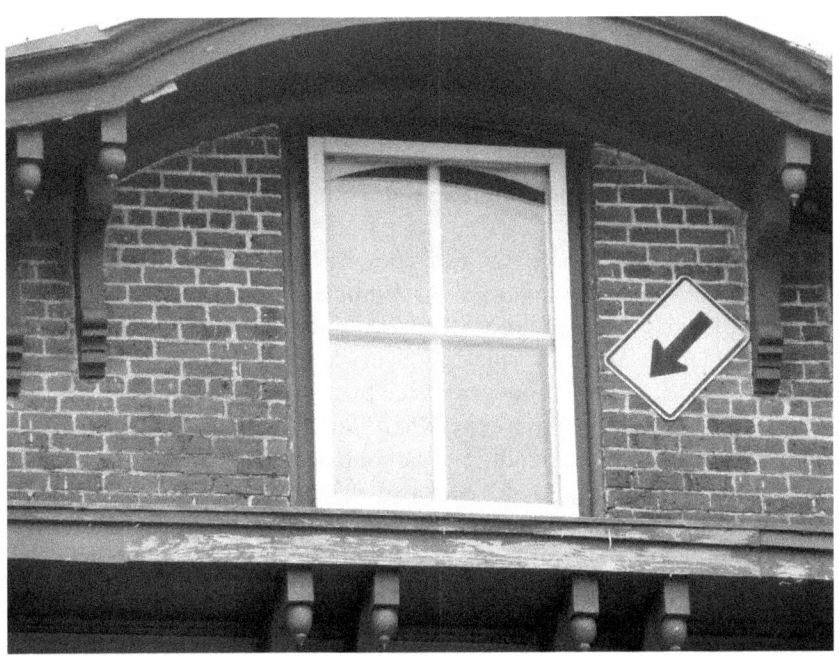

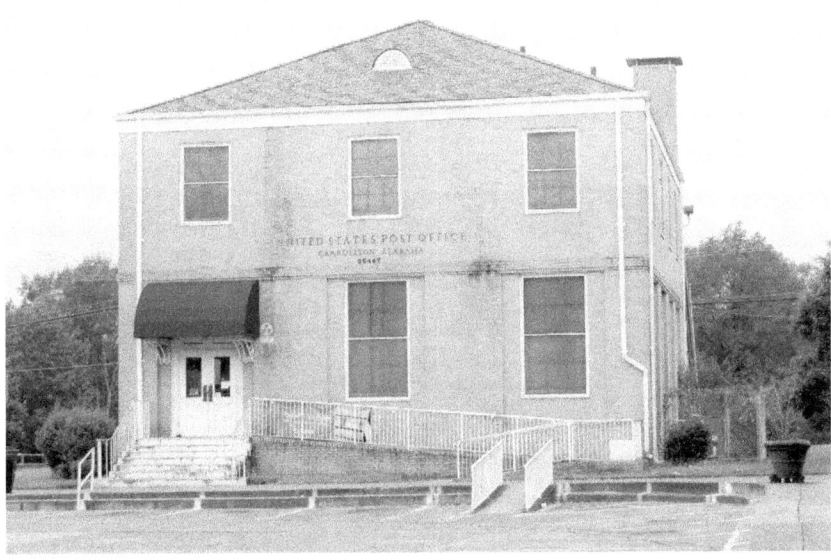

Top: An arrow marks the window where a face appears in the old Pickens County Courthouse in Carrollton, Alabama. *Bottom:* The Carrollton Post Office and Agriculture Building dates from 1940, which is somewhat later than the construction date of many other federal buildings. The brick building is still in use after three-fourths of a century.

Several local groups from the Carrollton area and even the Carrollton Postmaster had written to Washington to request that their town be given a mural. They had asked also that it depict Senator Bankhead, who had helped them secure the post office and federal building that they wanted the mural to decorate.

Stuart Purser of Louisiana, who complied with the thematic choice of the citizens of Carrollton, earned the commission for the Carrollton Post Office and Agriculture Building. The final panel shows Bankhead talking with a farmer in front of a typical Alabama farm using the newer methods of terracing and field rotation introduced by the Bankhead Tenant Farm Act and other related farm programs. When Purser completed the Carrollton mural, the head of the Carrollton Civic Club, wrote to the Section: "We are very proud of the mural and it looks so well in place. I think Mr. Purser caught the idea we had in mind and has put in the picture not only the atmosphere of our county but conveys as well the thought that Mr. Bankhead was particularly interested in that part of life."[4]

There is controversy over the identity of the politician in the mural. Edward Rowan with the Section of Fine Arts identifies in a letter the man in the dark suit as William Brockman Bankhead (April 12, 1874–September 15,

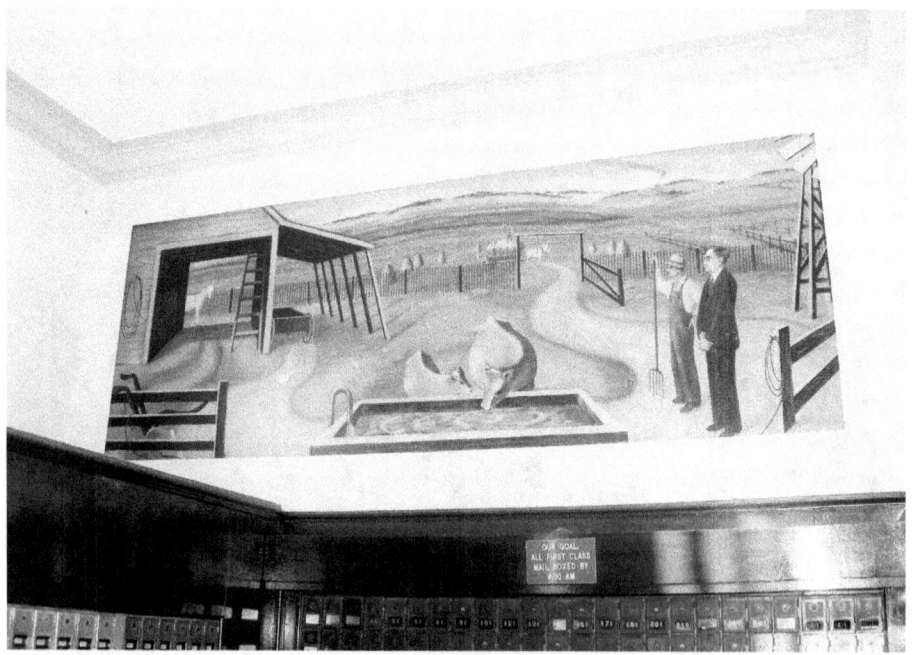

This mural by Stuart R. Purser is in the lobby of the Carrollton Post Office and Agriculture Building. Its year of installation was 1943.

1940), the Speaker of the U.S. House of Representatives. The title *Speaker of the House*, however, would make the politician pictured a Representative—not a Senator, as the mural title *Farm Scene with Senator Bankhead* has it.

There was a John Hollis Bankhead II (1872–1946) who was the brother of William Brockman Bankhead, the Speaker of the House of Representatives. John Hollis Bankhead II, who had taken his name from his father, was a senator and never served as Speaker of the U.S. House of Representatives, as Rowan suggested. Senator John Hollis Bankhead II (1872–1946) was the uncle of Tallulah Bankhead (1902–1968), the actress.

William Brockman Bankhead and his wife Adelaide were the parents of Tallulah. Adelaide died weeks after the birth of her daughter. Raised without a mother, Tallulah had an independent streak. In a ten-year period, she had been expelled from or had withdrawn from ten schools. At least one teacher suffered bites from Tallullah.

Fifteen-year-old Tallulah entered a contest that *Picture Play* magazine sponsored. She won! The prize was a weekly salary of twenty-five dollars, a trip to New York, and a chance to appear in a motion picture. Tallulah remained in New York until she was twenty. She earned the reputation of being "a hard-partying flapper with a wit as dry as a martini." A star in London, New York, and Hollywood, Tallulah was popular on the stage, radio, and screen. Her greeting of "Dahling" was a characteristic of the star. Tallulah died on December 12, 1968, of complications from pneumonia.[5]

The elder John Hollis Bankhead (1842–1920) also served in Congress. He was the father of both William Brockman Bankhead and John Hollis Bankhead II. He was an advocate of promoting federal aid for improving the roads in the state.

John Hollis Bankhead II served as a Democratic senator from Alabama. He was a proponent of agricultural interests and was an advocate of the New Deal; he was especially interested in needs of sharecroppers, tenant farmers, and large commercial farmers. Senator John Hollis Bankhead advocated the establishment of the Resettlement Administration (1935) to provide financial aid to needy farmers and to help in the resettlement of destitute farmlands. He worked with his brother William Brockman Bankhead to develop the Cotton Control Act; he co-sponsored the Bankhead-Jones Farm Tenant Act of 1937. This legislation helped provide tenant farmers with loans to purchase land or to improve their farms, as well as to help migrant farm workers. It was the Bankhead-Jones Farm Tenant Act that helped reorganize the Resettlement Administration into the Farm Security Administration.[6]

Rogers, Ward, Atkins, and Flynt remark that Bankhead

... proposed the most long-lasting effort to help the South's tenant farmers. A 1935 federal report, based on research in Georgia, Alabama, Mississippi, and Arkansas, concluded that the South's tenancy system had collapsed and could not be repaired.... Senator Bankhead introduced the Bankhead-Jones Tenancy bill in February 1935. It proposed $1.05 billion in capital to provide land, equipment, and livestock for resale to tenants on liberal credit terms. The bill passed the Senate but died in the House for lack of presidential support. Two years later Roosevelt decided to support a scaled-down version of the bill....[7]

John Hollis Bankhead II served in the Senate from 1931 to 1946. Both William Brockman Bankhead (1874–1940) and his brother John Hollis Bankhead II (1872–1946) died in office.[8]

Stuart R. Purser. The artist Stuart R. Purser painted *The Farm Scene with Senator Bankhead* in 1943. He was well-prepared for this task through his art education and through his life in the South.

Stuart's father Ed Purser had left Dayton, Tennessee, the day after a coal mine explosion in the mines where Ed worked. Ed moved to Stamps, Arkansas, and went to work in a sawmill.

In Stamps, Ed met Ora Olive Glass. The two married and had two children: Madelle and Stuart. When the sawmill closed, the family had to move from Stamps. Their move was to Good Pine, Louisiana.

In 1928, Stuart Purser earned his Bachelor of Arts degree from Louisiana College in Pineville, Louisiana. In 1929 Stuart left Louisiana with $14 in his pocket to study art at the Art Institute of Chicago.

The Great Depression was just beginning when Stuart enrolled in the Art Institute. He found it was necessary to work as many as four jobs simultaneously to complete his education. Stuart worked as a janitor at the Art Institute of Chicago and as a night clerk at the Palmer House Hotel.

After graduating in 1933 from the Art Institute, Stuart met Mary May, another art student. After Mary May and Stuart married, Mary dropped out of the Art Institute. She continued to paint with egg tempera; Stuart preferred oil.

On May 20, 1940, Mary gave birth to their son, Robert Stuart Purser. The same day the studio burned down. The fire destroyed most of the paintings and drawings inside.

When World War II began, Stuart tried to join the United States Marine Corps. He seemed, however, to be the only one with that goal in Louisiana. The Marines returned Stuart to Louisiana.

Purser signed a contract on January 22, 1942, to design, paint, and install a mural in Carrollton, Alabama, within 251 days. He earned $750 for this artwork. Purser created the mural through the use of tempera on panel. The place where he created the work, however, is uncertain.[9]

During the difficult war years, Stuart found a teaching position at Washington State College in Pullman, Washington. After only one year at Washington State, Stuart received—and accepted—an invitation to head the art department at the Southern college where he had studied: Louisiana College in Pineville, Louisiana. Mary taught design at Pineville.[10] For 1946–1947 Stuart accepted the position of building the art program at the University of Tennessee–Chattanooga.[11]

Like her husband, Mary competed to prepare a mural for a public federal building. She earned a commission to prepare a mural for the Clarksville, Arkansas, Post Office; she won this commission on the basis of her designs entered in the Vicksburg, Mississippi, Post Office competition. Mary May Purser received $470 to create the mural for Clarksville. She titled her 5' × 10' oil-on-canvas painting *How Happy Was the Occasion* (1939).[12]

Mary, too, took a teaching position with him at the University of Tennessee–Chattanooga. Jean, their daughter, was born on January 7, 1946.

In 1950 the family moved to "Ole Miss'" in Oxford, Mississippi. Stuart established the art program there. Mary completed a B.A. in fine arts from the University of Mississippi.

Purser found time to establish a summer art program near Biloxi, Mississippi. He became good friends with William Faulkner and encouraged many individual students.[13]

Stuart Purser exhibited regularly. He won the Art Association Prize in

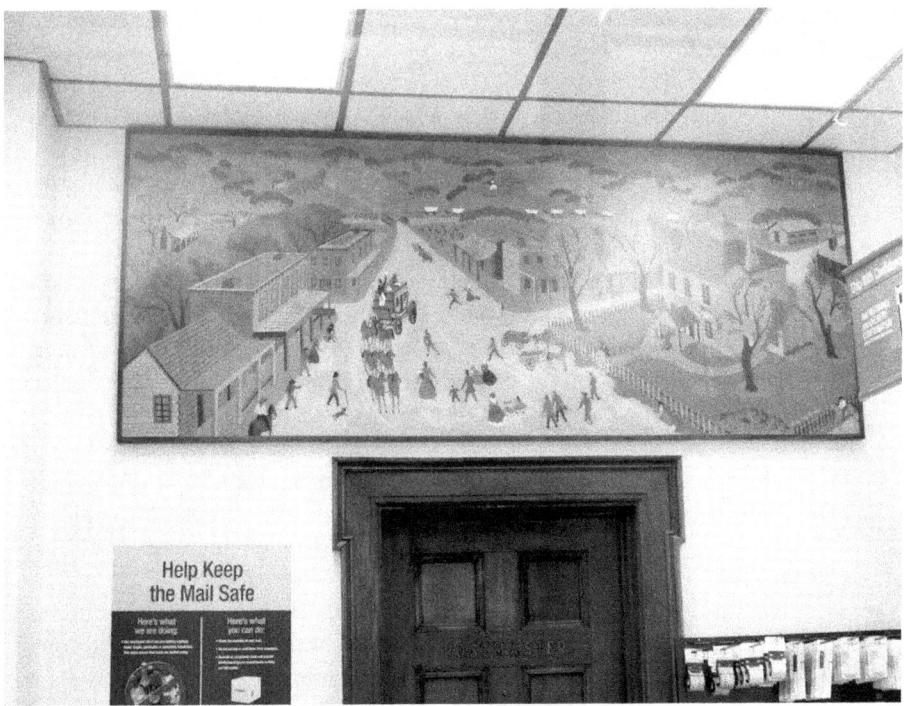

Mary Purser painted this mural in Clarksville, Arkansas.

New Orleans for three years straight: 1942, 1943, 1944. In 1942 he took the prize for the Mississippi Art Association.[14]

The family moved again in 1952. This time the move was to Gainesville, Florida, where Stuart became head of the Department of Art at the University of Florida. He served as chair until 1957, when he resigned to teach, paint, and write. Mary retired to paint and work in her church.[15]

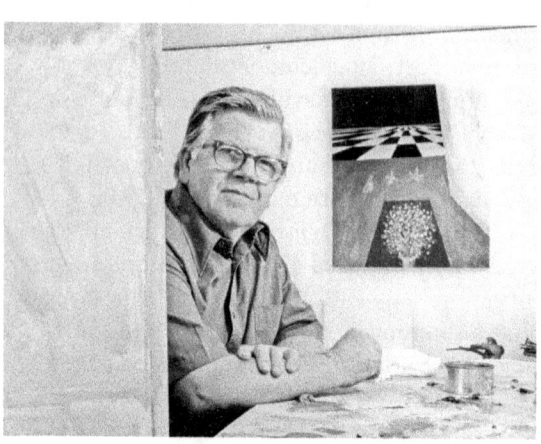

Stuart R. Purser published his first book in 1973. The autobiographical volume details Purser's life in Louisiana as a child and his friendship with an African American friend nicknamed "Applehead." Purser titled his book *Applehead*. In 1982 he published *Applehead: Part One and Part Two*, the play.[16]

Stuart R. Purser prepared the Carrollton, Alabama, mural in 1943 (Photo #6939–431245256–9140: State Archives of Florida).

In 1975 Purser published another book; for this one, he consulted with another artist. *Jesse J. Aaron, Sculptor* is the biography of an African American artist whom Purser helped and befriended. The volume describes life in the South for the talented sculptor, who began sculpting at the age of 75. The book was published in Gainesville, Florida. Both Purser and Aaron appear as authors.[17]

The University of Florida Department of Art, the University of Florida, the University Gallery, in Gainesville, Florida, and Stuart Purser published *A One-Man Retrospective Exhibition of Works by Stuart R. Purser: November 7th through December 19th, 1976* after Purser's exhibit. Worldcat.org still lists the publication after more than 30 years.[18]

In the same year (1976) as his *One-Man Retrospective Exhibition of Works*, Purser's professional book titled *The Drawing Handbook* appeared in print. Published in Worcester, Massachusetts, by Davis Publishing, copies of the book are often still for sale. Hardcover reprints of the book (1977) are still available from some sources.[19]

In addition to his concern for those not regularly included in educational opportunities because of their color or age or income, Stuart Purser had compassion for animals. He had a particular concern for dogs that were used for fighting; dog fighting was illegal, but some people still engaged in the "sport." To express his concern and to educate others about the cruelty to animals, he wrote and published a book about dog fighting: *Catahoula Cur.*[20] Published in Gainesville, Florida, the fiction book dates from 1984.[21]

Although dog fighting was illegal when Purser wrote his *Catahoula Cur*, the fights were still going on in the area. When Purser began to receive threatening phone calls from those engaging in the activity, Mary and he moved to a barn to limit the calls and to do away with other interruptions and visitors. The couple used the loft area for their artwork. They both began to change from oil to acrylics as the technology improved.

In 1984 the couple celebrated 50 years together. Their son Bob had a Ph.D. in architecture education and was teaching at Bellevue Community College near Seattle. Their daughter Jean was teaching high school art in Gainesville and was married.

Stuart Purser enjoyed having breakfast each morning at The Clock. He read the sports page every day. Both Stuart and Mary enjoyed painting.

The couple died within a few months of each other in 1986.[22]

Enterprise

Paul T. Arlt's federally commissioned, tempera-on-canvas mural titled *Saturday in Enterprise* (1941) was on display in the Enterprise, Alabama, Post Office building from 1935 until 1991 when the building was demolished. *Saturday in Enterprise* is now in the Enterprise Public Library at 101 East Grubbs Street, Enterprise, Alabama.

Enterprise, Alabama, is in Coffee County. The county has had two jurisdictional sections since 1907. The western section of the county uses Elba as its county seat; the Elba courthouse dates from 1903.

To help meet the needs of the people in the eastern half of the county, Enterprise became the branch seat of government in 1907. Enterprise did not replace the county seat in Elba, but merely began helping residents who lived in the eastern part of Coffee County. In 1999 a new courthouse in Enterprise began serving the eastern area; fire had destroyed the first two Enterprise courthouses. The third was razed for the construction of the new building.[1]

Enterprise is 25 miles north of the Florida state line. Like most of the state of Alabama, agricultural pursuits dominated the lives of most of the workers in Enterprise until the 20th century. Cotton was the major agricultural crop in Alabama until 1909 when the first boll weevil was discovered within the state's boundaries. The insect caused such enormous damage that within a decade the cotton acreage was reduced by a million acres.... The one-crop system had worn out the soil and when the weevil forced the farmers to diversify their crops, the future prospects of Alabama's agriculture were greatly improved.[2]

The boll weevil (*Anthonomus grandis*) is a beetle of the insect family *Curculionidae*. The weevil, which is about ¼" long, was a destructive pest in the United States until 1978; the aerial release of the Malathion insecticide helped to bring the beetles under control. By 2013 Texas was the only state that still had some areas infested with the weevil.[3]

The town of Enterprise did not always mourn the results of the boll weevil infestation. Instead, Enterprise would soon celebrate the crop diversity that the boll weevil brought to the area. Through donations and contributions, Enterprise was able to erect in the center of the town a monument to honor the pesky boll weevil. The sculpture was a thirteen-and-a-half-foot-tall Greek goddess who held a platter high above her head. A symbol for the boll weevil rested on the tray until 1949.[4]

The classical statue cost $1,800. An Italian sculptor created the monument, the world's only sculpture to honor an agriculture pest. Roscoe Fleming, a local resident, submitted the proposal for the downtown sculpture.[5]

A marker acknowledges the boll weevil monument in the center of Enterprise. The marker reads:

> December 11, 1919. In profound appreciation of the Boll Weevil and what it has done as the Herald of Prosperity[,] this monument was erected by the citizens of Enterprise, Coffee County, Alabama.[6]

Luther Baker did not like the fact that the Boll Weevil Monument did not have a replica of an actual boll weevil on the platter. In 1949, Baker decided to change that situation. He created a huge, fiberglass facsimile of the pest, which was added to the monument. After some vandals attacked the monument, a replica replaced Baker's damaged weevil. The Enterprise Depot Museum displays the damaged original.[7]

Perhaps the boll weevil did signal success for Enterprise. Beckham reports that Enterprise "revolves geographically, economically, and socially" about the statue.[8] Almost a century later (2014), the town has a combination of business, of industry, of military associations, and of agriculture. Its crops consist mainly of corn, hay, and cottonseed.[9]

In 2010, based on the recent census data, Enterprise received the nickname "Boom Town" of Alabama. The town had experienced a 25.3 percent growth in 10 years. With a population in 2010 of 26,574, Enterprise boasts that it is small-town friendly with the vitality of city life. Various opportunities in housing, education, recreation, and employment are available in Enterprise.

The mayor welcomed all in 2014: "Whether you are here to stay or just passing through, we hope Enterprise's southern hospitality and on-the-move lifestyle leaves a lasting impression on you."[10]

Post Offices and Libraries in Enterprise. Many changes have occurred in the locations of the post offices and libraries in Enterprise through the years. The first Enterprise Public Library dates from 1923; its location was in the old courthouse. The Enterprise Public Library moved to the Enterprise Banking Company on the corner of College and Main Street after the courthouse burned in 1924. Another move came in 1936 when the Enterprise City Hall facility accommodated the library.

After the post office moved to a new facility in 1970, the library moved to the 1935 building on April 1 of that year. The mural, however, remained in the 1935 post office building, which now accommodated the library.

When the library reached its capacity in 1991, the library association found a new location: the former First Alabama Bank building. After about 2.5 years of renovation, the location at 101 East Grubbs Street has been the current setting for the library and mural since the early 1990s.[11]

Saturday in Enterprise. The tempera-on-canvas mural *Saturday in Enterprise* was the work of artist Paul Arlt for the Enterprise, Alabama, Post Office. Arlt received the

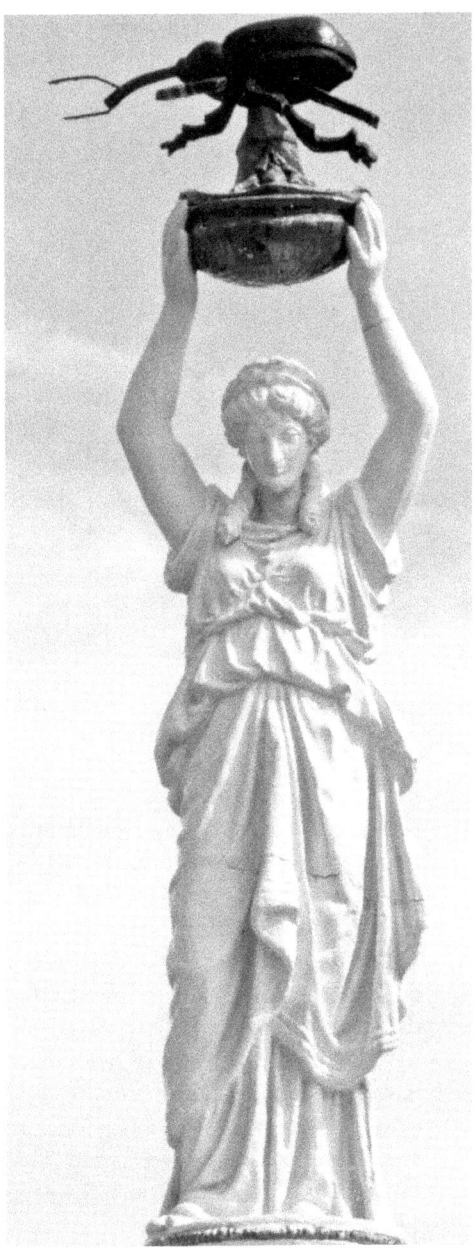

The monument in the center of Enterprise now shows a replica of a boll weevil on a platter that a goddess is holding above her head (Woodhaven-Historic. com).

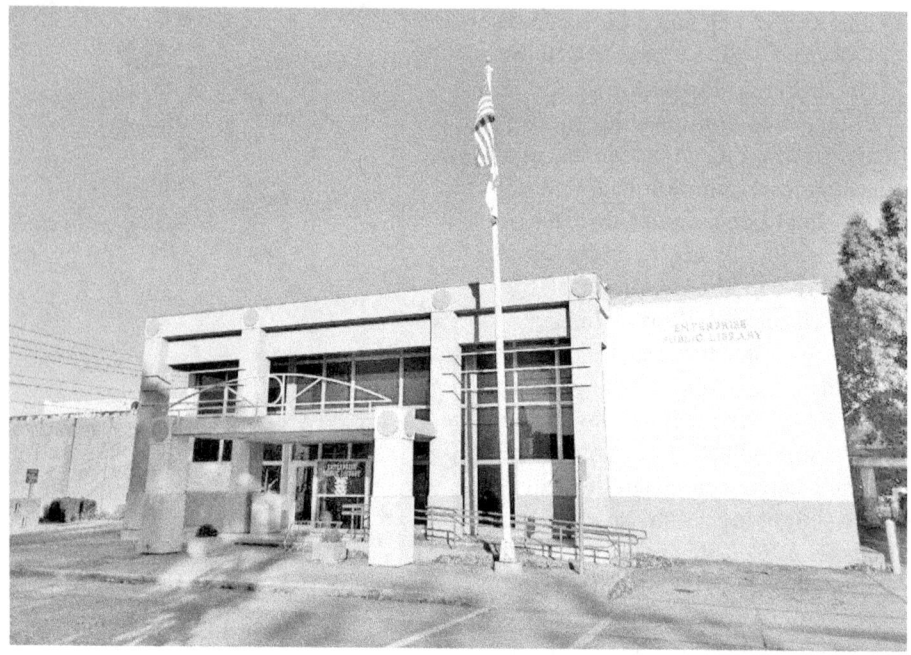

The Enterprise Public Library currently holds the mural by Paul T. Arlt.

commission to prepare the artwork on the basis of his entry in the Forty-Eight States Competition.[12]

Arlt did part of the actual painting of the mural at the Washington Inter-departmental Auditorium during "Art Week" in 1940. He worked on the cityscape as visitors filed by, observed, and asked questions. Holland describes the mural as including "a number of portrait drawings of townspeople and … [incorporating] the sketches into his mural, a lively street scene swirling around the town's downtown boll weevil monument."[13] Arlt's 1941 work depicts a city scene of downtown Enterprise. The famous boll weevil monument occupies the center of Arlt's mural, and a Saturday crowd fills the square. Advertisements project from the corner of a building. Street lights, a barber shop, Perlman's Dry Goods, a drug store, and a sign announcing City Café are visible to the careful observer. Visitors can still see the mural and identify on it the monument to the boll weevil and other landmarks.

Of particular importance in the mural are the people. All the individuals seem dressed in their best for the visit to downtown Enterprise on a Saturday. Arlt actually visited Enterprise and made sketches of the people on some Saturdays before he painted the mural. He depicted both African Americans and whites in the downtown area.

Many of the figures in the mural were recognizable to those who lived

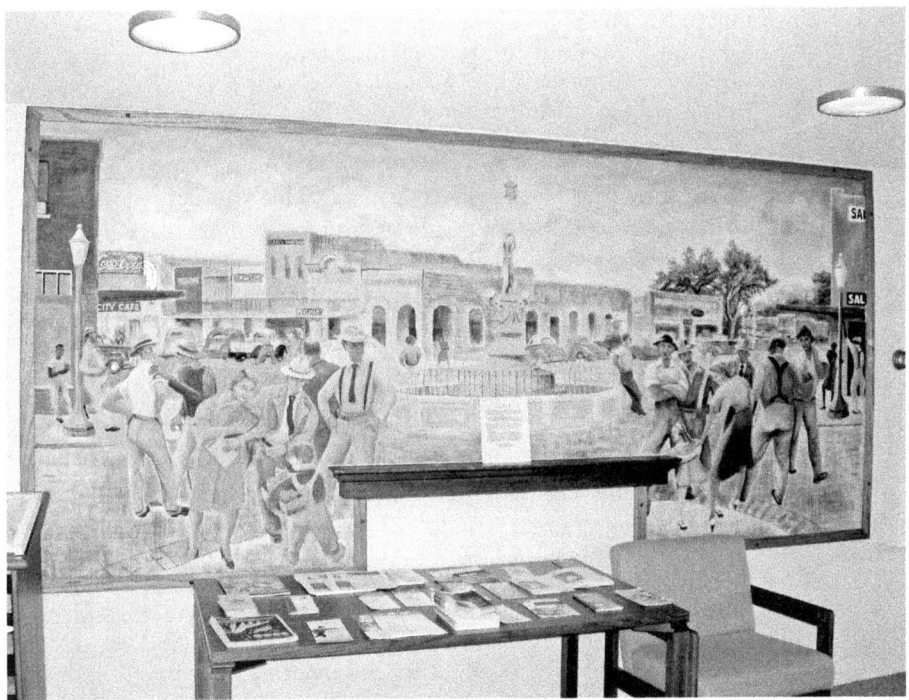

Paul T. Arlt prepared the tempera-on-canvas mural *Saturday in Enterprise* for the post office in Enterprise, Alabama; the mural is on display in the Enterprise Public Library.

in the town. Dan Stephens is the city policeman wearing the badge. Mrs. Warren is the lady with the little girl.

The mural recognizes the importance of peanuts to the area. Little Billy Warren is selling peanuts. Lint Warren—the mayor for twenty-four years—is purchasing peanuts.

Childhood Enterprise resident Lee Eudon Holland—later a successful CPA and CFP in Northville, Michigan—wrote a memoir-novel titled *Boiled Peanuts and Buckeyes*; the book details aspects of Holland's early life in Enterprise. Published in 2006, the book records events about the mural and other events from Holland's childhood.

Holland comments on the fact that Arlt was able to incorporate names and emblems—like Ford and Coca-Cola—into the mural. Holland indicates that "[s]uch inclusions apparently were understandably not sanctioned by the Section of Fine Arts."[14]

Lee Eudon Holland still recalls the sales jingle he used to sell the boiled peanuts:

Fresh boiled peanuts, five cents a bag;
fresh and fine, right off the vine.
If you don't have a nickel,
I can change a dime![15]

When the problem with the weevil prohibited the cultivation of cotton, Enterprise tried corn, potatoes, hay and sugarcane. These products flourished, but—as the painting suggests—the big cash crop was peanuts. The crop was so profitable that Enterprise labeled itself "the Peanut Capital of the World."[16]

H.M. Sessions, a local businessman, convinced C.W. Bastion to try planting peanuts as a crop, instead of cotton. When neighboring farmers found out that Bastion produced 8,000 bushels in that one year, they tried planting peanuts. In 1917 Coffee County celebrated the largest peanut harvest in the nation.[17]

Lee Eudon Holland reports in *Boiled Peanuts and Buckeyes* that Arlt received a call to come back to Enterprise after the painting's installation. Arlt recalled returning to Enterprise to change something in the mural that viewers in the area deemed improper:

Although Arlt did not remember precisely which characters were involved, or whether the controversy arose because of a juxtaposition that was deemed inappropriate or as a result of an offending gesture being made by one of the individuals, he did recall having to come to Enterprise to "fix" the mural. What is known is that black men in 1940s Enterprise had their place, and that place was at a clear and definite distance from white women.[18]

In her book *Depression Post Office Murals and Southern Culture: A Gentle Reconstruction*, Sue Bridwell Beckham indicates that the mural set in the "present" includes the dreams for the future. The joy and confidence the residents display include hopes for later rather than depictions just of the "here and now." The prosperity that Enterprise displays is a hope for the town climbing out of a period of deprivation and depression. Beckham comments on the way that Arlt placed the Greek woman with the boll weevil in the painting so that the town was visible and so that the pleasures of an afternoon without work are obvious. Blacks are in the mural, but they are outnumbered and do not occupy the foreground.[19]

Paul Theodore Arlt. Paul Theodore Arlt was born in Bronx, New York, on March 15, 1914. He graduated from Townsend Harris High School.[20] Arlt studied at Colgate University with Alfred Krakusin.[21] After his graduation, he lived in Greenwich Village and studied painting at Greenwich House. He studied also at the Corcoran and Phillips Gallery.

Paul Arlt worked at constructing ships for the Navy when World War II began. Later he joined the Marine Corps. Arlt served as a combat artist in the Marine Corps during World War II. To observe and capture the action,

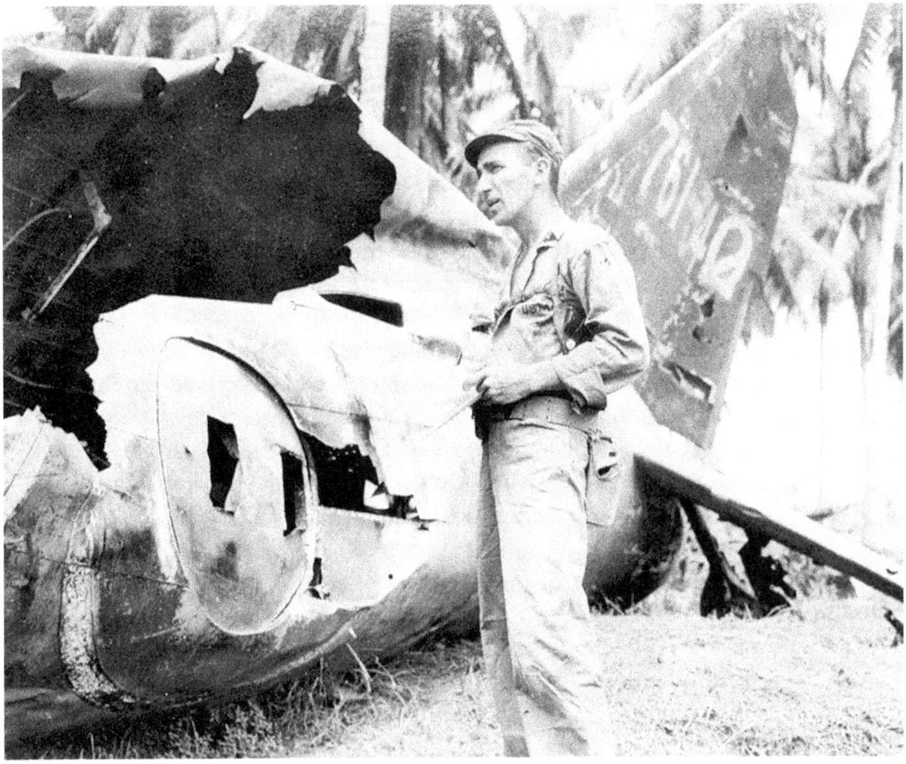

Paul T. Arlt was wounded in the Pacific while he served in the Marine Corps during World War II. He earned the Purple Heart (courtesy Ronay Arlt Menschel and used with her permission).

Arlt followed the troops to the front lines. He earned the Purple Heart after being hit by shrapnel as he ducked into a foxhole.[22]

From 1951 until 1956, Paul T. Arlt worked for the *New York Herald Tribune* as an editorial cartoonist. Arlt worked for trade publications until he moved to Washington, D.C., in 1965.[23]

NASA commissioned Paul Arlt in 1965 to create artwork that depicted the Gemini Program. In Washington, Arlt worked also as "a political cartoonist and graphic artist. He covered Capitol Hill hearings, drew images of elected officials

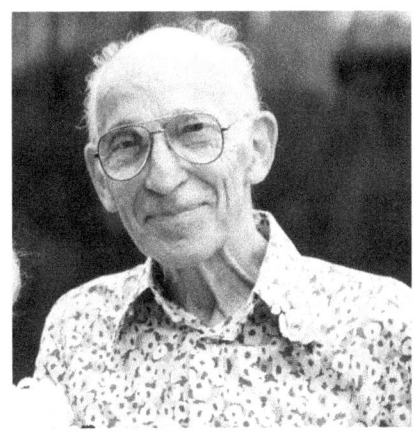

Paul T. Arlt in his later years (courtesy Ronay Arlt Menschel).

and captured Washington landmarks in his watercolors, drawings, and silkscreens. Over the years his work was exhibited at such famous locales as New York's Metropolitan Museum of Art and the Corcoran Gallery in Washington."[24]

Paul Theodore Arlt died at his home in Rye, New York, on September 20, 2005. This artist who had spent decades as a cartoonist and "in creating paintings of the powerful" died from congestive heart failure. May MacClaire Arlt (his wife of 65 years), Ronay Arlt Menschel (his daughter), Richard Menschel (his son-in-law), and three grandchildren survived the artist/cartoonist.[25]

May MacClaire Arlt died on December 21, 2007. She had been a member of the 1932 Class of Rollins College.[26] In 2001 she had received the honor of becoming a Life Member of the League of Women Voters.[27]

Daughter Ronay Arlt Menschel is chairman of Phipps Houses, a non-profit owner and developer of low- and moderate-income housing in New York City.[28] She and her husband, Richard, founded the Richard and Ronay Menschel Library within the George Eastman House. The facility contains a comprehensive collection of the literature of photography for information and a research-level collection of the literature of motion pictures and artifacts. Ronay is a recipient of the Frank H.T. Rhodes Exemplary Alumni Service Award from Cornell University.[29]

The contributions of the Arlt family continue.

Paul T. Arlt's works are still on display at many locations. The exhibit "75 Years of Marine Corps Aviation: A Tribute" included a brochure featuring the painting *Marine Ordnancemen* by Sergeant Paul T. Arlt, USMCR. The brochure with Arlt's art is available for public release and is obtainable online.[30] The Virginia Museum of Fine Arts, Watkins Memorial College, the Phillips Memorial Gallery, and the United States Marine Corps College still provide works by Paul T. Arlt for exhibit.[31]

Eutaw

Robert Gwathmey's federally commissioned mural *The Country-side* (1941) is on display in the Eutaw, Alabama, Post Office.

Eutaw, Alabama, is the county seat of Greene County, the least populous county in the state of Alabama. As of the 2010 census, the Greene County population was 9,045; the population of Eutaw was 2,934.

Eighty-one and one-half percent of the county respondents indicated in 2010 that they were African American. About 17.5 percent of these residents identified themselves as white. The remaining percentage identified themselves as Hispanic, Native American, Asian, or a combination of races or nationalities. The median income in 2010 for a household in Greene County was $22,352; the state of Alabama had a median household income of $40,547 in 2010 and a median income in 2012 of $41,574.

Based on soil composition and color, Greene County and its county seat of Eutaw are in the Black Belt of Alabama. Greene County is in the western, central part of the state. Because of its location near the Black Warrior River, Eutaw became a shipping and commercial center during the early 1800s.[1]

In 1819 the county received its name from Revolutionary War hero General Nathanael Greene. General Greene was in command of the army of the South after the Battle of Camden, South Carolina.

> He was an efficient officer and was able to inspire his men with hope and confidence.... [H]e made an efficient use of his little army.[2]
> Nathanael (sometimes spelled "Nathaniel") Greene was one of the most respected generals of the Revolutionary War (1775–83) and a talented military strategist. As commander of the Southern Department of the Continental army, he led a brilliant campaign that ended the British occupation of the South.[3]

The county seat of Eutaw in Greene County received its name from the Battle of Eutaw Springs. In this battle in South Carolina, General Nathanael Greene led his troops in the recapture of Charleston, South Carolina, from the British.[4]

Eutaw Post Office. The Eutaw, Alabama, Post Office dates from 1938. Henry Morgenthau, Jr., was the secretary of the treasury at the time of its construction, and James A. Farley was the postmaster general. Louis A. Simon was the supervising architect, and Neal A. Melick was the supervising engineer. Constructed before the passage of the 1990 Americans with Disabilities Act, the original Eutaw structure has more than 6 steps leading to the main entrance. The structure, which is more than 77 years old, is still in use—with modifications that include a ramp to allow ease of access for patrons.

The front of the Eutaw Post Office is symmetrical. The central front entrance has two windows on each side; each of these windows has 24 panes. An American eagle in relief poses above the door, which has the semblance of a column on each side. The black tiled, pitched roof has a centered cupola for interest.

***The Countryside* by Robert Gwathmey.** The largest competition that the Section of Fine Arts announced in the 1930s was the 48 States Competition of 1939. Artists across the nation submitted more than 3,000 entries for consideration; one post office in each state would receive a winning entry.

The artist Robert Gwathmey submitted an entry for the post office in

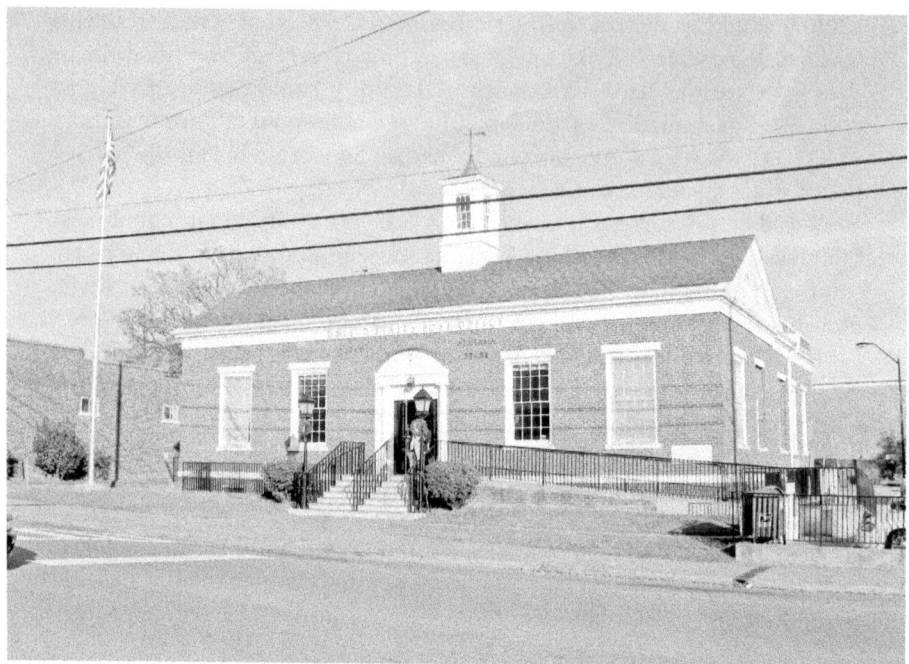

The Eutaw, Alabama, Post Office showing the centered main entrance and the series of steps leading to the front door. This structure at 227 Prairie Avenue, Eutaw, Alabama, holds Robert Gwathmey's mural titled *The Countryside* (1941).

Phoebus, Virginia. Phoebus is in the Chesapeake Bay area of Hampton Roads, Virginia, which is geographically much different from that of Eutaw, Alabama. Gwathmey had proposed a mural picturing a scene related to the nearby waters of Phoebus.

The jury offered $740 to Gwathmey to prepare a different, more appropriate mural for Eutaw, Alabama. Gwathmey agreed to prepare a painting suitable for the town.[5]

Life magazine on December 4, 1939, ran an article that pictured the winning entries and assigned a caption to each. Robert Gwathmey's entry for Phoebus, Virginia, was the first photo printed in the article because the state of Alabama comes first alphabetically. The picture and caption for Phoebus, however, were not appropriate for Eutaw, Alabama. The caption in *Life* read: "Robert Gwathmey's vivid mural will picture Negroes unloading and packing fish taken from nearby waters."[6]

James S. Coleman, editor of the *Greene County Democrat*, was concerned about the supposed selection for Eutaw. Coleman observed that Eutaw lay 200 miles from the Gulf of Mexico. Robert Gwathmey was teaching at the Carnegie Institute of Technology at the time. Coleman indicated that the selection of Gwathmey's work was another instance of a northern artist who was ignorant of the South and who was indifferent to the locale but nonetheless received an assignment.[7]

Gwathmey, however, did his homework. He visited Eutaw and discussed with the agricultural agent some ideas for a mural for the Eutaw Post Office. He decided to depict scenes from the local lumber industry and from the farms. In *The Countryside* some African Americans are stacking pine boards for drying, and some Caucasians are working in the fields.

Gwathmey's 13' × 4.5' scene created controversy. Even though whites were working in the field, many blacks objected to the fact that blacks were performing physical labor in stacking the lumber. Some observers objected to blacks and whites working together in the mural.

Eutaw Postmistress Julia J. Harkness wrote to the Section to verify the panel's final installation; she had originally asked for a mural showing Southern military heroism and scenes of the Confederacy.[8] With her verification of the completion of the work, she included a short note: "We have but one newspaper and I asked the editor to give the mural a write up in the next issue, and was told that he had nothing to say."[9]

In 1975 the mural was still generating controversy. Spiver Gordon of the Southern Christian Leadership Conference called the painting racist. In 1979 William McKinley Branch, a black probate judge in Greene County, used the

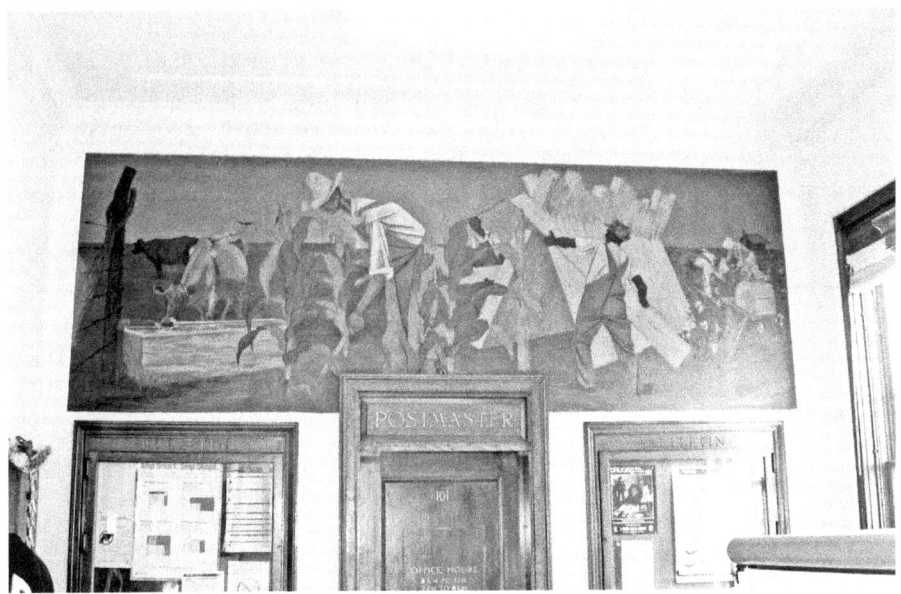

This oil-on-canvas mural titled *The Countryside* and painted by Robert Gwathmey is in the lobby of the Eutaw, Alabama, Post Office. Its year of installation was 1941.

word "dehumanizing" to describe the image of blacks in the artwork. The United States Postal Service authorized a study of the mural. The director of the Birmingham Museum described the mural as "a good picture, although not a great one"; the decision was that it should remain.[10]

Gwathmey returned to the Eutaw Post Office some years later. He described his work on the past mural as "fierce."[11] In *The Countryside*, Gwathmey depicted strenuous manual labor with an implication of racial integration. Showing whites and blacks working equally in a painting was unusual at the time, but Gwathmey wanted to stress that both groups had a mutual interest in freeing themselves from the economic and social systems that oppressed both of them. Some blacks, however, considered the work of the two racial groups to be unequal.[12]

Piehl cautions viewers, however, that one should not judge a work from the early 1940s against the social standards of the 1970s.[13] He also reminds readers: "The reality of the 'South' for Gwathmey was preserved quite literally in the mind's eye, a shared, complex visual memory of the people and the region out of which the artist came."[14]

The images of the documentary photographers of the Great Depression era influenced Robert Gwathmey's works.[15] These federal photographers included Arthur Rothstein (1914–1983), Dorothea Lange (1895–1965), Walker Evans (1903–1975), Marion Post Wolcott (1910–1990), and Jack Delano (1914–1997), among others.[16] The works of his wife, Rosalie Hook Gwathmey, were also influential to his style.

Robert Gwathmey (January 24, 1903–September 21, 1988). The artist Robert Gwathmey considered himself a Social Realist. Social Realists use art to communicate "social values in a critical yet constructive way."[17] Gwathmey explained it this way: "I'm a social being and I don't see how you can be an artist and be separate.... Artists have eyes.... You go home. You see things that are almost forgotten. It's always shocking."[18]

Robert Gwathmey received recognition for his depictions of rural life in the South. Having lived in the North and the South, he was able to depict both areas well.[19] Gwathmey had been born in Richmond, Virginia, on January 24, 1903. His father, also named Robert Gwathmey, had worked as a railroad engineer; he had died on May 27, 1902, when his locomotive exploded before his son was born.[20]

Gwathmey's depictions of Southern rural life presented dignified images of the African Americans. Gwathmey was one of the first artists to depict such positive images. He used bold coloration and many geometric forms in this work, which relied on his experiences in the North and the South.

Gwathmey's wife, photographer Rosalie Hook Gwathmey, was planning a documentary series on blacks in the South. Her work further inspired her husband.

Most art critics recognize that Robert Gwathmey was a social realist and ...
the first white American artist to produce dignified representations of black
Americans through painting. Gwathmey was a firm believer that artistic
expression and social issues could not be separated. Gwathmey was interested
in documenting the human condition, primarily as it pertained to the people
of his native south. He sought to portray human subjects as he saw them,
through observation, without over generalizing or romanticizing. Though
most well known for his iconic realist portraits of black southern agricultural
workers, Gwathmey produced portraits of both whites and blacks in urban
and rural landscapes, as well as still lifes.[21]

Robert Gwathmey's art training helped him to produce these items for which
he would later receive recognition, prizes, and awards.

During his studies at North Carolina State College in Raleigh (1922–
1923), Gwathmey had realized that business was not the work he wanted to
pursue.[22] Gwathmey took a job on a freighter to earn some money for further
education. He was able to transfer to the Maryland Institute of Design. He
completed four years at the Pennsylvania Academy of Fine Arts in Philadelphia.[23]

While Gwathmey was studying at the Pennsylvania Academy of Fine
Arts, he met fellow student Rosalie Hook from Charlotte, North Carolina.
Rosalie was particularly interested in photography, and most of her work
focused on her hometown. She began a series of photographs on blacks in
the South.

Rosalie Hook and Robert Gwathmey "kept company" for about six years.
The couple married on November 2, 1935, in Alexandria, Virginia.[24] Their
son Charles Gwathmey was born on June 19, 1938. Charles became a successful architect and designed dwellings for such well-known clients as Steven
Spielberg and Jerry Seinfeld. Charles died at 71 (August 3, 2009) from
esophageal cancer.[25]

Robert Gwathmey taught at Temple University in Philadelphia (1930–
1932); Beaver College in Glenside, Pennsylvania (1930–1937); and the Carnegie Institute of Technology in Pittsburgh, Pennsylvania (1939–1942). When
the war began, he became active in Artists for Victory, which helped artists
to assist in the war effort.[26]

Robert Gwathmey earned $740 for *The Countryside*. Installed in the
Eutaw Post Office in 1941, this painting demonstrated Gwathmey's skill as a
painter. Piehl observed that one of the things that made Gwathmey

a significant artist was his use of many southern stereotypes that existed in the
minds of both southerners and northerners in the mid-twentieth century....
In short, Gwathmey's art depended heavily on pictorial stereotypes to define
the reality of the region. This iconography is expressed in such diverse details
of the Eutaw mural as the red soil, men and women picking cotton, distinctive

vegetation and other visual features—sunbonnets, bib overalls, dilapidated fence posts and mailbox—in a southern context.[27]

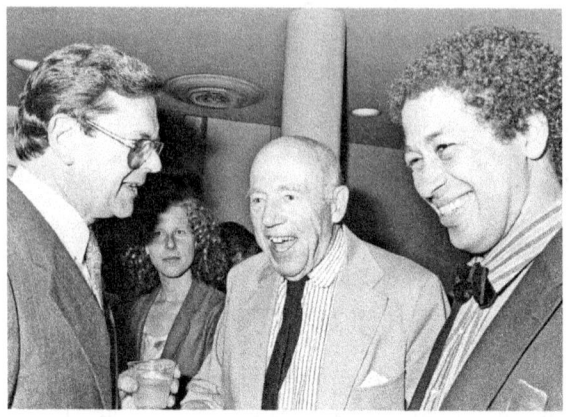

This 1985 photograph shows Robert Gwathmey at the opening of an exhibition at the Cooper Union. Alan C. Green, former vice-president of the Cooper Union, is at left. Roderick Knox, architecture adjunct professor at the Cooper Union, is at right (courtesy Cooper Union).

Piehl indicated that Gwathmey had a specific purpose in mind with *The Countryside.* He wanted to emphasize the mutual interest both the white and the black farm laborers had in freeing themselves from the oppressive economic and social systems of the day. Gwathmey demonstrated the hard manual work that both groups performed for a small white elite and depicted the solemn demeanor and style of dress characteristic of the tyranny under which they existed.[28]

In 1942 Robert Gwathmey began a twenty-six year teaching career at the Cooper Union in New York City. He retired from the Cooper Union in 1968.[29]

Even after his retirement, Gwathmey continued to work. He taught during 1968–1969 at Boston University. Despite his diagnosis of Parkinson's disease, Robert painted until four years before his death in 1988. He died from cardiac disease. The FBI observed him carefully because of his activism during the last twenty-seven years (1961–1988) of his life.[30]

Rosalie Hook Gwathmey. Rosalie Hook Gwathmey (September 15, 1908–February 12, 2001)—like her husband—came under attack because of her art. Rosalie joined the Photo League in 1942 and regularly attended its meetings. This group included people from all backgrounds and cultures. The members had a common ground, however; they were seeking "to raise consciousness about social conditions through the medium of photography."[31]

Rosalie noted that "when the McCarthy period came along ... we got wiped out. Everybody got scared." Rosalie remembers that "I just quit."[32] In 1955 Rosalie destroyed all her negatives, put her cameras away, and donated her prints to the New York Public Library. She was "tired of having to hide her work"; Rosalie just "walked away from photography."[33]

Rosalie Gwathmey worked as a textile designer through the 1960s and

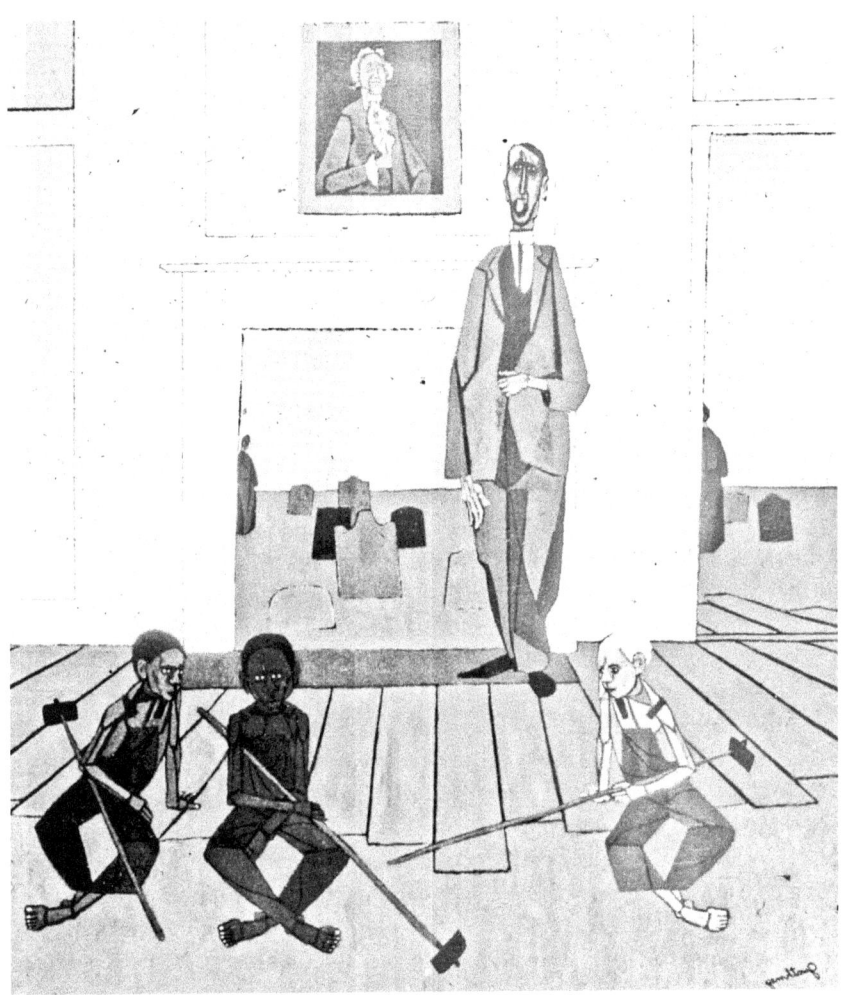

This old lantern slide titled *Ancestor Worship* is a part of the collection of co-author Anita Price Davis. The work by Robert Gwathmey bears the words A.C.A. Gallery; Gwathmey is satirizing Southerners who are arrogant about their ancestors. The slide gives no death date (just 1903–), indicating that it was prior to Gwathmey's 1988 death. The co-author purchased the lantern slide from eBay (from the collection of Anita Price Davis).

the 1970s. Her work experienced revival in 1994 with a solo exhibit of her work in East Hampton, New York.[34]

Rosalie Hook Gwathmey died at 92 in 2001. Her architect son announced that she had died at her home in Amagansett, New York. She "was noted for the warmth and artful simplicity of her pictures of black Southern communities."[35]

Fairfield

Frank Hartley Anderson and his wife Mary (Martha[1]) Fannin Fort Anderson painted the mural *Spirit of Steel* (1938) for the Fairfield, Alabama, Post Office.

Fairfield is in the western part of Jefferson County, Alabama. The city is about 97 miles northwest of Montgomery—the capital city of Alabama— and about seven miles southwest of Birmingham. The city of Fairfield is part of the metropolitan area of Birmingham, which is the largest city in the state of Alabama.[2]

The original name of the city of Fairfield was Corey. This name came from William E. Corey, the president of United States Steel Corporation. United States Steel purchased the Tennessee Coal, Iron, and Railroad Company (TCI) in 1907; this purchase saved TCI from bankruptcy and closure.

Birmingham developer Robert Jennison, Jr., formed the Corey Land Company in 1909. With Boston landscape designer George H. Miller to help him, Jennison began construction of an area for 15,000 people on 240 acres next to the U.S. Steel plant. The city would eventually encompass 2,100 acres; its development would extend over several decades. The plans for Corey would resemble the plans for Gary, Indiana.

In March 1911, former President Theodore Roosevelt spoke at Corey's main plaza for the founding ceremonies. He praised U.S. Steel, TCI, and the developers for their collective vision.

In 1913 U.S. Steel executives renamed the town of Corey. The new name of the Alabama town was Fairfield, the name of the hometown of United States Steel executive James A. Farrell. The incorporation of Fairfield, Alabama, dates from January 1, 1919. Fairfield Land Company—which had once been Corey Land Company—continued developing the town of Fairfield.

United States Steel continued to expand, and Fairfield grew with the increase in steel-related manufacturing—especially during World War I. A sheet-metal mill, new blast furnaces, and additional segregated housing for new employees—both black and white—resulted in an increase in the population of the area.

Three railroads serve Fairfield. The CSX Transportation, Inc.; the Norfolk Southern Railway; and the Birmingham Southern Railroad were and still are the three vital railroads.

Although Fairfield suffered during the Great Depression, TCI tried to protect its workers by dividing the workload among the employees. Fairfield Works remains one of the largest steel operations in the South.

Fairfield celebrated its centennial in August 2010. The population of

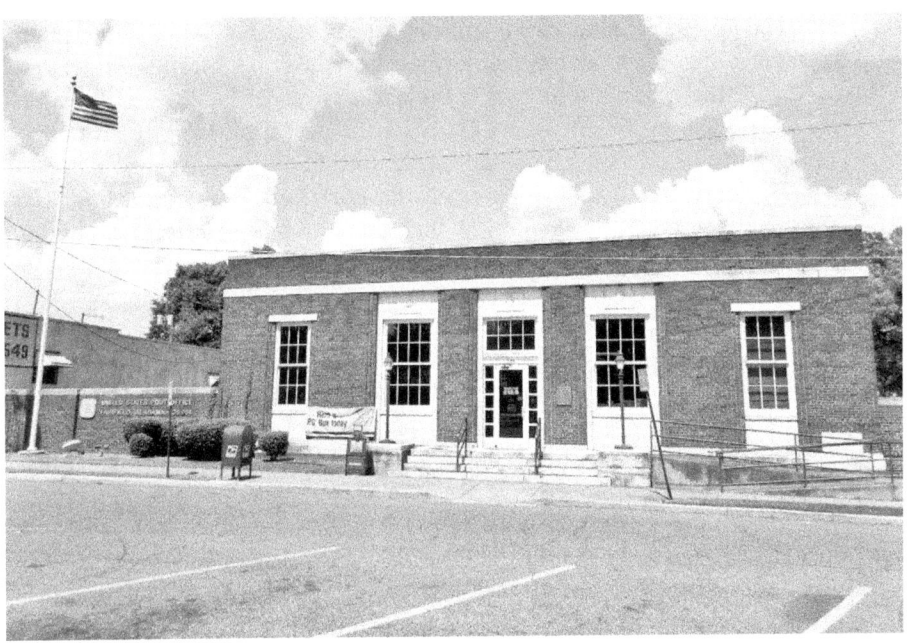

The Fairfield, Alabama, Post Office is still in use after more than 75 years. The structure has a flat roof and two windows on each side of the centered front door. Friezes decorate the areas above the windows.

Fairfield in 2010 was 11,117. More than 94 percent of the population was African American; only 4 percent was Caucasian.[3]

The estimated per capita income in Fairfield for 2012 was $17,084. The estimated median household income in 2012 was $32,712; the estimated median household income in Alabama for 2012 was $41,574.[4]

Interstate highways connect the Fairfield area with Atlanta in the east, Chattanooga in the northeast, and Mississippi in the west. The Birmingham-Shuttlesworth International Airport is only 15 miles away.[5]

Fairfield, Alabama, Post Office. The Fairfield Post Office, constructed in the 1938, is still in use. The red brick structure at 420 45th Street has five steps leading to the centered entrance. Transoms on either side of and over the front door serve to decorate and provide lighting.

A mural decorates the inside lobby of the Fairfield, Alabama, Post Office and provides information about the steel industry to customers. In her book, Beckham recognizes both Frank Hartley Anderson and Mary Fort Anderson as painters of the mural in Fairfield, Alabama.[6]

The Birmingham Historical Society Newsletter (November 2011) also gives credit both to Frank Hartley Anderson and to his wife Martha Fort Anderson for the work: "The Andersons designed and painted a still extant series of historical murals at Lakeview School and the *Spirit of Steel* mural at the Fair-field Post Office."[7] Other sources, however, credit Frank Hartley Anderson alone with the mural. For instance, the online sources "WPA Murals"[8] and "New Deal Art in Alabama Post Offices and Federal Buildings"[9] give only Frank Hartley Anderson's name as the creator of *Spirit of Steel*.

Frank Hartley Anderson and Martha Fort Anderson spent about six months in the mills of U.S. Steel in Birmingham around 1938. The couple was studying the operations of the company before preparing the mural for the post office in Fairfield.[10]

The Spirit of Steel. Frank Hartley Anderson wrote to the Section in 1938 to describe both the industry of Fairfield and the place where he was prepar-ing a mural. The Fairfield mural was probably the most direct image of a local industry produced by a federal artist.

Anderson informed the Section office that 99 percent of the people using the post office had connections with U.S. Steel. He noted that they all seemed pleased with the mural he was preparing.[11]

Marling observes that at the time (late spring of 1937) Anderson was preparing preliminary sketches for his mural in Fairfield, strikes were occur-

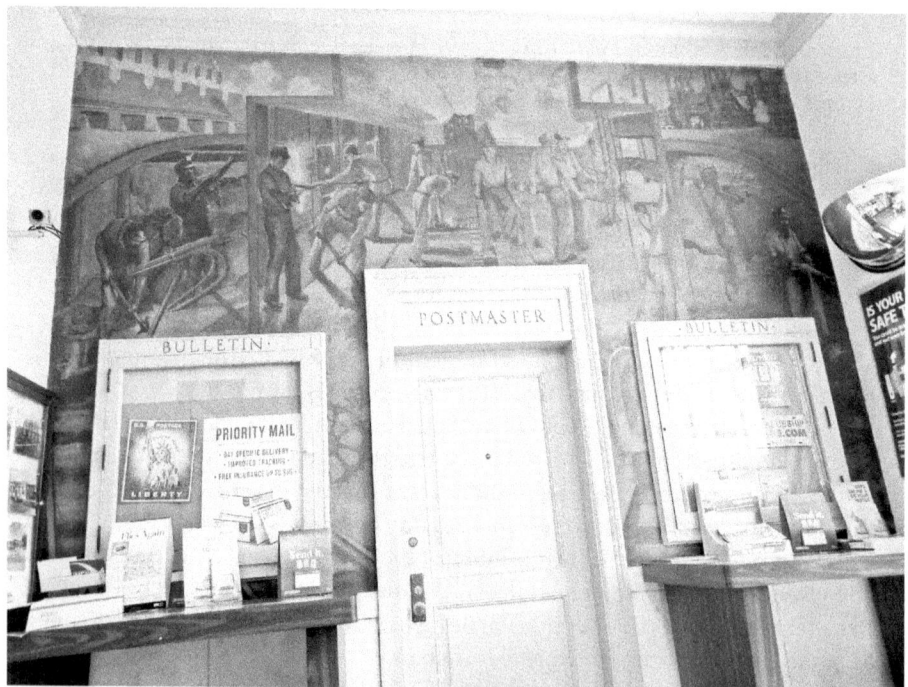

Frank Hartley Anderson and his wife Martha Fort Anderson prepared the mural *The Spirit of Steel*. The mural illustrates the steel-making process.

ring in many steel plants across the country. Workers were signing up with the Steel Workers Organizing Committee. Marling notes in eloquent, descriptive words the events that were going on in the painting and in the country at that time. She waxes poetic when she describes the workers and the work in the plants and in the mural.

> The steelworkers in the Fairfield post office look a bit thoughtful, as if they were remembering their CIO pledge cards and mulling over the odds that the union could keep them working forty-hour weeks with time and a half for overtime and a 10 percent wage increase. But "sad"? "Grim"? The working people of Mural America are too busy to worry about arranging their faces to please the Section, too energetic to pause for smiling daydreams, consumed by the will to work.... The workmen who stoke the blast furnace in Fairfield surmount the machinery on display in the lower reaches of the mural literally and figuratively. They work without a second to spare for posturing in "couchant" attitudes. They run the machines with no help from a mythical "Genius of Steel"; they are themselves "The Spirit of Steel," en masse. Heaps of ore and a film of coal dust internally lit by the glow of the converter hardly remind Fairfield steelworkers of the Augean stables. Besides, if a legendary hero strains in the murk, who might he be? The stoker? The miner? The crane operator? The foreman? Each man's effort matches that of his neighbor and each performs his ordinary job—a part of the larger enterprise—without a fuss.[12]

Marling refers to these manual laborers as heroes in the passages below:

> Heroes? It is the working people of Fairfield—and every person who works—who might merit that title were they not too caught up in the workaday rhythm of the four-to-twelve shift to flex their biceps and clench their jaws like regulation heroes—say, big strong Clark Gable in a denim workshirt saving the oilfield in the last reel of MGM's *Boomtown*.
>
> Work demanded the will to work and a collective commitment to grasp the tool, feelings to which histrionic stoicism and heroic eyeball rolling were emotionally superfluous. Work was the fiber of the past and the key to the future; it was the steady, business-as-usual heartbeat of Mural America. Grim or sad expressions, even pleasant ones, are hard to find there. The visages of the America workers are, at their emotional extreme, merely preoccupied; they hold their breath at the thrill of a job.[13]

"New Deal Art in Alabama Post Offices and Federal Buildings" includes a portion of the letter that Anderson wrote to the Section:

> Fairfield itself is entirely devoted to steel and iron, this covering of course the mining of coal and iron and the quarrying of limestone and dolomite, bringing them together and making iron, then steel, and into the finished bars, plates, structural steel, wire and nails. The central motif, in the center, rear, is the converter "up," which Fairfield knows to mean "all's right with the world." The flaming torch it makes as air is blown in lights up the sky for miles

around.... At the right and left are the stacks of the steel mill, with cooling towers, and the furnaces making pig iron. Below, at right and left, are the coal mines and the iron ore mines, both entirely underground. In the center, right and left, are the scenes "changing the furnace" and "making bottom," both important parts of the needed processes.[14]

A plaque at the Fairfield Post Office in Fairfield, Alabama, provides information to visitors about the mural:

The mural on the lobby wall above the postmaster's office is entitled "Spirit of Steel" and was painted in 1938 by Birmingham artists Frank Hartley Anderson and his wife, Mary. The mural shows the entire steel manufacturing process, from the mining of coal and oil, to the making of steel in open hearth furnaces, and on to the finished steel shaft. In the upper right corner of the mural the blast furnaces of the Fairfield works, a scene which still exists today.

The artists were commissioned by a Section of the United States Treasury which awarded its commissions on the basis of artistic merit. This practice differed from the more widely known "Works Progress Administration" (WPA) which considered the financial need of the artist in awarding of commissions.

Plaque placed 1991[15]

Frank Hartley Anderson and Martha Fort Anderson. Frank Hartley Anderson was born on June 10, 1890, in Boston. He studied at Harvard University,[16] at the Art Institute of Chicago, and at the Cleveland School of Art.[17]

Anderson was a member of the Northwest Printmakers. He authored articles in *American Architect, Architectural Forum, American Magazine of Art*, and in various newspapers.[18]

Anderson married Mary (Martha) Fannin Fort, who had founded the art program at the University of Alabama. She continued to illustrate, to teach, and to paint. The couple organized the Southern Printmakers Society in 1935. They enlisted in the Public Works of Art Project and in the Federal Art Project.[19]

Beckham hinted that Frank Hartley Anderson was arrogant. She suggested that the Section and the Southern communities did not like "arrogant artists." Beckham observed that Anderson "failed to show the submissiveness appropriate for a southern artist seeking government work."[20] When the Andersons received the form letter indicating that all entries in the Jackson, Mississippi, competition of 1935 had been rejected, Frank Hartley Anderson sent a handwritten note at the bottom of the form. Anderson's note read: "Will you answer these questions—Was our entry sent to you in Washington? If not—how can you know whether to reject it or not?"[21]

Edward Rowan sent Anderson a polite, firm reply that stated that the Section had indeed rejected Anderson's sketch and all the others. Frank Hartley Anderson continued to try. At last the couple received a commission for the Fairfield, Alabama, Post Office based on their entry in the Miami competition. William H. Gandy was the postmaster in Fairfield; he wrote a letter to Rowan on June 12, 1938, praising the mural. On June 19, 1938, Gandy mailed clippings praising the mural from the *Birmingham News-Age Herald.* He also sent Rowan clippings from the *Birmingham News.*[22]

Beckham concludes that Rowan did not like the Fairfield mural or Frank Hartley Anderson. Anderson continued to write to Rowan and to include articles about his work as a printmaker and about his status in the Southern Printmakers Union. In each letter, Anderson tried to persuade Rowan to give him additional commissions. Beckham observes that in the letters, "Anderson gets a little more belligerent; with each reply, Rowan gets more determined."[23]

The couple had many successes, but they lost their home in 1938. Frank took a job with the Army Corps of Engineers, and they moved into the home of Martha's parents. In 1942 Frank entered the U.S. Army as a captain; he received an assignment in Boca Raton, Florida.[24]

Frank Hartley Anderson died at the age of 56 (1891–1947). His wife Martha (1885–1968) lived more than twenty years after his death. Martha continued her career from the Fort family home in Mt. Airy, Georgia; she ran her home, Mountain Hall, as an art colony and continued to teach and paint until her death.[25]

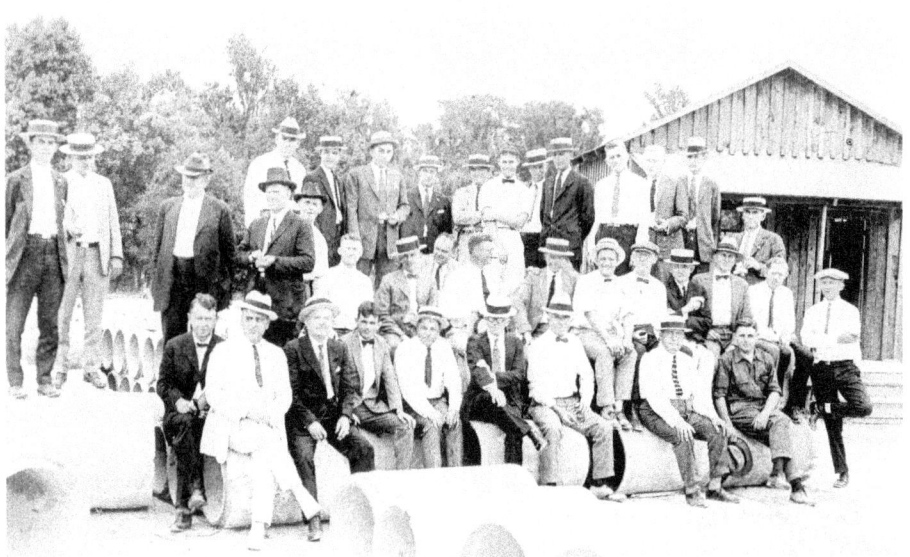

This photograph of Frank Hartley Anderson was made in Bartow, Florida. Anderson is the sixth from left on the second row (courtesy State Archives of Florida in Tallahassee).

The old Fort house—now the Glaze house—is still standing. Dr. Sidney Lanier, a cousin of the Poet Laureate Sidney Lanier, built the house as a tuberculosis sanitarium in 1899. The Fort family bought the house in 1904. Martha Fort Anderson lived in and owned the home until her death; at that time the house passed to Anderson's daughter Martha Fort Prince. Prince lived in New York; she was an heir to the home, but not a full-time resident.

After a hundred years it still occupies the most prominent point in Mt. Airy, Georgia. Ron Glaze, the current owner of the house, is beginning restoration of the house. He reports, "On a clear day one can see parts of eleven counties that surround us, including Oconee in South Carolina."[26]

Adjacent to the property where the art colony operated is East View Cemetery. Both Frank Hartley Anderson (June 10, 1891–April 17, 1947) and Martha Fort Anderson (June 22, 1888–December 10, 1968) rest there.

Fort Payne

Harwood Steiger painted the mural *Harvest at Fort Payne* (1938) for the Fort Payne, Alabama, Post Office.

In the early 1800s the site that is now Fort Payne, Alabama, was an important village to the Cherokees. When tribe members rebelled against the treaties imposed by the whites, federal troops "with the aid of militia from Alabama, Georgia and Tennessee, rounded up the hapless Cherokees like cattle in depots, or pens, and shipped them to the west."[1]

During the 1800s, Major John Payne and the United States Army built a fort to contain the Cherokee tribe members who stayed at the fort until their relocation to Oklahoma. The site of the fort associated with Major Payne is now Fort Payne, Alabama.[2]

Fort Payne, Alabama. Fort Payne, Alabama, has been the county seat of DeKalb County since 1878. Investors and workers from the North and New England flooded the Fort Payne area in the 1880s. Many of these people were working to take advantage of the coal and iron deposits discovered a few years earlier. This period carries the name "Boom Days."

Many of the historic buildings in Fort Payne date from the "Boom Days." These notable structures include the Fort Payne Opera House (1889) and the Fort Payne Depot (1891)—now the Fort Payne Museum.[3] The center structure in the group of three buildings in the photograph is currently (2014) Hunt Hall, the site of the mural painted by Harwood Magnus Steiger.

The hosiery industry was originally the base of the Fort Payne economy. At the turn of the 21st century, about 8,000 people worked at the 125 hosiery

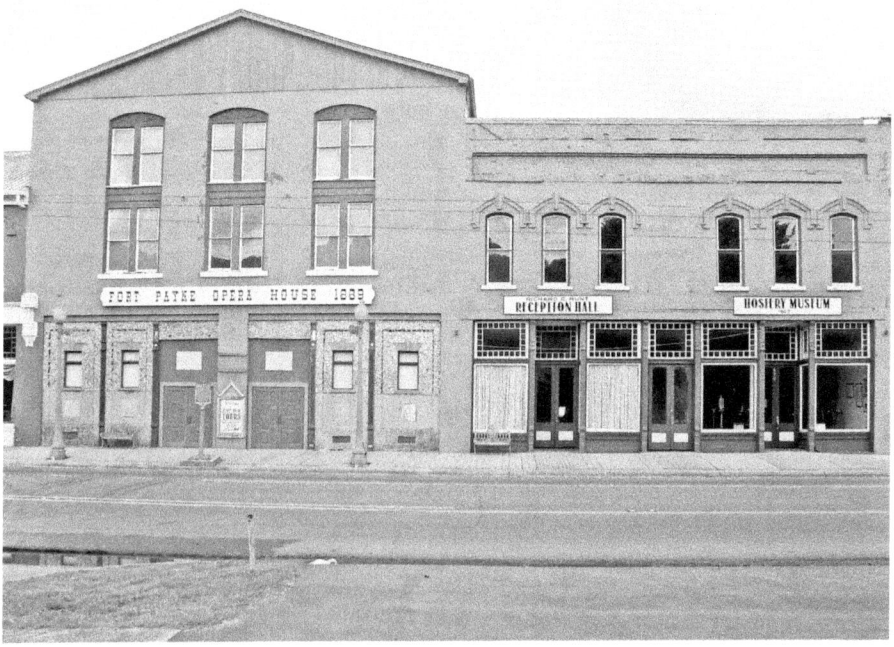

The Richard C. Hunt Reception Hall, center, holds the federal artwork (courtesy Landmarks of DeKalb County).

mills in Fort Payne, which had the nickname "Sock Capital of the World." By 2011, twenty mills in the area employed about 600 people.[4]

Fort Payne is the hometown of the award-winning country music group Alabama. Many visitors to the area visit the Alabama Museum. The group held a fundraising concert called "The June Jam" in Fort Payne each year for many years.[5]

The Fort Payne, Alabama, Post Office. The appropriated amount that the federal government allotted for the construction of the Fort Payne Post Office was $59,735. The official opening ceremony for the building was April 8, 1937; the event was the largest public gathering in Fort Payne history.

The speaker for the occasion was former judge of the 9th Circuit William Wallace Haralson. Haralson was 77; this event was one of his last public appearances before his death in the same year. Haralson introduced Congressman Joe Starnes, who had obtained the first federal building in his district—with the aid of Senator John Hollis Bankhead (the father of Senator Bankhead, featured in the Carrollton mural) and with the help of Senator Hugo Black (who later became an Associate Supreme Court Justice for the years 1937–1971).[6]

The city of Fort Payne grew and prospered over the next 40 years. The

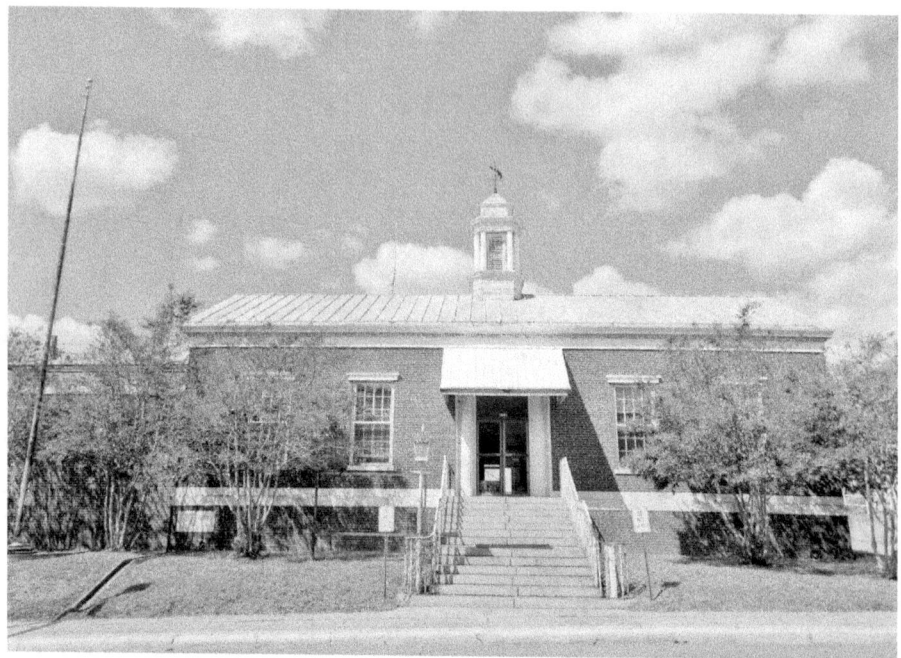

The Fort Payne Post Office is no longer in use as a post office. The building with its 10+ steps would prove difficult for those with disabilities to access.

year 1979 saw the beginnings of a new post office at the corner of First Street and Godfrey Avenue. On Friday, April 25, 1980, at noon, Postmaster Sam Baugh closed the window at the 1937 post office, lowered the flag there, and raised both the flag and the window at the new post office.

DeKalb County bought the 1937 post office building. The commission initially planned to raze it for parking along Gault Avenue. Luckily, a private individual purchased the post office to prevent its destruction.

Inside the 1937 post office was a mural that Harwood Magnus Steiger had painted through a federal commission. The new location of this mural, *Harvest at Fort Payne*, became the DeKalb County Courthouse in July 1980. The mural became accessible for viewing in the rotunda of the courthouse. It remained there for the next 20 years.

The next relocation of Steiger's mural for Fort Payne took place in 2000, when renovations began on the courthouse. These renovations would convert the courthouse into a judicial building only. *Landmarks* trustee and art expert Perry Morgan noticed the mural in the rotunda of the courthouse; potentially dangerous electrical wire dangled near the work. Morgan contacted fellow *Landmarks* trustee Judy Brown; they began the effort to protect the mural.

The county commissioners were cooperative from the beginning. There was, however, confusion about the actual ownership of the mural. After reviewing the original agreement between the United States Postal Service and the Dekalb County Commission, the Postal Service claimed ownership of the mural.

The commissioners argued that the impending construction on the courthouse and the removal of some of the public offices from the courthouse would lessen the number of people who could view the work. Finally, on June 5, 2001, the United States Postal Service and *Landmarks* signed an agreement; *Landmarks* would relocate and insure the mural for $25,000.

On June 11, 2001, *Landmarks* trustees Morgan and Brown supervised both the removal of the mural from the courthouse and its relocation in Hunt Hall in the Opera House Block. Hunt Hall, which is at 514 Gault Avenue and beside the Hosiery Museum, still displays Harwood Steiger's mural in the lobby on the north wall. The placard over Hunt Hall reads Richard C. Hunt Reception Hall; it is the center door of three, as shown in the earlier photograph in this section.

The door to the building on the left of Hunt Hall reads Fort Payne Opera House (1889). The door to the right of Hunt Hall invites visitors to the Hosiery Museum (1907).

Harwood Steiger and the *Harvest at Fort Payne* mural. In July of 1937 Harwood Steiger had learned of his selection to prepare the artwork for the Fort Payne Post Office. Steiger accepted the commission on August 2, 1937, and planned a trip south to Alabama when he finished with his art classes.

Steiger left for Alabama on September 12, 1937. His plans were to stay for one month and to make sketches of the local scenery to use as possible ideas for the mural. Twice, Steiger requested expense money for the trip; twice he received rejections.

Upon Steiger's arrival in Fort Payne, Postmaster John B. Davidson drove him to DeSoto Falls. Steiger found the scenery lovely, but the trip did not show the local day-to-day activities of the people.

Steiger decided to ride along the rural mail routes with Rob Dellinger. Forty years later Dellinger recalled his travels with Steiger. Dellinger noted that Steiger took a picture at Adamsburg where "Levi Baugh and his relative J.E. [Joseph Ernest] Owen [the grandfather of Randy Owen and great-grandfather of Teddy Gentry of the singing group Alabama] were making syrup." This scene became a part of the 1938 mural *Harvest at Fort Payne* for the Fort Payne Post Office.

Dellinger recalled that the large house in the center of the mural belonged to Charlie Doss on Sand Mountain near King's Chapel in the High Point community. Dellinger, however, regretted that Steiger chose to photograph only unpainted houses on his trips.

About a month after the trip to Fort Payne, Steiger corresponded with

Edward Rowan. Steiger indicated that he planned to add a cotton gin and hosiery factory to a scene of a cotton field.

Rowan made several suggestions about the sketch that Steiger had submitted. He wanted the mules in the center of the mural and suggested removing the mailboxes and the children.[7]

One member of the Section indicated that the depicted house, "while quite authentic for the locale, should be given more stability on its foundation."[8] Steiger, however, refused to change the house that he had painted directly from one he had seen on his rides across Sand Mountain. Steiger decided including a hosiery mill and a cotton gin in the scene would clutter the mural.

Correspondence between the Treasury and Steiger continued. Steiger finally received his contract in December of 1937 with stipulations that he

- would pay for all supplies and expenses.
- would receive $190 after the Section approved his sketch.
- would receive $150 when the mural was 50 percent completed.
- would receive the remaining $250 when the mural was successfully installed.

Steiger was planning to use the medium of tempera on gesso board. The necessary dimensions were 13'4" × 3'10.5". The Section expected the mural to weigh about 100 pounds.

The Section had a few more suggestions before it would approve the sketch that Steiger had submitted. One of these was to use chickens at the bottom of the scene.[9]

Harvest at Fort Payne. Farm laborers appeared often in the murals produced through the federal programs during the New Deal era. The depiction of subsistence farmers, however, was rare; most artists failed to admit having ever painted sharecroppers. The resulting paintings usually showed the farmers as strong, healthy, well-clothed, well-supplied, and successful.

Harwood Steiger's *Harvest at Fort Payne* was an exception to the rule. His mural depicts a twentieth-century farm with nineteenth-century equipment. Even the long skirts and the sunbonnets that the women wear are out-of-date.

A mule-drawn wagon replaces a more modern gasoline-driven tractor; a cistern for pumping water indicates that indoor plumbing is not available. Farm animals—not machinery— are grinding the cane for making molasses. Farm equipment appears severely limited in the mural. Gullies and erosion indicate other hardships that the farmers face.

In the upper left corner of the painting is an example of a "dogtrot" house. This housing style had a central hall with a door at each end. In warm weather, the occupants could open both doors to allow a breeze to blow through the house—or a dog to trot through the hall.

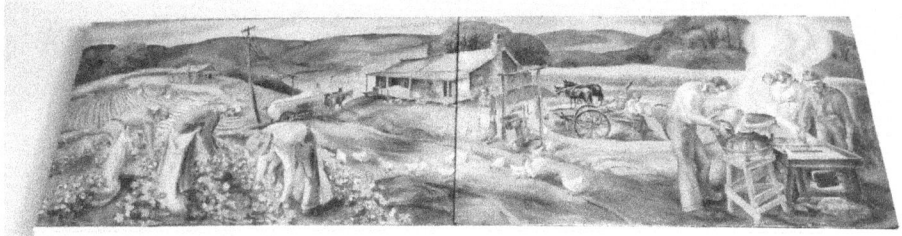

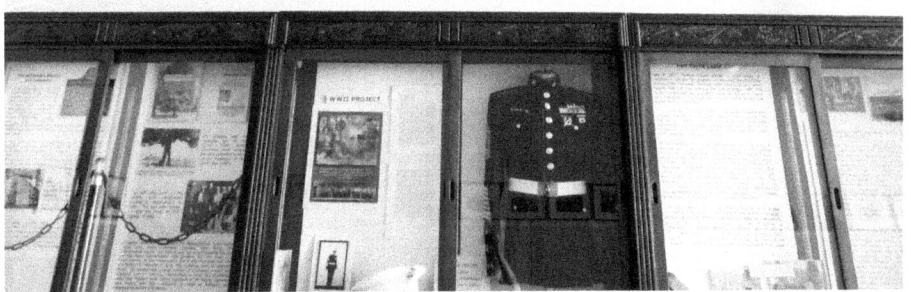

Harwood Magnus Steiger's mural for the Section shows farms and farmhouses as they appeared in many areas of Fort Payne, Alabama, during the Great Depression. He titled the mural *Fort Payne Harvest*.

Steiger did provide some signs of hope to the viewer of the mural. Contour plowing and electric lines—though as yet unconnected to the house—offer predictions of improvements in the future. Southerners were not offended by the problems evident in the scene because the artist hints that progress is coming.[10]

Harwood Magnus Steiger. When Harwood Magnus Steiger received the invitation to paint a mural for Fort Payne, Alabama, he admitted he had never been that far south. Up until this time, he had spent most of his life in New York, Pennsylvania, and Massachusetts.[11]

Steiger had spent ten summers teaching painting on Martha's Vineyard. Nevertheless, he made a trip to Fort Payne, and introduced himself to the postmaster, who viewed Steiger's sketches with interest.

Steiger asked the advice of the postmaster on the subject of the mural. Steiger had sketched two different scenes: a landscape and the cotton industry. The postmaster and the Section both chose the landscape.[12]

Steiger was not a resident of the Fort Payne area. His background as an artist, his visits to Fort Payne, and his willingness to seek the opinion of others helped make his work a success.

Harwood Magnus Steiger was born on January 2, 1900, in Macedon, New York. He spent his early years in Fairport, New York, with his family.

His art education was at Mechanics Institute in Rochester, New York; at the Academy of Fine Arts in Philadelphia, Pennsylvania, where he had a fellowship; and at Westchester and East End Art School in Provincetown, Massachusetts.

Steiger was also a teacher. He taught at a school he had attended, Mechanics Institute in Rochester. Through the years he was on the staff at various times at Oswego Training School, at the State Continuation School, at the YMCA department of art, at the Central School of Business, and at the Art School of the Rochester Atheaneum.

Harwood Steiger enlisted the aid of locals in building a studio for him in an unsettled area of Nova Scotia. The studio was on the Bay of Fundy and near Parker's Cove. The construction work was complete in fifteen days. Steiger would spend many summers painting and drawing in his studio.

In 1934 Steiger tried something new. He became a regular on a radio show in New York City. He lectured on both landscape and still life painting and taught from his studio on West 4th Street during the New York winters. He taught summer school at Edgartown, Massachusetts.[13]

On August 5, 1940, forty-year-old Harwood Magnus Steiger and 45-year-old Sophie Fredericka Halbwachs—a former student of his—married in Edgartown, Massachusetts.[14] The couple settled down near Red Hook, New York, and became avid gardeners. After a hurricane destroyed their studio,

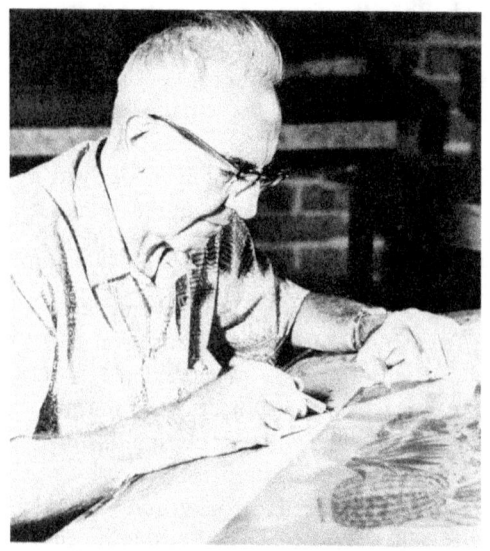

they worked on fabric design in Alamos, Mexico.

Tubac, Arizona. When Mexico did not prove to be profitable for the sale of their fabrics, the Steigers moved to Tubac, Arizona, in 1956. The Steigers returned to Red Hook for the summers and lived and worked in Tubac in the winters.[15]

Today about 1,000 people reside in the town, which is advertised as "Southern Arizona's growing artist colony." The area of Tubac, Arizona, is about 10.8 square miles of land in Santa Cruz County; it lists no water area.

Harwood Magnus Steiger designs a silk screen in Tubac, Arizona. He and his wife Sophie Halbwachs Steiger bought a lot and built a studio and shop in Tubac in 1958 after their move to Tubac in 1956 (courtesy Cynthia deVillemaretta).

Tubac is located in the Santa Cruz River Valley and boasts a 250-year-old Spanish history. Father Kino was first in charge of the mission along the Santa Cruz River. Today more than eighty shops and galleries feature sculptures, paintings, clothing, and hand-crafted items.[16]

Brownell notes that if one is traveling in the area, one must choose to visit the Tubac Center of the Arts, which serves as headquarters of the Santa Cruz Valley Art Association. Steiger was associated with the Tubac Center of the Arts and helped begin the Santa Cruz Valley Art Association.

Steiger objected to the use of customary advertising techniques. He preferred to use his beautiful designs on drapery fabrics and dress fabrics as their own advertisements. He soon "built a clientele of enthusiastic women across the country which became almost a cult. An oft-told tale is the story of two ladies meeting in Thailand, each exclaiming[,] 'Oh, I see you have a Steiger print!'"[17]

Steiger made certain that there was never a visible break between one inking and the next inking. Sophie—an herbalist who studied both plants and animals—made sure the structures of the plants and animals in the designs were accurate.[18]

By 1959 their silk screening store and studio on the Tubac Plaza was complete. By 1960 the couple would find it necessary to enlarge and remodel the Steiger Printed Fabric Shop.[19]

Sophie and Harwood Steiger had been among the founders of the Santa Cruz Valley Art Association. Harwood Magnus Steiger had sent out a letter on November 15, 1962, to encourage participation in the Santa Cruz Valley Art Association:

> There "ain't no" Santa Cruz Valley Art Association. We hope you will evolve one at a breakfast meeting 9 a.m. Sunday Morning, December 5, at Harwood Steiger's house in Tubac. Bring ideas for the 4th Annual Festival of Arts. Help us unearth treasures of arts and crafts in our hills and valleys, from Sells to Fort Huachica through Sonora…. Our interests will do much to develop and keep this talent alive (the Papago Indians are now doing pottery as well as basketry.) Let's keep our exhibitions regional, unique and interesting.[20]

In 1968 the Steigers added a screening room that was 130 feet long to their Tubac studio. In this facility they carried out the painstaking procedures of stretching the fabric, applying the screen, and printing the pattern.[21] "Many of his designs were inspired by the flora and fauna of the desert but he also produced many mid century [sic] abstract and geometric designs. This area of the Sonoran Desert is unusual as there are 2 rainy seasons. Harwood was especially fond of the desert road-runner!"[22]

The heavy linen placemat shows the roadrunners that Steiger liked to draw and print. The desert plants are true-to-form and typical of the dry area. The anatomy of the roadrunners is accurate, but they seem to project

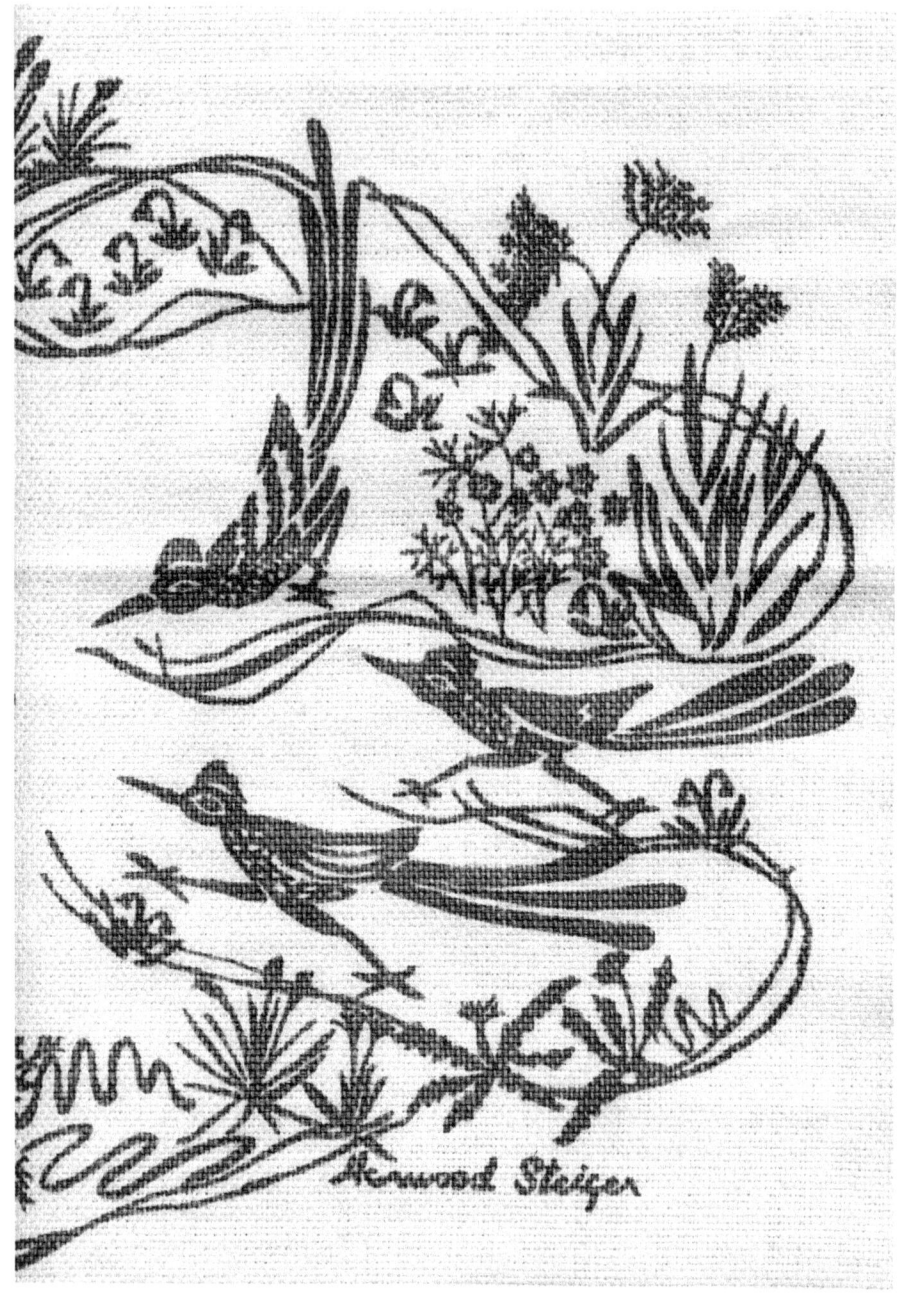

This fabric designed and printed by Harwood Magnus Steiger bears his name. The heavy linen fabric has fringed edges and is cut to serve as a placemat (fabric in the collection of author Anita Price Davis).

personality into the scene. Steiger called some of his prints with the scampering birds "Roadrunner Frenzies."

Harwood Magnus Steiger died in 1980. His burial was in Rhinebeck, New York.[23]

Sophie's niece Wanda Halbwachs managed their shop after the Steigers' deaths until 2006.[24]

Guntersville

Charles Russell Hardman painted the mural *Indians Receiving Gifts from the Spanish* for the Guntersville, Alabama, Post Office (1947).

A mural depicting the positive meeting and acceptance of the Spanish by the local tribes in 1541 was the topic that Charles Russell Hardman chose for the Guntersville Post Office in Alabama. The meeting of Hernando de Soto and the Native Americans that Hardman pictured occurred on McKee's Island.

Guntersville—Then and Now. The town of Guntersville took its name from the American pioneer John Gunter. Gunter was of Welsh or Scottish descent; in the late 1700s, he traveled south on the Tennessee River to a Cherokee village called *Kusanunnahi*, or Creek Path. Gunter settled there with the Cherokees; their local chief was Chief Bushyhead, head of the Paint Clan. Gunter married Chief Bushyhead's fifteen-year-old-daughter Ghe-go-he-li; Chief Bushyhead exchanged Ghe-go-he-li for salt from Gunter's mines. Gunter accepted the bargain and changed his bride's name to Katherine.[1]

The name of the village of Kusanunnahi became Gunter's Ferry. When flatboats began to stop at the town, Gunter's Ferry became Gunter's Landing. Finally, the growing town took the name Guntersville.[2]

Guntersville is in Marshall County. Today Marshall County, Alabama, has four main cities: Albertville, Arab, Boaz, and Guntersville. These four cities are near each other and create an urban-like area with advantages of both city and rural life.

Marshall County residents have many recreational opportunities. Water activities often focus around the Tennessee River and the 69,000-acre Lake Guntersville. Lake Guntersville is the largest lake in Alabama and is one of the three best bass-fishing lakes in America. The city of Guntersville is in the center of Marshall County; Guntersville offers easy access to Lake Guntersville.

The major cities of Birmingham and Huntsville are easily accessible from Guntersville. Birmingham—the largest city in Alabama—is only 70 miles away. Huntsville, Alabama, is only 35 miles to the north.[3]

The Guntersville Post Offices. The first post office in the Guntersville area was in 1833 in Helicon. In 1836 the post office became Van Buren; in 1844 it became Marshall, then Gunter's Landing, and finally Guntersville on January 21, 1854.

In 1910 Guntersville obtained its first dedicated post office building. Postal delivery began in the Guntersville area in 1922.[4] The *Guntersville Advertiser Democrat* noted in November of 1933: "Guntersville has a good chance of securing a post office at an early date. Material and labor are cheap and numbers of men are needing work, so now is a good time to build."[5]

After several delays, the federal Public Works Administration began constructing the United States Post Office in Guntersville in May of 1940. The architectural classification of the post office is a refrained Colonial Revival style of the 19th and 20th centuries. The facility reflects the contemporary trends of the day and the Great Depression limitations of financial resources.

The two-story building faces east. The lot is on a low hill and slopes upward from the front to the rear. Reinforced concrete retaining walls enclose

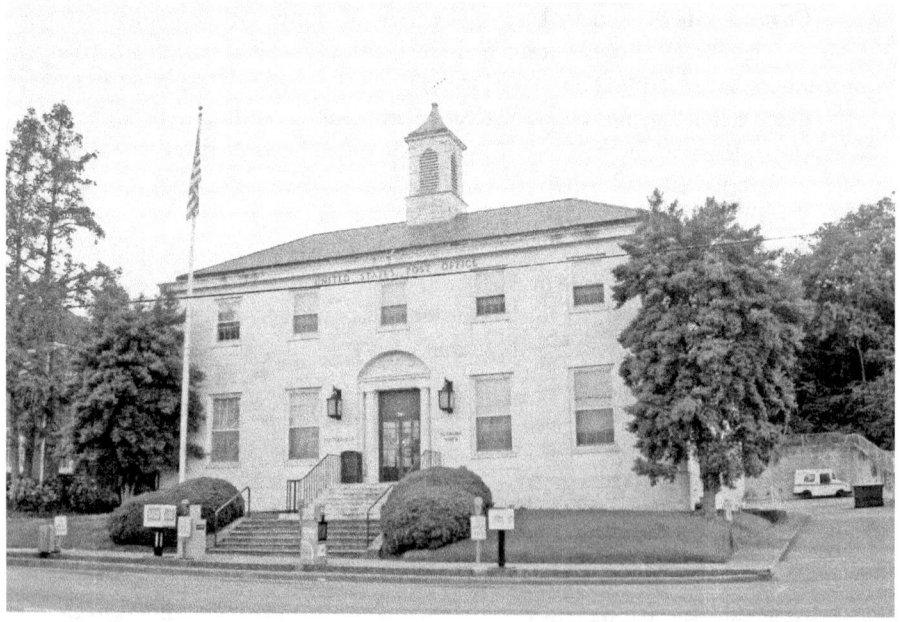

The Guntersville Post Office dates from 1940. It holds Charles Russell Hardman's mural *Indians Receiving Gifts from the Spanish* (1947).

the sides of the lot on the north, the west, and the south. The narrow front lawn slopes to the sidewalk.

The front door is centered. Two single double hung sash windows with twelve panes on top and twelve panes on the bottom flank each side of the front entrance. A decorative relief eagle adorns the area above the front door. On the second floor, five eight-paned windows add light, ventilation, and decoration to the building. Its final cost was $115,000. Louis Simon was also the architect for post offices in other Alabama towns, including Huntsville, Bay Minette, and Montevallo.

Sconces decorate and light each side of the front entrance. This principal entrance leads into a vestibule within a lobby that extends almost the full width of the building on the east wall. A counter window occupies part of the wall opposite the main entrance. Banks of post office boxes extended along the walls of the hallway on the north, south, and west.[6]

A cornerstone is on the south corner of the post office. It cites those who participated in the construction of the Guntersville post office. The cornerstone reads:

JAMES A. FARLEY
POSTMASTER GENERAL

JOHN M. CARMODY
FEDERAL WORKS ADMINISTRATOR

W. ENGLEBERT REYNOLDS
COMMISSIONER OF PUBLIC BUILDINGS

LOUIS A. SIMON
SUPERVISING ARCHITECT

NEAL A. MELICK
SUPERVISING ENGINEER

1940[7]

On November 20, 1940, a ceremony marked the laying of the cornerstone "of this magnificent building that is nearing completion."[8] A dedication ceremony on June 2, 1941, celebrated the completion of the building funded through the Public Works Agency, part of President Franklin Roosevelt's New Deal.

In 2007 the City of Guntersville obtained both the property on which the New Deal Post Office stood and the structure that had housed the old Guntersville Post Office. The city paid $425,000 for the structure and the property. By this time, the United States Postal Service had moved its services into a new facility on Blount Avenue and no longer had need of the older building.

The United States Postal Service retained rights to the mural *Indians Receiving Gifts from the Spanish* by Charles Russell Hardman; the mural dates from 1947. The National Register of Historic Places added the Guntersville Post Office to its list of historic places on August 16, 2010.[9]

The Guntersville Post Office is an example of the Colonial Revival style of architecture. Such building styles typically have symmetry of the front façade, the inclusion of sidelights and fanlights at the front entrances, and doorways with pediments. In the 1940s the two-storied buildings of this style often had hipped or side-gabled roofs. The Colonial Revival style of architecture was popular for public buildings like post offices, government offices, and libraries.[10]

Upon the opening of the post office in Guntersville in 1941, the *Guntersville Gleam* commented on "the most interesting thing in the whole building." The article states that this point of interest is

> the "lookout" built for use of the postoffice [*sic*] inspectors. These men come and go without warning, usually without anybody knowing they have been here. The lookout has three entrances—from the basement, first floor and second floor. Only the inspectors can get in.
> Once inside they can see everybody in the postoffice, but nobody can see them. They look out through narrow slits in the walls onto the first floor and even into the basement. The employes [*sic*] never know when they are being watched.[11]

Indians Receiving Gifts from the Spanish. The Alabama Historical Commission in its *Preservation Report* notes that there is no indication who commissioned the mural on the north wall of the Guntersville Post Office. The title of the mural is *Indians Receiving Gifts from the Spanish* and is the work of Charles Russell Hardman, a Florida artist. The installation of the mural dates from 1947, which was after the mural program ended. The United States Postal Service, however, reserves rights to the mural in the Guntersville Post Office. The 2007 deed that transfers the property to the City of Guntersville "expressly reserves the right for the Post Office to 'remove and take away said mural.'"[12]

Beckham in her *Depression Post Office Murals and Southern Culture* does not recognize *Indians Receiving Gifts from the Spanish* as a federally commissioned work.[13] Other sources like the *Huntsville Times* indicate, however, that the mural was a product of a Treasury Department program.[14] The Alabama Department of Archives and History indicates that "there are no files or documents in the National Archives relating to it."

The mural depicts a group of Native Americans meeting with a group of Spanish soldiers. The theme is one that is prevalent in the paintings of the period, and the meetings were not uncommon in history. "Local tradition holds that explorer Hernando Desoto [*sic*] met with Native Americans at a village near present-day Guntersville."[15]

To the observer, the mural seems familiar. Such paintings seem almost

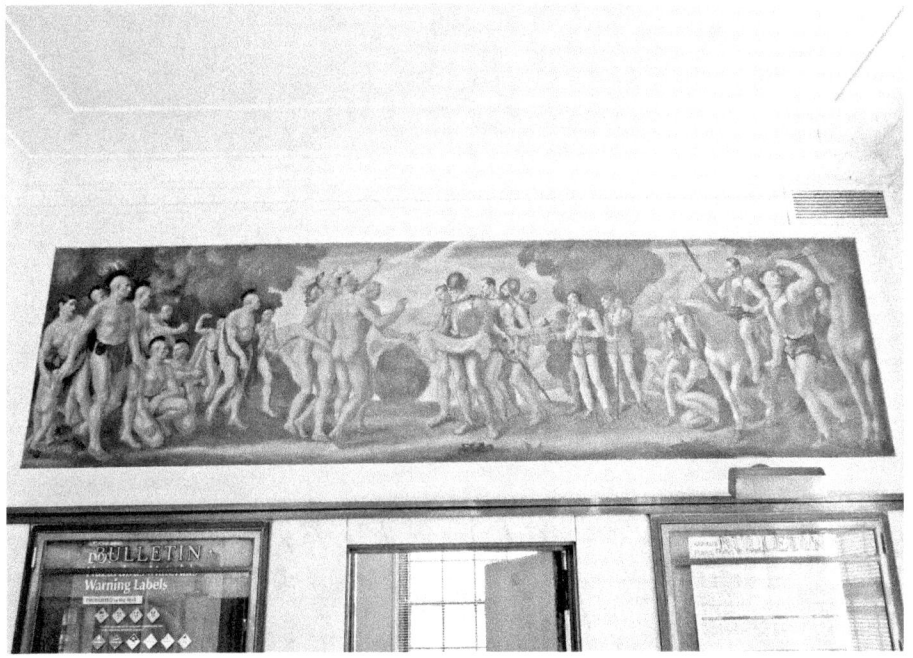

Indians Receiving Gifts from the Spanish (1947) **is by Charles Russell Hardman. The source of the funding for the work, however, is unclear.**

"an overgrown, line-by-line replica of the famous 1564 Jacques Le Moyne gouache in the New York Public Library, showing Rene de Loudonnier meeting Chief Athore."[16] Nudity is prevalent in the mural, but because the people unclothed are not white, objections were fewer than what they might have been.

Charles Russell Hardman. Georgia artist Charles Russell Hardman painted the Guntersville mural and the mural in Miami Beach, Florida. Little biographical information, however, is available about Hardman either in Florida or in Alabama.

The Miami Beach Post Office structure that holds Hardman's *Episodes from the History of Florida* is not the typical building constructed in the 1930s and 1940s for the postal department. The Miami Beach Post Office dates from 1937; it is an Art Moderne structure. Howard Lovewell Cheney designed the Miami Beach building, which is in the Art Deco section of Miami Beach at 1300 Washington Avenue.

Howard Lovewell Cheney (1889–1969) was both an architect and engineer. He designed the Miami Beach Post Office (1937) and the Washington National Airport (1940–1941), now the Reagan National Airport. The Miami Beach Post Office has a central, drum-shaped main feature; wings or sections

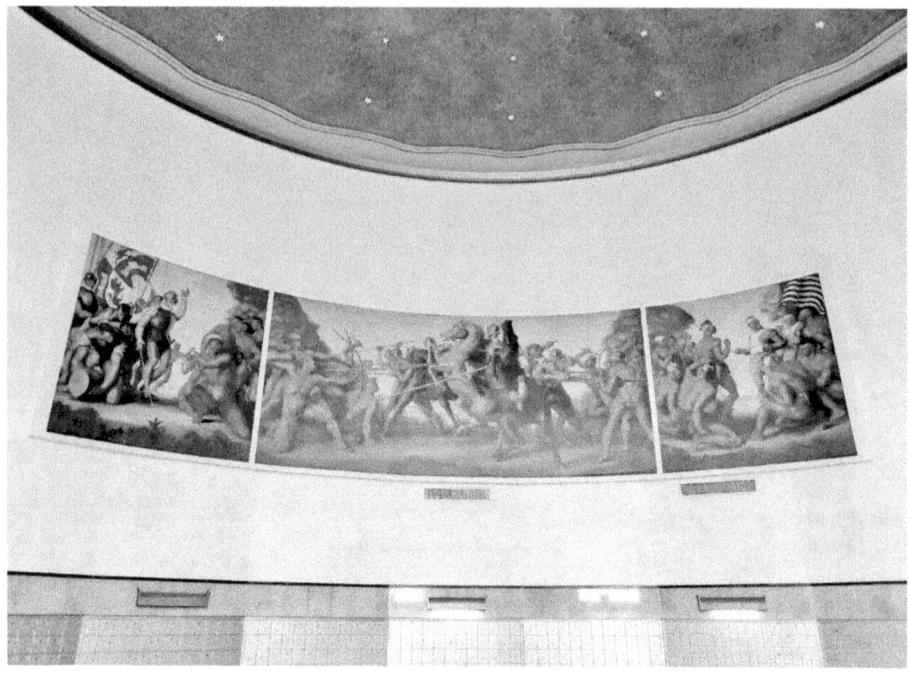

Charles Russell Hardman's murals for the Miami Beach Post Office (1940) show his interpretation of the relationships of the explorers to the Native Americans in Florida. The content is suggestive of the later mural *Indians Receiving Gifts from the Spanish* (1947).

extend from the large, rounded portion. Inside the structure is a fountain and Charles Russell Hardman's murals that depict Ponce de Leon's invasion of Florida; an art fixture that resembles the sun provides light for the lobby.

There are other Art Deco structures in Miami Beach. The distinguishing features of the Art Deco style are simple, streamlined, clean shapes. The construction materials frequently include both man-made and natural substances.[17]

Hardman's art murals for the post office in Miami Beach were products of the 1940s. He titled the works *Episodes from the History of Florida*. The first image to the photographer's left is *Discovery*. The subject matter follows the pattern of many murals: it show members of a tribe meeting with visitors to the area. In this instance Hardman shows Ponce de Leon (ca. 1460–1501) and a few Indians at an encounter in Florida.

The second mural in the series of three depicts an altercation between Hernando de Soto (1497–1542) and the Native Americans. Hardman titled this middle painting *De Soto and the Indians*.[18] Beckham describes it as "a raging battle between Spaniards and Indians." She observes that the overdeveloped horses are rearing in fright. She finds the human figures to be believable even though they are somewhat exaggerated:

> They writhe; they suffer; they make war on one another. ... [T]he Indians in Miami stand on both feet and the conquistadors cling to Renaissance painting, not a medieval one.[19]

The third mural shows Quartermaster General Thomas Sidney Jesup (1788–1860) conferring with Seminoles in Florida. President Andrew Jackson had ordered him to Georgia and Alabama to deal with the Creek tribe; next, President Jackson placed Jesup in command of all the U.S. troops in Florida during the Second Seminole War (1837–1842).[20]

Hardman worked on the mural for Guntersville for about five years and earned $800 for the work. He painted the mural on canvas in the New York apartment he shared with his wife. She accompanied him to Guntersville to install the work.

Hardman explained that he sketched each figure on the mural many times before transferring it to canvas. He said that he lost money painting the 12'3" × 3'3" work.

He particularly liked the subject, however, because it allowed him to contrast the beautifully clad Spaniards with the nude figures of the Native Americans. He also enjoyed painting the Tennessee River, the nearly life-sized figures, and the spirited horses.

Mrs. Hardman said that it was difficult for her to leave the mural in Guntersville after living with it in their New York apartment for five years. "As they left the post office, Mrs. Hardman paused a moment for a last look over her shoulder...."[21]

Personal information on the artist Charles Russell Hardman is very limited. He was born in Augusta, Georgia, on July 16, 1912. His burial on December 16, 1995, was in Magnolia Cemetery, in Augusta, Georgia.[22] Falk's *Who Was Who in American Art* notes only that Hardman developed a mural for Miami, Florida; no mention is made of Guntersville or any other place where Hardman's work resides.[23]

Haleyville

Hollis Holbrook painted the mural *Reforestation* (1940) for the post office in Haleyville, Alabama.

Hollis Holbrook contracted to prepare a post office mural for Haleyville, Alabama. The mural and its installation were complete in the Alabama city by 1940. Holbrook based the Haleyville mural on an appropriate theme: *Reforestation*.

Haleyville, Alabama. Haleyville is in the foothills region of the Appalachian Mountains and is in the northwestern part of the state of Alabama in mountainous Winston County. Winston County had the nickname "Free State of Winston" during the Civil War because it seceded from the state of Alabama.

Winston County comprises 614 square miles with six incorporated communities and four county commissioners. The Sipsey Fork of the Black Warrior River rises in the Bankhead Forest in Winston County; it flows into Smith Lake, which then eventually gets to the Black Warrior River. Waterways were vital to the development of the county. Winston County has a population of 24,484 (2010 census) and marks its founding date as February 12, 1850. Haleyville is its largest city.[1]

The first dwellers in the Haleyville area were the Cherokees. They settled near the place where the waters divide: "the division of the waters." At this place of separation (sometimes called "the continental divide"), water runs north to the Tennessee River, south to the Warrior River, and west to the Tombigbee.

Alabama became a state in 1819. In 1820, Richard McMahan of Lauderdale County established the first permanent English settlement in Winston County near what is now Haleyville.

The original development of Haleyville as a town was along the railroad tracks. The population of the Haleyville area continued to expand mainly because of the railroads, the roads, and the job opportunities.

When the white settlers tried to force the Cherokees out of the area in 1836, however, some refused to go and found places to hide. Many names in the area today have Cherokee roots.[2]

Haleyville is part of the Cumberland Plateau physiographic section. Low, rolling hills with evergreens give way to mountainous areas with hardwood trees. A portion of Winston County is in the William B. Bankhead National Forest. Stuart R. Purser recognized the Bankhead family in his mural *Farm Scene with Senator Bankhead* for Carrollton, Alabama.[3]

Much of the region around Haleyville has coal deposits. Erosion is apparent in some areas.[4]

Haleyville: The First 911 Call. The very first 911 call in the United States was in Haleyville, Alabama, in 1968. Great Britain had used 999 since 1937 to summon the services of the police, medical aid, or the fire departments. Although the first investigations of a universal emergency number in the United States had begun in Congress in 1958, it was 1967 before the passage of the legal mandate for the use of the number 911.

Alabama House Speaker Rankin Fite placed the first 911 call from Haleyville on February 16, 1968. Congressman Tom Bevill answered the call.

The requirements for the new emergency number were that it be an easy number to use and that it be three numbers that were not in use in any telephone number or area code in Canada or the United States. AT&T and the Federal Trade Commission announced plans to build the first 911 system in Huntington, Indiana.

Bob Gallagher, who was president of Alabama Telephone at that time, was annoyed that there had been no consultations with the independent phone companies. He completed the first 911 emergency service in Haleyville before AT&T could do so in Huntington, Indiana.[5]

This recent photograph is of the historic (old) Haleyville Post Office. The structure served as the Haleyville Post Office from 1939 to 1970; it now serves as the Haleyville Public Library.

An architectural feature of the Haleyville Post Office is dentil molding along the roofline. Dentils are rectangular blocks that—when placed closely together—can form a band or decorative molding; in this case the dentil molding is below the cornice of the Haleyville Post Office/Public Library.

The front of the Haleyville Public Library is symmetrical. Two windows on either side of the front door provide decoration and ventilation.

Four steps with wrought iron railings allow patrons to enter the building more easily than they could some of the other early post offices. The 1940

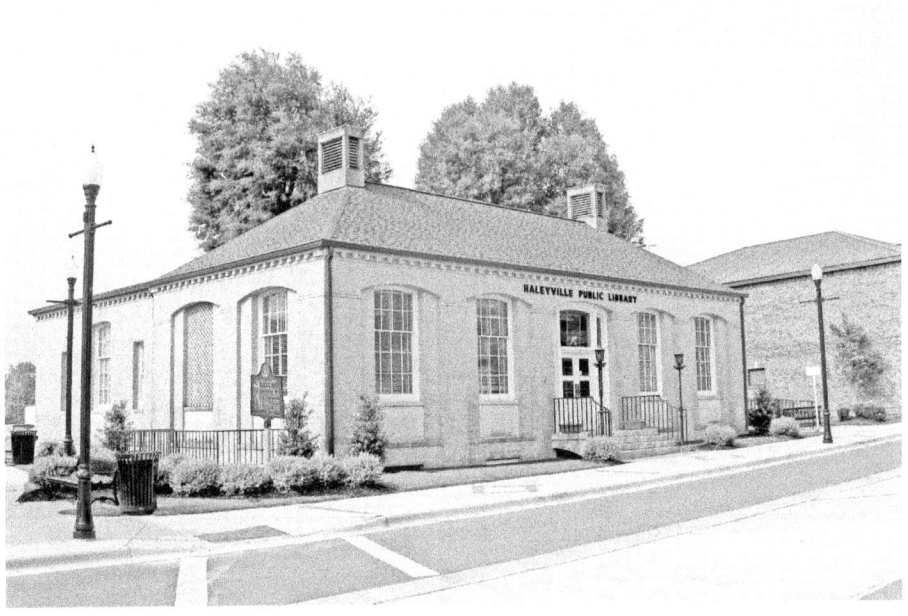

The current Haleyville Public Library served as the Haleyville Post Office from 1939 to 1970. Dentil molding decorates the building.

buff brick post office holds the painted-over original mural and houses the replication of *Reforestation.*

Reforestation (1940). Artist Hollis Holbrook visited the area around Haleyville shortly after he received his commission to prepare public art to display in the Haleyville Post Office. Holbrook wrote to Edward Rowan, the assistant to the Chief of the Treasury Department's Section of Fine Arts, about his visit and about his ideas for the public art.

Holbrook observed the countryside around Haleyville and wrote to Rowan that the land was "laid bare to deep gashes caused by erosion."[6] In the mural he was to prepare, Holbrook expressed a desire to "show the benefits of land terracing and the benefits of the top soil in contrast with the old worn out methods of burning the grass and of pulling up the roots of trees, etc."[7]

The Civilian Conservation Corps (CCC) had been at work reforesting, terracing, and improving the area around Haleyville.[8] Holbrook, therefore, had some examples of terracing and reforesting—in addition to some erosion—to observe when he visited in Alabama. In *Reforestation* (1940), Holbrook placed examples of reforesting, terracing, recent conservation work, and bountiful crops in the forefront of the mural. Holbrook included in a prominent place Ranger Thomas Wilson, who had requested that the mural represent more than a "pretty picture." Holbrook also placed a Civilian Conservation Corps (CCC) worker on the mural in order to recognize the work of the CCC in the Black Warrior Forest.[9]

Hollis Holbrook painted *Reforestation* in egg tempera on the lobby wall of the Haleyville Post Office in 1940. He matched the blue in the sky with the blue of the post office wall. When he installed the work, he used 36 brown eggs from Haleyville to mix his paint. He listened to the comments of patrons and shared them with Rowan.[10]

> I have never felt so well rewarded as I have for this task. The people of Haleyville have lauded my efforts with exhaustive praise. Honestly they are starving for some good art works.... [One says,] "Doc, that sure is the prettiest sign paintin' I've ever seen." Another says, "By God, that sure is the prettiest thing I've ever seen!"—another—"Ain't that the prettiest doggone thing you've ever seen!" Somewhat the same but there have been hundreds of the same thing. I've heard that a picture isn't so good when it is liked by all but right now I want to say "Who cares?"[11]

In a September 26, 1940, clipping sent to Rowan, Holbrook noted that he enjoyed his work in Haleyville. He described the residents as "the most sincerely cordial and likeable people he had ever met."[12]

Holbrook contrasted erosion and "unscientific farming" (shown in the background of this replication of the mural) with the work of Ranger Wilson and the CCC "boys" (indicated in the foreground of the duplicated work).

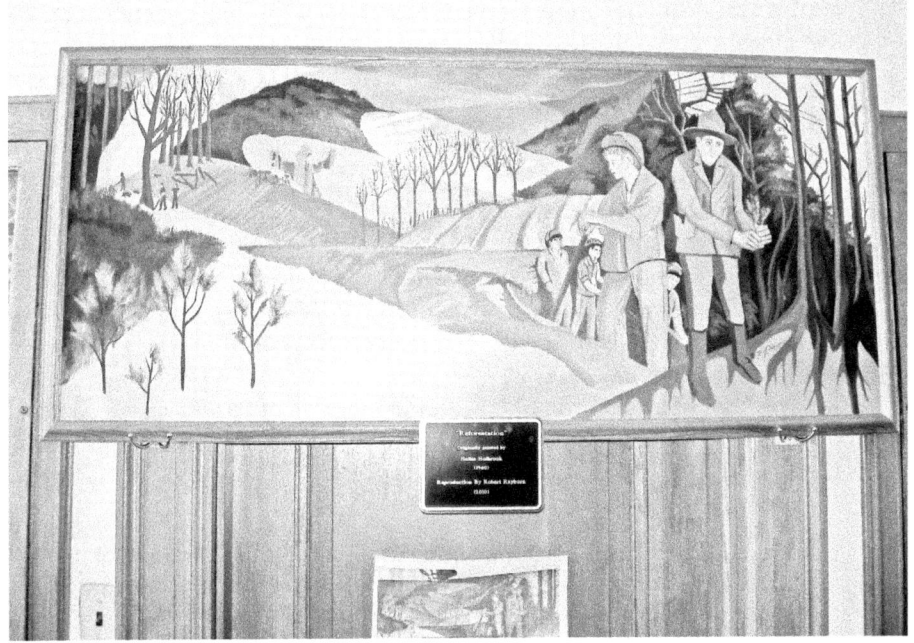

The placement of the reproduction *Reforestation* in the Haleyville Post Office.

Holbrook warned—through the medium of his artwork—about the consequences of continued disregard for the land.[13]

Hollis Holbrook had painted the original New Deal mural titled *Reforestation* in 1940. Around 1970, during the renovations of the post office building for the Haleyville Public Library, someone covered the mural with paint. The Haleyville Historical Society had a conservator uncover 3 quarter-sized areas on the wall where the mural had been originally. The conservator confirmed that the mural is still on the wall of what is now the Haleyville Public Library. The Haleyville Historical Society commissioned Robert Raburn, a local artist, to replicate an image of Hollis Holbrook's *Reforestation*. The Historical Society is currently (2014) trying to raise funds to uncover and restore the original mural.[14]

Hollis Howard Holbrook. Hollis Howard Holbrook was born in 1909 in Natick, Massachusetts. He attended and graduated from the Massachusetts School of Art in 1934; he graduated also from the Yale School of Fine Arts in 1936.

Holbrook joined the University of Florida as a faculty member in 1938. Shortly thereafter, he founded the university's art department. Holbrook taught at the University of Florida until he retired from there in 1978 as a professor emeritus. Throughout the years, he created murals, sculptures and paintings for exhibitions and competitions. Hollis Holbrook died in Gaines-ville, Florida, in August 1984 at the age of 75.[15]

Meghan Navarro indicates that Hollis Holbrook received commissions for six different post office murals. She lists three: *John Eliot Speaks to the Natick Indians* (1937) in Natick, Massachusetts; *Reforestation* (1940) in Haleyville, Alabama; and *Sugar Cane Mill* (1941) in Jeanerette, Louisiana.[16] The website at http://www.wpamurals.com lists only the three murals above, however, and makes no reference to other works by Hollis Holbrook.[17]

C.W. Short and R. Stanley-Brown in their *Public Buildings: Architecture Under the Public Works Administration: 1933 to 1939* note a mural by Hollis Holbrook in the Painted Desert Inn in the Petrified Forest in Arizona. They cite the completion date as 1939.[18]

The setting of Holbrook's mural titled *John Eliot Speaks to the Natick Indians* (1937) was the place of Hollis Howard Holbrook's birth: Natick, Mas-sachusetts.

Park says:

> In this very sympathetic portrayal of Indians, Hollis Holbrook shows John Eliot in 1675 surrounded by shackled Natick Indians whose women and chil-dren carry their goods as best they can during their removal by the English.... The artist had been born in Natick, and the community approved of his paint-ing this unhappy beginning of the town.[19]

The topic of the mural for Natick, Massachusetts, was a controversial one. Navarro describes the subject matter as an 18th-century episode of removal of the Natick Indians to Deer Island in Boston Harbor and cruel intern-ment of the local Indian people.

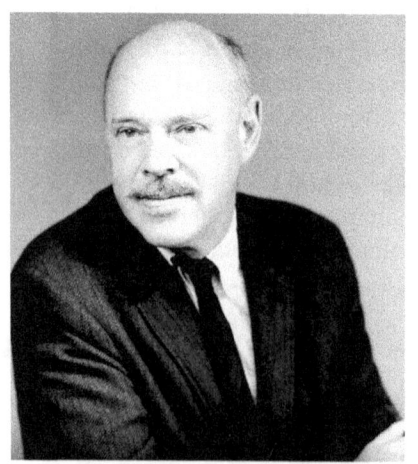

Near midnight on October 30, 1675, the Natick inhabitants were ferried out to Deer Island, and left with little clothing or provisions. When the arrangements were made for the Praying Indians to be interned on Deer Island, the island's owner, Daniel Henchman of Boston, expressly forbade the cutting down of trees, hunting of game, and lighting of fires on the island. Many, particularly the young and old, pregnant and sick, died from starvation, disease, and exposure to

Hollis Holbrook, professor of art at the University of Florida from 1938 to 1978, painted *Reforestation* and other paintings for the Section of Fine Arts (courtesy University of Florida Photograph Collection, George A. Smathers Libraries, Uni-versity of Florida).

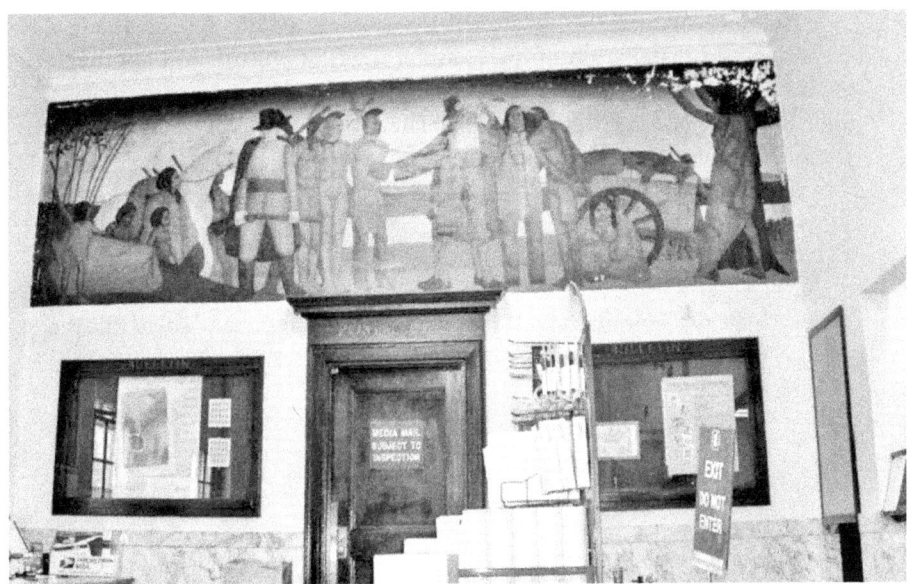

Hollis Holbrook painted the Natick, Massachusetts, mural in 1937. The work is still on display.

the elements…. Indians captured in the fighting were also imprisoned on Long Island in Boston Harbor…. Hollis Holbrook's mural captures the moment at The Pines when the Natick were being taken away in chains and were seeking comfort from John Eliot. Holbrook is reported to have taken his likeness of Eliot from a historical image, but the figure of Chief Waban was actually modeled on the postmaster at the time of Holbrook's painting, P. Victor Casavant…. Many among the Indians in Massachusetts today regard this mural as an important reminder of the cruel treatment of their forbearers. The mural was restored in 2007 after it suffered damage from a roof leak and a local Native leader described the restoration as "a spiritual restoration and reconciliation[.]"[20]

Dallan Wordekemper, the federal preservation officer for the United States Postal Service, noted in 2007 that 1,200 murals were a part of the New Deal program to place art in public buildings. In 2014 Wordekemper noted that 1,100 murals remained. The costs of the restoration project for Hollis Holbrook's Natick mural were an estimated $10,000.[21]

A letter from Edward Rowan to Hollis Holbrook on September 26, 1939, reminds readers of the origin of the Haleyville mural. Rowan indicated to Holbrook that on the basis of his "competent designs submitted in the St. Louis, Missouri, Post Office Mural competition," the Commissioner of Public Buildings wanted to consider Holbrook's designs for Haleyville. The proposed 12' × 5' painting would be placed over the door of the postmaster.

Rowan explained in the letter that there was a $700 appropriation for execution and installation of the painting for Haleyville. Upon approval of the preliminary sketches, Holbrook would receive $150; he would earn $225 upon approval of the full-size cartoon. The final $325 was available upon the completion, installation, and approval of the mural.

Rowan concluded:

> It is required that the work be completed and installed within a year's time. Further information for your consideration in connection with this project is attached hereto.
>
> We hope that you will be able to undertake this project and would like the opportunity of reviewing your preliminary designs at your earliest convenience.[22]

Hartselle

Lee Roland Warthen prepared the federally commissioned mural titled *Cotton Scene* (1941) for the Hartselle, Alabama, Post Office. It is now in the Historic Train Depot (Chamber of Commerce).

The City of Hartselle dates from 1870. The site for the original village was a location along the South and North Railroad (later named the L&N Railroad). When the railroad company found that the incline of the land selected for the village was inappropriate for a train stop and depot, the railroad asked the village to relocate.

The village moved, as the railroad had requested. The village took its name from George Hartsell, an owner of the railroad and a founder of the village. In 1873 the United States Post Office added an *e* to the name of the town; Hartsell became Hartselle. In 1875 the state of Alabama chartered the town of Hartselle.

A horrendous fire destroyed the 21 buildings in Hartselle in 1916, but the residents did not surrender to the devastation; instead they rebuilt. The reconstruction of the business district of Hartselle was primarily near the railroad, hence its name Railroad Street. In 2014 the Alabama Historic Register identified Hartselle as the Alabama city with more historically contiguous (adjacent) buildings than any other city in the state.[1]

Hartselle's Great Bank Robbery of 1926 is an event that the town has celebrated as a part of the Depot Days Festival since 1980.[2] The Chamber of Commerce of Hartselle calls the Great Bank Robbery "The Community's greatest claim to fame—or infamy."[3]

Hartselle, Alabama: The Great Bank Robbery. At 1:00 a.m. on March 15,

1926, fifteen thieves used eight blasts of nitroglycerin to storm their way into the bank. Before forcing their way into the facility, the burglars had used a saw to cut the cables linking the Hartselle telephone lines with other towns. The robbers held the town at bay for four hours while they took all of the gold and the cash and even some of the silver coins from the depository.

The criminals bound and gagged seven men in the back of the bank. Fortunately, only one person was injured in the crime.

Although the thieves took about $15,000, the bank had insurance against such loss. The managers were able to open the next day—with help from some other banks. Despite the efforts of all concerned, no one ever captured or even identified the robbers.[4]

The Depot Days Festival in September each year reminds visitors of the history of Hartselle, especially the Great Bank Robbery; pays tribute to the railroad and acknowledges its contribution to the development of Hartselle and the north Alabama area; and provides an opportunity for socialization and enjoyment. The popular events—in addition to the live music, children's rides, art, games, and food—typically include three re-enactments of the Great Bank Robbery by the College Street Players. Attendees of the Depot Days Festival and visitors throughout the year often visit the historic train depot to view the mural titled *Cotton Scene*, painted by Lee Roland Warthen.[5]

Hartselle is the second largest city in Morgan County, Alabama. Hartselle is about 30 miles from the Tennessee state line and about 10 miles from Decatur; Hartselle is a part of the Decatur Metropolitan Area.[6]

The National Register of Historic Places added the Hartselle Downtown Commercial Historic District to its sites on April 22, 1999. The city has a total area of 14.9 square miles, only .07 percent of which is water. Hartselle carries the nickname "The City of Southern Hospitality."[7]

In September of 2010 the descendants of George Hartsell met for a reunion and to witness the unveiling of a new historical marker on Railroad Street. The Alabama Tourism Bureau provided the sign, which is printed on both sides. The marker is in front of the Chamber of Commerce in the historic train depot on Railroad Street. The marker reads:

> Hartselle, named after early pioneer George Hartsell (with no "e"), rose from modest beginnings to an important position in the growing economy of Morgan County. Founded in 1870, the town owes its existence to the construction of the North and South Alabama Railroad (later the L&N), which began construction through the area in 1869 in an effort to connect the mineral rich areas in the southern part of the state with major shipping areas in north Alabama. Originally a mile north of the depot's current location, Hartselle consisted of a general store and saloon for workers. The town was relocated to its present site in 1873 and grew quickly around the first depot building, a converted boxcar. Railroad construction opened the Hartselle area to agriculture and timber production and the town became an important shipping point.

The town's growth followed the fortunes of the railroad and farmers for more than 60 years. The Great Depression took a heavy toll on the local economy. Railroad and farming are no longer mainstays of today's economy.[8]

The 2000 census indicated that there were 12,019 people in Hartselle, Alabama. The population density was 809 people per square mile at that time. The percentage of whites in the city was 92.25 percent. The percentage of blacks was 5.2 percent. The remaining races made up the other 2.55 percent.

In 2000 the median income for males in Hartselle was $40,211. The median income for females was $24,142. About 8.6 percent of the Hartselle population lived below the poverty line in 2000.[9]

The CSX, the Historic Hartselle Train Depot, and the Hartselle Chamber of Commerce. The birthday of the CSX line is July 1, 1986. That was the date when the Chessie System and the Seaboard System Railroad combined.[10]

The CSX has a "passing siding" in Hartselle. A passing siding is a section of track that is parallel to a through line and is connected to the through line at both ends by *switches*. These passing sidings allow trains moving in opposite directions to pass each other; the passing sidings can also allow faster trains to pass slower trains moving in the same direction.[11]

The depot in Hartselle dates from 1917. When train passenger service to Hartselle stopped in the late 1960s, the railroad donated the train station to the city; by 1976 the restoration of the train depot was complete. The restoration of the freight station produced another site for visitors to see; a variety of specialty shops in and near the freight station is another attraction for tourists and residents alike.

The historic Hartselle Train Depot now houses the Hartselle Chamber of Commerce. The station is an attraction to visitors and residents alike. The brick structure with a hip roof and a variety of windows and doors has a total of twelve openings on the west façade and ten openings on the east façade, including doors with transoms and double-hung windows.

Inside the Chamber of Commerce located in the restored train depot is the mural created by Lee R. Warthen; the work was originally on display in the 1939 post office with its hip roof of asphalt shingles and cupola. The relocation of the Lee R. Warthen mural from the 1939 post office to the Chamber of Commerce, housed in the historic Hartselle Train Depot, came in 1984. Hartselle Utilities acquired the Hartselle Post Office, and the Hartselle Chamber of Commerce obtained the artwork.[12]

The mural *Cotton Scene* is currently on display on a brick wall in an office in the Chamber of Commerce in the Hartselle Train Depot. The painting now hangs behind the desk of the director of the Hartselle Chamber of Commerce.

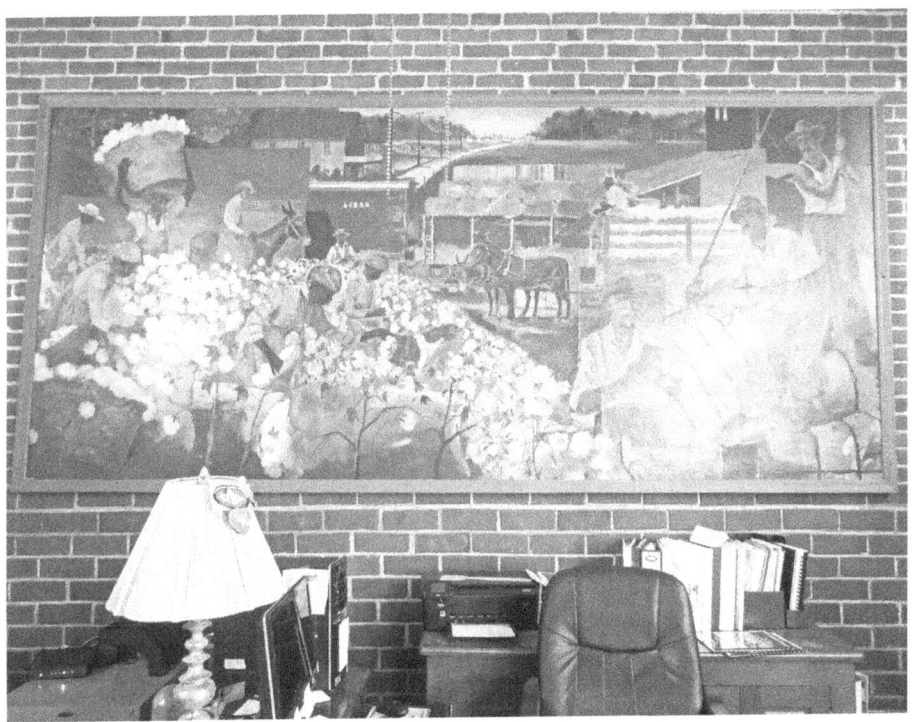

The 5'3" × 12' mural by Lee Roland Warthen is on display in the Hartselle Depot.

Cotton Scene (1941) is an example of Social Realism. The mural depicts the social hierarchy, racial segregation, and the work environment as they existed at the time. The art itself is realistic without any abstract figures, and shows workers producing a crop of cotton.[13]

Lee Roland Warthen studied the Hartselle area and talked with some Hartselle residents before submitting his sketches to the postmaster in Hartselle for approval. Warthen's granddaughter Kathryn Smith—herself an artist—shared with the author copies of Warthen's May 20, 1941, correspondence with the postmaster. Warthen's letter mentions the two topics of the railroad and of agriculture as possible themes for the federally funded painting.

Warthen indicates in the letter that he had done some research on Hartselle and on Morgan County in the Congressional Library. When his investigation of Hartselle "yielded nothing" and his exploration of Morgan County revealed "very little," Warthen indicated that he "had a talk with Rep. John J. Sparkman, representing your district and born in Hartselle, who kindly gave me some useful information about your own.... [Sparkman] concurs in my personal opinion that the cotton story would be a good subject."[14]

In the painting, the artist Lee R. Warthen divides the labor between the African American workers and the white workers as it would have been in the 1940s. The workers who are harvesting the crop are in the background in *Cotton Scene*; they are distinctly black laborers who are performing manual work.

The white workers seem to be engaged in the commercial handling of the cotton. These white figures occupy a prominent place in the foreground and do not appear to be engaging in strenuous physical labor. Black women and white men work together in the scene. Black workers are more prominent in the background. Park describes the scene as one of "peaceful productivity."[15]

Lee R. Warthen of Washington, D.C., painted the mural for the Hartselle Post Office as a result of his selection in a competition sponsored by the Section of Fine Arts. The competition was for an artwork for the War Building in the District of Columbia. While some offices of the War Department moved into the building for a few years, the building never became the War Department Headquarters.[16]

Warthen's mural originally occupied the Hartselle Post Office. The one-story structure has a hip roof, asphalt shingles, and a cupola. The building is a listing on the National Register of Historic Places.[17]

Park and Markowitz note that Warthen's painting has a "distinctly static quality." They observe that the stagnant southern economy was dependent on labor-intensive agriculture, that the South maintained a rigid caste system with segregation, and that African Americans remained subordinate by working on white-owned farms.

In the Alabama mural the African Americans are in their typical subservient positions. The whites are depicted as overseers or foremen. The artist may have been "opposed to segregation nevertheless observed it and therefore recorded the subordination of blacks to whites."

Park and Markowitz indicate that in the Hartselle scene and in many other scenes from the South, the artists do not "convey a sense of independence and individual worth. In this they depart from a national image and set the South apart from the rest of the nation."[18]

Lee Roland Warthen. Lee Roland Warthen had a short professional career because he lived only 56 years. Born in 1893, he died in McLean, Virginia, in 1949. A private with the 499th Aero Squad Air Service, Lee R. Warthen is buried in Arlington National Cemetery in Section 17, Site 24073-19.[19]

Lee R. Warthen's works are still on exhibit in the Department of the Interior in Washington, D.C. On display are his dioramas depicting the Hoover Dam, the meeting of Washington and Lafayette at Morristown, and other topics; Warthen himself constructed the scenes, the sculpted figures, and the painted scenery. His dioramas and illustrations often concern Indian

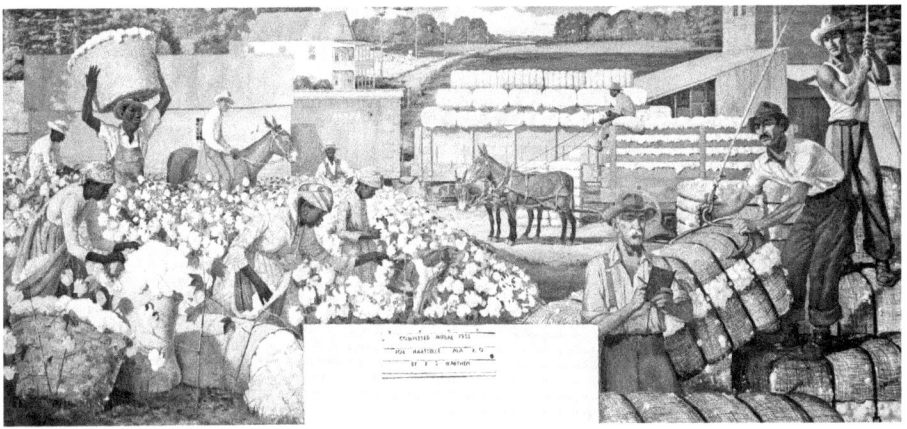

This photograph from the estate of Lee R. Warthen shows the study of the mural titled *Cotton Scene*. Lee Roland Warthen had executed and installed the work in the Hartselle Post Office by August of 1941 (courtesy Kathryn Lee Smith).

affairs and land management. Warthen has other exhibits within the National Parks Service throughout the country.[20]

Lee R. Warthen's wife was Ferol Katherine Sibley Warthen, who was also an artist. Ferol was born on May 22, 1890, in Aberdeen, South Dakota, and died in Silver Spring, Maryland in 1986. She is best known for her white-line prints. For 35 summers she worked in her studio in Provincetown, Massachusetts, to perfect her techniques and her work.[21]

With a white-line print or Provincetown print, the artist Ferol Sibley Warthen used one block of wood for her image. She perfected cutting a tiny groove between the parts that required separate colors on the wood block. She would apply watercolor to paint one small section of the wood block at a time before lowering the paper onto the wet paint; the grooves cut into the block to separate the colors would produce a white line on the print.[22]

Swedish immigrant Bror Julius Olsson Nordfeldt (1878–1955) had studied printmaking in London and had helped bring these techniques—including white-line prints—to the United States; his 1907 etchings, however, were not popular at first with a population that supported realistic images. The methods he brought to the United States soon caught on in the Provincetown area.[23]

Lee and Ferol Warthen's daughter is Sibyl M. Warthen Smith; their granddaughter is Kathryn Lee Smith, who is an artist like her grandparents. Kathryn learned to prepare white-line prints at the feet of her gifted grandmother. Works by Kathryn Smith and Ferol Sibley Warthen are on display in the James R. Bakker Antiques, 359 Commercial Street, Provincetown, Massachusetts.[24]

Painter and block printer Ferol Katherine Sibley Warthen attended

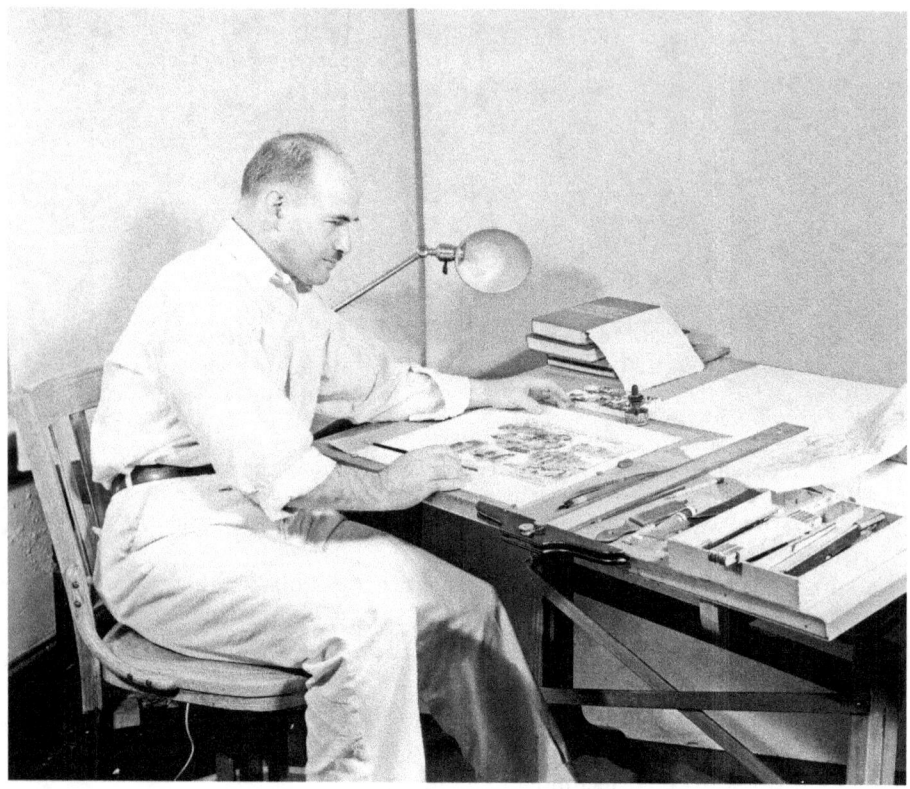

Lee Roland Warthen, date unknown (courtesy Kathryn Lee Smith).

Columbus Art School and graduated from Ohio State University, B.S. She studied from 1910 to 1912 at the Art Students' League in New York with William Merritt Chase and Kenneth Hayes Miller. Ferol Warthen began printmaking studies in 1950 with Blanche Lazzell in Provincetown, Massachusetts. She studied painting with Karl Knaths in Washington, D.C. She continued with white line printmaking from 1950 until her death in 1986. Her distinguished prints have been acquired by galleries and museums around the world; they appear in exhibits in Boston, the Provincetown Art Association and Museum, the Smithsonian Institution, and the National Museum of American Art in Washington, D.C.[25]

Kathryn Lee Smith. Ferol Sibley Warthen's education, training, and experience helped her to inspire and educate her granddaughter, Kathryn Lee Smith, whose work is available for viewing in such prestigious settings as the FitzWilliam Museum in Cambridge, England; the Boston Public Library, the New Britain Museum of American Art, the Cape Cod Museum of Art, and the Provincetown Art Association and Museum. Kathryn's works and exhibits date from as early as 1972. She and her grandmother—together and separately—held many exhibits featuring white-line prints.

Smith hosted a yearly one-person exhibition at Hell's Kitchen Gallery in Provincetown, Massachusetts for eight years. In addition to her many exhibits and the preparation of the catalogues that accompanied the events, Smith found time to conduct the White Line Printmaking Workshop in Kami Gori, Japan, and write about it in the journal *InPrint*, 14 (September 2003). Kathryn Lee Smith has also written *Down the Line: Tracing the Path of the Provincetown Print* (1998) for Express Publishing in Provincetown.

Smith has found from her thirty years of technical experience that the warmth of the natural wood, the use of hand tools, and the pulling of the print are all vital to white-line woodblock printmaking. These actions repeat themselves over time and have formed their own unique signatures.[26]

Smith, at the age of four, learned the method of printmaking developed in Provincetown in 1915. Her grandmother Ferol Sibley Warthen—wife of Lee R. Warthen, herself a noted artist, and a past student of Blanche Lazzell's—helped bring all this to pass.[27]

Summary of Federal Artist Lee R. Warthen. Kathryn Smith's grandfather Lee R. Warthen made his own contributions is his own short lifetime. He produced many oil paintings of landscapes and prepared countless portraits. He studied at the Art Students' League from 1910 to 1912 before serving his country in World War I. During the 1930s he also produced oil paintings as illustrations for books and magazines; most of these works had a human interest theme. His *Cotton Scene* (1941) is still on display in Hartselle, Alabama.[28]

Huntsville

Xavier Gonzalez (1898–1993) prepared the 1937 mural *Tennessee Valley Authority* for the Huntsville Post Office and Courthouse in Huntsville, Alabama.

Huntsville serves as the county seat of Madison County, located in the central, northernmost part of the state of Alabama. Huntsville is the fourth-largest city in the state. Its population grew from 158,216 in 2000 to 176,645 in 2008.

Huntsville: Early History. Huntsville dates from 1805. Leroy Pope, a lawyer and prominent local resident, asked that the area be called Twickenham, a name from Alexander Pope's English home. On November 25, 1811, however, the name of the town became Huntsville to honor the first settler,

John Hunt; this incorporation made Huntsville the first incorporated city in Alabama.[1]

In June of 1819, President James Monroe arrived unannounced in Huntsville. The residents organized a welcoming party for him when they found out he was entering the city and arranged a public dinner the very next day. After many business meetings, trips to Washington, and much correspondence, the legislators learned that on December 14, 1819, President Monroe had signed the resolution that admitted Alabama as the twenty-second state.[2]

Through the years, Huntsville has continued to grow and expand; it has added textile mills, munitions factories, NASA's Marshall Flight Center, and—at the Redstone Arsenal—the United States Army Aviation and Missile Command. Huntsville currently extends into Limestone County.[3]

Kiplinger Personal Finance named (2009) Huntsville as "America's Best City."[4] Huntsville received the honor also of being named by the National Trust for Historic Preservation to its "America's Dozen Distinctive Destinations for 2010" list.[5]

One federal program of the 1930s that directly affected Huntsville was the Tennessee Valley Authority. In May of 1933, Congress authorized the formation of the Tennessee Valley Authority (TVA) to improve flood control, generate and disperse electricity, develop the area, and improve navigation. The TVA was controversial in Alabama—and elsewhere; the program met with criticisms and the challenges posed by private power companies, people who owned land needed by the government, and the consumers of the generated electricity. The TVA in the Huntsville area eventually resulted, however, in increased availability and consumption of power—often by those who had never before had electricity.[6]

Huntsville was able to offer its residents electricity, water, and natural gas through Huntsville Utilities (HU). HU still purchases and resells power from the Tennessee Valley Authority. The two TVA plants that provide much of the electricity to the HU are the Browns Ferry Nuclear Power Plant in Limestone County and the Guntersville Dam in Marshall County.[7]

Beckham describes the TVA as "the government's most ambitious investment in the South's future." The South was grateful when things went right, though

> when there was scandal or when some particular dam project threatened to disrupt people's lives, then the TVA became the biggest carpetbagging scheme of the century ... but few seem to have had so many reservations that they refused to take advantage of the agency's flood control and conservation efforts, its offer of cheap electricity and its programs to control disease.[8]

In the 1930s, in particular, the federal government was at work in the state of Alabama and in Huntsville in other ways besides the TVA. One obvi-

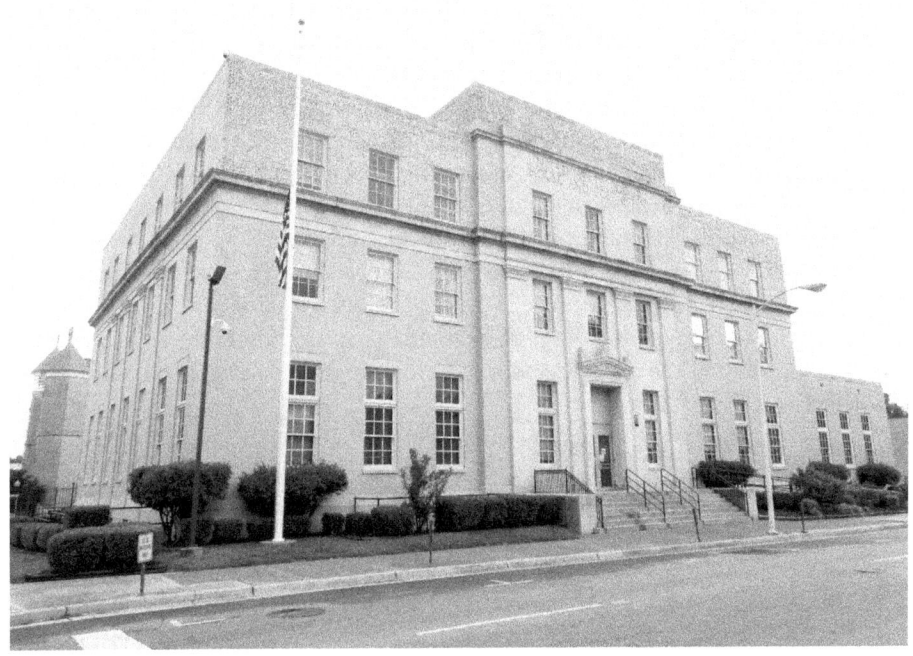

The original United States Courthouse and Post Office Building in Huntsville, Alabama, is still in use—but not as a post office. The courtroom is still in use regularly.

ous example of the work of the federal government in Huntsville was the construction and decoration of a public building—specifically the United States Courthouse and Post Office in Huntsville.

The federal construction of the United States Courthouse and Post Office in Huntsville, Alabama, dates from 1936,[9] according to the General Services Administration.[10] The buff-brick, three-story building with limestone ornamentation is in Greek Revival style, which follows certain rules of proportion and form.[11] Its main functions originally were as a courthouse, federal building, and post office.

The recessed main entrance has above it a tympanum, which is a triangular enclosed space, or a pediment. The pediment over the door at the Huntsville Post Office has decorative reliefs. Above the tympanum are three anthemions (leaves in a radiating arrangement); these anthemions add interest and design.[12]

The architects for the project were Edgar Love, who was an architect in Huntsville, and the Birmingham firm of Miller, Martin and Lewis.[13] The federal architect Gilbert Stanley Underwood may have supervised the project because it was a federal building.[14]

In the center of the 2nd floor of the United States Courthouse and Post Office located in Huntsville is the main courtroom. A 4' wainscot of wood surrounds the room. Plaster crown molding painted with blue rectangular fields and gold highlights adds additional decoration to the formal setting.

Pilasters are rectangular supports with a base and a capital; pilasters are similar in function to columns, except that they project partially from a wall. The pilasters in the Huntsville courtroom add decoration and interest at regular, 2' intervals throughout the room. The blue rectangles on the frieze between the pilasters are small and include a drawing of a sheaf; the rectangles directly above the pilasters are larger and include a scroll.

The flat-roofed building has a basement in addition to the three stories. The basement has a few small offices, but its main uses are as a service, mechanical, and storage area.

The Huntsville Courthouse and Post Office facility had 18 restrooms. Eight are still in their original condition.[15]

The U.S. government had approved $200,000 for the construction of the 1932 Huntsville Courthouse and Post Office. The final cost, however, was only $169,000.[16]

The Tennessee Valley Authority. The GSA noted that possibly the most striking feature in the courtroom is the mural of Belgian linen on canvas behind the rostrum. The mural uses primarily zinc white, earth tones, and cadmium yellow colors. The setting of the scene is characteristic of the environment of Huntsville and includes five main figures symbolizing different phases of society. The figures represent youth, scientific agriculture, work, artistic endeavors, and motherhood.

Two men, three women, and a small child are evident in the mural. One of the men is holding a cornstalk; he represents scientific agriculture. The other man is using an anvil and hammer; he represents industry. The three females represent the work of a young girl, the arts, and motherhood and a happy home, including a young child helps. Gonzalez used symbolism in this work.

The Section of Painting and Sculpture commissioned the mural. Its installation date was October 27, 1937.[17]

The Alabama Department of Archives and History summed up the Huntsville artwork in this manner:

> The Huntsville mural was the largest and most expensive panel commissioned in Alabama and the only one placed in a federal courthouse rather than a post office. Gonzalez received the invitation for the panel based on designs he had submitted for a competition in Jackson, Mississippi, in 1936. He originally proposed a rather odd allegorical panel that the Washington office criticized for both its style and its lack of meaning for the people in Huntsville. Instead of making allegorical allusions it was suggested that Gonzalez place emphasis

on the realities of life. Using a realistic style and basing his new theme on the work then being done by TVA in northern Alabama, he redesigned the panel several times.[18]

The artist Xavier Gonzalez described Huntsville and the TVA favorably:

Huntsville, Alabama, is situated in the lower angle of the Tennessee River and has profited immensely by the benefits derived from the Muscle Shoals Project. Before this undertaking was begun, the country, being unprotected, was at the mercy of floods and calamities. The benefits of electricity were a privilege of the few who could afford the exorbitant price, the soil of the country was being washed away by the floods, and industry and agriculture were underdeveloped due to the uncertainty of land conditions. Since the completion of this project, tremendous benefits have been received [including] the control and proper use of water resources; … conservation and preservation of land resources; … [and] the disposition of surplus electric energy created as a by-product of the irrigation and flood control.[19]

In the mural by Gonzalez, the viewer can identify the Wilson Dam, the First National Bank, the Tennessee River, and the Huntsville Post Office. Furrows and a rock wall are examples of conservation techniques illustrated.

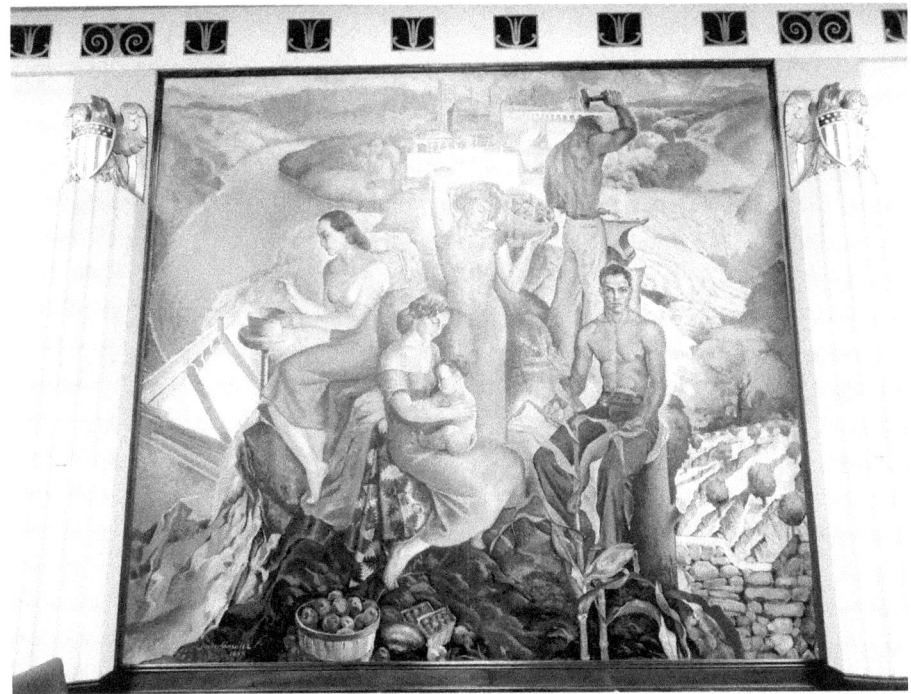

The mural that Xavier Gonzalez prepared in the Huntsville Courthouse had the title *Tennessee Valley Authority*. The mural is still on display at limited times.

Xavier Gonzalez. Xavier Gonzalez was born in Almeria, Spain, on February 15, 1898. He often said that he "slid into art."

Before coming to the United States in the early 1920s, Gonzalez had trained in mechanical engineering by correspondence. He went to work for a manufacturing company after immigrating to America and busied himself at his desk making caricatures, portraits, and sketches of his co-workers; to prevent them from seeing the drawings, Gonzalez would throw the papers into the chute leading to the shipping room in the basement.

When a friend goaded him into sliding down the chute, he found his sketches pinned to the walls where the shipping clerks had placed them. He was thrilled![20]

Xavier enrolled in night school at the Art Institute of Chicago (1921–1923). He assisted his uncle José Arpa at the school he opened in Mexico in 1926. He studied at the Academy of San Carlos in Mexico City, in Paris, and in the Far East. His career in art had begun![21]

Gonzalez achieved his United States citizenship in 1930. He taught summers from 1932 to 1940 at the Sul Ross State Teachers College—now Sul Ross State University—in Alpine, Texas. He also served as the (sometimes) Director of the Summer School of Art at Sul Ross State University from 1933 through 1959.[22]

After accepting the position of teacher at Sophie Newcomb College in 1931, Xavier Gonzalez met the student he would marry:

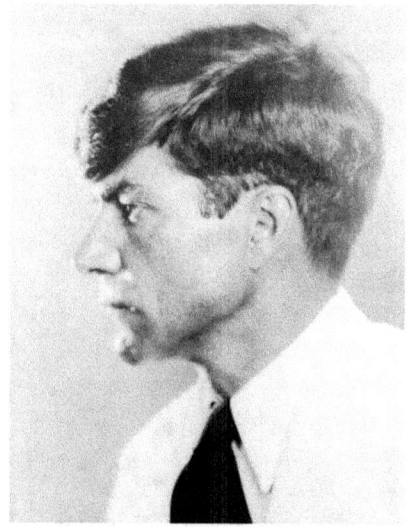

In the summer of 1935 Gonzalez married one of his Sophie Newcomb students, a New Orleans girl named Ethel Edwards, in a ceremony in Alpine. She was 21, and Gonzalez was 36. The bride's brother, Bruce Edwards, recalls that his parents were delighted with the match because his sister had a beau in New Orleans who [sic] they considered to be something of a bad actor, and that in fact the wedding was held in Alpine for fear that he might disrupt it if it were held in New Orleans. Edwards also remembers that Gonzalez was unfamiliar with Protestant usage and kept addressing the Methodist minister as "Uncle." The marriage lasted until Gonzalez' death

This image of Xavier Gonzalez dates from the time that he taught at Alpine, Texas (Sul Ross State University Collection; Archives of the Big Bend, Bryan Wildenthal Memorial Library, Sul Ross State University, Alpine, Texas).

in 1993 at the age of 94. Gonzalez' papers at the Smithsonian include hundreds of illustrated love notes that he wrote to his wife over the years.[23]

Gonzalez had emerged as one of the prominent American muralists. His painting for the San Antonio Municipal Auditorium (1933) was one of his first. Gonzalez intended it to represent the decadence of war. The mural with its bleeding palm (a socialist symbol to some viewers) and clenched fist (interpreted as a communist symbol by some) created so much criticism—especially from the American Legion—that in 1935 Mayor Charles Quinn ordered the removal of the painting on canvas and its return to the Civil Works Administration.

Gonzalez was able to prepare seven murals in 1934. One was his mural of the Chisos Mountains currently on display in the Big Bend Museum. The other six—picturing airplanes flying over identifiable sites, like the Eiffel Tower—were for the Art Deco Shushan Airport in New Orleans.

After completing the Huntsville mural in 1937, he received a commission from the Section of Fine Arts to prepare four murals (1940) for the Kilgore (Texas) Post Office. Gonzalez's wife, also an artist, received a commission the same year (1940) to prepare a mural for the Lampasas (Texas) Post Office. Another commission was forthcoming for Xavier Gonzalez in 1941. This assignment was for the Mission (Texas) Post Office.

Lonn Taylor shares a story about the postmaster at the Mission Post Office. The postmaster wrote to the Assistant Postmaster General and suggested, "If we have any choice, we prefer having a new adding machine."[24]

Beckham writes that Gonzalez's final product was the sixth version of the mural. Although Xavier Gonzalez was teaching in New Orleans at the time he was working on the mural for Huntsville, he had to go to Alpine, Texas, to work because his New Orleans studio was too small to accommodate the work. Edward Rowan of the Section of Fine Arts had criticized the central woman on Gonzalez's original design[25]: "She was apparently both too old and too symbolic for Rowan. He suggested that she should be 'less lugubrious' and that she should be 'a figure of great beauty and need not be associated with senility.'"[26] After the installation of the mural, however, Rowan wrote to Xavier Gonzalez. "[T]he reaction of the general public to your work is most gratifying and, of course, those are the people for whom the work was intended, not the postmaster alone."[27]

When World War II began, Xavier Gonzalez worked in the War Department. He served as an art director and created a series of maps and posters for the U.S. Navy.

After the war, Gonzalez opened a summer painting school in Wellfleet, Massachusetts. He divided his time between New York City and Cape Cod. In 1947 he received a prestigious Guggenheim Fellowship. His work included teaching at the Art Students' League, serving as artist in residence at Western Reserve University in Cleveland (1953–1954) and at the El Paso Museum of Art (1965), and fulfilling commissions from *Life*, the city of New York, and the Department of the Interior.

His wife, Ethel Edwards Gonzalez, reported in 1993 that ninety-four-year-old Gonzalez had died of leukemia at Calvary Hospital in New York. By this time his work was in such collections as those at the Metropolitan Museum of Art, the Whitney Museum of American Art, the Boston Museum of Fine Arts and other American museums. His sculptures, friezes, and murals appeared throughout the United States.[28]

Ethel Edwards. Ethel Edwards was born in 1914 in Opelousas, Louisiana. She always gave New Orleans, however, as her city of birth. Her father wanted her to attend business college in New Orleans and complete secretarial courses. She resisted and secured a scholarship to Newcomb College.

In 1935 Ethel enrolled in H. Sophie Newcomb College, where she studied art under Xavier Gonzalez. The two married in 1936. The couple lived and worked together in New York, Washington, Texas, and Massachusetts. They

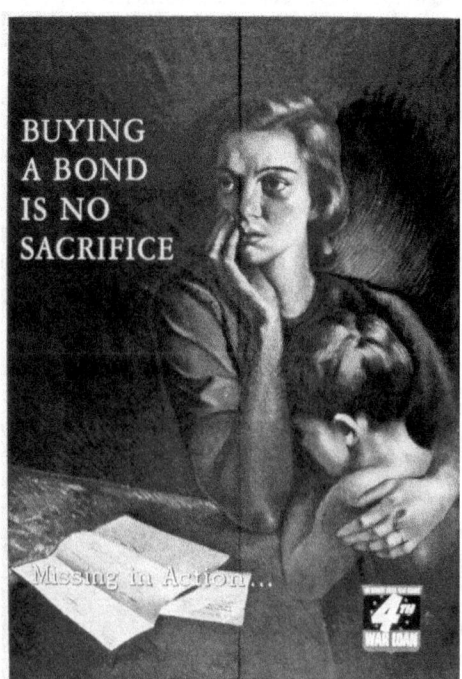

both taught at the Art Students' League, at Wellfleet, and else-where.

In 1939 Ethel won the Forty-Eight State Competition in Lampasas, Texas. Her mural had the title *Afternoon on a Texas Ranch*; it remained in the Lampasas Post Office until 2002, when it was moved to City Hall. She painted also a mural for Lake Providence, Louisiana, as a commission from the same competition.

After her death on January 24, 1999, the obituary for Edith Edwards Gonzalez appeared in the *New Orleans Times-Picayune*. It called her "an artist for all seasons, full of warmth and with an intense discipline to create."[29]

The ashes of both Xavier Gon-

During World War II Xavier Gonzalez created this poster that reminds the reader that "Buying a Bond Is No Sacrifice" (photograph from Office of War Information, 1942–1945; National Archives at College Park, ARC Number 514014).

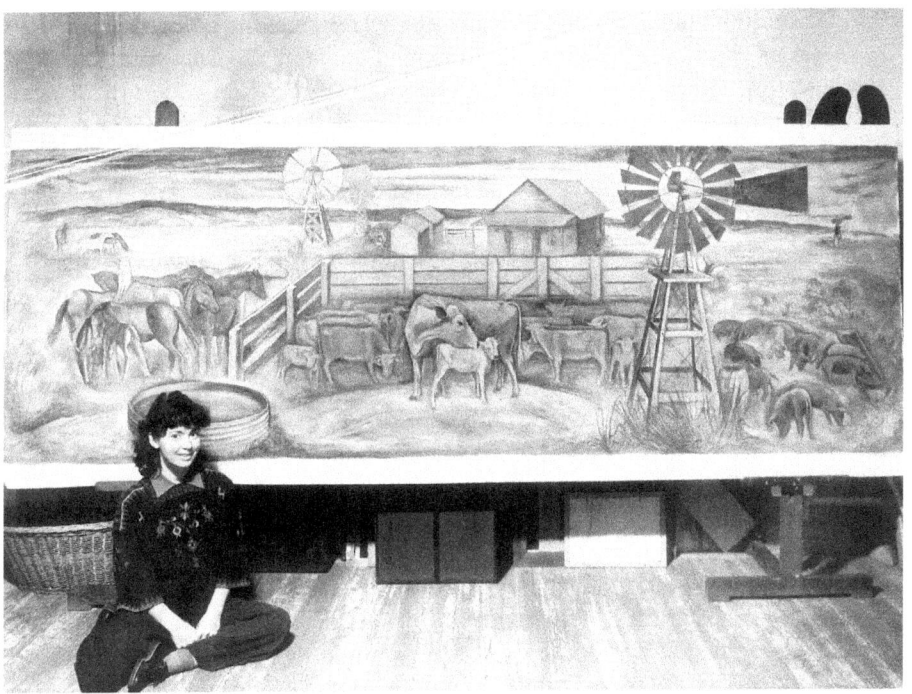

Edith Edwards sits in front of the mural *Afternoon on a Texas Ranch* that she prepared for the Lampasas Post Office after winning the 1939 competition (Ethel Edwards Gonzalez, Photographer unknown, Newcomb College Photographic Collection, Number 3251, Newcomb Archives, Newcomb College Institute, Tulane University, New Orleans, Louisiana).

zalez and Ethel Edwards were scattered over Central Park. They chose the location because it was just a few blocks from their last residence.[30]

Gonzalez has no grave marker. His "monument" includes 17 important murals across the United States. His wife also has such "monuments" in Louisiana and Texas.

Luverne

Arthur K. Getz prepared the mural *Cotton Field* (1942) for the post office in Luverne, Alabama.

Luverne, Alabama, heralds itself as "The Friendliest City in the South." The small town that serves as the county seat of Crenshaw County takes pride both in its past and in its present qualities.[1]

In 2001 the Internet Company ePODUNK measured every place in America and ranked Luverne as a "top ten home town in the United States." These "great home towns" all have deep roots, churches with good attendance, historic buildings, and locally-owned businesses. The power of Place prevails.[2]

Crenshaw County took its name from Andrew Crenshaw. Crenshaw was from South Carolina, but in the early 1800s he had settled in adjoining Butler County. The newly organized county took its name from the distinguished man from South Carolina. The Alabama State General Assembly created the county of Crenshaw by its act of November 24, 1866.[3]

An important community—now city—in central Crenshaw County was Luverne. Its name came from the wife of realtor M.P. LeGrand. The 1889 founding of the town in central Crenshaw County was with a main purpose: to become the end of the line of the Montgomery and Florida Railroad Company. The community grew with the success of the railway station. The residents of Crenshaw County in 1893 voted to make the more populous Luverne the county seat in place of Rutledge.[4]

Luverne is at 31.716° north latitude and at -86.263° west longitude. Its elevation is at 354 feet. Luverne is in the Central Time Zone. Its 2003 estimated population was 2,570.

Luverne has a state-licensed airport, but there are no commercial flights from it. One has to travel 45 miles to Montgomery to find a commercial carrier, like Delta.[5]

In Luverne almost half (47.8 percent) of the citizenry aged 25 and older has no high school diploma.[6]

Each fall since 1970 the Crenshaw County Shrine Club has held its annual Luverne event: the World's Largest Peanut Boil. The Shriners Club boils and bags about 17 tons of peanuts for the World's Best Boiled Peanut Festival, which starts the Thursday before Labor Day and continues until the club sells all of its peanuts.[7]

Luverne Post Office. The Luverne Post Office is a red brick building. The front entrance is centered between four windows. Each window has 15 panes. The front door has a covered entrance. Six steps lead to the small front porch. Two columns support the front of the porch; two pilasters appear on the back wall.

The Luverne Post Office is at 29 East 3rd Street, Luverne, Alabama. On January 14, 2005, the Luverne Post Office and 185 other structures became a part of the Luverne Historic District and joined the Alabama properties listed on the National Register of Historic Places. First and Sixth Streets and Le Grande, Glenwood, Folmar, and Hawkins Avenues bound these properties dated 1887–1942.

Inside the Luverne Post Office is a mural commissioned by the Treasury

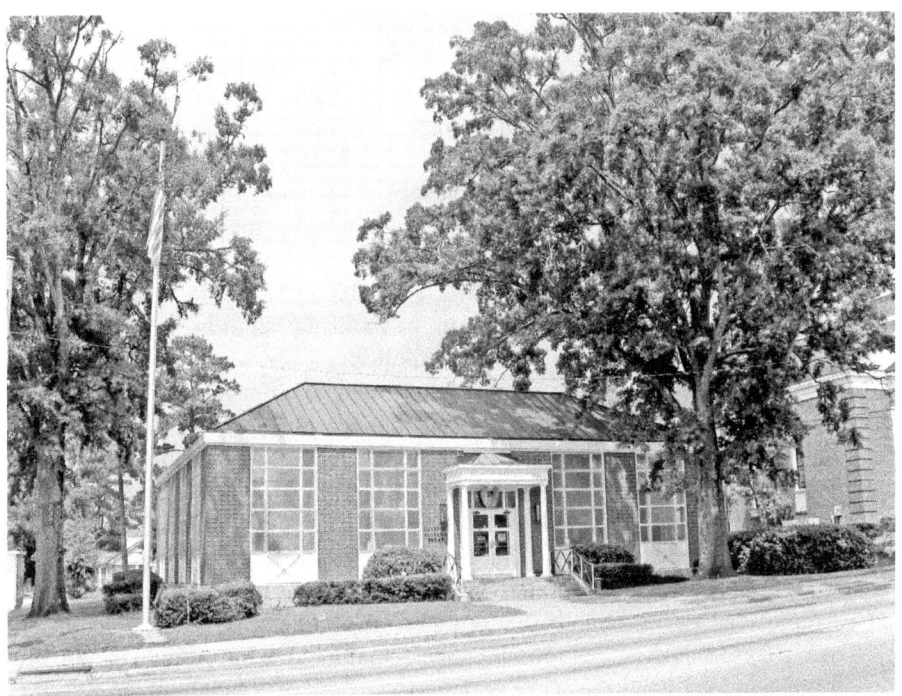

The Luverne Post Office holds the mural *Cotton Field* prepared by Arthur Kimmig Getz.

Section of Fine Arts for 1942. Arthur Getz earned the commission on the basis of designs he had submitted for the War Department Building Competition.[8]

War Department Building Competition. During the early 1930s, the National Capital Park and Planning Commission was planning the development of the section of the District of Columbia that was between C, E, Eighteenth, and Twenty-third Streets. This section had the nickname of "Foggy Bottom."

The War Department in the 1930s was occupying several different buildings on the Mall. Consolidation in one building was a high priority, and the Foggy Bottom site was large enough to accommodate just such a building. The plans were to construct the facility in two phases.

Gilbert Stanley Underwood and William Dewey Foster designed the building during 1938–1939. Construction began in 1940. By the time that the first phase of the building was complete in 1941, however, several agencies had observed that the War Department had already expanded beyond the capacity of the building. These concerns turned out to be well-founded.

While some offices of the War Department moved into the building for a few years, the building never became the War Department headquarters; the facility would become the site for the State Department. After expansion of the State Department Building in 1956–1960 and its dedication in 1961, a renaming of the building occurred in 2000. The official name of the State Department Building became the Harry S Truman Federal Building.

Congress appropriated funds to begin constructing the Pentagon for the War Department early in 1941. In 1955 allocated funds from Congress enabled the expansion of the Pentagon.[9]

Arthur K. Getz earned the 1942 commission for *Cotton Field* for the Luverne Post Office in May of 1941 on the basis of designs he had submitted for the War Department Building Competition.[10] The Section warned Getz, a Northern artist: "It will be necessary for you to acquaint yourself thoroughly with the appearance of a cotton plant as the individuals using this post office will be especially observant on this point…."[11] Getz did his homework. He talked with Southern painters and investigated the production of cotton.

Cotton Field. Getz researched the harvesting and the weighing of the cotton in the fields. He found that the "cotton pickers"—who were often tenant farmers and their families—wore a "pick sack" over one shoulder and/or around their necks. Usually the mother of the home made these sacks from heavy cotton ducking or from flour sacks that had held the family supply of flour. The lengths of the sacks varied according to the height of the cotton picker, with children, of course, having shorter sacks. The lengths, then, varied from 3' to 4' for the children to 12' to 15' for the taller family members. The closed bottom of the sack typically dragged the ground as the picker filled the sack.

A strong strap or even a part of the sack itself went over the neck and/or shoulder. The sack was about 16" in diameter. The cotton pickers would often compete to see who could pick the most cotton.

The laborers often had to make some decisions to achieve an advantage in the daily contest. If the picker used a large sack, he/she did not have to empty it as often; the sack was, however, heavier to drag. If the picker used a smaller sack, he/she was not slowed down by the extra weight; the worker, however, had to empty the sack more often, and this shortened his/her time for picking.

At the end of the day, the crop owner or the overseer weighed each sack. This was done by tying the sack to one end of a board or beam and by hanging a weight—called a "P" weight—from the other end of the board.

The overseer or crop owner would use a large "P" weight for heavy sacks and a smaller "P" weight for lighter sacks. The smaller "P" weighed 16 pounds. The overseer would move the "P" along a beam or board until the arm balanced. The beam might be propped on the shoulders of two workers, on the tongue of a wagon, or even on a tripod.[12]

On the beam or board where the "P" was hung, the official "weigher" could see numbers recorded on the board. These figures along the scale beam or board indicated the weight; one side had calibrations for heavy sacks, and the other side had calibrations for lighter sacks.

The "weigher" kept a record of the amounts gathered by each cotton picker before the picker placed the cotton from the emptied sacks into the wagon—or the truck in later times. The owner usually took the cotton to the gin.

In *Cotton Field* (1942), Arthur K. Getz pictured the balance beam used in the fields to weigh the amount of cotton harvested during the day by each picker. He also showed the cotton plant with some of the cotton still in the bolls.

The Luverne mural dates from 1942. Two mules pull a wagon with high sides to hold the harvested cotton. The overseer who is weighing the cotton is a white man; the laborer is a black man. The mural is an example of Social Realism.

In *Cotton Field*, large baskets appear on the right side of the mural. On some farms the workers emptied their sacks into the large, woven baskets.

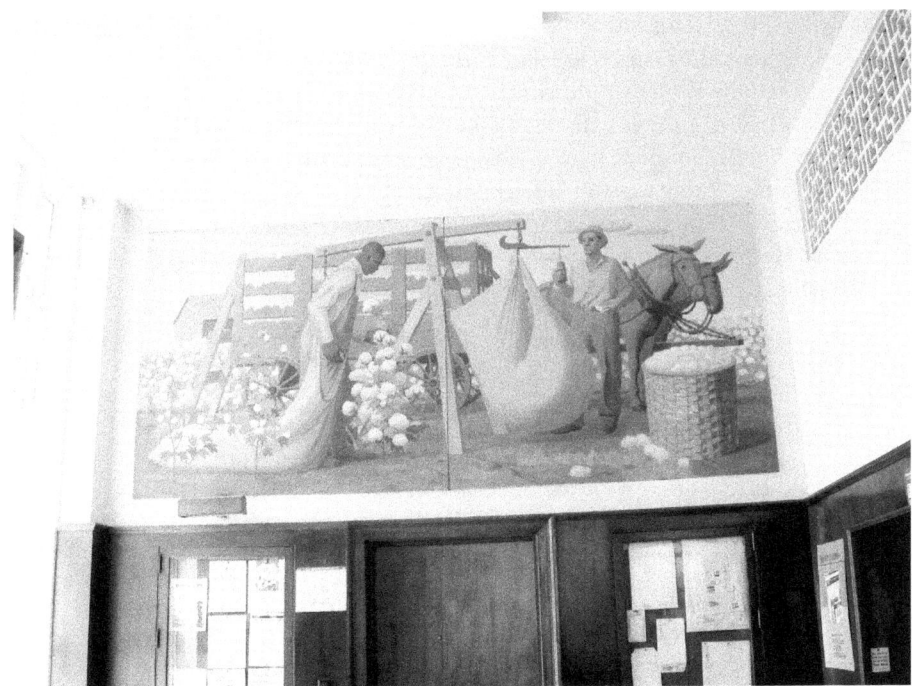

This is the mural *Cotton Field* prepared by artist Arthur Kimmig Getz for the Luverne Post Office.

On other farms, however, the overseer did not believe that the baskets held enough cotton to justify the added expense; these overseers had the workers dump their picked cotton on a sheet until time to "weigh in."

Both men seem neat, clean, and content in their work. They appear in good health, unlike some of the field workers that Federal photographers like Dorothea Lange and Jack Delano captured during the Great Depression in the Southern fields. There is no evidence in the mural of the child workers or family laborers that were prevalent during this time period.

Arthur Kimmig Getz. The American illustrator, artist, writer, teacher, muralist, and painter Arthur Kimmig Getz[13] was born in Passaic, New Jersey, to Madeline Kimmig Getz and Anthony Getz on May 17, 1913.[14]

Arthur's mother ensured that her son would get an education. After his graduation from high school, he had joined the merchant marines. After he spent a year at sea, his mother destroyed his papers because she knew he belonged elsewhere. Getz was able to attend Brooklyn's Pratt Institute on a full scholarship. In 1934 he graduated with honors from Pratt's School of Fine and Applied Art. The Depression had hit New York with a vengeance, but Getz did not surrender to the hard times. In 1936, he sold his first drawing to *The New Yorker*. His first cover illustration for *The New Yorker* dates from July 23, 1938.[15] This cover was a map of Larchmont, New York. He depicted tiny yachts sailing on Long Island Sound.

The New Yorker would run 210 of his covers before 1988. This was more covers than any other artist had contributed.[16] In fact, sometimes *The New Yorker* published more than one Getz cover in a single month.

Painter Philip Guston befriended Arthur Getz. Guston taught his young charge how to mix casein tempera, which was often used for murals. Guston urged Getz to apply to the Section of Fine Arts for a mural commission. Getz earned four commissions over the next four years:

- 1939: Post Office, Lancaster, New York
- 1939: Textile Building, 1939–1940 World's Fair
- 1941: Post Office, Bronson, Michigan
- 1942: Post Office, Luverne, Alabama[17]

Edward Rowan with the Section of Fine Arts looked at Getz's sketches for the Luverne Post Office. Rowan declared Getz's idea for the post office mural as "rather appealing in its simplicity."[18]

The story of the completion of Getz's mural was all too familiar late in the Section program. He had received the commission for the Luverne mural in May of 1941. In February of 1942, while completing the project, he needed a letter for his draft board from the Section to allow him to finish the work. Getz seems to have managed to complete the mural and send it to Luverne for installation only a week or ten days before he was to be inducted into military service.[19]

Arthur Kimmig Getz served as a first lieutenant of field artillery during World War II.

After Getz and Margarita Gibbons (an artist) divorced in 1963, Getz married Anne Carriere, a writer. In 1969 the couple moved from New York City to Sharon, Connecticut.

Arthur Kimmig Getz lived the rest of his life in Connecticut. One can observe a change in his covers for *The New Yorker* after his move; the cover illustrations began to include more rural scenes than city-related works.

Getz began something new for him. He began to write and illustrate books for children. There are four of these: *Hamilton Duck* (Golden Books, 1972); *Hamilton Duck's Springtime Story* (Golden Books, 1974); *Tar Beach* (Dial Press, 1979); and *Humphrey, the Dancing Pig* (Dial Press, 1980).

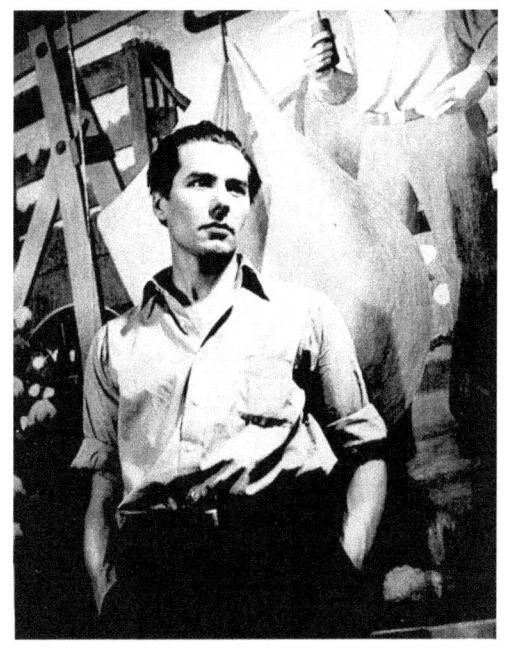

Arthur Kimmig Getz near his mural *Cotton Field*, which he prepared for the Luverne Post Office (used with permission from the Estate of Arthur Kimmig Getz. All rights reserved).

Before their divorce in 1973, Arthur Kimmig Getz had illustrated *Jennifer's Walk*, which his wife Anne Carriere authored. He also illustrated *Double Trouble* by May Garelick (1958), *Mr. Goat's Bad Good Idea* by Marileta Robinson (1979), *Gator & Mary's Traveling Band* by David Martin (1981), and *Prisoners of the Good Fight* by Carl Geiser (1986).

Arthur Kimmig Getz's final cover for *The New Yorker* appeared on August 29, 1988. He was 75 years old.

In 1994 Getz suffered a stroke that left him blind in one eye. Yet he continued to draw and paint until his death on August 29, 1996. He was 83 and had left his mark on the world.[20]

Lee Lorenz, a former art editor for *The New Yorker*, commented on Getz's covers over the fifty-year period of 1938–1988. Lorenz stated that Getz's works seem to have been primarily about the joy of painting.[21]

Monroeville

Arthur Leroy Bairnsfather's first federally commissioned artwork was *Harvesting* (1939), a mural for the Monroeville, Alabama, Post Office (constructed in 1937).

Arthur Leroy Bairnsfather's mural *Harvesting* (1939) for the Monroeville, Alabama, Post Office shows the cutting of wheat by a thresher pulled by mules. The family dog sets the pace for the farmer who follows and for the three animals towing the mower.

Bairnsfather was from Kentucky. His interest in the South is evident both from his choice of subjects and from the detail he was able to bring to his work. The mural *Harvesting* by Bairnsfather is still in place over the post-master's door in the post office in Monroeville.

Monroeville Post Office. The front view of the Monroeville Post Office shows six windows—two of which are sealed. The front door has a covering for the protection of the patrons; an aluminum sash and glass door with side-lights now replaces the original door. The door has pilasters to either side; a decorative wooden fanlight is above the door. Partially surrounding the fan-light is a round, arched, modern awning.

The roof of the brick structure at the corner of Alabama Avenue and E. Claiborne Street and across the street from the old Monroe County Court-house is flat. Four steps with wrought-iron handrails make entrance to the building accommodating to most patrons.

Inside, the mural *Harvesting* by Arthur Leroy Bairnsfather is on view. The post office—constructed more than seventy-five years ago—has with-stood the test of time and still serves the Monroeville area. The post office in Monroeville with its mural is one of the sites recommended to visitors by the Chamber of Commerce.

Monroeville serves as the county seat of Monroe County. Founded in 1815 on lands ceded by local tribes of Native Americans, Monroeville origi-nally had the name of Centerville. The name of Monroeville came from Pres-ident James Monroe, who visited the area; the incorporation of Monroeville dates from April 15, 1899.

Monroe County is just north of Escambia County. Escambia County is the location of the city of Atmore and the site of Anne Wilson Goldthwaite's oil-on-canvas *The Letter Box*. Escambia County is also the site of Brewton and its missing mural.

At the 2000 census the population of Monroeville was 6,862. The U.S. Census Bureau reported in 2000 that Monroeville had a total area of 13.1 square miles. Of this, .08 percent was water.

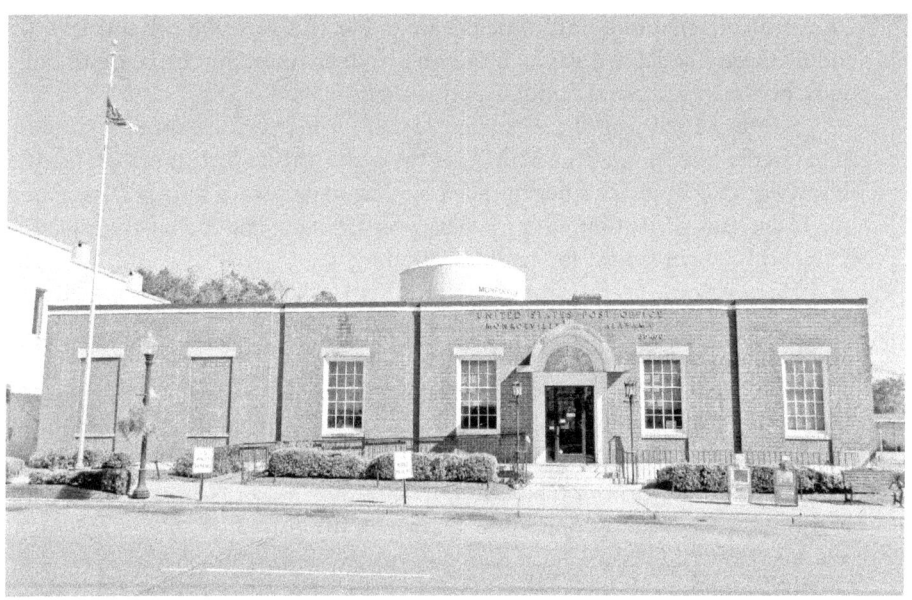

The Monroeville Post Office was constructed in 1937 at the corner of Alabama Avenue and E. Claiborne Street.

The population density of Monroeville in 2000 was 525.8 people per square mile. Of the 2000 people, 53.09 percent were Caucasians, 44.84 percent were African American, and 0.38 percent were Native American. Asians, Hispanics or Latinos, and those from two or more races made up the remaining 1.69 percent.[1]

Monroeville and the Monroe County Chamber of Commerce have developed a walking tour to highlight points of interest to visitors to Monroeville and to the immediate area.[2] One of the sites that the brochure from the Chamber recommends that tourists visit is Bairnsfather's *Harvesting*, which is still in the Monroeville Post Office.[3]

In 1997 the Alabama State Legislature declared Monroeville to be the "Literary Capital of Alabama" because of the famous writers who have lived there. Nelle Harper Lee (April 28, 1926–) is one acclaimed American novelist who has always lived in Monroeville; she wrote her 1961 Pulitzer Prize–winning *To Kill a Mockingbird* in and about the town where she was born. She called Monroeville by the name Maycomb in the book. Harper Lee still resides in Monroeville. The Chamber of Commerce capitalizes on the literary heritage of Monroeville in its advertisements.[4]

To Kill a Mockingbird won the Alabama Library Association Award (1961) and the *Bestsellers'* paperback award in 1962. Also in 1962, *To Kill a Mockingbird* was made into a movie starring Gregory Peck and released by

Universal-International. After the release of the movie *To Kill a Mockingbird* and its three Academy Awards, Monroeville, the author Harper Lee, and the book became even more familiar to the public.

Gregory Peck won the Academy Award for his performance as *Atticus Finch* in the film; he was the 35th actor to receive this award since the Academy Award for Best Actor began. The 1963 Academy Award for Art Direction of a black-and-white film went to Alexander Golitzen and Henry Bumstead, along with Oliver Emert for set decoration.

Horton Foote used Harper Lee's *To Kill a Mockingbird* as the foundation for a movie script. He received the 1963 Academy Award for a movie screenplay based on material from another medium.[5]

As a child, Truman Capote (September 30, 1924-August 25, 1984) began spending summers with relatives in Monroeville. He, Harper Lee, and Harper's brother Edwin Lee became fast friends. Capote is another writer who helped establish the reputation of Monroeville as the Literary Capital of Alabama. Capote is perhaps best-known for his novel *Breakfast at Tiffany's* and his true-crime book *In Cold Blood*.[6]

Since 1991, the Mockingbird Players have annually performed the play *To Kill a Mockingbird* in the courtroom of the old Monroeville Courthouse. The performances have been sell-outs—even when the players traveled in Washington, China, and Israel to act out Harper Lee's story.

The Chamber of Commerce brochure encourages tourists to visit the south lawn of the Old Courthouse in Monroeville and observe the monument to the fictional character Atticus Finch. The Alabama Bar Association erected the monument in 1997 and designated the monument as "the first commemorative Legal Milestone in the state's judicial history." The association chose the fictional character to stand as a model for all people working for equal justice for all. The monument is another example of Monroeville's serving as the Literary Capital of Alabama and is a reminder of Harper Lee and *To Kill a Mockingbird*. The Chamber of Commerce and the Visitors Center at the Monroe County Heritage Museums encourage everyone to visit Monroe County and for each to write his/her own story.[7]

Harvesting. Arthur Leroy Bairnsfather entered an open competition conducted by the Treasury Section of Painting and Sculpture, which was under contract to the Works Progress Administration. The offered prize was $680 to paint a mural above the postmaster's door inside the Monroeville, Alabama, post office in 1939. Bairnsfather won the contest.

The subject Arthur Leroy Bairnsfather chose for the painting in the Monroeville Post Office reminds the viewer that the Monroeville community in southwestern Alabama was primarily agricultural in its early days. He titled his mural *Harvesting*; the artwork shows three mules, a threshing machine, a farmer, and the family dog in an Alabama field.[8]

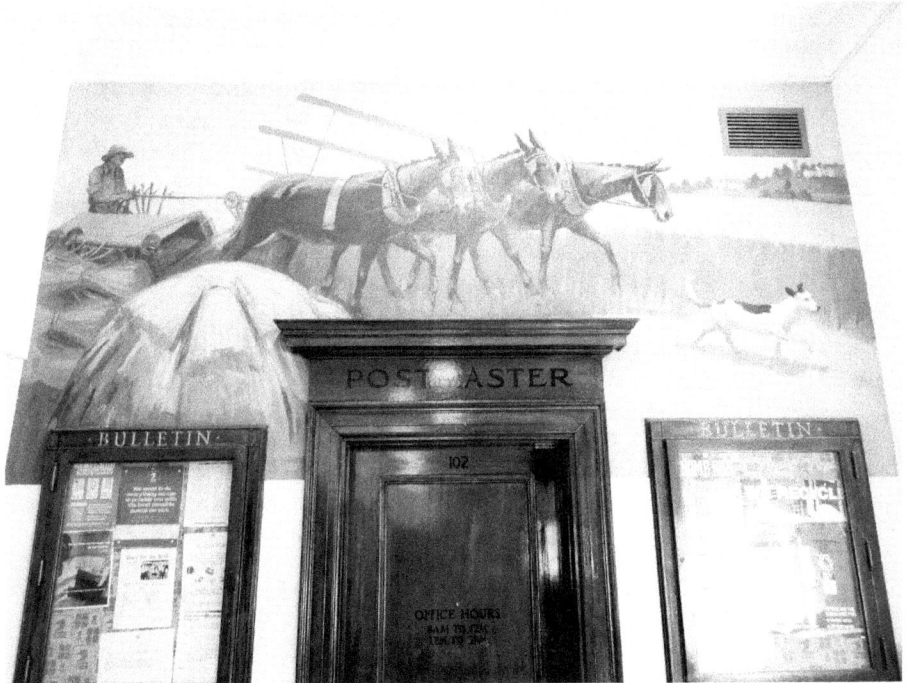

Arthur Leroy Bairnsfather painted the mural *Harvesting* in 1939 for the Monroeville Post Office.

In a 2004 article for the *Monroe Journal*, George Thomas Jones quotes John Lee Betts, a postal employee working at the time of the creation of the mural. Betts, upon looking at the mural, had remarked, "Whoever heard of three mules ever being hitched to anything in this part of the country?"[9]

The Monroe County Chamber of Commerce and Monroeville (its county seat) have developed a brochure for visitors to Monroeville and the immediate area. One of the recommended sites for tourists is Bairnsfather's mural *Harvesting*, which is still over the postmaster's door in the Monroeville post office. *Harvesting* was Bairnsfather's first federal commission.[10]

Arthur Leroy Bairnsfather followed *Harvesting* with a federal contract (July 12, 1939) to complete two murals for Burlington, North Carolina, within the coming year. Bairnsfather earned $1,900 upon completion of *Cotton Textiles* and *Historical Railroad Station*.[11] *Historical Railroad Station*, now located in the federal building in Burlington, is included in the National Register of Historic Places (August 1988).[12]

Bairnsfather's work in Burlington, North Carolina, was popular. Whitehurst wrote: "Unlike the artwork in other places in the nation, there are no evidences of any controversy or, indeed, of any reaction from Burlington citizens at the time the work was completed. The murals are still on the walls of the building."[13]

Arthur Leroy Bairnsfather. Arthur Leroy Bairnsfather was born in Kentucky on April 14, 1883. The 1910 United States Federal Census indicates that the twenty-seven-year-old Bairnsfather was residing in Manhattan Ward 21, New York. The young artist/illustrator was already experiencing some success in his profession. Soon, however, he would return to the South to live.[14]

In 1938 *Time* ran an article on Bairnsfather and his successes.

> Last week Arthur Leroy Bairnsfather of Birmingham, Alabama, could not get over his surprise at what had happened down in Montgomery. A big, bushy-haired artist who once studied under Frank Duveneck (*Time,* April 25, 1938), Mr. Bairnsfather never goes far afield for his subjects. Last summer he spent about 30 hours, smoked about 60 pipes, doing a brown and silver study of Dr. George Washington Carver, famed old Negro chemist at Tuskegee Institute. When the Southern States Art League, proud nurse of regional consciousness among artists from New Orleans to Charleston, held its 18th annual exhibition last month in Montgomery, Arthur Bairnsfather sent in his portrait. What surprised him, as a Southerner, was that it got the Blanche S. Benjamin prize of $250 for "the loveliest painting of a Southern subject." Jury's reason: "Spiritual rather than physical loveliness" inspired this breach with a tradition of landscape prize winners.[15]

Bairnsfather found commissions for artwork with the federal government during the Great Depression. First, he painted the mural in 1939 in Monroeville, Alabama, which is still an important part of the Walking Tour in Monroeville.

> Inside the Post Office is a WPA [Works Progress Administration] mural, titled *Harvesting.* The subject is a farmer using a three-mule team to pull a threshing machine across a wheat field.... Bairnsfather was hired to paint the mural after he won an open competition conducted by the Treasury Section of Painting and Sculpture.... [H]e was paid $680.[16]

After the Section issued Bairnsfather an invitation to prepare a mural for the Monroeville Post Office, he submitted three sketches to the Section for their approval. The Treasury Section of Painting and Sculpture chose a scene showing the harvesting of grain; Bairnsfather mentioned to the group that the area around Monroeville grew very little grain, but the Treasury Section kept their choice. After the installation of *Harvesting* in January of 1939, the postmaster and public asked if they could have another mural for the opposite lobby wall.[17] The Treasury Section and Bairnsfather did not fulfill the request.

Bairnsfather's two 1940 murals for Burlington, North Carolina, were important to the area—and also to Bairnsfather. His contract specifies that he would receive $1,900 for successful completion of the two murals for the

Alamance County Federal Building within a one-year period. Each mural was to be twenty feet by eleven feet upon completion.[18] The finished Burlington pictures measured twenty-one feet by twelve feet, however.[19]

Cotton Textiles depicts a room at a textile mill where workers are completing the slashing process, which is applying sizing (a protective coating) to the material or yarn and dried in an oven or on hot cans or rollers after the application. He pictured also a device called a *lease* that separates the sheets of yarn into separate strands after the sizing.

The second mural that Bairnsfather prepared for Burlington was *Historical Railroad Station*. The painting depicts a pre–Civil War Burlington—or Company Shops as some people called it. The railroad station and the train served Burlington and the South by tying them to the outside world.[20]

The murals by Bairnsfather for Burlington are still in the former United States Post Office and Federal Building at 430 South Spring Street. The 1936 structure is an example of Classical Revival Style and Art Deco Style. Architect R. Stanley Brown—working under Louis A. Simon, the head of the Office of Supervising Architect—designed the building, which still houses two important wall murals reflecting the history of Burlington and painted by Arthur L. Bairnsfather.

On November 3, 1987, Roche Biomedical Laboratories bought the building. The former post office became a part of the National Register of Historic Places on September 23, 1988.[21]

Arthur Leroy Bairnsfather died on April 1, 1974, in Birmingham, Alabama. He was just a few days short of his ninety-first birthday.[22]

Bairnsfather had many accomplishments in his life. His education was a first step toward his goals. Besides studying with Frank Duveneck, Bairnsfather studied with Vince Nowottny and attended the Cincinnati Art Academy. He was a member of the Salmagundi Club, established in 1871; this early, important art club in New York City held regular exhibitions and formed a collection.

Bairnsfather was also a member of the Southern States Art League, established in 1921. In 1929 at its exhibition in San Antonio, Texas, he took the prize; in 1938 at its exhibit in Montgomery, Alabama, he again won an award.[23]

Bairnsfather's work remains on display at the University of Alabama. His photograph in this article shows Bairnsfather before his death with a mural he prepared for Doster Hall there.[24]

George Thomas Jones writes in 2003 of a controversy in Monroeville as to who actually painted *Harvesting*. Jones reports that J. Kelly Fitzpatrick, an artist from Montgomery, originally had his signature on the mural; the date "9-1-39" followed the signature, according to Jones. Other people had other ideas.

To clear up the discrepancy, the *Monroe Journal* invited citizens to share

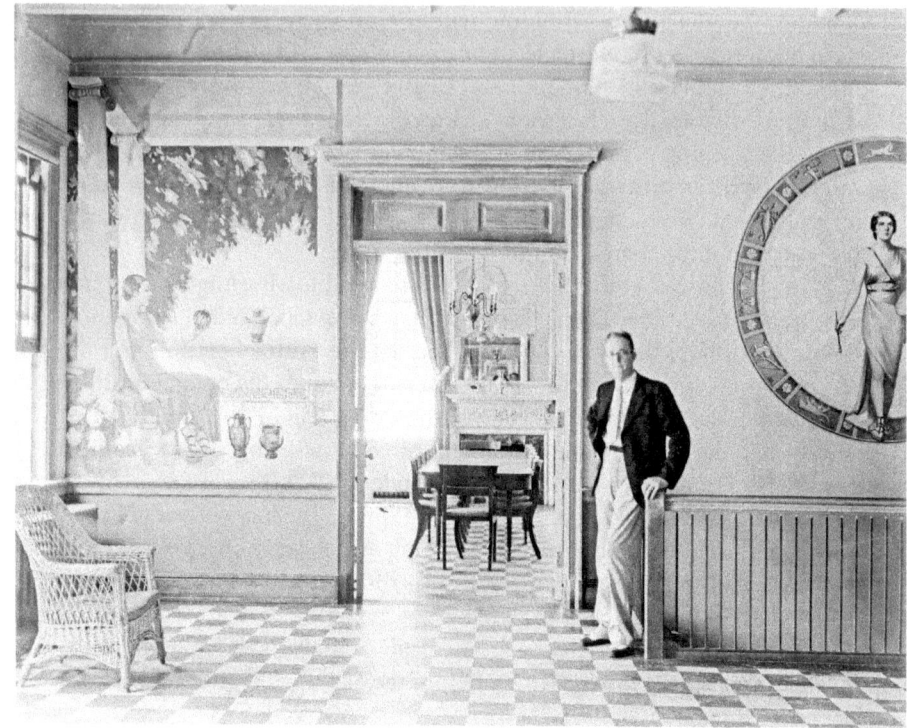

Arthur Leroy Bairnsfather with one of his murals, in Doster Hall at the University of Alabama (courtesy Alabama Department of Archives and History, Montgomery, Alabama).

information on who actually prepared the painting. The paper could not contact Bairnsfather to solve the 1985 controversy because he had passed away some time ago.

Cornelia Sawyer shared a letter she had received from Karen Yasko. Yasko was with the General Services Administration in Washington; at the time she had written the letter, Yasko was a counselor for fine arts and historic preservation. Yasko stated that Arthur Leroy Bairnsfather had painted *Harvesting* in 1939 after winning an open competition by the Treasury Section of Painting and Sculpture.

John Bertalan, a Birmingham native specializing in art restoration, had earned the job in 1985 of restoring the 1939 *Harvesting*. Bertalan contacted a postal supervisor at the United States Postal Service in Atlanta. He received a letter telling him to credit Arthur Leroy Bairnsfather with the painting. Bertalan complied and painted "A.L. Bairnsfather" over the words "J. Kelly Fitzpatrick."

John Bertalan received a telephone call from artist Arthur Stewart.

Stewart told Bertalan that he knew an A.L. Bairnsfather, who was a portrait painter in Birmingham. Stewart speculated that Bairnsfather had tried to model his rural scene from that of Fitzpatrick. Stewart further speculated that Bairnsfather had signed Fitzpatrick's name to the work to ease his conscience.

Jones concludes that at last the mystery of the source of the Monroeville mural was solved. He concludes: "Now, Monroeville can boast of at least two things unlike any other. The architecture of the 1903 courthouse and the 1939 mural painted on the wall of the post office."[25]

Montevallo

The 1939 federally commissioned mural *Early Settlers Weighing Cotton* by William Sherrod McCall is still on display in the Montevallo, Alabama, Post Office.

The postmaster in the town of Montevallo reported in 1940 that the public was pleased with the artwork that William Sherrod McCall had completed for the Montevallo Post Office the previous year. McCall's mural *Early Settlers Weighing Cotton* (1939) reflects the history of Montevallo.

Montevallo, Alabama. The city of Montevallo is close to the exact geographic center of the state of Alabama; cotton was vital to its history and growth. A marker prepared by the Alabama Tourism Department and the City of Montevallo alerts visitors and citizens alike as to something of the history of the town and its exact geographic location at

33° 6'18" N 86° 51'46" W. In 1814, Jesse Wilson laid claim to Wilson's home located above Shoal Creek, making it the oldest settlement in Shelby County, Alabama. In 1817, after General Andrew Jackson defeated the Creek Indians on the Coosa River, homesteaders like Wilson and his family and friends settled in the area. During this time, the area was known as "a little mountain in a valley," and Montevallo is thought to have derived its name from this geographical reference. The direct Italian translation of Montevallo is "on a mound in the valley."[1]

Montevallo originally had the name Wilson's Hill. Jesse Wilson had come to Alabama from Georgia. He built a log house in 1817 near Shoal Creek and on top of a hill, subsequently known as Wilson's Hill. This was before Alabama had been admitted as the twenty-second state in 1819.

Edmond King from Georgia soon came to the area and built "the finest house" visitors had ever seen. He built also a brick store on the Reynolds lot, where their warehouse now stands. The Creek Indians lived here also. Arrowheads are still sometimes visible in the local fields. Near Davis Falls one could still find a beech tree at the turn of the century. The name McHenry and the date 1821, attesting to the age of the settlements, were still legible.

The Bowdons, the Powells, the Nelsons, the Killoughs with their saw and grist mills, the Lahons, and the Walkers are other recognizable names from the past of Montevallo. The two-story house built by Fred Watrous is the oldest structure still standing in Montevallo.

The Bell Hotel was the first hotel in the area. The Bell Hotel was in the storehouse building used by H.C. and W.B. Reynolds.

In the 1850s railroad fever raged in the Montevallo area. Edmond King donated an engine valued at $15,000 and another $20,000 in cash. The Alabama & Tennessee River Railroad laid its iron in Montevallo in 1855.

Montevallo became the largest market in North Alabama for a few years with its ease of accessibility and its increase in population. Calhoun, Talladega, Blount, St. Clair, Jefferson, Walker, Bibb, and Tuscaloosa Counties marketed their cotton in Montevallo for a while.

The old books from the railroad show 24,000 bales of cotton shipped to the area. A heavy bale of cotton at the time brought $300; cotton brought as much as 50 cents a pound.[2] "In addition to the financial opportunities in Montevallo, the panorama is delightful … the wealth in coal and iron and limestone and timber, which lie almost at its doors, extends with limitless profusion."[3]

The population of Montevallo in 2012 was 6,452. The estimated median household income in Montevallo in 2012 was $29,250; it was down from $30,541 in 2000. The median income of a household in Alabama in 2012 was $41,574.[4]

Fertile lands, a temperate climate, and close proximity to mining and manufacturing towns make Montevallo attractive to prospective citizens and tourists alike.[5]

Another marker posted by the Alabama Tourism Department and the City of Montevallo offers residents and tourists additional information about Montevallo:

> Montevallo's rich history and deep roots left behind treasured buildings and places that remain integral parts of the community. The classic main street is just one example, with buildings dating back to the late 1800s. Seventy-three homes and buildings in Montevallo have earned their place on the National Historic Register including Reynolds Hall and other buildings on the University of Montevallo campus. Some areas have even taken shape as tourist attractions for the city, such as the Aldrich Coal Mine Museum and Farrington Hall.[6]

The city of Montevallo continues to try to maintain its original character. The University of Montevallo also preserves and values its rich historical heritage.

The University of Montevallo. In October of 1896, a school to educate women to be self-supporting opened in Montevallo. Named the Alabama Girls' Industrial School (AGIS) the school enrolled some 150 young women from across the state of Alabama. These women had come for training as teachers, bookkeepers, artists, musicians, dressmakers, telegraphers, and milliners; the students hoped to escape field work, mill work, and dependence on another person for support in a poverty-stricken state.

In 1911 AGIS became Alabama Girls' Technical Institute (AGTI). Curriculum changes enabled AGTI to become Alabama Girls' Technical Institute and College for Women in 1919. In 1923 the school became a degree-granting institution: Alabama College, State College for Women.

With the enrollment of two men in January of 1956 and 33 more in September, the name of the school and also the curriculum changed again; Alabama State College for Women became the University of Montevallo. Its colleges included arts and sciences, education, business, and fine arts. The University of Montevallo remains the only public liberal arts university in Alabama. With degree programs in 70 academic areas and a student-faculty ratio of 17 to 1, the University of Montevallo continues to scale the ranks of America's Best Colleges in the list of *U.S. News & World Report.*[7]

Montevallo Post Office. Montevallo's historic post office is on the corner of Main and Vine Streets.

> During the Great Depression the town of Montevallo received a grant from the Works Progress Administration in 1936 to build a new post office. Completed in 1937, the $52,000 building had a redbrick exterior with white Georgian marble trim in the interior. The interior also features a large mural painted by William Sherrod McCall.[8]

After climbing two sets of steps that total ten, visitors originally had to manage six more steps to gain admission through the centered front door. This series of steps made entry to the facility difficult for some patrons. To ease entrance for the disabled, a ramp with wrought iron banisters now provides easier access for many customers.

Two lampposts provide lighting and decoration to the front of the Montevallo Post Office. An awning protects the front entrance, which is centered between four windows. The double-hung sash windows have 12 panes above and 12 panes below the centerpiece.

The Montevallo Post Office was one of twenty-four buildings in Alabama to receive artworks through the Section of Fine Arts of the Treasury Department. Twenty-three of the buildings in Alabama that originally received the federal artwork were post offices.

Early Settlers Weighing Cotton. The Section of Fine Arts commissioned William Sherrod McCall to paint a mural for the Montevallo Post Office.

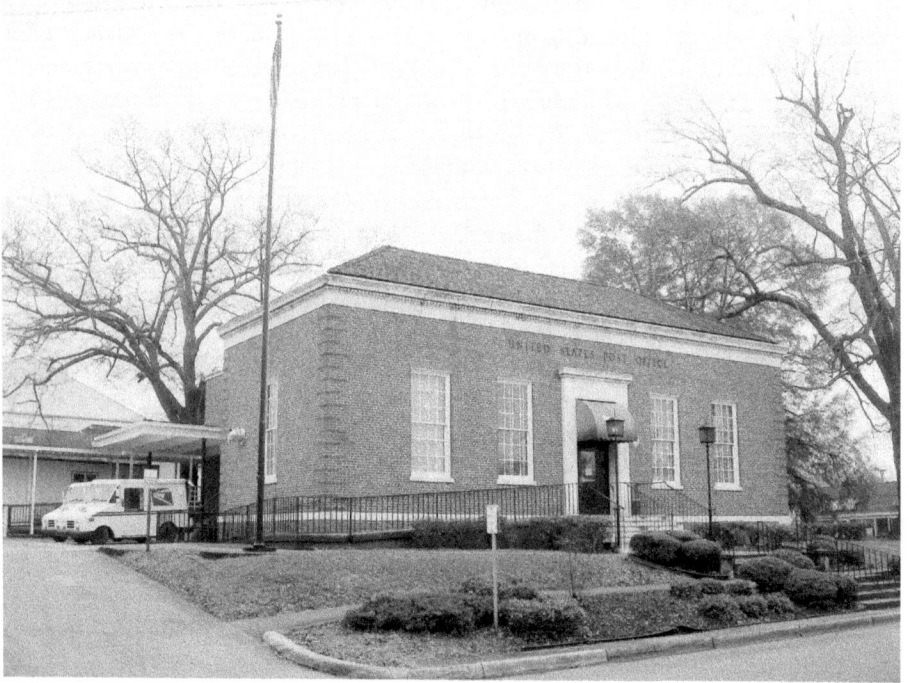

The Montevallo Post Office—constructed in 1936—was a red brick structure that is still in use.

McCall was a resident of Jacksonville, Florida, at the time he received his commission for Montevallo. He earned the commission on the basis of designs he had submitted for a competition in Miami, Florida.[9]

Upon notification of his commission for the Montevallo mural, McCall visited the Alabama site immediately. He chose the themes of cotton and the settlement of the region for his 1939 mural titled *Early Settlers Weighing Cotton*. The topic of cotton growing, harvesting, and ginning had not been and would not be an unusual one for Alabama murals.

- Franc Epping prepared (1941) a terracotta relief titled *Cotton* for Alexander City.
- Lee R. Warthen painted (1941) the mural *Cotton Scene* for Hartselle.
- Arthur Getz painted (1942) *Cotton Field* for Luverne.
- John Kelly Fitzpatrick exhibited (1939) his oil-on-canvas *Cotton* in Phenix City.

In a letter to the Section, William Sherrod McCall justified his topic. McCall wrote, "Montevallo was a very important little town to the cotton industry of the State in the early days."[10]

The postmaster, in the letter he wrote to the Section to verify the installation of the mural, commented:

> I would like to state that the citizens find the work a beautiful addition to our building and wish to thank the Federal government for this contribution. The heads of the Departments in our Alabama State College, as well as those students who are able to comment upon Mr. McCall's workmanship, join me in saying that it is one of the best pieces of work seen in the State.[11]

McCall wrote a letter to the Section in which he commented upon his royal treatment in Montevallo. He provided the Section with a description of the panel and its historical source.[12]

> In the frontier days of Alabama History, cotton planters from Virginia and the Carolinas migrated into the Alabama Territory where the possibilities of acquiring new soil lay open before them. In the center and south eastern [*sic*] sections of the new State [*sic*] they settled where the climate and soil were favorable. Some were wealthy and brought along many slaves to work in the fields. Other, less fortunate, did their own work, the women and children joining in the harvesting of the crops. These were a fine and sturdy people. Their descendants make up the backbone of Alabama.
>
> The scene depicted in the panel is one that might have been typical of the period.[13]

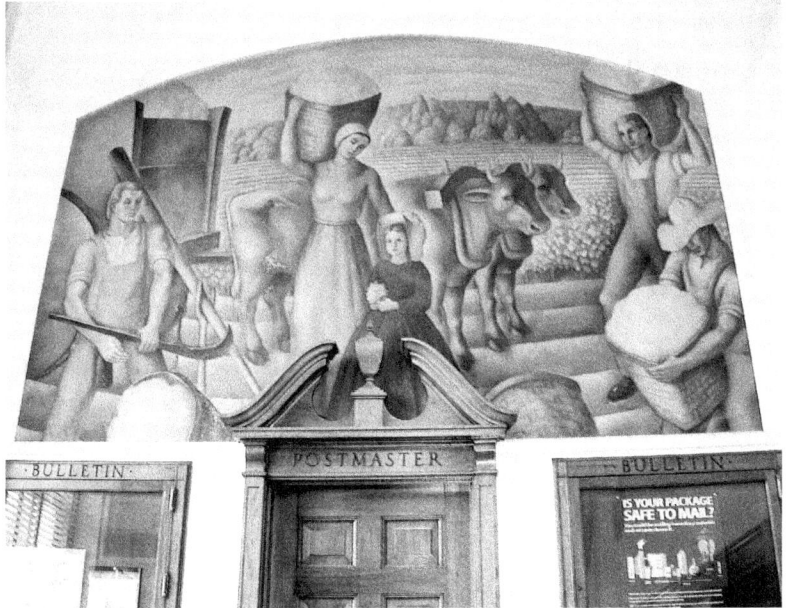

The 1939 mural that William Sherrod McCall prepared for the Montevallo Post Office is still on display in the post office. Its title is *Early Settlers Weighing Cotton*.

McCall went on to identify the actual people who are pictured in the mural panel for the Montevallo Post Office:

My cousin, Eugene Mitchell posed for the three older male figures. He is a farmer, still working the same soil that three generations of Mitchells had worked before him.
The youth at the right, is one of my pupils. He is not a farmer but his lean type is to be found all over Alabama. His name is William Cox.
The little girl in the center is the child of an artist friend of mine [Eunice Lytle] Her quaintness of character made her a perfect subject.
The mother was posed by one of my pupils and very dear friends [Mrs. Price Chalker]. Her people helped to found the City of Jacksonville, Florida.
The oxen were developed by drawings made from a very gentle and lovable old beast that I found, turning the grinder of a cane mill.[14]

The Section of Fine Arts has presented its own description of the mural:

In the frontier days of Alabama history, cotton planters from Virginia and the Carolinas migrated into the Alabama territory to acquire new soil. In the center and southeastern sections of the new state they settled where the climate and soil were favorable. Some were wealthy and brought along many slaves, but others did their own work, the women and children joining in the harvesting of the crops. These were a fine and sturdy people, and their descendants make up the backbone of Alabama. The scene depicted in this mural is one that might have occurred in those early days.[15]

William Sherrod McCall. William Sherrod McCall wrote his own autobiography for the Section of Fine Arts. It is important to observe the facts that the artist himself deems as most important.

McCall mentions that he was born on January 31, 1900, in Quincy, which is in Gadsden County, Florida. His maternal ancestors (Smiths) had migrated to Florida from Virginia in the 1800s. His paternal ancestors came to Florida about 1780 from South Carolina. Both families were planters of cotton and tobacco.

Before he joined the Navy in June of 1917, McCall finished his public school education and one year of preparatory school at Columbia College, which was in Lake City, Florida. McCall served in the Mine Fleet in Foreign Waters during World War I.

McCall describes 1920–1926 in his own words. He says he spent those years "in trying to adjust myself to many various types of work, none of which pleased me. Spent my spare time in drawing and painting, knowledge of which was self-taught."[16]

In 1926 McCall worked for three years as a hospital janitor on the West Coast while he attended the Otis Art Institute. McCall summarizes his next years before painting the mural for Montevallo:

Painted four canvases on P.W.A.P. after which was given work on W.P.A. Returned to Florida in 1936 and became School Manager at Jacksonville Federal Galleries, which position I have held until present time.[17]

McCall notes his painting of one mural in Phoenix, Arizona; one at Howard University; one at Pomona College; one at Los Angeles Junior College; one at the Negro Public Library in Los Angeles; and six murals in Jacksonville.[18]

McCall returned to duty during World War II. He again had contact with the military when he received his diagnosis of illness from the Oteen Veterans Administration Hospital in Buncombe County, North Carolina. McCall had "Bronchogenic carcinoma, left lower lobe with extension into mediastinus and pericardium." McCall died in the Oteen Hospital on April 26, 1963—8 months after the onset of the disease. His burial was in Green Hill Cemetery in Waynesville, North Carolina.

William Sherrod McCall's spouse, Marguerite Horn McCall, joined him in the Green Hall Cemetery in Waynesville (Haywood County), North Carolina, after her death on June 25, 1978. She, like William, had been born in Florida.[19]

In addition to the legacy of his artwork, William Sherrod McCall is remembered for his service to others in the U.S. Navy (World War I), the U.S. Army (World War II), and his service as assistant supervisor for a WPA recreation program. He helped to build service centers for men in Fort Myers, in Sebring, in Avon Park, and in Clearwater. From 1940 to 1941 he directed the St. Petersburg WPA Art Center, which was a federally funded center, before returning to service in World War II.[20]

Oneonta

Aldis Birdseye Browne II's federally commissioned mural *Local Agriculture—A.A.A. 1939* (1939) is on display in the Oneonta, Alabama, Post Office (constructed in 1938).

Oneonta, Alabama. Oneonta is in the eastern part of Blount County, Alabama. The Alabama Territorial Legislature created Blount County from the lands that the Creek Indian Nation ceded. The name Blount County came from the Tennessee Governor W.G. Blount, who provided troops under Andrew Jackson during the Creek War. Oneonta has been the county seat since 1889. From 1825 until 1889 Blountsville had functioned as the county seat.[1]

The city of Oneonta is 35 miles northeast of Birmingham. The location of Oneonta is in the Murphree Valley. Red Mountain and Sand Mountain are to its northwest; Straight Mountain is to Oneonta's southeast. After John Hanby discovered a rich iron ore seam in Oneonta in 1817, the area became a mining community.[2] Most of the Oneonta citizens seek to preserve and remember the past; the Blount County Museum reminds residents and visitors alike of this heritage.

Oneonta began as a small town with only a train depot, a post office, a telegraph office, three stores, and twelve residents. Many citizens remember that Oneonta operated a small prisoner of war camp just outside of its city limits during World War II. The town today covers fifteen square miles and (according to the 2010 census) consists of 6,567 residents. About 14.7 percent of the population was below the poverty line in 2010.[3]

By 2012 the estimated median household income in Oneonta was $30,810. This median yearly income for a Oneonta household was up $2,190 from 2000. The Alabama median household income in 2012 was considerably higher than that in Oneonta; the median income for a household in Alabama in 2012 was $41,574.[4]

Blount County has the nickname the "Covered Bridge Capital of Alabama." A covered bridge is one with trusses made from timbers; the roof and sidings—usually of wood—create an almost complete enclosure. Three covered bridges remain in Blount County: the Easley Covered Bridge, the Horton Mill Covered Bridge, and the Swann Covered Bridge, which is 324 feet long and the longest in Alabama. All three of these bridges are on the National Register of Historic Places.

The Easley Covered Bridge dates from 1927. It is the oldest of the three covered bridges in Blount County.

The Horton Mill Covered Bridge is the tallest covered bridge in the United States. The bridge is 70' above water. It dates from 1934.

A third covered bridge in Blount County is the Swann Bridge, which dates from 1933. It is the longest covered bridge in Alabama.

Oneonta—the county seat of Blount County and the site of three covered bridges—hosts the Covered Bridge Festival each year on its Main Street.[5] The 31st Annual Covered Bridge Festival was in 2014; the Blount-Oneonta Chamber of Commerce calls the event officially the Blount County Covered Bridge Festival.[6]

Oneonta is home to Heritage Golf and Limestone Springs Golf. The Locust Fork River and the Mulberry Fork River provide whitewater rapids for adventurers.

While still preserving small-town charm, Oneonta provides its visitors and residents with the services and shops they desire. Properly trained police and fire personnel are readily available for the community. The Oneonta school and athletic system are in high demand; the high school won state

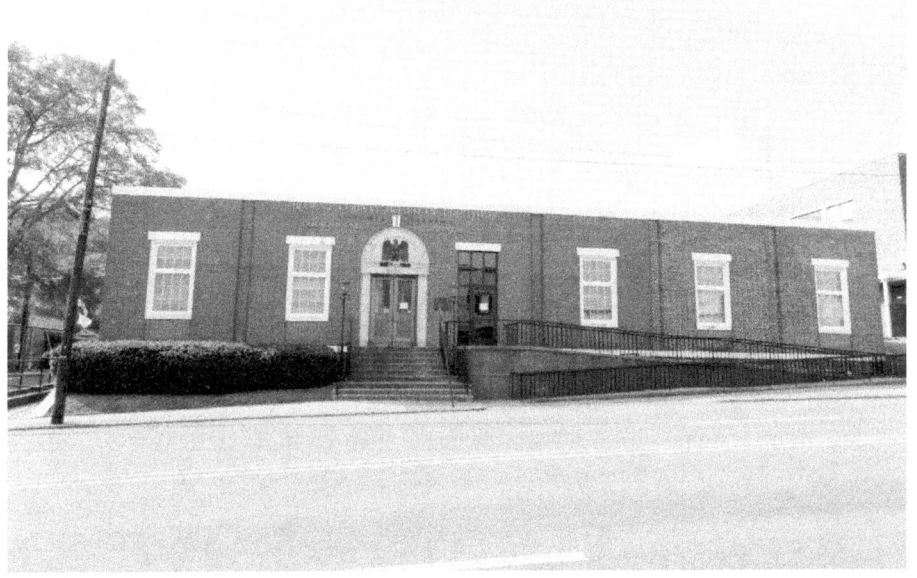

The Oneonta, Alabama, Post Office dates from 1935.

titles in football (2013), girls' basketball (2013–2014), boys' golf (2012), and boys' individual track and field (2013). The airport, public library, local churches, airport, and local hospital meet the needs of residents and visitors.[7]

Oneonta Post Office. The Oneonta Post Office was originally at 204 2nd Avenue, East, in Oneonta, Alabama; the cost of the lot was $4,750. The federal builder and architect was Neal A. Melick. The dedication of this federal building costing $66,000 was August 6, 1938.

The location of the one-story building of red brick laid in English Bond Style was on the former site of the H.C. McPherson Home. The Blount County Children's Shelter moved into the relocated home.

The 1938 post office has a full basement; the building has 4,938 square feet of area on each floor. The windows are double-hung wooden sash with 8/12 lights. The lobby of the building has a brick floor.

The front entrance to the structure has a bronze eagle with a semicircular arch around it. Two lampposts help with both the decoration and the lighting for the front entrance. A 1965 addition to the building changed the front appearance to a bilateral design with four windows on one side of the door and two on the other. The cost of this addition was $185,000; Davis, Speake and Thrasher of Birmingham was the architectural firm.

A ramp with metal banisters, added in 1991, makes the facility more easily accessible to the handicapped. During the remodeling, a door replaced one of the windows on the front of the building to allow patrons to gain a less difficult entrance to the services inside. The building is on the Alabama Register of Historic Places.

In 1995, upon completion of a new post office facility, the postal service left the 2nd Avenue building. The Blount County Court House Annex moved into the facility. Today the Board of Education occupies the structure, which is still identifiable at 204 2nd Avenue, East by the American eagle over the door and the flat roof.[8]

Local Agriculture—A.A.A. 1939. Aldis B. Browne II received the commission from the Section of Fine Arts to prepare the mural *Local Agriculture—A.A.A. 1939* for the Oneonta Post Office. The 12' × 4' mural still hangs in the old Oneonta Post Office building that the Board of Education now uses.

The Browne mural references in its title and in its content the A.A.A. [Agricultural Adjustment Administration]. A definition of the A.A.A. is in order here:

> In May of 1933, the government established by law the Agricultural Adjustment Administration (AAA) to aid the nation's beleaguered farmers and ultimately the nation. This organization helped to educate the farmer, to encourage effective agricultural techniques, to assist both the small and the tenant farmer, to control the market, and to make benefit payments to those employing soil conservation measures and limiting crops. This was the beginning of the "alphabet soup" of programs to follow as a result of the New Deal legislation.[9]

Browne accepted some of the suggestions of the residents of Oneonta as to the subject matter to incorporate in the mural for the Oneonta Post Office. Browne came to Oneonta in the South from Connecticut. Each day he painted directly on the wall of the post office.[10] Many of the local residents made a daily visit to the post office to use its services and to check on the progress that Browne was making.

Browne wrote to the Treasury Section of Fine Arts about his work in Oneonta. Browne reported that he was "nuts" about the county seat of Blount County; he remarked also that the residents of the dry county were engaged in serious debate as to whether the jug he had painted on the wall held corn whiskey.

Browne heeded the requests of the postmaster and the local citizens to include behind the figures certain scenes and buildings. He painted on the left the Birmingham Dam, which was only seven miles from Oneonta. On the right, Browne added a local strip mine. Browne painted the post office, the local sawmill, the courthouse, the jail, the cotton warehouse, the Baptist church, and the Methodist church across the top of the painted scene. He included also a house with a tin roof, a barn with a cyclone cellar, and a covered bridge, which was fitting for a town noted for its covered bridges.

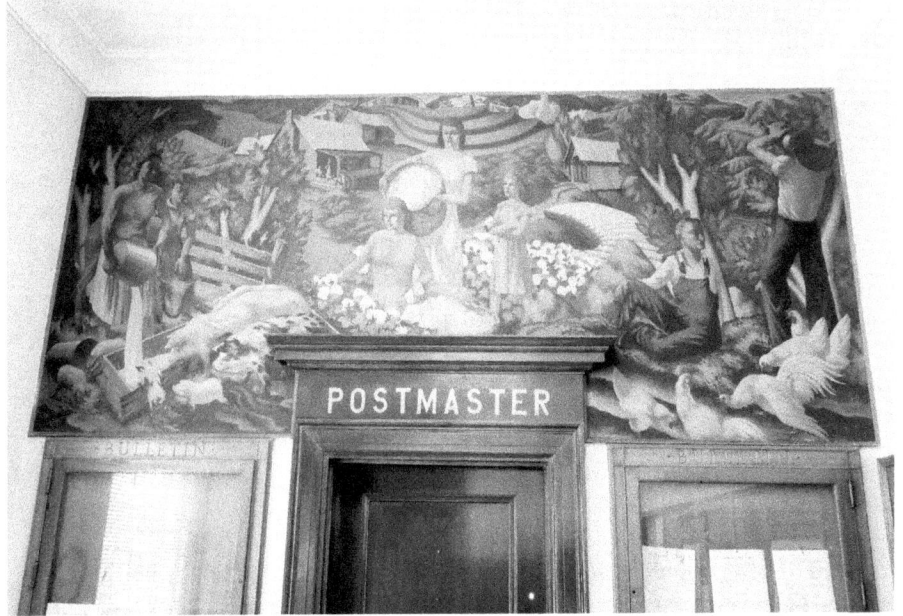

Aldis Birdseye Browne II's federally commissioned mural *Local Agriculture— A.A.A. 1939* (1939) is still on display in the old Oneonta, Alabama, Post Office.

In the center of the scene are two fields: one that is terraced and one that is the product of erosion. Browne reported that the local agricultural office was already using the mural to demonstrate to farmers the benefits of modern, scientific methods of planting. In the center of the scene, female farm workers gather the cotton; on the right the viewer notes a boy with a calf and a woman feeding the hogs. Two men are resting on the right in the scene.

Other Alabama murals show the effects of and prevention methods of erosion also. These murals include the ones in Montevallo (1939), Haleyville (1940), and Huntsville (1937).

"The Living New Deal"—sponsored by the Department of Geography at the University of California at Berkeley—indicates the reaction of the postmaster to the Browne mural. The website indicates that the postmaster's letter verified to the Section of Fine Arts the installation of the mural. The letter was "effusive in its praise for the Section, Browne, and the mural." The mural was oil on canvas.[11]

NewSouth Books in Montgomery, Alabama, published Eddie Wayne Shell's book *Evolution of the Alabama Agroecosystem: Always Keeping Up, but Never Catching Up* in 2013. Aldis Birdseye Browne II's mural is referred to in this book.[12]

Aldis Birdseye Browne II. Aldis Birdseye Browne was born in Washington, D.C., on August 2, 1907. His namesake was his grandfather Aldis Birdseye Browne, a lawyer in Washington, D.C. *A History of the City of Washington: Its Men and Institutions* (1903) lists Attorney Aldis Birdseye Browne as one of the best-known corporate lawyers in Washington.[13]

For most of his early life, Aldis Birdseye Browne II lived in Essex, Connecticut, where he became a founding member of the Essex Art Association. Despite the fact that both his father and grandfather were lawyers, Aldis did not pursue the legal profession. He instead entered the Yale School of Fine Arts in 1928. His interests were in watercolor, imaginative composition, and decoration. His further work included portraits, which have been carried out in various mediums. In 1934 he earned the B.F.A. from Yale.[14]

Through the Treasury Art Project, Aldis B. Browne painted historical murals in the Henriques Room, which was originally the library room of the United States Coast Guard Academy. The room was named for Captain John A. Henriques (1826–1906).

Henriques had been the first superintendent of the Coast Guard Academy. In 1841 he had joined the merchant marine and in 1854 he had enlisted in the revenue marine. In addition to serving as the superintendent of the Revenue Cutter School (the precursor of the Coast Guard Academy) until 1883, Henriques had run the first cadet training ships: the *Dobbin* and *Chase*.[15]

When Browne was installing his historical murals at the United States Coast Guard Academy as part of a Treasury Art Project, "Browne and the Superintendent, then Captain E.E. Jones, had their differences. On one occasion Browne, who was a dwarf, rose to his full four feet and threatened to paint Jones' [*sic*] face on the figure of a smuggler in one of the murals."[16]

The January 1, 1940, *Life Magazine* contains an article featuring Aldis Birdseye Browne II and his paintings of icebergs. Browne captured the scenes while he was on a seven-month iceberg patrol aboard the United States Coast Guard cutters *Tahoe* and *Pontchartrain*. Browne's permission to accompany the Coast Guard Service and to paint the Ice Patrol in action was a "rarely-granted honor to civilians." Browne had received this honor after completing the murals for the Coast Guard Academy in New London, Connecticut; his work won favor with the Coast Guard officials because it was responsible for "depicting the Service's long and valiant history."[17]

Browne worked under the government programs TRAP (Treasury Art Project) and the PWAP (Public Works Art Project). He and fellow artist Vincent Mondo completed two panels for the Fair Haven Junior High School in New Haven, Connecticut, in 1934. Of course, Browne also prepared a mural for the Oneonta Post Office.

In 1966 Browne married for the first time. He was 59 years old. He married fellow artist Patricia (Glazier) Kreis in Essex, Connecticut. He moved into her house in Essex. Patricia was the widow of Henry G. Kreis, a prominent sculptor, who had died in Essex in 1963. Aldis Birdseye Browne II and Patricia divorced in 1973.

Aldis relocated to Anna Maria Island, Florida, after the divorce. He later moved into a retirement home in Davenport, Florida. Browne was suffering from emphysema. He died on May 7, 1981, in Davenport. He was seventy-four years old.[18]

Opp

The 1938 federal post office in Opp, Alabama, was the site for the original installation of Hans Mangelsdorf's federally commissioned sculpture: *Opp* (1940).

Opp, Alabama, is in Covington County. With its slogan "City of OPPortunity," Opp suggests a positive image to visitors and residents alike.

The total area of Opp is 24.6 square miles. Of this total area, water covers 0.9 square miles.[1]

The elevation of Opp is 338 feet. One can compare this elevation with that of Mobile, Alabama. Downtown Mobile has an elevation range of 10 feet on Water Street; the elevation is 211 feet at the Mobile Regional Airport.[2]

The highest point in Alabama is Cheaha Mountain in Cleburne County. Cheaha Mountain has an elevation of 2,407 feet, which is considerably above the 338 feet of Opp.[3]

The first white settler in what is now Opp was Walker Patrick. In 1880, Patrick bought 160 acres in the area. He used it for a farm, a house, and a store. The locals referred to it as Hallton or as Cool Springs. In the late 1800s postal services became available at the first post office in the area.

When the Louisville & Nashville (L&N) Railroad came through the area, the city of Opp grew up at a point where the line ran south and east. Alex Hart, a local entrepreneur, bought land along its route. The lots he subdivided from his purchase made up the downtown area.[4]

The city of Opp on its official website reminds residents and visitors of its history. The name came from a lawyer, Henry Opp, who worked for the Louisville & Nashville Railroad. Opp practiced law in Andalusia, Alabama, and served as mayor of Andalusia (1899–1906). When the L&N tried to complete a survey of lands in Covington County and determine a right-of-way into the county (1901), the Central Georgia Railroad tried to block this survey from occurring. Opp defended the case for L&N and was successful in his argument that L&N be able to complete its survey. Ultimately, the L&N was able to establish its railroad line through the area that is now Covington County.[5]

In 1819, President Monroe signed a resolution admitting Alabama as the twenty-second state.[6] At one place there was a well-defined branch in the tracks of the L&N railroad. One split went distinctly east, and the other division went noticeably south. This junction was a good turning place for trains, and there were already some settlers at this point. The L&N encouraged a town at this branch. The town, with the encouragement of the L&N Railroad, took the name Opp to recognize Henry Opp, who had been directly responsible for the location of the L&N in the area. The town received its charter in 1901.[7]

In the 1980s change would come to the L&N, the railroad that had been so important to Opp. On November 1, 1980, the Seaboard Coast Line Industries merged with the Chessie System and formed the CSX Transportation System. The CSX and the L&N merged on December 29, 1982. The resulting railroad system is the Seaboard System Railroad.[8]

The Alabama & Florida Railway operated a short line railroad from south central Alabama, eastward through Opp and on to Geneva. The L&N operated it between 1901 and 1982; the Seaboard System operated the short line from 1983 to 1986. The Pioneer Railcorp controlled this short line railroad for a while before selling 33 miles of track from Georgiana to Andalusia, Alabama; the buyer was Three Notch Railroad (TNR). Some railways in Opp are still in use. The Alabama Farmers Co-op in Opp has been a steady industrial customer of the railroad.[9]

There are individuals and organizations at work to preserve the history of the L&N, which was vital to the history of Opp; some of these groups are working also to preserve the equipment of the L&N. These organizations include the Historic Railpark and Train Museum in Bowling Green, Kentucky; the L&N Historic Society; and the Kentucky Railway Museum.[10]

The 2010 population of Opp in Covington County, Alabama, was 6,659. The racial makeup of Opp was 80.9 percent white and 16.7 percent black. The remaining 2.3 percent of the population was Native American, Asian, Hispanic or Latino, and a combination of two or more groups. About 18.2 percent of the population was below the poverty line.[11]

The Opp Rattlesnake Rodeo. Opp has been the site of a controversial festival for more than half a century. The Opp Jaycees and J.P. Jones developed the event: a Rattlesnake Rodeo. Only six states—Alabama, Georgia, Kansas, New Mexico, Oklahoma, and Texas—hold these contests at which hunters bring in as many snakes as they can catch in a year, slaughter their catch, and sell the skin and meat. Kaetz indicates that the attendance for the weekend affair has numbered 20,000.

Arts and crafts, food, beauty contests, snake shows, music, games, races, karaoke, buck-dancing exhibitions, and a Rattlin' Country Concert are some of the usual events during the weekend rodeo at Opp.[12]

> A recent study analyzing 50 years of roundup data found eastern diamondback rattlesnakes in sharp decline due to roundup pressure and habitat loss. Rattlesnakes play a key role in the food web, especially in terms of rodent control.
> And roundups are harmful to many species, not just rattlesnakes. To catch snakes for the event, hunters spray gasoline into tortoise burrows, destroying the burrows and often killing the animals inside. More than 350 species depend on tortoise burrows for food and shelter.... Handling venomous snakes in front of the public and then killing the snakes is the opposite of wildlife education.
> Nor do roundups protect public health. There are many more annual fatalities in the United States from dog bites, lightning strikes and bee stings than from venomous snake bites. And in fact, the majority of snake bites occur when humans try to capture or kill snakes—so rattlesnake roundups themselves endanger public health by encouraging the public to do just that.
> Finally, roundups are far from necessary to generate community revenue....[13]

The Center for Biological Diversity opposes the Rattlesnake Rodeos because of the wildlife—in addition to the rattlesnakes—that suffer harm from the roundups. The Center filed a notice in 2013 of its intent to sue the United States Fish and Wildlife Service because of its failure to protect the rattlesnake. The Center also circulated petitions with signatures of those who prefer festivals without the killing of animals. Some success is already evident.[14]

Opp Post Office. The Opp Post Office in Covington County received the wood relief titled *Opp* in 1940. The brick post office facility (1938), located at 101 N. Main Street, is currently in use by the Opp City Hall.

The cornerstone of the building lists many familiar names. Henry Morgenthau, Jr., was the Secretary of the Treasury in 1938. James A. Farley was Postmaster General during the construction of the Opp, Alabama, Post Office. Louis A. Simon was the Supervising Architect, and Neal A. Melick was the Supervising Engineer in 1938.[15]

Centered between the four windows is the front entrance. Two double-hung, 8/12 windows are on either side of the paned front door. Two plain, undecorated, square Doric columns support the roof of a front porch that protects patrons using the front door. Six steps lead to the front entrance; wrought-iron banisters make the steps more easily accessible to those entering the public building. Two black, wrought-iron light fixtures provide decoration and the necessary lighting needed at times for safety.

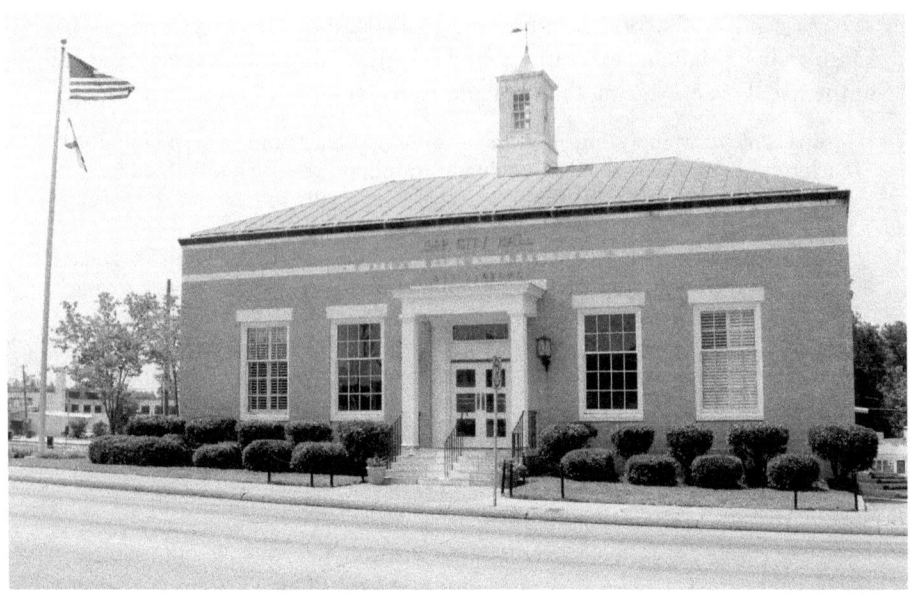

The United States Postal Service used the building until the late 1990s when a new post office was constructed. The old structure houses Opp City Hall.

A cupola is centered on the roof of the former post office building. This ornamentation adds interest to the structure. The Opp Federal Post Office building is still in use by the city, though it no longer serves as a post office.

***Opp,* a Wood Sculpture.** Hans Mangelsdorf earned a commission from the Section of Fine Arts to prepare an artwork (1940) for the Opp Post Office. Within a month after receiving the commission and the invitation to visit Opp, Mangelsdorf, who had been residing in New Orleans at the time, was in Alabama.

After visiting Opp and after talking with the residents and the postmaster, Mangelsdorf sent two things to the Section. He sent projected sketches of the artwork and his assertion that he had incorporated the suggestions of the people of Opp into the prospective work. Mangelsdorf indicated that he had made certain to include especially the locals' recommendations of the essential things to represent Opp.[16]

Mangelsdorf planned to employ relief for the decoration of the Opp Post Office. A relief is any work which projects from a background; a relief is different from sculpture in the round and three-dimensional works. With the three-dimensional sculpture in the round, the artwork has form on all sides; one can view sculpture in the round from any angle.

There are two main types of reliefs. In high relief, the figures project "at least half of their natural circumference from the background."

By contrast, in low relief (*basso-relievo, bas-relief*) the figures project only slightly from the background; no part of the artwork is detached from the background. With *crushed relief* the figures barely exceed the background. Another type of low relief is hollow relief; with hollow relief the carving lies within a hollowed-out area below the surface.[17]

Hans Mangelsdorf's sketches for his work in Opp, Alabama, and the work itself illustrate high relief. The local newspaper described the work after its installation.

In the relief agriculture is personified by the

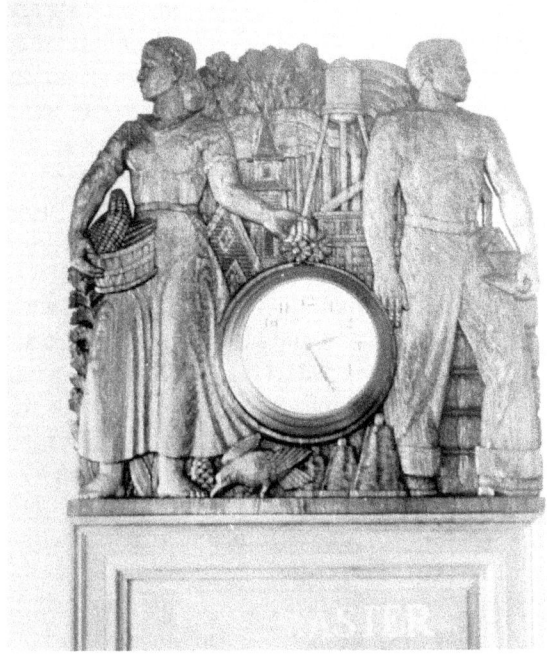

This image is that of the wood relief that Hans Mangelsdorf carved (1940) for Opp, Alabama. The carving is lost at this time (courtesy National Archives).

woman holding a basket of corn in one hand and flowers in the other hand, and the church in the background indicates home, life, and education. The goldenrod, the State flower, and the Flicker, the State bird, are also shown on the relief. Industry is personified by the man holding a spool, symbolizing the main industry of the town, the cotton mills. The water tower, symbol of the industrial progress, shows in the background, and in the back of all is the long leaf pine.[18]

The Opp wood carving by Hans Mangelsdorf is currently missing. When the United States Postal Service moved from the 1938 federal building into the new postal facility in Opp, the carving was lost. Its location is still unknown, but the investigation into its whereabouts is ongoing. Anyone with information should contact the postmaster of the Opp post office or the Historic Preservation Office of the United States Postal Service.[19]

Hans Mangelsdorf. The artist Hans Mangelsdorf was born on November 22, 1903, in Leipzig, Germany. Mangelsdorf was able to study under the prestigious German-born artist Max Klinger, who lived between 1857 and 1920. Mangelsdorf's training included work with other artists in both Germany and Vienna.[20]

On June 27, 1937, thirty-four-year-old Hans Mangelsdorf agreed to an interview with William Weathersby of the *New Orleans Times-Picayune*. The sculptor and painter Mangelsdorf had, according to Weathersby, seen as much of the rest of the world on as little money as anyone else.

In 1919 Mangelsdorf had become a soldier in Germany at sixteen, but he gave up his military career to continue with his studies in art. His studies took him to Munich, to Augsburg in Bavaria, and to Vienna. His studies ended in Vienna, and he went to work in a porcelain factory before his traveling days began. His chief means of travel was walking. Because he had no particular destination in mind, he stopped when he needed to rest or to work for money. His art and his travels were first in his life at the time.

Hans Mangelsdorf traveled through Switzerland, Italy, Hungary, Russia, and Czechoslovakia. Mangelsdorf's travels took him also into France and Spain. Weathersby reported that "when Europe became small to him," Mangelsdorf went to Canada and took a job on a ranch near Calgary in Alberta. Mangelsdorf found that his experience in breaking in horses and leading hunts on the Hungarian plains, together with his familiarity with guarding cattle in the Swiss Alps, had prepared him well for his new work on the Canadian ranch. Mangelsdorf admitted that he had even learned to like the weather—including the storms and blizzards—and the solitude of the Canadian ranch.

Mangelsdorf next found his way into Arizona and Texas. Later he drove into New Orleans in a Model T car. In Louisiana, Mangelsdorf earned a commission to prepare a series of sketches for a museum. He decided to base these works on legends that explain things that we do not understand.

The German-born artist had been on his way to Mexico when he had stopped in New Orleans in 1935. Between 1935 and 1937, Mangelsdorf worked on a plantation in the area and opened his own art studio.

Mangelsdorf concluded his interview with Weathersby by expressing his desire to continue the things he liked best in life: art and traveling.[21]

When World War II came about five years later, Hans Mangelsdorf soon joined the United States Army. Along with his military service, Mangelsdorf was able to produce some works of art.

As Allied forces moved across the Pacific, they had to establish supply bases and airfields on conquered islands to ensure advancement to the next island. The transformation of the island of Saipan, however, began even before the Allies had cleared it of enemy forces and before Army engineers had begun the task of developing the island into "the most powerful base in the Pacific.... American forces landed on the island in June 1944, and by November B-29 Superfortresses were flying bombing missions from the runways the engineers had cleared from the hard coral rock."[22]

The military provided the following caption for this image:

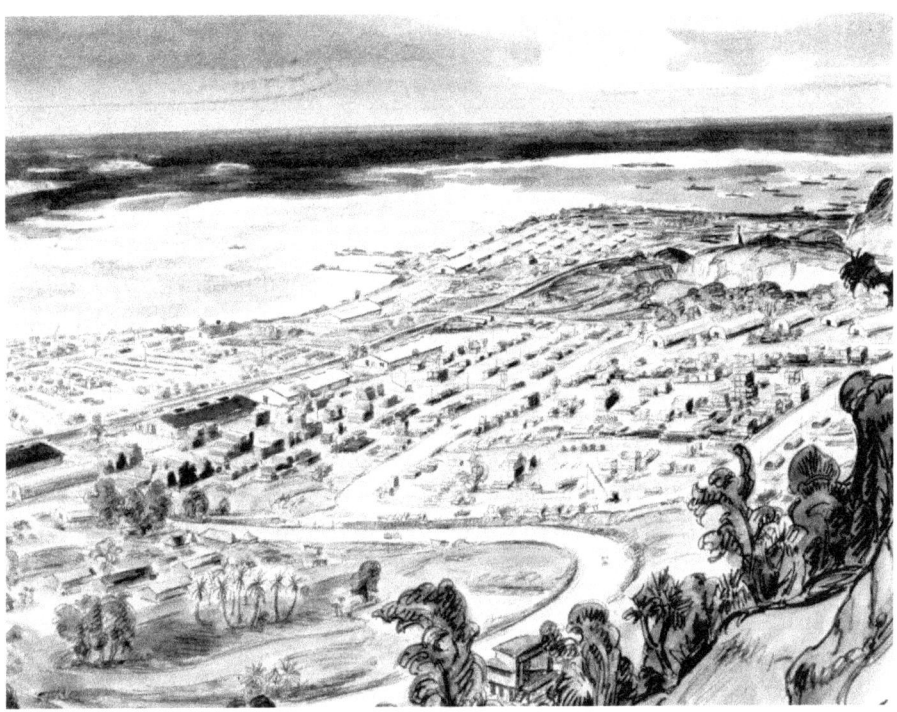

This drawing of the "U.S. Army Engineer Base Yard" in Saipan is the work of Hans Mangelsdorf (http://www.history.army.mil/html/artphoto/pripos/finalstages.html).

Saipan is the largest of fifteen islands in the western Pacific Ocean known as the Marianas. Japanese forces held the strategically significant island on 15 June 1944 when America launched its amphibious attack.

A magnificent drawing of Saipan's Tanapag Harbor, by Hans Mangelsdorf, is part of the Army's Art Collection. It depicts the massive forces that were launched to capture the island. The Empire's hero of Pearl Harbor, Vice Admiral Chuichi Nagumo, was in command of Japanese forces. It would be his last battle.

Image of a drawing called *Tanapag Harbor, Saipan, Pacific*, by Hans Mangelsdorf. This military work of art depicts the naval vessels, offshore at Saipan, which delivered the invasion forces.[23]

After a fierce battle, the Allies secured the island. The tide of war, by the summer of 1944, had turned against the Empire of Japan. One can still obtain Mangelsdorf's copyright-free drawing *U.S. Army Engineer Base Yard: Saipan* that he prepared while he was in the United States Army by contacting U.S. Army Center of Military History.[24]

The German-born artist specialized in sculpture, painting, murals, and crafts. He was a member of the Southern States Art League and was a PWA and WPA, Public Works Project Participant. He died in 1991 at the age of 88.[25]

Ozark

John Kelly Fitzpatrick's federally commissioned mural *Early Industry of Dale County* (1938) is on display in the old post office building (now the Sheriff's Department) in Ozark, Alabama.

John Kelly Fitzpatrick originally installed his federally commissioned mural *Early Industry of Dale County* (1938) in the Ozark, Alabama, Post Office. When the postal service moved from the building, the mural remained. *Early Industry of Dale County* (1938) is currently in the Dale County Sheriff's Department Building.

Ozark, Alabama. The oral history behind the name of Ozark, Alabama, is that a visitor to the area observed that the place reminded him of the Ozark Mountains in Arkansas. Ozark seemed to have its name.

The first European known to reside in what is now Ozark was John Merrick, Sr. Merrick, a Revolutionary War veteran, settled in the area in 1822. In honor of him, the town became Merricks. The town later became Woodshop. In 1855, the town—at the request of the citizenry—became Ozark. This third name stuck!

Ozark is in Dale County, which had as its county seat the town of Newton. In 1870 Ozark became the county seat.

Three sites in Ozark are on the National Register of Historic Places. Two are houses—the Samuel Lawson Dowling House and the J.D. Holman House—and one is a church: the Claybank Log Church.

A part of the Wiregrass Region, Ozark has a total area of 34.5 square miles. Most of this area—34.2 square miles—is land; only 0.2 square miles is water.[1]

The population of Ozark grew from 512 in 1880, to 1,570 in 1900, to 2,518 in 1920. During the Great Depression of the 1930s, Ozark had a population of 3,103. By 1960 its population had tripled to 9,534.

By 1970, the population of Ozark had increased to 13,555. This trend of growth would not continue indefinitely. In 1980 the total population had decreased by 2.7 percent to 13,188. The population decline continued; in 1990 the population was only 12,922—a 2 percent decline. The year 2000 saw a 17 percent increase in population. The population was 15,119 in 2000; this was the highest recorded. The number, however, had dropped to 14,907 by 2010;

this was a 1.4 percent loss.[2] Projections for 2013 were for another slight drop (–0.3 percent) in population to 14,860.[3]

The racial makeup of the city of Ozark in 2000 was 68.28 percent white, 28.3 percent black, and 3.42 percent other. The median age of the Ozark resident in 2000 was 39 years. Nineteen percent of the population and 14.8 percent of the families were living below the poverty line.[4]

The Ozark City Schools, the Dale County Schools, and three private schools serve Ozark. Enterprise State Community College offers a program in aviation maintenance technology at the Alabama Aviation Center at Ozark; other college courses are also available.

Dothan Regional Airport, a commercial airport, serves Dale County. Dothan has a Delta connection and a Northwest airlink. Blackwell Field, with its lights, repair facility, 5,000-foot runway, and hangars, is also available to Ozark.[5]

The Muscogee (also spelled Muskogee) people originally inhabited the area that is now Ozark. Also known as the Creek, the Native Americans traditionally occupied the southeastern woodlands.

The Muscogees who still live in Alabama may be descendants of the Mississippi tribe who often built mounds of earth. Walter Williams, the historian, wrote that Spanish explorers encountered ancestors of the Muscogee in the 16th century. Many of the Muscogees were relocated to Indian Territory in 1830.[6]

Ozark Post Office. In 1843 the first Woodshop Post Office opened; it was a log building. After a petition for change, the name of the town officially changed to Ozark in 1855.[7]

The year 1936 marked the construction of a new post office in Ozark, Alabama. The cornerstone of the federal building indicated that the erection occurred when Henry Morgenthau, Jr., was the Secretary of the Treasury; when James Farley was Postmaster General; when Louis Simon was Superintendent of the Archives; and when Neal A. Melick was the Supervising Engineer.

The flat-topped structure is made of red brick with decorative inserts. Four windows across the front of the building serve for decoration and for lighting and ventilation. A front door is in the center of the windows. Two sets of five concrete steps allow access to the front entrance; an awning offers some protection from the elements to patrons of the facility.[8]

The 1936 Ozark Post Office building is no longer in use as a post office facility; a new post office building dates from 1987. The 1936 structure now carries the name Creel Richardson Building. The artwork by John Kelly Fitzpatrick still occupies the lobby of the building.[9] The Dale County Sheriff's Department uses the Creel Richardson Building, the former Ozark Post Office.[10]

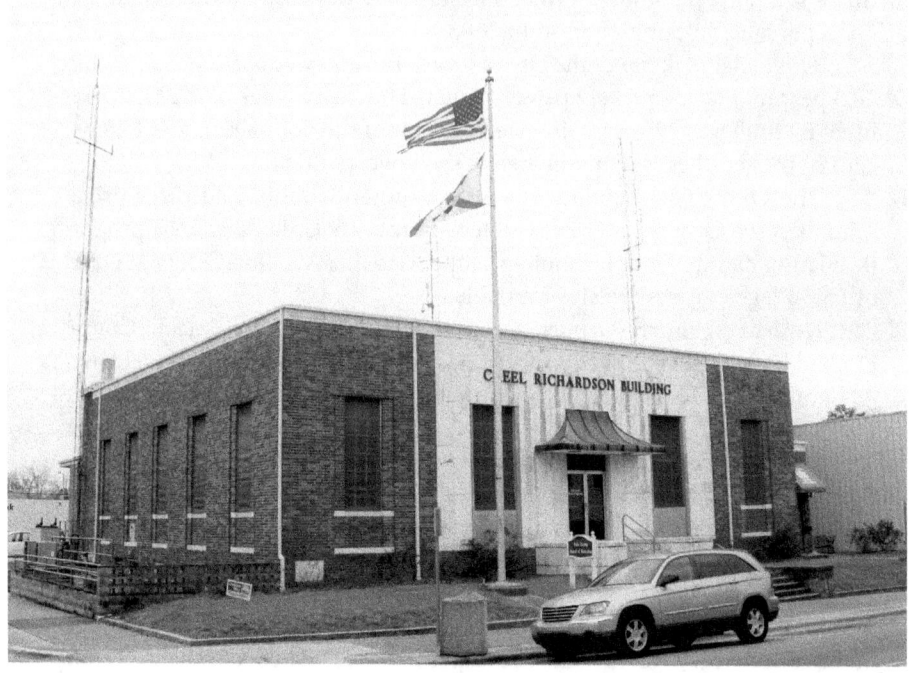

The Ozark, Alabama, Post Office building dates from 1936. The structure still stands, but it is now the Creel Richardson Building. Its use has changed to the Dale County Sheriff's Office.

Early Industry of Dale County **(1938).** John Kelly Fitzpatrick created *Early Industry of Dale County* through a commission from a New Deal Agency, the Treasury Section of Fine Arts. The painting is still on display.

Early Industry of Dale County was one of two federal murals that John Kelly Fitzpatrick painted for Alabama. Fitzpatrick had earned the commission on the basis of his works. Fitzpatrick suggested several different themes for his mural for the Ozark Post Office. His proposed topics included a depiction of the battle between Samuel Dale and the locals, an allegorical panel, and a panel illustrating postal history.[11]

The Section, however, had its own suggestion. President Franklin Delano Roosevelt had chosen John Kelly Fitzpatrick's painting *The Water Mill* to hang in the White House. President Dwight David Eisenhower later liked *The Water Mill* so much that he had it moved to his private office. The work captured the bright colors and the use of light that Fitzpatrick had studied in the European works.

TRAP proposed that Fitzpatrick depict a local Ozark industry and use his previous Public Works of Art Project *The Water Mill* as a model for the

Ozark Post Office mural. TRAP approved Fitzpatrick's sketch of the water mill. After the installation of the painting now titled *Early Industry of Dale County*, the local newspaper praised the work highly.[12]

Fitzpatrick "strongly believed that only a Southern artist could truly capture the essence of his or her own section of the country, putting him at the heart of the regional art scene in the 1930s and 40s."[13]

John Kelly Fitzpatrick painted other Alabama industries of the 1920s and through the Great Depression. He captured Alabama's rural landscape, its inhabitants, and their businesses at a time when rapid change was underway. Some other industries besides *The Water Mill* that Fitzpatrick preserved in his art were his 1934 *The Saw Mill* (oil on Masonite), his 1934 *The Cotton Gin* (oil on canvas), and his 1933 *The Cane Mill* (oil on canvas). These last three works were gifts of the Works Progress Administration to the Montgomery Museum of Fine Arts in Montgomery, Alabama.[14]

John Kelly Fitzpatrick (1888–1953). John Kelly Fitzpatrick was born in 1888 near Wetumpka, Alabama. After high school he attended briefly the University of Alabama in Tuscaloosa. He also enrolled for a short time at the Art Institute of Chicago. In 1918 Fitzpatrick enlisted in the United States Army and signed up for active duty in France. Four months later he experienced a life-changing event.[15]

> On July 19, 1918, to the sound of blasting whistles and shouted commands, thirty-year-old J. Kelly Fitzpatrick clambered out of his trench and, in the words of World War I doughboys, went "over the top." To his left and right, fellow soldiers of the 12th Machine Gun Battalion, Fourth Infantry Division, joined Fitzpatrick in an awkward trot as they lugged their weapons and ammunition across the barbed-wire landscape toward the distant German trenches.
>
> Within minutes, unseen German machine guns chattered to life as artillery

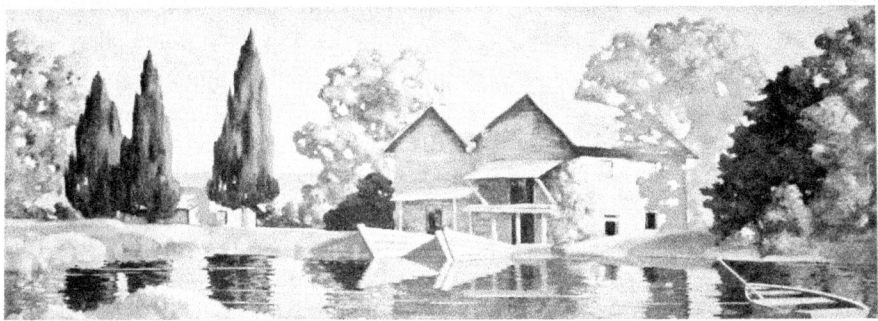

The mural by John Kelly Fitzpatrick still resides in the 1936 Ozark, Alabama, Post Office—now the Creel Richardson Building. The bright colors and the light that Fitzpatrick incorporated into the work are still visible.

shells rained down on the advancing Americans. The enemy fire tore Fitzpatrick's company to pieces. The shrapnel of one exploding German shell
ripped through Fitzpatrick as he struggled to continue the advance. As he lay
wounded, most of the rest of his unit died around him. He was one of the few
survivors....

His war experience left Fitzpatrick with two legacies: disfiguring scars on
his face, neck, and chest, and a new-found belief that, having been "through
the furnace of war, nothing mattered but the spiritual things of the world."[16]

Upon his discharge, Fitzpatrick returned to Wetumpka. Despite his bad
experiences during the war, Fitzpatrick returned to Europe for a while in
1926 to study at the Academie Julian in Paris. He studied the bright colors
and the use of light in the European works. He "was inspired by the work of
the Fauves and the Post-Impressionists. When he returned to Alabama the
following year he incorporated bright colors and exaggerated lines into his
depictions of the Southern landscape."[17]

John Kelly Fitzpatrick contributed to art in the State of Alabama. He
was a founder both of the Alabama Art League and of the Montgomery
Museum of Fine Arts in Birmingham. As the 1920s ended, Fitzpatrick—like
so many others—encountered financial problems. He struggled to hold onto
his home. The Treasury Department's Public Works of Art Project brought
some relief to him. Fitzpatrick took the position of a decorator of federal
buildings for the PWAP. He earned $38
per week.

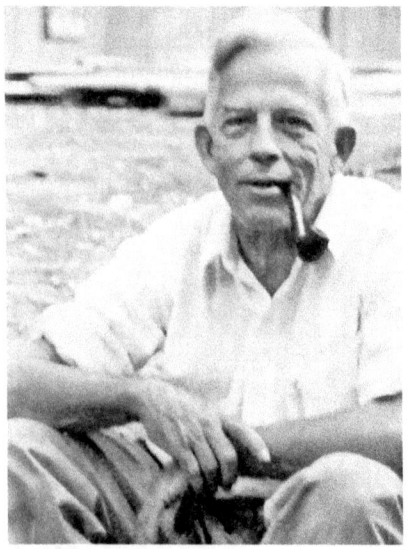

Fitzpatrick also found work with the
Treasury Department. The Treasury
Department at the time was responsible
for the construction of federal buildings;
1 percent of the cost of each building was
to go for artwork and decoration. An
artist working with TRAP usually earned
about $700 for a mural and $3,000 for a
courthouse. Alabama received commissions for the decoration for one courthouse and for the decoration of twenty-
three post offices. Through the Treasury
Department, John Kelly Fitzpatrick earned
commissions for two post offices in Alabama: Ozark (1938) and Phenix City (1939).

John Kelly Fitzpatrick some time after his military service. His birth-town of
Wetumpka, Alabama, has the John Kelly Fitzpatrick Memorial Gallery, which fur-
nished the photograph (courtesy Kelly Fitzpatrick Memorial Gallery, Wetumpka,
Alabama).

John Kelly Fitzpatrick was the first director of the Montgomery Museum of Art School. He taught at the Dixie Art Colony at Lake Jordan, Alabama.[18]

John Kelly Fitzpatrick dedicated his life to promoting the arts in his home state of Alabama.... Following the war, Fitzpatrick returned to Alabama and worked as a landscape and genre painter. In 1926 he traveled to Europe once again.... [Later in] Alabama Fitzpatrick became a leading figure in promoting the arts of his home state. Prior to 1930, artists had very few venues to display their work, so Fitzpatrick led a small group of artists, known as the Morningview Painters, and founded the Alabama Art League with the intent of finding places to hold exhibitions. The success of the resulting exhibitions led to the formation of the Montgomery Museum of Art in 1930. Fitzpatrick served on the original board of directors and the exhibition committee for the newly opened museum.

In 1933 Fitzpatrick and his friends Sallie B. Carmichael, Warree Carmichael LeBron, and Frank Applebee founded the Dixie Art Colony, also known as *Poka-Hutchi*, a Creek Indian expression meaning the "gathering of picture writers." It was located on the banks of Lake Jordan near Wetumpka, Alabama. Guest artists to the colony included Anne Goldthwaite, an Alabama native who taught at the Art Students' League in New York [See Chapters Two and Twenty-four], and Lamar Dodd, head of the art department at the University of Georgia.[19]

Although John Kelly Fitzpatrick painted portraits and still-lifes, his landscapes are perhaps his best-known works. Partly as a result of his studies in France, Fitzpatrick promoted painting *en plein air*, or in the open air out of doors; he often took his students to picturesque countryside locations in the Alabama area.[20]

Fitzpatrick's mature style can be classified as Regionalist, referring to a movement that rejected abstract art in favor of more traditional scenes, usually depicting a local, rural way of life.

Kelly Fitzpatrick produced many idealized images of his home state. His positive images were well-received by his fellow Alabamians and he influenced many upcoming artists through his teachings.[21]

John Kelly Fitzpatrick painted throughout his life. He had just finished *Swing Low, Sweet Chariot* for the Alabama Department of Archives and History when he suffered a massive heart attack and died on April 18, 1953.[22] His resting place is the Wetumpka City Cemetery in the place of his birth: Wetumpka, Alabama, in Elmore County.[23]

John Kelly Fitzpatrick (1888–1953) left behind his influence and more than 400 paintings and sketches.[24]

Phenix City

The 1939 federally commissioned oil-on-canvas mural *Cotton* by John Kelly Fitzpatrick is currently on display in the Phenix City, Alabama, Post Office.

Phenix City, Alabama, has not always carried that name. Beginning as a trading post on the west bank of the Chattahoochee River, the name of the post originally (pre–1820) was Girard, in recognition of the Philadelphia philanthropist Stephen Girard, who owned much of the land in the area.

The location of Girard was inside Creek Indian Territory. About eight miles to the south of Girard was Coweta, the capital of the Creek Nation. The northern boundary of Girard, Fifteenth Street North, eventually became the northern boundary of Russell County.

Opposite Girard on the east side of the Chattahoochee River was a white settlement designated as Marshall's Reserve; Ben Marshall had sold the area originally for $35,000. This community later sold for $100,000 and would later become Columbus, Georgia.

December 18, 1832, marked the formation of Russell County. The designated county seat of Russell County was Girard. The first session of court to convene in Girard was on October 14, 1833.

Samuel G. Ingersoll and his associates applied for a charter to build a railroad from Ingersoll's Hill in Girard to Crawford, Alabama, which was about 11 miles to the west. The chartered railroad later became the Central of Georgia.

An Act of the Alabama legislature, H.B. #585 on February 23, 1883, incorporated the town of Brownville. Brownville was just north of Girard in Lee County. The southern boundary of Brownville was the northern boundary of Girard, or Fifteenth Street North.

On February 19, 1889, an Act of the Alabama legislature (H.B. #679) changed the name of Brownville to Phenix City. The name came from the Phenix Mills in Columbus.

The incorporation of Girard did not occur until December 8, 1890. This incorporation was a result of the passage of H.B. 333 by an Act of the Alabama Legislature. With its incorporation (1890) and with the earlier advent of the railroad (1846), the population of Girard continued to grow.

The Federal Census records these populations of Phenix City before the annexation of the city of Girard:

- 1900—3,840
- 1910—4,214
- 1920—4,942

August 9, 1923, was the date of the consolidation of Girard and Phenix City. The total population at that time was 10,374.[1] In 1935 Phenix City became the county seat of Russell County.

Phenix City has had to overcome some hardships. During the Great Depression, Phenix City declared bankruptcy. It had accumulated debts of more than $1.1 million. By 1933 Phenix City

> was operating under a federal receiver. At the time, local authorities rationalized widespread crime and corruption in Phenix City as being a necessary revenue producer in the absence of other businesses. City leaders took advantage of this activity and enforced a system of fines and licensing for gambling and for the use and sale of liquor to raise money for the city's treasury, while not addressing the illegal activities themselves. By 1945, the city was collecting more than $228,000 a year in fines.[2]

Among other Alabama municipalities, Phenix City had a reputation as the "bad boy." The main industries of Phenix City by 1950, according to Lyles, included prostitution, gambling, racketeering, and other vices; on Fourteenth Street alone, there "was a cornucopia of gambling, prostitution, drugs and alocohol."[3]

The year 1938 marked the date of the construction of the present Russell County Courthouse. Built by Murphey Pound, the new building was the

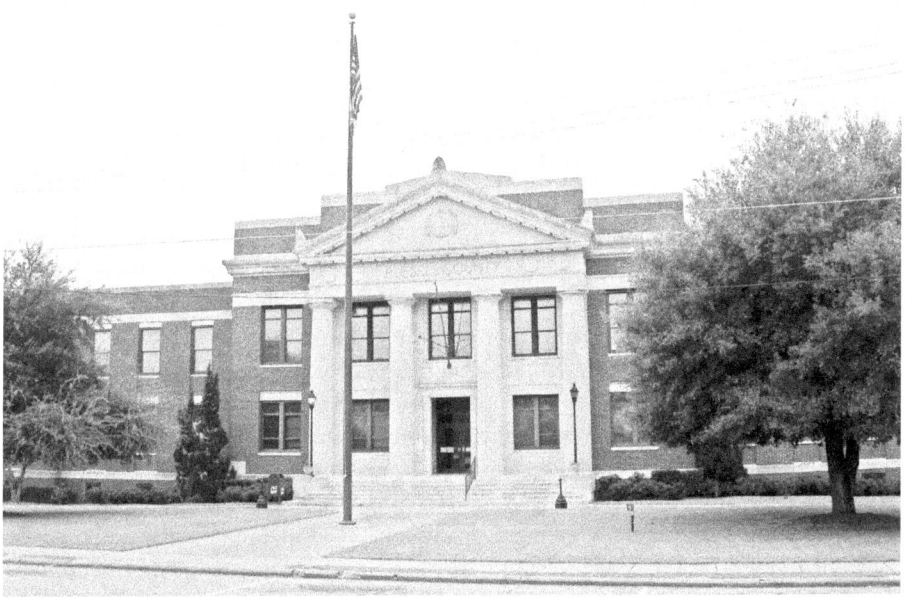

The Russell County Courthouse in Phenix City, Alabama.

design of J.J.W. Biggers and housed all the county offices; the Russell County Courthouse in Phenix City is a Classical Revival structure.

In 1944 the county building received an addition on its north side. The newer section held the Chamber for the County Commissioners and the offices of the county clerk. An eastern addition in 1949 used the design of J.J.W. Biggers; this time J.D. Stillwell was the builder. Jimmy S. Emerson, DVM, noted that it was possible to see the courthouse of Muscogee County, Georgia, from the front lawn of the Russell County Courthouse.[4]

The form of government for Phenix City has changed through the years. Since 1977, however, Phenix City has employed the council and the city manager form of government.[5]

Phenix City Post Office. The year 1938 marks the date of the erection of a new postal facility for Phenix City, Alabama. The cornerstone attached to the front of the Phenix City, Alabama, Post Office building credits the 1938 structure to Henry Morgenthau, who was Secretary of the Treasury at the time; James A. Farley, who was Postmaster General; and Neal A. Melick, who was Supervising Engineer at the time.

The name of only one architect, Louis A. Simon, is on the cornerstone. The Treasury Department had found that using numerous private architects for its many small architectural projects was neither economical nor time-effective. Using only one supervising architect was more efficient for the federal government.

A series of some ten steps with a platform about halfway up leads patrons to the front entrance of the red brick building. Four windows with the front door centered between them provide a controlled appearance to the building.

A decorative eagle rests above the front entrance. Two pilasters decorate the front of the building and provide interest; one white pilaster is on either side of the centered door.

Two wrought-iron electric lanterns on posts function as decoration and for utilitarian purposes; they are about halfway up the series of front steps. The wrought-iron banisters on the steps complement the lanterns and provide a contrast to the white front door and the red brick.

An elaborate cupola rests on the black roof. Centered on each side of the cupola is a window with six panes on the top half and six panes below. Inside the building is the mural that John Kelly Fitzpatrick created for the federal building.

After the postal service left the building in 1964, the public library used the facility for a while. When the library obtained its own building, the post office building remained vacant. A private individual now owns the building.

Cotton. When one considers that during the Great Depression the cotton

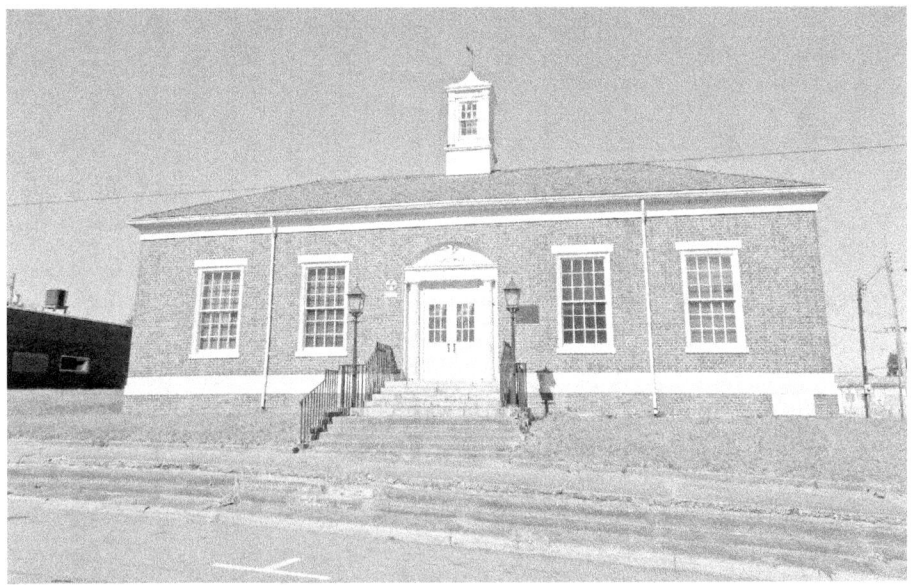

The "old" Phenix City Post Office houses the John Kelly Fitzpatrick artwork.

belt was three hundred miles deep and sixteen hundred wide, it is not surprising that the theme of cotton was common in the art of the South.[6]

New Deal Art in the federal buildings of Alabama focused frequently on cotton also.

- Terracotta reliefs in Alexander City by Franc Epping in 1941 included *Cotton.*
- Lee R. Warthen's 1941 mural for Hartselle had the title *Cotton Scene* and focused on the baling of cotton after the harvest.
- Arthur Kimmig Getz's mural for Luverne in 1942 has the title *Cotton Field.*
- William Sherrod McCall's 1939 oil-on-canvas for Montevallo was *Early Settlers Weighing Cotton.*
- Alabama native John Kelly Fitzpatrick chose *Cotton* for his 1939 oil-on-canvas artwork for Phenix City, Alabama.

Fitzpatrick's *Cotton* was the second of two murals that the artist from Wetumpka had prepared for federal buildings in his home state. His *Early Industry of Dale County* (1938) for Ozark had been his first for Alabama.

Before the installation of the Phenix City mural, with its theme of the cotton in the South, the Montgomery Museum of Fine Arts exhibited the work. The newspaper described the work by John Kelly Fitzpatrick:

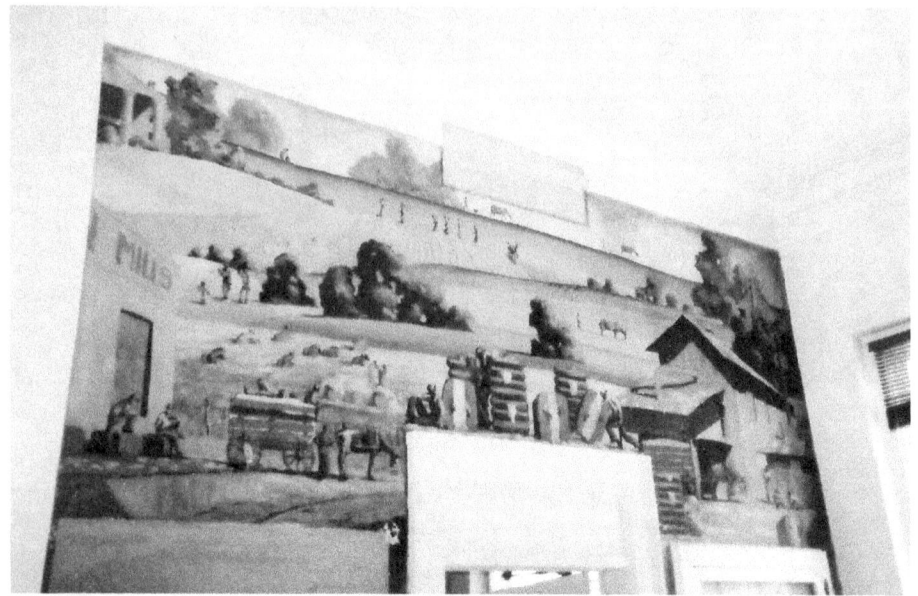

The mural that John Kelly Fitzpatrick prepared for the Phenix City Post Office, titled *Cotton,* **reminds viewers of the importance of agriculture to early Phenix City.**

The subject of the mural is a cotton growth cycle showing the various steps from the planting of the seed to weaving it into cloth. The scene is a typical east Alabama landscape where one gently rolling hill rises above another and on each succeeding level a period of growth is depicted.[7]

The mural still hangs in the old post office.

John Kelly Fitzpatrick. Painter, educator, and proponent of the arts, John Kelly Fitzpatrick (1888–1953) spent most of his art career presenting his rural Alabama to others, emphasizing the importance of art, and helping others succeed.

John Kelly Fitzpatrick had been born to Phillips Fitzpatrick (a physician) and Jane Lovedy Fitzpatrick, who lived near Wetumpka, Alabama, before the turn of the century (1888). Their home was in Greek Revival style and dated from the mid–1840s. John Kelly resided in the family home even after the deaths of his parents and for most of his life.

Called "Kelly" by his family and friends, Fitzpatrick took pride in the fact that his grandfather (Benjamin Fitzpatrick) was Alabama's governor from 1841 until 1845. He was proud that his grandfather was also a United States Senator representing Alabama.

Kelly found the 1920s and the Great Depression turbulent both socially and economically. Fitzpatrick, however, focused his attention on Alabama's rural landscape and its inhabitants during the troubled time. An artist and art teacher, Fitzpatrick was a prominent and important advocate for art and art education.

Kelly had attended both Starke University School in Montgomery and the University of Alabama (1908–1910); he did not graduate, however. He had studied at the School of the Art Institute of Chicago in 1912 and in the 1920s at the Académie Julian in Paris. His travels and his observation of the works of artists were other sources of his education, as the section on Ozark in this volume discusses.

John Kelly Fitzpatrick found some relief, like many other artists, from the New Deal programs. The biographical sketch of Fitzpatrick in the section on Ozark in this volume explains more about his work the Public Works of Art Program, known as PWAP, in 1933–1934, and his commissions for murals in both Ozark and Phenix City under the Treasury Section of Painting and Sculpture.

The section in this book on Ozark gives information on Fitzpatrick's military career and his horrific injuries during World War I. That section also discusses his outlook on life after suffering his war wounds.

In addition to art making, Fitzpatrick taught and promoted such art organizations as the Montgomery Museum of Fine Arts and the Alabama Art League. Fitzpatrick was an original member of the board of directors of the Montgomery Museum of Fine Arts, founded in 1930.

Kelly Fitzpatrick chaired the exhibitions committee at the Montgomery Museum of Fine Arts. He was able to establish the original art collection through personal donations and with the assistance of his contacts in the federal relief programs. The Montgomery Museum of Fine Arts is a repository for examples of the work of John Kelly Fitzpatrick, "a popular and beloved art teacher."[8]

Back home in Alabama, Fitzpatrick established the Dixie Art Colony in 1933. It was the first such art colony in the Deep South, and Fitzpatrick happily settled into the role of the colony's lighthearted, carefree leader. "All he took seriously," one member of the colony recalled, "was art and courtesy." Materialism, status, business, and responsibility were all treated with amused disdain as he worked to develop the artistic talents of his students.[9]

The section on Ozark in this volume gives an additional description of the Dixie Art Colony, the purpose of the organization, and its founding. The last meeting of the Dixie Art Colony was in 1948.

Fitzpatrick, however, worked with Genevieve Southerland of Mobile, Alabama, to facilitate colonies on the Alabama coast in the mid–1940s and at Coden in 1950. Fitzpatrick allowed the amateur artists to pursue their own work; he guided and critiqued but did not offer formal instruction.

Although he did complete some still-lifes and some portraits, Fitzpatrick primarily used the Alabama landscapes—particularly the area around his home in Wetumpka—as his subjects; this is Regionalism. He specialized in

> rural dwellings, county crossroads settlements, and genre scenes that depict the day-to-day life of the predominantly black population that labored in agricultural activities in the area.... Fitzpatrick's signature style [was] a light-filled composition dominated by the natural environment of trees, hills, and clouds, with the human inhabitants blending seamlessly into the landscape.... The strong shadows convey the midday heat of an Alabama summer, and the contrast created by their dark forms intensifies the brilliance of the color.[10]

Fitzpatrick's painting style was unique. When he was composing his paintings, he did very little drawing. He created the forms using a variety of brushstrokes. To produce weight and volume, he used short choppy strokes. To produce expanses of sky and land, he employed long, sweeping paint applications.

Fitzpatrick created an uneven surface on his works; this thick, uneven texture is known as *impasto*. To achieve this surface, he applied paint thickly and built up layers.[11]

His Alabama audience received his work with favor. Unlike documentary photographers and some other artists of the era who emphasized the deprivation and hardships of the Great Depression, Fitzpatrick presented images of a peaceful, ordered society. He was able to do this because of his own love of the people and the land; this positive view came from his personal experiences with the land and its people.[12]

In a letter to a former art student, John Kelly Fitzpatrick summarized his view of art. He declared that art

> is the most important thing in life, to me ... for art, I have given up a well-satisfied, comfortable, useful life, without wife and children, with debt, leaky roofs, ragged clothes, and a thousand evils that should make me ashamed and miserable but do not! ... I feel that I am doing what I was created for and not bucking the game.[13]

Like the book that included the biography of John Kelly Fitzpatrick, the artist always had his heart in Dixie.[14]

Russellville

Conrad Alfred Albrizio (spelled Albrizzio in some sources) created the federally commissioned mural *Shipment of First Iron Pro-*

duced in Russellville (1938) that is on display in the Russellville, Alabama, Post Office.

Russellville is the county seat of Franklin County, Alabama. It has played an important role in Franklin County and in Alabama history.

Russellville, Alabama. Russellville received its name from William Russell, an early settler to the area; Russellville has served sporadically as the county seat since 1818. In 2010 the population of Russellville was 9,830; it was the largest city in Franklin County.

Franklin County is in the northwest corner of Alabama and is in the Central Standard Time Zone. Its elevation is 764 feet above sea level.[1]

The creation of Franklin County dates from February 4, 1818. Benjamin Franklin was its namesake. The county originally comprised more than 1200 square miles. It extended from Marion County to the Tennessee River. There were at the time only two towns: Russellville, incorporated on November 17, 1819, and Big Springs, which now carries the name Tuscumbia. The 1819 incorporation of Russellville was three weeks before the admission of Alabama as a state.

In 1818—even before its incorporation—Russellville became the County Seat of Franklin County, a position it held until 1849.

In 1849, an election moved the county seat to a more central location within Franklin County. The new county seat, Frankfort, served as the county seat of Franklin County until 1879. With brick made in Frankfort, the new county seat had both a courthouse and a jail.

Some citizens in the northern section of Franklin County began to push the Alabama Legislature to create a new county. The Alabama Constitutional Convention on February 6, 1867, created Colbert County. The new Colbert County had 570 square miles; of this area 190 square miles was in the Tennessee Valley and 380 square miles was in the mountains. Franklin County had 657 square miles.

About 8 months later (November 29, 1867), Colbert County again became a part of Franklin County. Two years later (December 9, 1869), Colbert County became a distinct county again; Belgreen became the county seat of Franklin County until December 4, 1890, when fire destroyed the courthouse and most of its contents.

A very close election resulted in Russellville's again becoming the county seat of Franklin County. Russellville received 1228 votes, and the town of Isbell received 1147 votes.

Russellville received a new courthouse in 1893. The three-story brick structure had a steeple and bell and a four-sided clock.

On January 13, 1953, fire again destroyed the area courthouse. Construction began soon thereafter. Made entirely of native limestone, the new

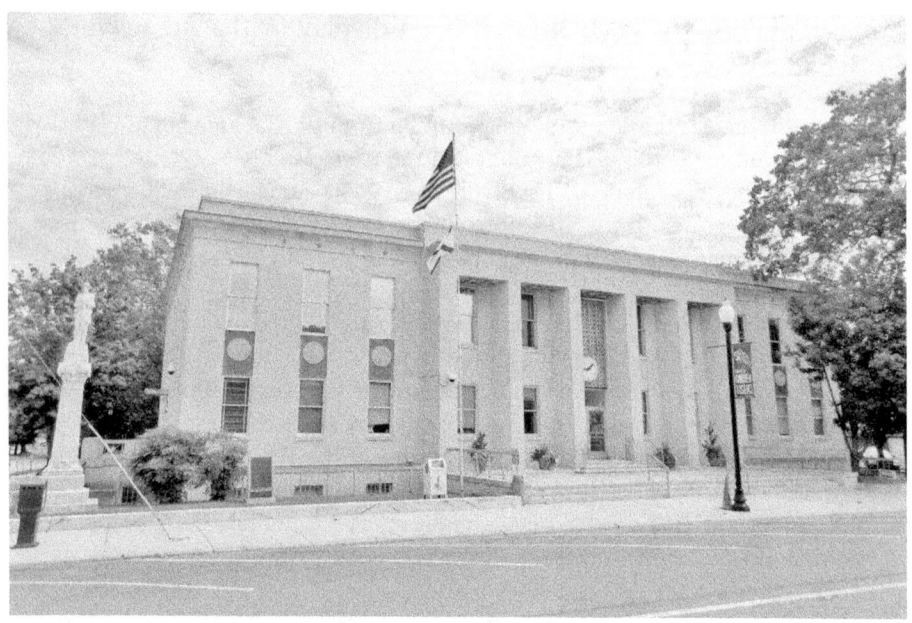

The Franklin County Courthouse, constructed after the fire of January 13, 1953, destroyed the previous courthouse. This courthouse is made entirely of native limestone.

courthouse—which is still in use—has 52 rooms and 5 vaults. The salvaged original bell is still on display.[2]

The 2010 Census reported that the population of Franklin County was 31,704. Most (83 percent) identified themselves as white; 14.9 percent indicated that they were Hispanic, and 3.9 percent noted that they were African American. The remaining 2.6 percent were Asian, Native American, or a combination of two or more races. (The figures total more than 100 percent because of an overlap between the count of whites and Hispanics.)

The median household income for the state of Alabama as a whole was $40,547; the median household for Franklin County was $33,380. The annual per capita income in Alabama was $22,732 as compared to the annual per capita income for Franklin County of $17,610.[3]

Morton reminds readers of some interesting facts about Franklin County.

- What is now Franklin County was once land that the Creeks, the Cherokees, and the Chickasaws held.
- Vice-President Aaron Burr secreted himself in the northeastern part of Franklin County for two weeks in 1806 after killing Alexander Hamilton in a duel.

- Andrew Jackson and his troops built Jackson's Military Road through the county between 1816 and 1820.
- The first railroad in Alabama—the Tuscumbia Railroad—opened in 1832 in Franklin County.[4]

The fact that Franklin County became one of the chief iron manufacturers in Alabama is a major theme of the mural installed in the Russellville Post Office.

The Russellville Post Office. Constructed in 1934, the flat-topped, red-brick Russellville Post Office would house Conrad Alfred Albrizio's fresco titled *Shipment of First Iron Produced in Russellville* (1938). At the time of its construction and at the time of the installation of the cornerstone on the building, the federal staff included Secretary of the Treasury Henry Morgenthau, Jr.; Postmaster General James A. Farley; Supervising Architect Louis A. Simon; and Supervising Engineer George O. Von Nerta.

Four windows for lighting, ventilation, and decoration are on the front of the Russellville Post Office. The two windows that are on either side of the front door have 30 panes. Fifteen of the panes are above the midpoint of the window; fifteen panes are below the midpoint of the windows. A nine-paned smaller window is beside each of the larger windows.

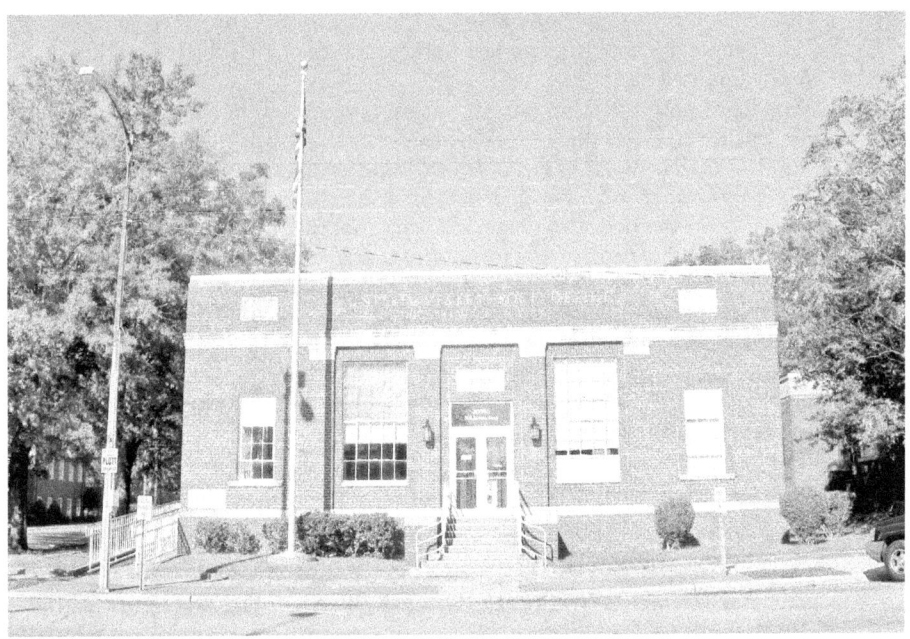

The Russellville Post Office, showing the flat-topped brick building and the centered front entrance.

The two glass front doors have a clear glass transom above them. Eight steps lead to the front entrance; iron banisters make accessing the front doors easier for patrons. Two wall-mounted, wrought-iron lanterns on either side of the door give light and decoration to the symmetrical front of the building. A recently added ramp helps ensure ease and safety for the patrons who need the additional accommodation.

Shipment of First Iron Produced in Russellville. Franklin County was one of the leading iron manufacturers in Alabama. The iron that the Cedar Creek Iron Works produced helped both the Mexican and Civil War efforts. During Union General Lovell H. Rousseau's raid through the Russellville area, the troops destroyed the furnace in 1864. With this history, John M. Clark with the Natchez Trace Association, protested the humdrum scene chosen for the Russellville fresco.[5]

The mural for Russellville was one of the most controversial artworks in Alabama. After Albrizio received an invitation to participate in preparing the Russellville mural, he submitted two sketches of local industry: a local quarry and an early iron mine. The Section selected the local quarry in early July 1937 as the topic of the work Albrizio was to produce.[6]

Clark wrote to the Honorable W.B. Bankhead on August 19, 1937; Bankhead is introduced in "Chapter Five: Carrollton" in this volume. Clark insisted:

> The people of Russellville protest the acceptance of the subject [of the art-work] submitted.
> The first iron furnace built in Alabama was erected in 1817 a few miles out from this town. It was there the iron and steel industry in Alabama had its birth. It is the one point of *great historic value* in this vicinity. It is *that* that we want in our mural.
> …We know the Bee Hive shape of all charcoal furnaces erected at that date. We know that this furnace and forge were motivated by water power through a race that still exists. We know they used a five hundred pound hammer to shape the pig—we still have the hammer. We know the ore was collected by slave labor and hauled in ox carts to the furnace … and we have the records where it sold … for one hundred dollars per ton. The rock wall foundation of the warehouse still stands along the creek bank … here is a site of great historic value that is rapidly disappearing.
> We insist that an Artist can give a magnificent conception of the true appearance of the old furnace.[7]

Urgent telegrams from others who were interested in preserving local history followed Clark's letter. Edward Beatty Rowan (1898–1946) with the Treasury Department's Section of Painting and Sculpture wrote to Conrad Alfred Albrizio on August 30, 1937. Rowan asked that Albrizio consider creating a design that would satisfy the artist himself and that would also satisfy Dr. Clark and his group.

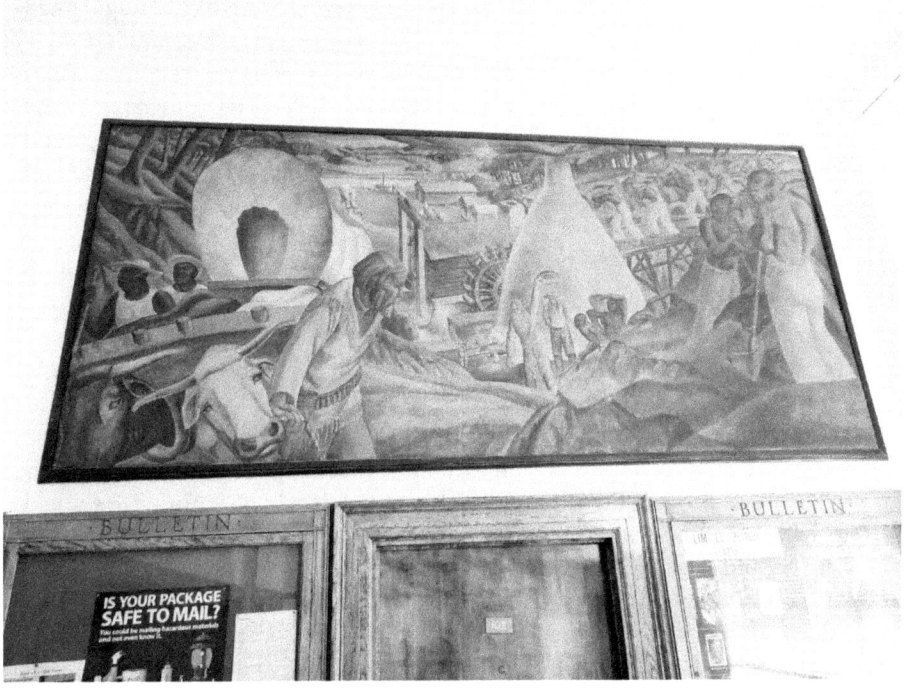

The completed Albrizio mural in the Russellville Post Office.

Beckham in the book *Depression Post Office Murals and Southern Culture* reported that Albrizio's fresco

> was a singularly unlovely mural. The furnace rises in the center middle-ground behind rather unlikely hills. Slaves labor in the foreground and in the background ... a gigantic covered wagon looms over the hills.... The result, however, is a confusion of sizes and shapes. The most sympathetic object in the picture is the ox in the left foreground, his head larger even than the wagon he pulls ... the town's inhabitants and its postal employees are not only comfortable with him; he has become an especial favorite.[8]

Conrad Alfred Albrizio. Conrad Alfred Albrizio was born on October 20 or 27, 1894, in New York City. Much of his work, however, would be in the South.

Conrad Alfred Albrizio was the son of Italian immigrants. Alfonso Albrizio, Conrad Albrizio's father, was an architect. Conrad's brothers, Humbert (1901–1970) and Joseph, became sculptors.[9]

Conrad Alfred Albrizio's first formal studies in architectural drawing were in 1911 at the Cooper Union. In 1912 he received employment as a draughtsman. In 1918, at the age of 24, Albrizio studied at Beaux Arts with

Frederick Hirons; Albrizio's employment in New Orleans as a draughtsman and designer followed.[10]

While Albrizio studied and worked in New Orleans, he met other artists and writers who were living in the French Quarter. His associates in the French Quarter included William Spratling, William Faulkner, and Sherwood Anderson. Albrizio and other interested individuals formed the Arts and Crafts Club of New Orleans; this club influenced art and literature in New Orleans for decades.

While he was in New Orleans during the 1920s, Albrizio began painting on canvas. His style was impressionistic, and he had two one-man shows sponsored by the Arts and Crafts Club in New Orleans.[11] With impressionism, the artist excludes unnecessary detail, avoids harsh outlines, and uses only pure colors.[12]

Albrizio's art education continued in 1923 at the Art Students' League in New York and abroad. To finance his education and travels, he worked part-time at Boring and Tilton, an architectural firm in New York. He studied in Paris, learned fresco in Rome, studied at the Fontainebleau School in France, and traveled throughout Europe.[13]

Most people know Conrad Albrizio best for his murals. For these works he usually employed frescoes (paintings on moist plaster), mosaics (inlaid stones, tiles, glass, or other materials), and oils that he usually applied on canvas. Albrizio's themes in the 1930s were much like that of the artists of the Regionalist School and of the American Scene; both schools were popular during the 1930s. Albrizio often employed his art to depict agricultural and industrial scenes and to represent historical events.

Barry Cowan found that Conrad Alfred Albrizio's first major federal commission was to paint two fresco panels in the New State Capitol building that was under construction in Baton Rouge. The panel that was in the Court of Appeals is no longer in existence.

The panel that was in the Supreme Courtroom would later be relocated to the governor's press room; that work showed Albrizio's interpretation of Biblical passages on justice.

Albrizio began serving as an instructor of art at Louisiana State University in 1936. He continued in this role until his 1954 resignation. Despite his eighteen years with Louisiana State, Albrizio still found time to exhibit his works in various venues and to fulfill various orders for his works.

Albrizio prepared frescoes for the Louisiana State Capitol in Baton Rouge and for the United States Post Office in DeRidder, Louisiana; the 1936 mural for the DeRidder Post Office was his first federally commissioned work. The DeRidder mural had the title *Rural Free Delivery*; it particularly found favor with the Treasury Department because it focused on the history of the postal service.[14]

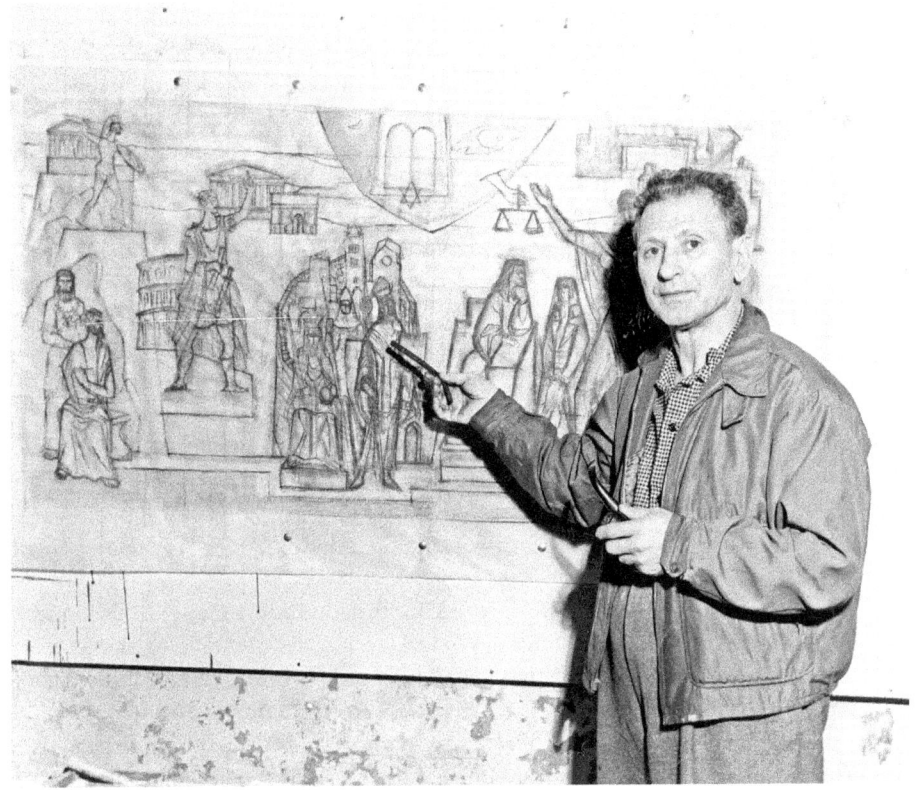

Conrad Alfred Albrizio with a sketch of a mosaic (about 1955) (courtesy Conrad Albrizio Papers, Mss. 33349, Louisiana and Lowes Mississippi Valley Collections, Libraries, Baton Rouge, LA).

Albrizio painted—among other things—murals for the Russellville Post Office in Alabama; the Parish Court House in New Iberia, Louisiana; and the Louisiana State Office Building in Baton Rouge.[15] In 1938, Albrizio painted four panels in fresco for the portico of the Louisiana State Exhibit Building in Shreveport. Two of these panels depicted views and industries of both northern and southern Louisiana.

Later in 1938, Albrizio painted four frescoes on panels for the Capitol Annex in Baton Rouge. These panels represented the state's recent achievements under Louisiana Governor Richard W. Leche (1936 to 1939).[16]

Conrad Alfred Albrizio used a medium that he did not normally employ when he prepared panels for the Church of St. Cecilia in Detroit, Michigan, of the 14 Stations of the Cross (the 14 points that Jesus reached on his path to the Cross). Albrizio used gesso for these panels.[17] Gesso is a coating that combines chalk or whiting with a glue or casein solution. It is sometimes the ground for paints. Sandpapering produces an ivory-like, smooth surface. Gesso material is ideal for tempera and watercolor painting.[18]

In 1940 Conrad Alfred Albrizio painted his last artwork for the federal government. The work was a fresco titled *The Struggle of Man* for the New Iberia Courthouse. The theme of this Albrizio mural is the continual struggle that all people face in order to achieve their physical and moral goals.

Albrizio's work has appeared in the Whitney Museum of American Art in New York City. *Jordan*, his oil depicting an African American baptism, was an exhibit at the 1939 San Francisco World's Fair. His other achievements include a fellowship (1945–1946) from the Julius Rosenwald Fund, a one-person show at the Passedoit Gallery in New York City, a one-person show at what is now the New Orleans Museum of Art, and frescoes displayed at the Waterman Steamship Building in Mobile. His 60' × 8' fresco (one of the largest in the United States) in the Union Passenger Terminal in New Orleans proved to be Albrizio's last fresco.

Governor Huey Long contracted with Albrizio to prepare artwork for the Louisiana State Capitol. This work halted temporarily when Huey Long was shot on September 8, 1935.

Albrizio's mosaics appear in the Louisiana Supreme Court building in New Orleans, in the City Court in Gretna, and in the Mental Health Center in Algiers. Mobile, Alabama, has several Albrizio mosaics, including works for Mobile General Hospital, the YMCA, and the municipal auditorium.

In 1965, when Albrizio's health began to decline, he moved to the Baton Rouge General Hospital's Guest House. In 1972, he was able to paint a mural there; the work—with a religious theme—depicted exercise. Albrizio died on January 6, 1973.[19]

His artworks, memories that others have of him, and his home remain. "Jeff" writes:

> I now own Albrizio's house in the French Quarter, my wife and I have been here 20 years. It has a giant mural in the front hall, and an elderly neighbor (also an artist) said that all the figures in it, all masked and in costume for Mardi Gras, were all neighbors. I knew several of them, and it is true. After we bought the house, we found out that a good friend of ours grew up in it and knew Albrizio well! Her mother was an artist and evidently he was quite a charmer. When renovating this house (in the 1950s) he went to Italy to buy Venetian glass and tile, etc. He rode back on the cargo ship with all the stuff and when they arrived at the port in Houston there was a strike ... and he refused to get off the ship! He was worried his things would be stolen or lost. So there he stayed for several weeks until the strike was over. My friend has many tales....[20]

Scottsboro

Constance Ortmayer, an artist specializing in sculpture, prepared the federally commissioned bas-relief sculpture *Alabama Agriculture* (1940) for the Scottsboro, Alabama, Post Office.

Although Constance Ortmayer was in the state of Florida and teaching at Rollins College in 1940, she earned the federal commission to prepare a sculpture for the Scottsboro Post Office in Alabama. Her work proved enduring in Scottsboro, an area that has changed considerably through the years.

Scottsboro, Alabama. Originally, Cherokee Indians inhabited the area now known as Scottsboro. The Cherokees did not have large settlements at the time that the first white settlers arrived in the area, but there was a Cherokee town called Crow Town near the current city of Scottsboro, which is now in Jackson County.[1]

As potential settlers began exploring the area around what is now Scottsboro, they found the Tennessee River area to be a good resource for food, for water, and for transporting supplies to and from other cities. One of the earliest settlers to the area was John Hunt (1805). The settlement near his log cabin became Huntsville, Alabama, in 1811. Huntsville is about 45 miles due west of Scottsboro.[2]

Jackson County, created by an act of the legislature, dates from December 13, 1819. Its name came from General Andrew Jackson. Jackson was visiting in Huntsville at the time and was racing his horses at the Old Green Bottom Race Track. The next day—December 14, 1819—marks the admission of Alabama as a state. Jackson County, then, is older than the state of Alabama.[3]

In late 1834 Congress passed a law ordering the relocation of Cherokees from Alabama, Georgia, and Tennessee to Indian Territory. Cherokee Chief John Ross in the Jackson County area agreed with General Winfield Scott to move his people himself. Ross marched more than 10,000 Cherokees overland in separate groups and by different routes to help ensure adequate food and water on the hazardous journey. Still, sixteen hundred perished en route.[4]

Scottsboro in the spring was—according to a visitor—a "charming village" situated in "pleasant, rolling hills." The green of the hills contrasted with the red of the freshly turned soil. Scottsboro had grown slowly until it became a stop on the Memphis and Charleston Railroad in 1870.[5]

Robert Thomas Scott receives credit as the founder of Scottsboro. For many years Scott and his wife had been the managers of a hotel in Bellefonte, which is only about 7 miles away to the northeast. In addition, Robert Thomas Scott served in the Alabama legislature for some 20 years. Between 1850 and

1853 the Scotts moved southwest from Bellefonte to the area that is now Scottsboro.

Scottsboro had various names before 1870. Some of its early monikers included Sage Town, Scott's Mill, and Scottsville. After the 1857 construction of a railway station for the newly established Memphis and Charleston Railroad (a stretch of railroad that runs from Memphis, Tennessee, to Charleston, South Carolina), the area took the title Scott's Station. The Alabama legislature finally incorporated the population center as Scottsboro in January of 1870.[6]

Scottsboro is now the county seat of Jackson County, Alabama.[7] At the 2000 census, the city had a population of 14,762.

Scottsboro and First Monday. Scottsboro boasts the fact that it is "the home of the oldest trade day in the country." Called "First Monday" by the locals, the event dates from the beginning of the 1900s and continues today. Those who attend say, "You never know what you might find there."[8]

The Scottsboro Case. Most people associate Scottsboro, Alabama, with a 1931 court case in which two white women on a freight train moving across northeastern Alabama accused nine African American young men, aged twelve to nineteen, of raping them. The result was one of this country's most famous and controversial court cases and a tragic and revealing chapter in the history of the American South.

All nine of the defendants received rapid trials, and eight received the death penalty. The age of the young men, the hastiness of their sentencing, and the harshness of their punishment brought national attention to Scottsboro and the South during the 1930s—and afterward. The Supreme Court heard the case in 1937. The death sentences were commuted, but it was almost twenty years before the last of the nine left prison.

Dan T. Carter used the Scottsboro case as the topic for his doctoral dissertation. His research officially began in the 1960s. His book *Scottsboro* (1970) brought new interest to the case. Two autobiographies, several docudramas from Hollywood, and many articles followed Carter's work.

Instead of simply using the collective term "Scottsboro Boys" to refer to the nine young men charged in the case, Carter gives their names when appropriate. He refers to Charlie Weems, Ozie Powell, Clarence Norris, Olen Montgomery, Willie Roberson, Haywood Patterson, Eugene Williams, Andrew Wright, and Leroy Wright as people and gives them the dignity of using their names.[9]

The Unclaimed Baggage Center: The Only Lost Luggage Store in the United States. An important feature of Scottsboro today is the Unclaimed Baggage Center, which is almost half a century old. Doyle Owens borrowed a pickup truck and $300 and went to Washington, D.C., in 1970 to pick up his first load of unclaimed baggage. Initially, he sold the contents of the baggage on card tables in a rented house. Owens, his wife Sue, and their two sons had just opened the only lost luggage store in the United States. Scottsboro, Alabama, began to receive that attention of the media and of visitors from across the globe. Everyone, it seemed, wanted to visit the store and examine the unclaimed treasures.

In 1995, Doyle's son Bryan purchased the Unclaimed Baggage Center. Today this business covers more than a block. Each year over a million visitors from every state and from more than 40 countries visit the Unclaimed Baggage Center, making it one of the top tourist attractions in the state of Alabama.

Only 0.5 percent of the baggage is lost in travel. Passengers pick up the remaining 99.5 percent of the items at the carousel. The airlines search extensively for the owners of the unclaimed luggage and attempt to reunite the items with their owners. The result is that only a small fraction of a percent of the baggage remains separated from the owners after three months. The airlines pay the claims on the lost bags before selling the unclaimed baggage to the Unclaimed Baggage Center in Scottsboro.

Today, Bryan Owens does not pick up the lost items in a pickup truck. Tractor-trailers bring the items to the Unclaimed Baggage Center for sorting, cleaning, testing, and pricing. About half of the items are discarded. Many salvageable items are donated through the Reclaimed for Good Program of the Unclaimed Baggage Center to help others.

The goal of the Unclaimed Baggage Center "is to sell, donate, recycle and repurpose everything we can, finding a new home for what was once lost."[10]

Scottsboro, Alabama, Post Office. The Scottsboro Post Office is at 101 South Market Street in the city named for Robert Thomas Scott.

The cornerstone affixed to the side of the Scottsboro Post Office building credits the 1938 structure to Henry Morgenthau, who was Secretary of the Treasury at the time; James A. Farley, who was Postmaster General; and Neal A. Melick, who was Supervising Engineer at the time.

The name of only one architect, Louis A. Simon, is on the stone. The Treasury Department reported that using numerous private architects for its many small architectural projects was neither economical nor time-effective. Using only one supervising architect was most efficient.

Architect Louis A. Simon (1867–1958) began working with the federal government as an architect in 1896. In 1933, at the age of 66, he began serving as the federal supervising architect in the Treasury Department. He designed federal buildings, including post offices, across the nation until 1939. In that year the office of the supervising architect moved from the Public Works Administration to the Works Progress Administration. Simon was 72 years old in 1939 when he retired from his federal office.[11]

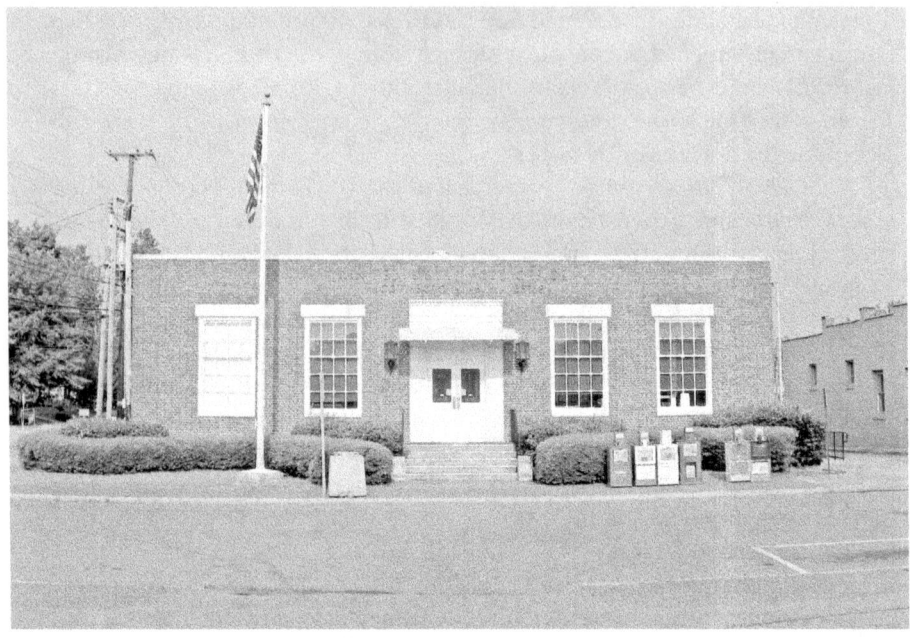

The New Deal era Scottsboro Post Office (1938). The red-brick building is still in use. The symmetrical design is typical of many of the structures constructed by the federal government during the Great Depression era.

The Scottsboro Post Office (completed in 1938) was one of twenty-four structures in Alabama to receive art decoration through the Treasury Section of Fine Arts. One courthouse received an artwork; the other twenty-three Alabama artworks at the time went to post offices.

The Scottsboro Post Office is a flat-topped, red-brick building. No cupola, dome, or turret decorates the rooftop. On each side of the centered front door of the post office are two windows; twenty panes—eight above the center lock and twelve below—provide interest, ventilation, and light to the inside area.

Five centered outside cement steps lead visitors to a concrete landing. Wrought-iron banisters on either side of the steps make entry easier for patrons. A metal awning protects the centered double entrance, which has a glass panel on each door. The symmetrical front of the Scottsboro Post Office provides patrons with a pleasant view.

On either side of the double front door is a black, wrought-iron lantern to match the railing on the front steps. These electric lights provide decoration and lighting for safety purposes for the Scottsboro Post Office.

The Scottsboro Post Office structure is typical of many of the post offices that the federal government constructed during the Great Depression. Historians understand and appreciate the value of these post offices. A group, Save the Post Offices, is at work to preserve and maintain these federal buildings.[12]

Alabama Agriculture. Constance Ortmayer was teaching at Rollins College in Florida when the Treasury Section of Fine Arts invited her to prepare a panel for the Scottsboro Post Office. For her theme, Ortmayer chose Alabama agricultural products; she focused especially on cotton and corn.

The topic of cotton was not a new one for the federal artwork in public buildings in Alabama during the period. Alexander City had terracotta reliefs that included cotton. Eutaw had cotton on its mural. Fort Payne had two oil-on-canvas panels that detailed harvest; Hartselle had a mural titled *Cotton Scene.* The federal artwork in the post offices in Luverne, Montevallo, and Phenix City all featured cotton prominently.

Constance Ortmayer described her art for the Scottsboro Post Office in these words:

> Three phases of cotton growing form the theme of the central panel. On the right the cultivation of the crop is symbolized by the young man working with a hoe among the new plants. Opposite a young woman is depicted picking ripened bolls, and for the background, the processing and shipping of cotton is represented by the bales and the strong figure of a second young worker standing between them. Both of the flanking panels interpret the growing of corn. The young man and woman shown on the right are examining the fruit on the ripened stalks and the couple on the left are represented as workers who have harvested the new crop.[13]

The Treasury Section of Fine Arts wrote about the work by Ortmayer in Scottsboro, Alabama: "In a sculpture characterized by clean, flowing lines, Miss Ortmayer gives an exceptionally effective representation of the youthful strength and grace that each new generation brings to the agriculture of the south."[14] The work in Scottsboro was not the first—or last—for this woman artist.

Constance Ortmayer (1902–1988). Constance Ortmayer was born in New York City on July 19, 1902. This sculptor, educator, coin designer, artisan, and professor of sculpture has achieved lasting recognition beginning with her successful education.

Constance's father, Rudolph Joseph, was a lithographer. Her mother was Mildred (Cerny) Ortmayer. Constance received her high school education (1914–1916) at New York High School. Young Ortmayer attended the summer school at Bryn Mawr, where she could "showcase her talent for art."[15]

Ortmayer studied at and graduated from the Royal Academy of Fine Arts of Vienna, Austria. Her teachers included Austrian-born sculptor Franz Plunder and Josef Müllner from 1930 until 1932.[16]

When Ortmayer returned to the United States (1932), she found it difficult to secure employment. One of her friends, who tutored Secretary of the Treasury Henry Morgenthau and Morgenthau's wife Elinor, recommended Constance Ortmayer for a position in the Section of Painting and Sculpture.

Ortmayer secured employment in the Section. There, she organized competitions that enabled young artists both to enter contests with more established figures in the arts and to begin applying for and securing governmental commissions.

Ortmayer found, however, that she could not pursue her own artistic interests at the Section because of time constraints. In 1937 Ortmayer resigned the position with the Section after five years.[17]

Constance Ortmayer found a position as instructor in sculpture at Rollins College in Winter Park, Florida, in 1937. She would remain at the college in various positions—including as Professor of Sculpture and Chairman of the Department of Art—for the next thirty-one years. She formally retired from Rollins College at age 66 (1988).[18]

After Ortmayer gave up her position with the government, she could enter competitions and submit designs for federal commissions. Ortmayer earned commissions to design two bas reliefs for federal post offices.

Constance Ortmayer would complete one of these federal commissions in Arcadia, Florida, in 1939. The bas-relief that Ortmayer created for the

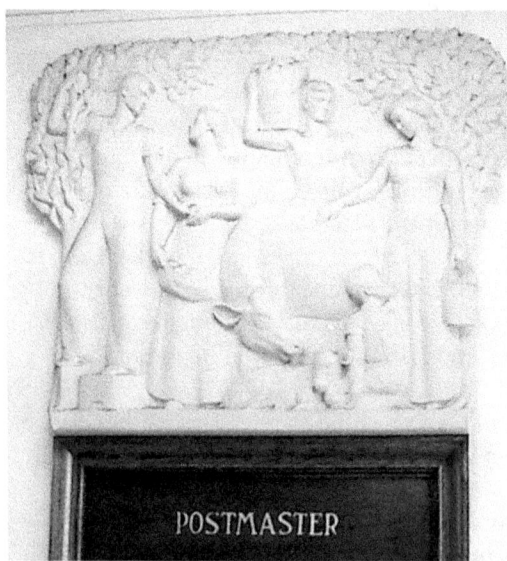

Arcadia post office depicts a group of four adults (two men, two women) and a child (a boy); along with the human figures are a cow and her calf. The pastoral relief set in an orchard bears the title *Arcadia*.

In 1940 Ortmayer completed her second federal commission for the Scottsboro, Alabama, Post Office. The red-brick, flat topped post office with a symmetrical appearance is typical of many federal buildings of the New Deal Era.

This pastoral scene with a cow and calf in an orchard includes two couples and a boy harvesting fruit from the orchard. Constance Ortmayer placed this bas-relief in the Arcadia, Florida, Post Office.

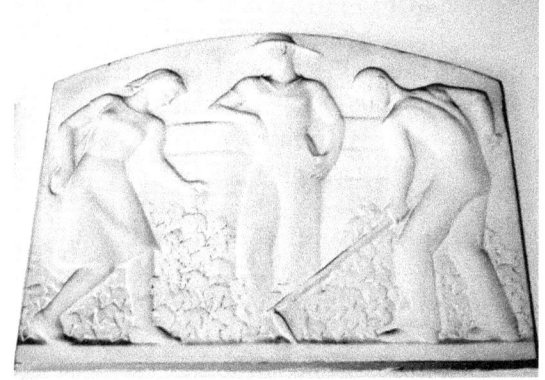

Above: **The Constance Ortmayer artwork is in place over the postmaster's door in the Scottsboro Post Office. The artwork is in bas-relief.** *Right:* **This close-up of the bas-relief by Constance Ortmayer shows the theme of agriculture.**

This artwork is a series of three different panels that she titled *Alabama Agriculture.*

On the left is a man and woman examining ears of corn. The middle and largest panel exemplifies a familiar theme for the Alabama artworks: cotton. The third panel—on the right—depicts the corn harvest.[19]

In 1941, Ortmayer earned the promotion from her original position as instructor of sculpture to assistant professor of sculpture at Rollins College. In 1945 she advanced to the rank of associate professor, and in 1947 Constance Ortmayer achieved the highest faculty rank at Rollins College: professor.[20]

During her time at Rollins, Ortmayer created a number of coins and medals, most of which she designed at the request of the administration of

Rollins College to honor faculty and staff. She also created some medals and coins on the national level.[21]

The American artist Constance Ortmayer (July 19, 1902–May 15, 1988) is perhaps best known on the national level for her 1936 design of a half dollar to commemorate the fiftieth anniversary of the Cincinnati Music Center. On March 31, 1936, Congress had passed an act that authorized the issue of commemorative coins for the Cincinnati Music Center; interestingly, there was no anniversary to celebrate. Cincinnati did not even host any special musical events in 1886.

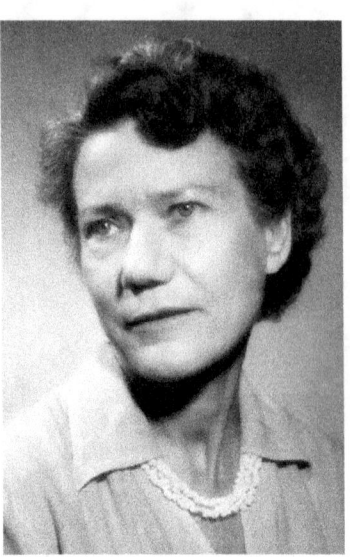

The Congressional act, however, prescribed the production of a total of 15,000 silver half-dollars to commemorate "the fiftieth anniversary of Cincinnati, Ohio, as a center of music, and its contribution to the art of music for the past fifty years." The Cincinnati Musical Center Commemorative Coin Association, headed by Thomas G. Melish, intended that all three mints—Philadelphia, Denver and San Francisco—would produce some of the coins. Constance Ortmayer would design the Cincinnati Musical Center Commemorative Coin as her first numismatic item for the general public.[22]

Constance Ortmayer in a Rollins College Yearbook (courtesy Department of College Archives and Special Collections, Olin Library, Rollins College, Winter Park, Florida).

The author has in her collection a replica of the 1936 Cincinnati Musical Center Commemorative Coin. The Franklin Mint Sterling Silver Replica of the Stephen Foster coin enables one to study the details of the obverse side of the coin.

The obverse side of the coin features a bust of Stephen Foster, who is facing right. Across the top of the coin are the words *UNITED STATES OF AMERICA.* The words *STEPHEN FOSTER AMERICA'S TROUBADOR* appear as an identifying label below the bust. The denomination—*HALF DOLLAR*—appears at the bottom of the coin.

Stephen Foster (1826–1864) was an unusual musician for inclusion on the commemorative coin. Foster had lived in Cincinnati only briefly in the 1840s when he was clerking at his brother's firm. He wrote his compositions elsewhere—primarily Pennsylvania. His most important songs include "My Old Kentucky Home," which is the state song of Kentucky and the official song of the Kentucky Derby. Other important songs by Foster include "Jeannie with the Light Brown Hair" and "Old Folks at Home." Foster contracted a fever and died impoverished at the age of 37.[23]

The reverse side of the commemorative coin shows a kneeling figure representing music. The young woman is holding a lyre. The writing on the reverse side of the coin reminds the holder of the anniversary dates (*1886–1936*). Other information is that the coin is a product of the *UNITED STATES OF AMERICA*. Other messages on the reverse side include *IN GOD WE TRUST*; *E PLURIBUS UNUM*; *LIBERTY*; and *CINCINNATI A MUSIC CENTER OF AMERICA*.[24]

Some of Ortmayer's exhibitions included the Vienna Secession (1932), the 1935 National Association of Western Painters and Sculptors in New York. She also exhibited for the Allied Arts at the Brooklyn Museum (1936), the National Sculpture Society at the Whitney Museum of American Art in New York City (1940); and the Pennsylvania Academy of Fine Arts (1941).

Constance Ortmayer earned numerous prizes. Some of these awards included the Anna Hyatt Huntington Prize from the National Association of Women Painters and Sculptors (1935); the Henry O. Avery Architectural Prize from the National Sculpture Society (1940); and the Award of Merit from the Florida Foundation of Art (1948). Her works remain at Brookgreen Gardens in Myrtle Beach, South Carolina, and elsewhere.[25]

Constance Ortmayer died in 1988, the same year that she retired from Rollins College.

Top: This sterling silver replica of the 1936 Cincinnati Musical Center Commemorative Coin shows the bust of Stephen Foster on the obverse side. The writing declares *STEPHEN FOSTER AMERICA'S TROUBADOR Bottom:* The reverse side of the 1936 Cincinnati Musical Center Commemorative Coin is a tribute to the goddess of music; she holds a lyre. The writing indicates the value of the coin (a half dollar), the country, a tribute to God, and the years of the centennial (both photographs: The Franklin Mint replica of the half-dollar coin designed by Constance Ortmayer are from Davis's collection).

Tuscumbia

Jack McMillen's federally commissioned mural *Chief Tuscumbia Greets the Dickson Family* (1939) is on display in the Tuscumbia, Alabama, Post Office.

In the 1700s some French settlers attempted a permanent community "near a bountiful big spring in the foothills of the Appalachian Mountains"; this is now the current site of Tuscumbia, Alabama. The original French settlement, however, was unsuccessful.

Next, the Chickasaw Indians built a town near the big spring. The Michael Dickson family settled in the same area about 1815. The relations among Chief Tuscumbia, the Chickasaws, and the Dicksons were good. It was this congeniality that the New Deal artist Jack McMillen depicted in the mural he prepared for the Tuscumbia Post Office; he titled his work *Chief Tuscumbia Greets the Dickson Family.*

The federal government constructed a road for military purposes through the town in 1817–1819. General Andrew Jackson approved the construction of this "superhighway" that opened the area for trade.

In 1820 the town incorporated as Ococoposa. The name of the town next became Big Spring.

In 1822 the name of the town changed again. The new name of the village became Tuscumbia, in honor of the Chickasaw chief who lived in the area. Two choices had been on the ballot: Tuscumbia and Anniston (a designation derived from Anne, the first white child born in the town). The town became Tuscumbia by one vote. After the election, Chief Tuscumbia took a pair of moccasins to little Anne for consolation.[1]

When steamboats became more numerous on the Tennessee River, Tuscumbia capitalized on the opportunity. The town built a landing on the river in 1824 just two miles from town. An immense trade business grew, and the river landing soon became too small. The local merchants built another landing. This landing was up river from the first landing and connected by rail to Tuscumbia. This railroad became the Tuscumbia Railway Company in 1830. The Tuscumbia Railway Company was the first railroad on the American frontier.

Another railroad promptly followed because of the success of the Tuscumbia Railway Company. The second line went from Tuscumbia to Decatur; it bypassed forty-three miles of rapids—Muscle Shoals—on the Tennessee River. The new line was complete by 1834; its name was the Tuscumbia, Courtland and Decatur Railroad. Being on the main route from the East to the American Southwest brought growth and importance to Tuscumbia. In

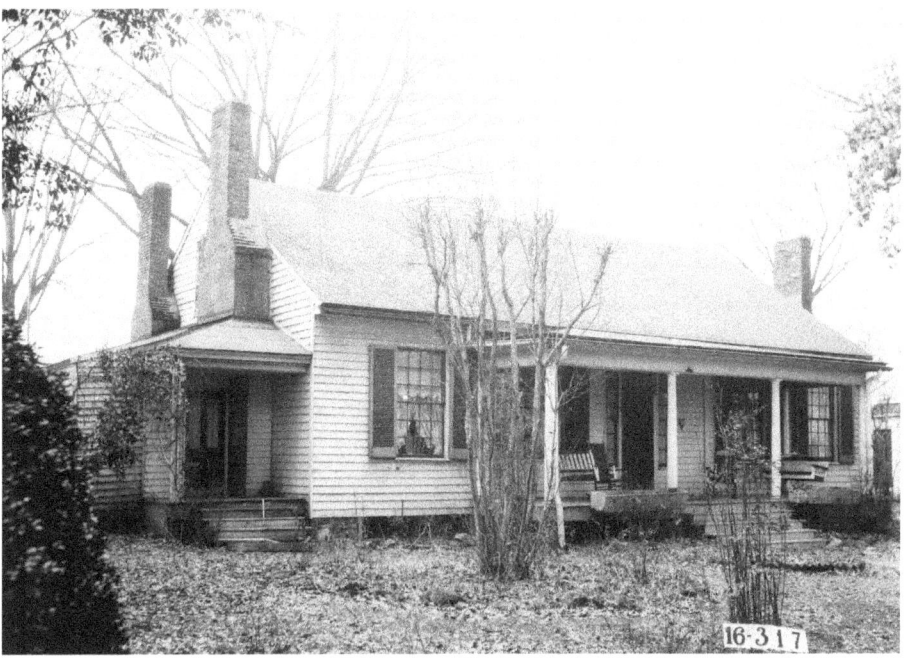

Helen Keller's home is in Tuscumbia, Alabama. The site is a frequent visiting place for locals and tourists alike (Library of Congress, HAB ALA, 17-TUSM,4-1).

a two-year period Tuscumbia doubled in size. With 41 stage departures and arrivals each week, the Tuscumbia Post Office grew in just two years to be one of the most important post offices in the southwest. The Civil War, however, took its toll on the town, and postal service became limited.

Tuscumbia became the county seat for Colbert County (1867). It is also well known as the birthplace of Helen Keller (1880–1968), the first person who was both blind and deaf to graduate from college. Helen Keller's home, Ivy Green, is still open daily for visitors.[2]

Tuscumbia Post Office. A marker on the side of 1936 Tuscumbia Post Office building recognizes that Henry Morgenthau was Secretary of the Treasury at the time. The marker names James A. Farley, as Postmaster General, and Neal A. Melick, as Supervising Engineer at the time.

The name of only one architect, Louis A. Simon, is on the stone. The Treasury Department had found that using only one supervising architect was most efficient.

Architect Louis A. Simon (1867–1958) had started work with the federal government as an architect in 1896. In 1933 he began serving as the federal supervising architect in the Treasury Department. He designed federal buildings, including post offices, across the nation until 1939. In that year the office

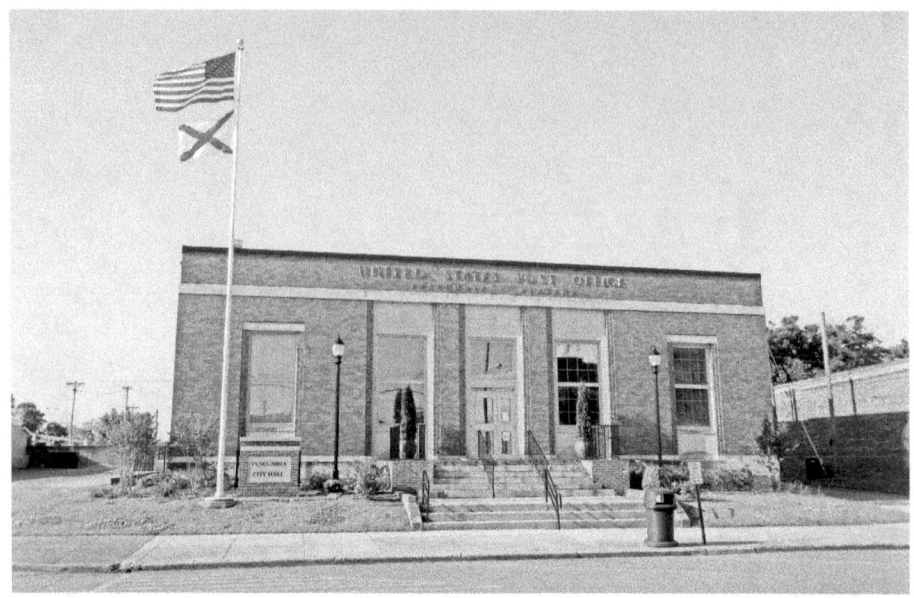

The 1936 Tuscumbia Post Office vacated the building in 2004. In 2011 the building began serving a new purpose: Tuscumbia City Hall.

of the supervising architect moved from the Public Works Administration to the Works Progress Administration. Simon was 72 years old when he retired from his federal office.[3]

The Tuscumbia Post Office (completed in 1936) was one of twenty-four structures in Alabama to receive art decoration through the Treasury Section of Fine Arts. One courthouse in Alabama received an artwork; twenty-three Alabama post offices received federal works of art. One of these was in Tuscumbia.

The 1936 red-brick Tuscumbia post office has a symmetrical appearance from the front. Four windows across the front of the building help with ventilation and lighting; each of windows has twenty-four panes: twelve above the sash and twelve below the sash. The paned front door is centered between the four windows.

Three steps in the front of the structure lead to a landing. Five steps take the patrons from the landing to the front door. A wrought-iron lamp on either side of the door adds decoration and lighting.

The Tuscumbia Post Office vacated the building in 2004. The City Hall moved into the building in 2011. The New Deal mural remains in the lobby.

***Chief Tuscumbia Greets the Dickson Family* (1939).** The artist Jack McMillen prepared the mural for the Tuscumbia Post Office—now the Tuscumbia City Hall. The painting depicts a very important event in Tuscumbia's

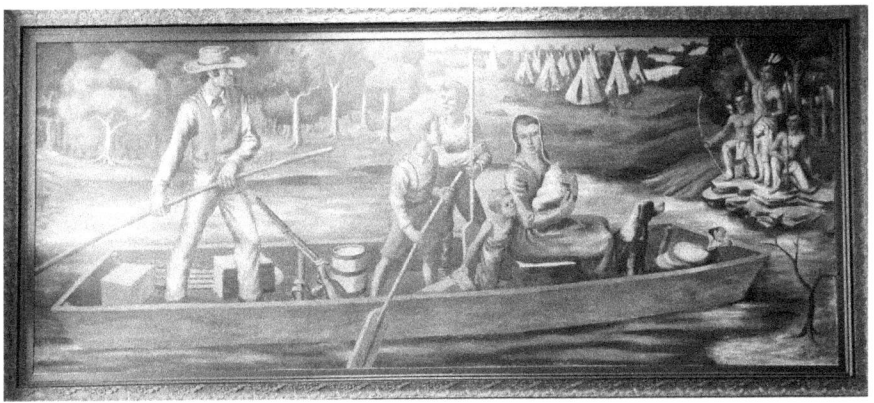

The Tuscumbia Post Office received the mural prepared by Jack McMillen. The work shows Chief Tuscumbia, some Chickasaws, and the Dickson family meeting congenially.

history: the reception of the Dickson family by Chief Tuscumbia and members of the Chickasaw Tribe.

Jack McMillen's son—Dr. Brian A. McMillen in the Department of Pharmacology and Toxicology, Brody School of Medicine at East Carolina University—remembers hearing his father speak of the medium that he preferred at that time. Jack McMillen often painted with tempera pigments mixed in egg yolks in the 1930s and 1940s; he often applied this mixture directly onto the wall as a fresco. He sometimes used the paint on a Masonite board.

Dr. McMillen was impressed that Tuscumbia was able to preserve and restore the mural that his father prepared. McMillen remembered asking his father about the mural. Jack McMillen had told his son that to move some of his murals, one would "have to take the wall."[4] The Tuscumbia mural, however, is now framed after the post office moved out of its earlier building.

Artist Jack McMillen had originally planned to prepare a mural on the life of Tuscumbia-born Helen Keller. The Section noted pleasure in his proposed topic of Helen Keller's life. The committee had remarked that most murals focused on either the land, the Native Americans, or the pioneers; they welcomed a change.

When Keller attended an anniversary celebration for the town, however, there were some problems. Tuscumbia decided it did not want a mural on Helen Keller's life at this time. Jack McMillen "on the quick" found the story of the Dickson family and Chief Tuscumbia. The Section approved the substitute mural. This second submission is in the Smithsonian.

Dr. Brian McMillen recalls that his father thought the proposed mural of Helen Keller's life was one of his better works. The location of the entry is unknown.[5]

Jack McMillen. The artist Jack McMillen was born in Portchester, Connecticut, in 1910. He studied at the University of Kentucky; the University of Illinois; Minneapolis School of the Arts; the University of Missouri; and the Art Students' League. His work remains in Walter Reed Hospital; the Presbyterian church in Kirksville, Missouri; the College Park, Georgia, Post Office; the Tuscumbia Post Office (now the City Hall) in Alabama; and elsewhere.[6]

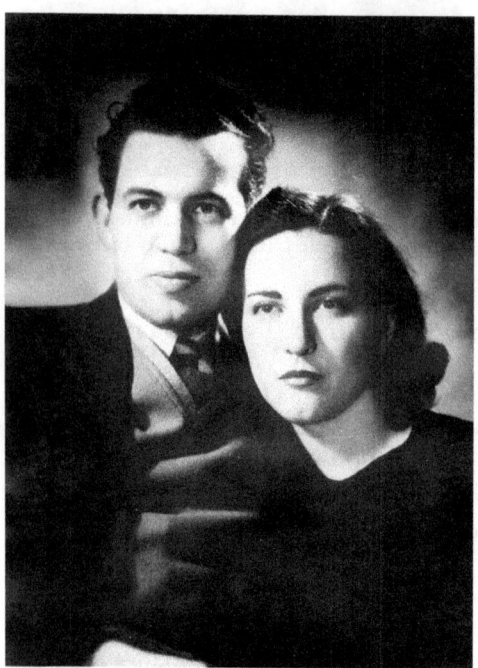

Beatrice Allen and Jack McMillen met in 1936 at the Art Students' League in New York City—"a pair of starving artists."[7] They married in 1940.

When he was 32 years old, Jack McMillen received his draft notice from the U.S. Army. As one of his assignments in 1943, he traveled across the United States setting up art shows in different towns and cities as part of a bond-raising program. One of the Hollywood stars of the time who attended and performed at some of these bond-raising events was Linda Darnell.[8]

During World War II, after his bond show assignment was over, Jack McMillen received orders for

Jack McMillen and Beatrice Allen McMillen in their 1940 wedding photograph (courtesy Dr. Brian A. McMillen).

training for the engineers and [he] became very ill. They got him sent to Walter Reed Hospital where they performed life-saving surgery. While recuperating he did a 10' × 7' mural that is hanging in the National Cemetery Museum of Health and Medicine, but the legend on it states he painted it under contract from the Section. I have twice told them that is wrong, just a GI grunt in recovery who did the painting probably both as therapy and as a thank you.[9]

The April 17, 2006, issue of *Pieces of Eight* from East Carolina University features an article titled "Professor Finds Father's Lost Art in National Museum" by Nancy McGillicuddy. The article describes how Dr. Brian McMillen found his father's artwork from 1944 when he searched "Jack McMillen" on the Internet. The artwork had hung in the National Museum since 1998 (the year before the death of Jack McMillen), but McMillen and

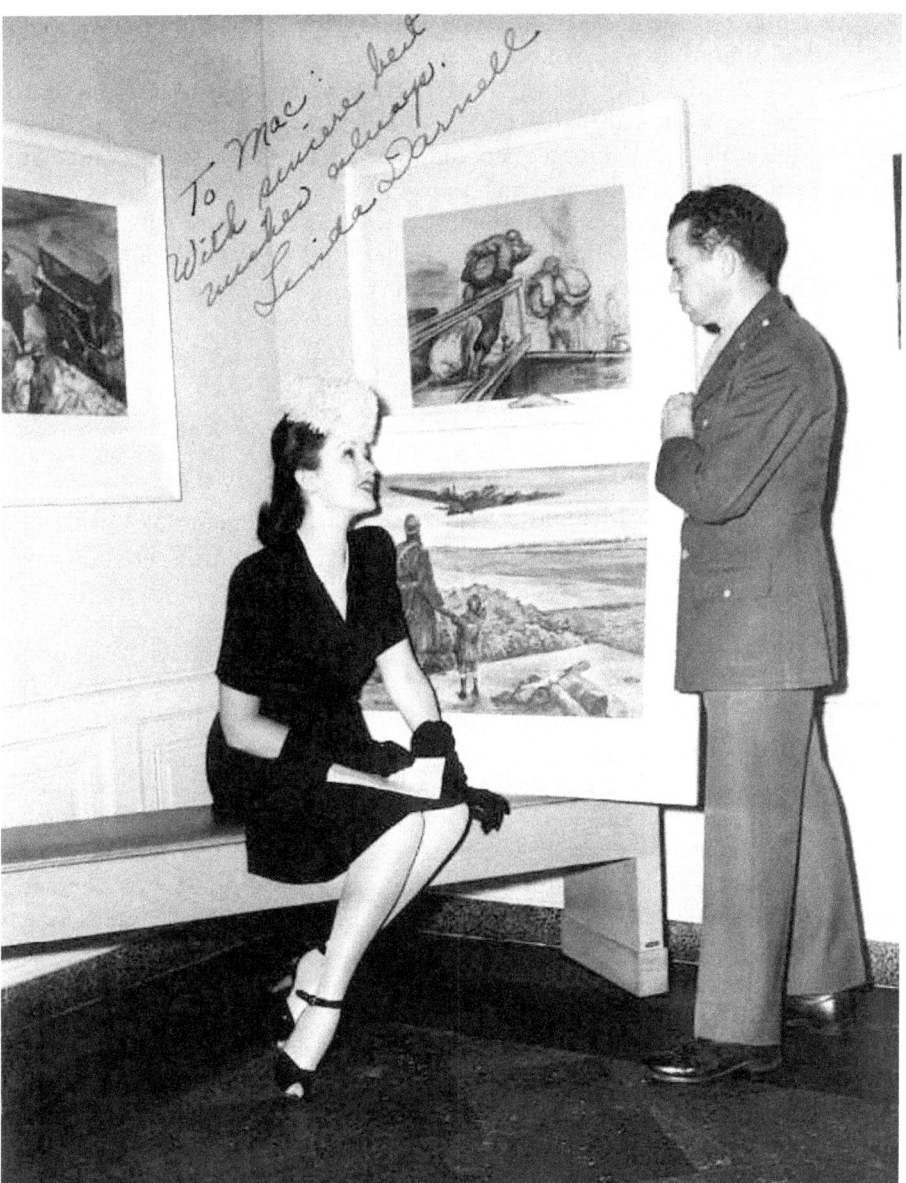

On one of the art show tours of the United States to raise money for bonds, Jack McMillen and Linda Darnell (a prominent Hollywood star) appear together. In the background is some of the artwork Jack McMillen was "carting around" (courtesy Dr. Brian A. McMillen).

his family did not know its location. The article pictures Angie and Brian McMillen in front of the 7.1' × 10.6' mural.[10]

Dr. Brian A. McMillen ("BAM") recalls pestering his father to start painting again after the elder McMillen retired from commercial art. Jack McMillen did start painting again, but Brian recalls that his father said that he "was too old to crack eggs anymore."[11]

Jack McMillen lives on through his work at Tuscumbia City Hall, the work displayed at the museum of the Walter Reed Army Medical Center, in the book *Military Psychiatry: Preparing in Peace for War*, and his other work elsewhere.

Tuskegee

Anne Wilson Goldthwaite prepared the oil-on-canvas painting titled *The Road to Tuskegee* for the Tuskegee, Alabama, Post Office in 1937.

The settlement of what is now Tuskegee (a word meaning "Warrior") dates from shortly after the French and Indian War (1754–1763). As a result of the treaty ending the war, the French surrendered; both their fort and the land that is now Tuskegee went to the English.

After the end of the American Revolution, the United States took possession of the area that became part of the Mississippi Territory. In 1819 some of this area became a part of Alabama.

Macon County dates from 1832. One year later (1833), General Thomas Simpson Woodward selected Tuskegee for the county seat. The Creek Nation still heavily populated the area. The name *Tuskegee* came from Taskigi, a Creek leader in the area.

After the Creek left the area in 1836, white settlers began to infiltrate the Tuskegee locale. The incorporation of Tuskegee dates from 1843. The area's first local newspaper was the *Tuskegee News*, first published in Tuskegee in April 1865.[1]

In particular, two nineteenth-century African Americans—Booker T. Washington and George Washington Carver—helped bring progress and positive publicity to Tuskegee.

Booker T. Washington (1856–1915) and George Washington Carver (ca. 1865–1943). Born a slave in Hales Ford, Virginia, Booker T. Washington was a graduate of Hampton Normal and Agricultural Institute and Wayland Seminary. Booker Taliaferro Washington founded Tuskegee Normal and Industrial Institute in 1881. Washington served as president of Tuskegee Insti-

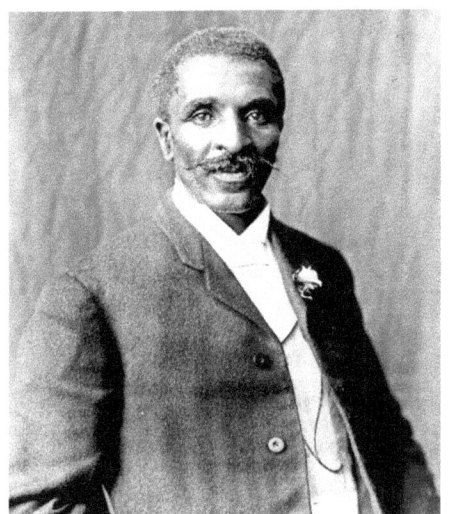 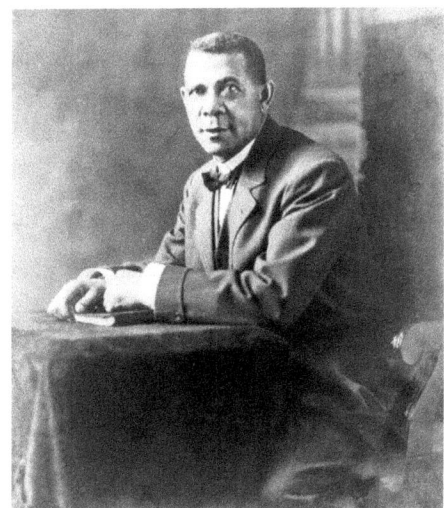

Left: This portrait from the Tuskegee Institute shows George Washington Carver (1864?–1943). Frances Benjamin Johnston (1864–1952) was the photographer (courtesy Library of Congress, LC-J601–302). *Right:* This photograph shows Booker Taliaferro Washington (1865–1915) seated at a small table. Washington served as president of Tuskegee Institute/University for many years (courtesy Library of Congress, LC-USZ62–57959).

tute—now known as Tuskegee University—until his death in 1915. Tuskegee Institute grew from a school of 30 enrollees to a world-famous college.

Booker T. Washington's autobiography *Up from Slavery* has been translated into more than 20 languages and dialects. After his death in 1915, Washington was buried on the campus of Tuskegee University.

In 1940 the United States government selected Booker T. Washington to be one of five educators honored with a commemorative postage stamp. In 1956—the hundredth anniversary of his birth—the United States government honored Washington again with a commemorative postage stamp.[2]

A statue on the campus of Tuskegee University shows Tuskegee President Booker T. Washington "Lifting the Veil of Ignorance" from a black man's face.[3]

George Washington Carver (ca. 1865–1943). In 1896 Booker T. Washington invited George Washington Carver of Missouri to serve on the faculty of Tuskegee Normal and Industrial Institute. Carver helped increase the prestige of the science program at Tuskegee Institute through his research on such products as peanuts, cotton, sweet potatoes, and soybeans.[4]

The Notorious Tuskegee Syphilis Study (1932–1972). In Tuskegee, Alabama, a controversial study of syphilis among African Americans began during the Great Depression (1932) and continued until 1972—a forty-year period. The U.S. Public Health Service (PHS) informed most of the hundreds of participating African American men that they were being treated for their late-stage syphilis. In actuality, this was not always true. These men—without their consent and knowledge—were being used in a public health study on the effects of untreated syphilis.

> Susan M. Reverby (in her *Examining Tuskegee: The Infamous Syphilis Study and Its Legacy*) offers a comprehensive analysis of the notorious study of untreated syphilis, which took place in and around Tuskegee, Alabama, from the 1930s through the 1970s.[5]

On May 16, 1997, President William Jefferson Clinton assembled the survivors of the study in the East Room of the White House. He stated that it was time to end the silence and stop turning our heads away from what happened. President Clinton said, "[W]hat the United States government did was shameful, and I am sorry."[6]

Tuskegee Airmen. Tuskegee received positive recognition during World War II as the training site for more than 1,000 pilots. The Tuskegee Airfield was the location of the Tuskegee Airmen. President Franklin D. Roosevelt had ordered the Army Air Corps to set up a pilot training program for African Americans in Tuskegee. These "Red Tails" received much favorable publicity for their contributions to the World War II effort.[7] The airfield is now known as the Tuskegee Airmen National Historic Site.

Present-day Tuskegee. In 2010 Tuskegee had a population of 9,865. Participants identified themselves as:

African Americans	95.8 percent
White	0.7 percent
Asian	0.7 percent
Hispanic	0.7 percent
Native American	0.2 percent

The median household income for families in Tuskegee in 2010 was $26,325. The per capita income in Tuskegee was $14,920.[8]

Tuskegee carries the nickname the "Pride of the Swift Growing South." Tuskegee invites locals and visitors to spend some time at the home of Booker T. Washington; this historic home is The Oaks.

Dedicated to preserving and communicating the history and the legacy of the Tuskegee Airmen, the National Park Service (NPS) established a landmark to honor the Tuskegee Airmen. The NPS encourages visitors and locals alike to come to the Tuskegee Airmen National Historic Site.

The campus of Tuskegee University—the first black college to be listed as a National Historic Landmark—and the George Washington Carver Museum are other sites to visit. The City of Tuskegee hopes "that you will visit our city and immerse yourself in the history and the captivating spirit that is alive and well right here in Tuskegee, Alabama!"[9]

The Tuskegee Post Office of 1935. The marker on the side of the old Tuskegee Post Office building at 201 South Main Street indicates that the building dates from 1935. Henry Morgenthau, Jr., was the Secretary of the Treasury in that year. James A. Farley was Postmaster General during the construction of the Tuskegee, Alabama, Post Office. Louis A. Simon was the Supervising Architect, and Neal A. Melick was the Supervising Engineer.

The 1935 red-brick former post office building has a symmetrical appearance. Between the four windows on the front of the building are centered, double, glass-paned front doors. Dentil molding decorates the roof-line of the building. A cupola occupies the center of the gable roof. Two steps lead from the sidewalk to a landing, and six more steps lead from the landing to the front entrance.

When a new post office opened in 1996 in Tuskegee, Alabama, Dyann Robinson purchased the 1935 downtown Tuskegee Post Office building for her own use and the use of the community. She re-opened it as the Jessie Clinton Arts Centre, intending the structure to house the offices and the teaching/rehearsal/performance space necessary both for the school and for

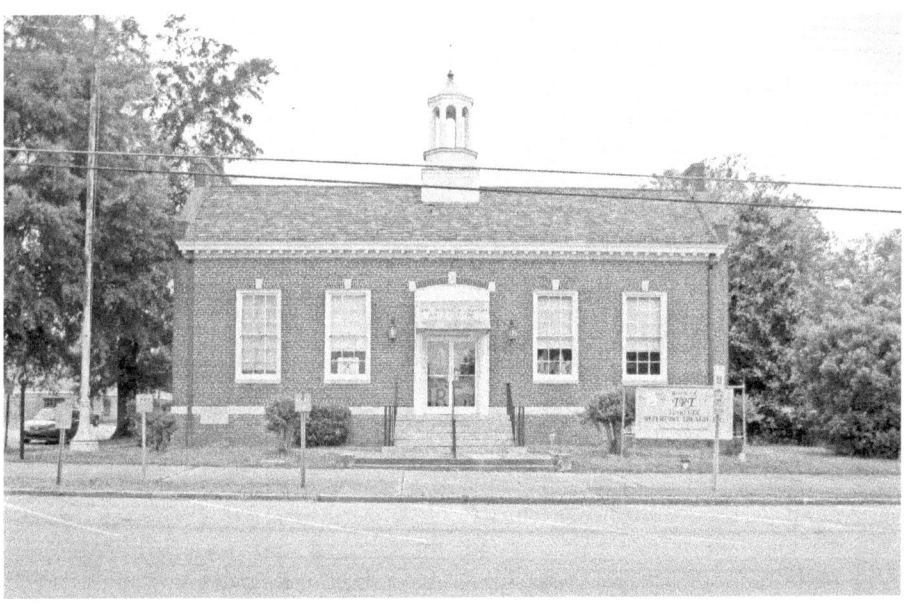

The Tuskegee building at 201 South Main Street formerly housed the Tuskegee Post Office. The structure now holds the Jessie Clinton Arts Centre and the performance space of the Tuskegee Repertory Theatre (courtesy Dyann Robinson, director of the Tuskegee Repertory Theatre).

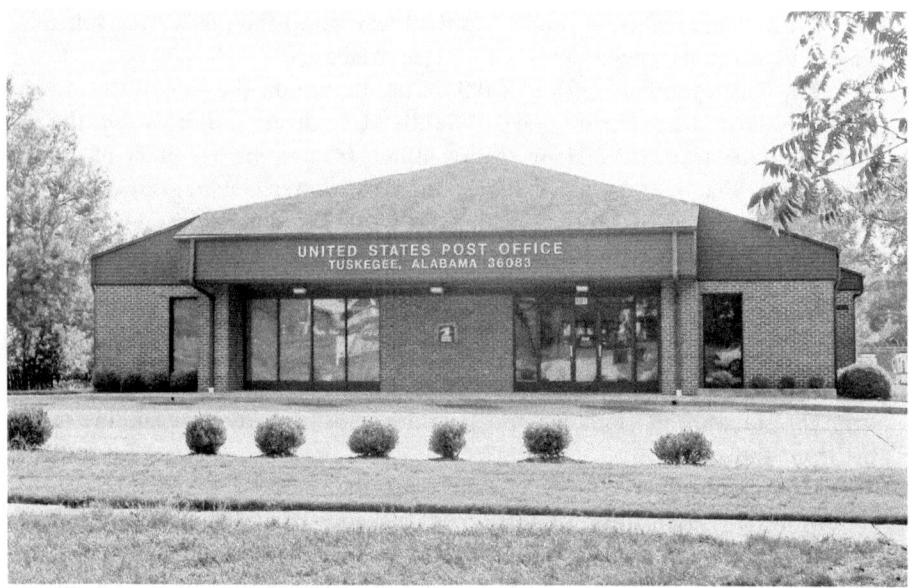

The current post office in Tuskegee, Alabama.

the theatre company that Robinson directs, the Tuskegee Repertory Theatre, Inc. Seats for up to 80 are available in the performance area.[10]

The Tuskegee Post Office of 1996. An updated Tuskegee Post Office opened on North Elm Street in Tuskegee, Alabama, in 1996. No steps lead to the front entrance, which is on ground level. A double-paned glass door on the right side of the covered porch provides entrance to the building. The four windows on the left side of the porch provide the necessary balance to achieve a symmetrical appearance to the front of the building; these four, single-paned windows reach from the floor of the covered porch to the top of the porch.

The red-brick structure houses, of course, the services and the equipment of the United States Postal Service. The federal mural *The Road to Tuskegee* that Anne Wilson Goldthwaite had prepared in 1937 also has found a place in the new facility.

The Road to Tuskegee. Anne Wilson Goldthwaite would prepare the mural for the Atmore Post Office in 1938; she incorporated both the theme of postal history and local scenes into the murals she prepared for the Atmore (1938) and the Tuskegee Post Offices (1937). The mural that Goldthwaite prepared for the Section of Fine Arts titled *The Road to Tuskegee* suggests the many transportation methods over time—horse-drawn wagons, vintage cars, trains, and airplanes—for conveying people and the mail. In the scene, Goldthwaite depicts many separate incidents—such as plowing the land, car-

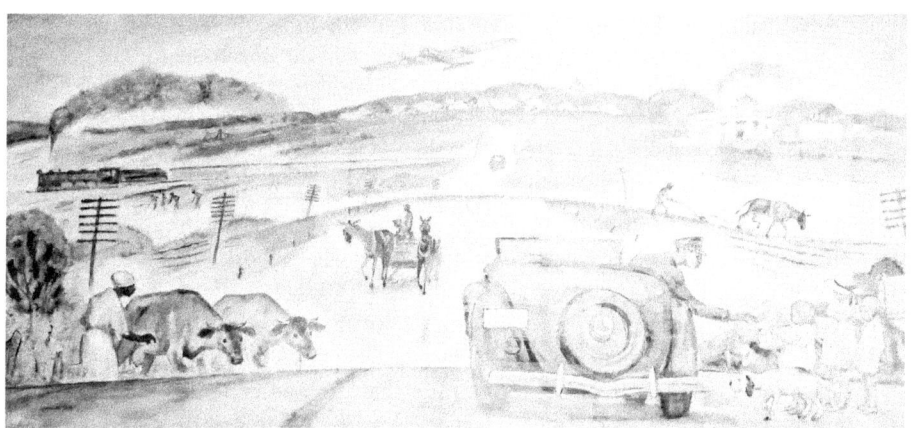

The Tuskegee mural by Anne Wilson Goldthwaite is currently on display in the Tuskegee Post Office.

ing for the cattle, receiving the mail from the mail carrier, the beginning of rural electric power—typical of the time and place. The restoration of the oil-on-canvas painting and its transfer to the 1996 Tuskegee Post Office have helped ensure its existence for some time to come.

Anne Wilson Goldthwaite (June 28, 1869–January 29, 1944). Anne Wilson Goldthwaite was the only woman to receive federal commissions for two artworks in the state of Alabama.[11] She prepared the oil-on-canvas *The Letter Box* for the Atmore Post Office in 1938. Explicit details about her life are available in the section on Atmore in this volume. Ausfeld adds some additional personal facts about her and about her painting style.

Growing up in Montgomery, Alabama, "[t]he high-spirited young woman bridled at the usual invitations to country club dances and the endless search for beaux.... [S]he insisted on wandering the town alone, pad and pencil always at hand for sketching.... [W]omen as a rule undertook artistic activities only casually."[12]

Goldthwaite began her memoirs late in her life; she never finished the work, however. The same cannot be said about her numerous works of art that she completed and that are still on display; she seemed to have completed most of that which she began.

In Paris in the early twentieth century, Goldthwaite led a "decorous" life—a decided difference from the bohemian lifestyle of many artists in that time and place. When World War I forced her to leave Paris, Anne Wilson Goldthwaite used commissions from portraits as a source of income. Ausfeld describes in detail Goldthwaite's style of mixing colors and painting:

> Her method of dabbing and blending paints, varying the thickness to stain some areas and building up layers in others, is indicative of her study of works

by Cézanne and his contemporaries and is ideally suited to her spontaneous, abbreviated designs. Her emphasis is primarily on the linear qualities of her subjects, sketching in the major elements with a strong black line and using the color to "finish" work by degrees. Compared to her other efforts her portraits are more tightly rendered, with surer contours and modeling.[13]

Goldthwaite expressed the intent of the art that female artists prepared. "We want to speak to eyes and ears wide open and without prejudice," she said in 1934, to "an audience that asks simply—is it good, not—was it done by a woman."[14]

Ausfeld summarizes her opinion of Anne Wilson Goldthwaite: "That she could flourish in such a climate is a testament to the determination of a remarkable person. Her art demonstrates that she was a talented and creative one as well, justifiably recognized as 'the leading painter of the South.'"[15]

Appendix:
Federal Art Projects
Between 1933 and 1943

Between 1933 and 1943, the federal government spent $83,500,000 on art projects.[1] Twenty-four towns in the State of Alabama would benefit directly from the money allocated for public art. These federal projects extended throughout the entire state of Alabama.

The purpose(s) of these expenses varied with the project, of course. Some of the projects were intended to embellish public buildings. Many of the funded projects had the purpose of providing art for the American public; other programs provided some relief for unemployed artists. Still other agencies professed to a combination of goals. The projects, the programs, the goals, and the products of the federal art projects sometimes overlapped.

Most Americans—even at the time—expressed confusion about the projects. These citizens tended to lump all the programs together and to call all the resulting artworks "WPA art"—even though the category might be inaccurate.

Hopefully, the tangled web of projects, programs, products, and purposes will untangle in the following analysis of each project between 1933 and 1943.

I. Civil Works Administration (CWA): 1933–1934

In November 1933, President Franklin Delano Roosevelt by executive order established the Civil Works Administration (CWA). Its purpose was the creation of a program of work-relief and aid to Americans during the hard winter months. The CWA established about one hundred professional and white job classifications, which included artists.

II. Public Works of Art Project (PWAP): 1933–1934

The same month (November 1933) that President Roosevelt established the Civil Works Administration, planning began to establish an Advisory Committee. This group would suggest methods for promoting art and develop plans to assist artists who were in need and who had the necessary professional ability. Members included Chair Frederick Delano; Harry L. Hopkins, commissioner and later administrator of the Federal Relief Administration; Rexford G. Tugwell, assistant secretary of agriculture; Edward Bruce, artist; and others. The advisory committee met for the first time in December of 1933. Edward Bruce (1880–1943) served as acting secretary.

George Biddle, an artist and friend of the Roosevelts, helped to organize the project; he and others recommended Edward Bruce as the director of the Public Works of Art Project (PWAP), which was under the aegis of the Treasury Department.

Edward Bruce had been a successful attorney and businessman. In 1922, at the age of 43, Bruce gave up these two careers to become a full-time artist. He—like many other artists of the 1920s and 1930s—found it impossible to succeed financially during the time. In 1932 Bruce took a job as a lobbyist for the Calamba Sugar Estate of San Francisco.

Biddell summed up the Advisory Committee and Bruce by saying: "It would be difficult to appoint a more intelligent and liberal group to look after the interests of American artists, and Bruce as the active administrator of the committee deserves the greatest credit for its far-reaching results."[2]

When Bruce (1879–1943) received an offer to work full-time with the PWAP, he agreed to help with the first federally supported arts program. In 1933, he accepted the position as director of the Treasury Department's Section of Fine Arts. Bruce envisioned the artists as working *with* the government. His task was to organize the project and to help provide work for the thousands of unemployed artists across the nation.[3] Bruce helped organize a program to create murals, sculptures, and artworks for public buildings. Professional ability and need would help determine the selection of the artists.

The Civil Works Administration (CWA) funneled $1,312,000 into the Public Works of Art Project (PWAP). Housed under the Treasury Department's Procurement Division and funded by the Civil Works Administration, the PWAP was President Roosevelt's first large-scale art program.[4]

Forbes Watson (formerly the editor of *The Arts*) became the head of the technical staff of the PWAP. The PWAP hired the first artists on December 12, 1933, and eventually employed 3,700 artists during the six months of its existence; these artists produced 15,663 artworks. The cost of the program was about $1,312,000.

Bruce determined that the artists and sculptors would not engage in "busy work." Because public money paid for the work, the work would belong to the general public and would be on display in buildings and parks that taxes—state, federal, or municipal—supported. Some of the artists received an hourly wage; other worked as artists with the PWAP as their patron. The PWAP was a crash relief program, without strict relief tests in the Treasury Department.[5]

The results of the PWAP included 1400 sculptures and murals, 2600 works of graphic art, and 7000 easel paintings and watercolors. The PWAP provided employment for thousands of artists on relief rolls.[6]

The CWA ended in 1934. The Emergency Work Relief Program (under the Federal Emergency Relief Act, or FERA) assumed the unfinished PWAP projects.[7]

III. The Treasury Department's Section of Painting and Sculpture: 1934–1938

Henry Morgenthau, Jr., the Secretary of the Treasury, issued an order on October 14, 1934, to establish the Treasury Department's Section of Painting and Sculpture. Among others, its goals included

1. securing suitable, quality art to embellish public buildings;
2. carrying out the work in order to reward talent and develop art in the country;
3. employing local talent;
4. securing the cooperation of others to advise and to critique works; and
5. encouraging competitions to give all artists opportunities to participate.[8]

The primary goal of the Section of Painting and Sculpture was to transform federal buildings into art galleries for the people. During its nine years (1934–1943), this federal program—which would undergo several name changes—would eventually employ 850 artists and commission 1,371 artworks; most of these artworks were on display in federal post offices and courthouses around the nation.[9]

To decorate the public buildings, the Section of Painting and Sculpture—later the Treasury Department Section of Fine Arts (1938–1939) and the Section of Fine Arts (1939–1943)—used anonymous competitions.

Headed by Edward Bruce (an artist), painter Edward Rowan (1898–1946), and art critic Forbes Watson (1880–1960), the Section had as its chief administrators these three persons with artistic backgrounds; none of the three were part of the established political bureaucracy. The three "combined their skills to create an efficient artistic sphere where new ideas could prosper."[10]

Each of the three administrators assumed different roles. Bruce, who had helped develop the idea for the Section, handled the bureaucracy and the general policies of the Section of Painting and Sculpture. Rowan and Watson both served as art critics. Rowan, however, was the one who dealt directly with the artists and served as an advisor to them. Watson served as publicist; he promoted general awareness of the federal programs and publicized the federal works in magazine and newspaper articles.

To fund the artwork in the buildings, one percent of the cost of the new federal buildings went for the embellishments that artists would provide. The average cost of each artwork was $600, or one percent of the building's cost. Under the New Deal construction programs, the average space covered by the federally funded post office decorations was twelve feet by five feet; the space over the postmaster's door was the typical location for the artwork.

The surface for decoration in the courthouses was often larger and, therefore, more costly. The commission might be $3,000. From the allotment, however, the artist had to purchase all the necessary supplies. Not all of the New Deal structures, however, received a decoration.

To eliminate favoritism and to give opportunities to the young and the old, to women and men, to the known and the unknown, the Section of Painting and Sculpture did not use financial need as the prime requisite for the employment of the artist. It used anonymous competitions. A later program (the Treasury Relief Art Project, directed by Olin Dows from 1935–1938), however, would take into account the relief rolls.

Over the nine-year-period that they were in operation, the programs of the Section sponsored 190 competitions, most of which were regional; only 15 of the contests were national. More than 15,426 artists submitted sketches, which numbered 40,426.

The regions of the country appointed a committee and a chair after the designation of the specific federal building to receive the artwork. The selected chair of the regional committees was usually a museum director or an art school principal or director; this appointed chair selected a jury. The groups would organize a contest, notify artists of the competition through mailings, run announcements in newspapers, and write promotions for *The Section Bulletin*, a publication that had a readership of more than 8,500.

Contestants in the competitions had to submit unsigned entries. Their names and contact information had to be in sealed envelopes taped to the back of their entry or entries. The judges opened the envelope only after they determined the winner.

Step One in the process was the submission of both a black-and-white and a color sketch by the contestants; the scale was one inch to one foot. The committees recommended the submission of four sketched ideas; these multiple sketches might help to ensure the selection of one of the artist's ideas by the committee.

The jury usually based its contract on the color sketches. Edward Rowan himself often critiqued the entries; he frequently encouraged the artists to make adjustments to their work and/or to their depiction of the scene. Hereafter, the administrators usually saw the artist's actual work only in photographs of the paintings and/or sculptures.

Step Two was a "cartoon," which the artist submitted to the administrators. The cartoon was a black-and-white drawing to scale. The artist would photograph this image and submit the photo to the administrators.

Artists who were preparing sculptured murals would prepare a clay model (maquette) after they had prepared the sketch. Edward Rowan would often critique the modeling, the perspective, and the composition of the sculpture; he frequently offered his advice to the sculptor.

The Section of Painting and Sculpture supervised the progress of the artists by mail. The group—composed of nineteen people—met regularly and submitted critiques of the artworks that were in progress. Edward Rowan, however, was the one who corresponded with the artists.

Step Three was the creation of the artwork by the artists under contract.

Step Four was the installation of the art. Some artists might install the work themselves; others gave explicit written directions for the installation.

Contestants often had another chance for a commission even if their work was not the first selected for a particular region. Judges might grant an artist a commission if the artist received "runner-up" status. If a federal building was under construction in the artist's locale, an artist showing "exceptional promise" might receive special consideration and might submit a sketch appropriate for the new site—without the formal competition. If the committee for the new site and the Section of Painting and Sculpture approved the work, the artist might receive a contract.

Artists under contract received an installment of their pay as they completed each stage. The first—and smallest—payment came upon approval of the initial sketch by the Section of Painting and Sculpture. Upon receiving approval of the cartoon or the clay model, an artist received a second payment. The largest payment came after the installation of the artwork and after a statement confirming the completion of the work from the local official. The monetary amounts varied, but mural painters received about $20 per square foot.[11]

The 850 contestants selected by the Section of Painting and Sculpture included only three African-American artists and only 162 women. The anonymity of the process, hopefully, ensured that there had been no deliberate discrimination at work. Melosh, however, notes: "Women were distinctly a minority among Section artists, and to some extent they were second class citizens. Section records contain gendered language that expressed and enforced female marginality."[12] Park and Merkowitz report the number of selected women artists as evidence of the inclusiveness of the judges and administrators. These two authors give the number of women as 150—slightly lower than Melosh reported. Still, they maintained their opinion that women were included.[13]

The anonymity of the entries ensured that both Democrats and Republicans were among the chosen; in addition, however, Communists, Socialists, and members of other radical political parties were among the selected artists. Rumors were that some "well known artists quite often refused to enter the competitions, stating that their already recognized ... reputation adequately demonstrated their ability."[14]

The competitions helped to ensure that the artists used only certain artistic styles. Realism and American scenes were generally favorable; cubism, modernism, and abstractions were generally unfavorable. Sculptures and murals were preferred media. The administrators generally approved "dignified work," readily accessible locations, and subjects with which the residents could identify.[15]

Artists with contracts created their work within a studio and later installed it in the designated building. The administrators and judges encouraged each artist to visit the town scheduled for their artwork. The reasoning was that communicating with the locals within the community would help in designing an accurate art piece. Because travel was expensive and difficult, many overly-confident artists neglected to heed the suggestion. Sometimes the results were the works by an artist who had never been to the area. The communication gaps at times caused problems.

The federal programs to aid artists and advance art for the public continued through the next few years under various names and with overlapping programs. Before these federal programs for art and artists faded away in 1943, these federal programs awarded 1400 contracts and spent $2,571,000, most of which went for salaries.

IV. The Treasury Department Section of Fine Arts: 1938–1939

When the Treasury Department Section of Painting and Sculpture became a part of the Federal Works Agency in 1938, its name changed on October 13, 1938, to the Treasury Department Section of Fine Arts (1938–1939). Its director at the national level was Edward Bruce, who had directed the Section of Painting and Sculpture.

The Treasury Department Section of Fine Arts was not primarily a relief program. Through regional and national competitions—not financial need—

the artists received their contracts. The program had the goal of decorating new federal buildings with artwork of the highest quality.[16]

V. The Section of Fine Arts: 1939–1943

The transfer of the art programs to the new Public Buildings Administration brought another name change. The Section of Fine Arts—directed by Edward Bruce—endured from 1939 until 1943. Like the programs immediately before it, the Section of Fine Arts was not a relief program. Regional and national competitions were the means of gaining employment in the Section of Fine Arts. The Section endeavored to provide the highest quality work to decorate the new federal buildings; it was in these ways like the Treasury Department Section of Fine Arts (1938–1939).

During the transition months (July 1939 until about April 1940), the Section of Fine Arts conducted its famous national competition. "The Forty-Eight State Competition" was—as its name implies—a national contest; its goal was contracting artworks for a designated federal building in each state.[17]

This competition was the largest one that the Section of Fine Arts ever sponsored. There were over 3,000 entries. One post office in each state received a mural. The winning entries were on exhibition around the country. *Life* magazine in December of 1939 reproduced the winning drawings for each state.[18]

There was some confusion in the scene represented for Alabama, created by artist Robert Gwathmey. Gwathmey would produce an artwork for Eutaw, Alabama.

VI. Treasury Relief Art Project (TRAP): 1935–1939

Congress signed a congressional appropriation of $4.8 billion earmarked for relief on April 8, 1935. The agency to administer the funds, however, was the discretion of President Roosevelt.

On May 6, 1935, President Roosevelt created—by executive order—the Works Progress Administration (WPA). Roosevelt assigned Harry Lloyd Hopkins as Administrator of the WPA and Francis Clark Harrington as Assistant Administrator. In December 1938, Hopkins would assume the post of Secretary of Commerce and hold the post for two years; next, he would help manage President Franklin Delano Roosevelt's 1940 presidential campaign, lead the Lend-Lease program with the United Kingdom (1941), and serve as advisor to President Roosevelt throughout World War II.[19]

When Harry Hopkins left the WPA in 1938, Harrington became the administrator; later Harrington became commissioner when the Works Progress Administration became the Work Projects Administration. Howard

Owen Hunter was Francis C. Harrington's successor (acting commissioner, 1940; commissioner, October 1941–1943) of the WPA.

To respond to the need for art relief, the plans initially specified drama, music, writing, and the plastic arts. These components would fall under the Treasury Department, which already had structures set up for art. After Edward Bruce and Secretary of the Treasury Henry Morgenthau, Jr., expressed hesitancy in accepting responsibility for such a diverse plan, the WPA set about developing its own plans for administering the project. The result was the Federal Project Number One, more about which follows in the next section.

The Treasury Department did accept funds in the amount of $530,784 from the WPA (July 1935). These funds would establish a relief program to help decorate public buildings. From July 1935 the program had Olin Dows as its director. Cecil H. Jones succeeded Dows as the director. TRAP functioned until about December of 1938. Its liquidation occurred in June of 1939. The programs of the Treasury Relief Art Project (TRAP) overlapped in time with some of the programs of the Section.

Whereas the Section (under Edward Bruce) provided the government with the best professional art for its financial investment, the Section never had the goal of alleviating unemployment among artists in the nation.[20]

The Treasury Relief Art Project (TRAP) intended to commission art primarily from unemployed artists. Its goal was to decorate both existing and new federal buildings that did not have money in their construction budget for artworks. As beneficiaries of a relief program, 90 percent of the TRAP artists in the beginning had to come from the relief rolls; later the percentage changed to 75 percent. With its heavy accent on relief for artists, TRAP differed from the Section of Painting and Sculpture, the Treasury Department Section of Fine Arts (1938–1939), and the Section of Fine Arts.[21]

Most of the TRAP sculptures and the murals were for small post offices and other federal buildings. The focus of TRAP was primarily on those structures that did not have provisions in their budget for artistic decorations or those existing public buildings that had no embellishments.

With TRAP, a "master artist"—not necessarily one on relief—received assignment to a project; often this individual received the appointment because of submissions to competitions. This appointee organized relief-roll artists to help in the execution of the work. For 96 hours of work for a month, the going wage was $69 to $103.

O'Connor summed up TRAP in this way:

[t]he procedures of TRAP assured a high level of professional artistic competence while at the same time providing, on a small scale, much needed employment. In all, 89 murals and 43 sculpture projects were completed for federal buildings and housing projects. In addition, about 10,000 easel paint-

ings were allocated to government institutions and embassies. These works were done by about 446 artists. Its scope as a relief program, however, was limited and it was left to the Federal Art Project of the Works Progress Administration—which began a month after the start of TRAP—to effectively meet the problem of the unemployed artist.[22]

VII. The Federal Art Project (FAP) of the Works Progress Administration (WPA): 1935–1943

President Franklin Delano Roosevelt created the Works Progress Administration (WPA) on May 6, 1935. He put Harry Hopkins, his chief relief manager, in charge of the WPA.

The Federal Art Project (FAP) of the Works Progress Administration (WPA) operated from 1935 until 1943. Several name changes occurred within its jurisdiction and within its time frame, however. Holier Cahill served as the national director of the Federal Art Project (1935–1943); he considered the artists as working *with* the government. Thomas C. Parker served as the assistant director of the WPA/FAP.

During the period of 1939–1940, when Cahill worked on the New York World's Fair, however, Parker substituted for Cahill. Parker left the WPA/FAP to become director of the American Federation of Arts (1940–1952).

John Michael Carboy oversaw the WPA's Federal Art Project, which was primarily a relief program. The WPA/FAP lasted from August 1935 until September of 1939 and reached its peak in 1936.[23]

O'Connor described the Federal Art Project as the most extensive program of the New Deal art programs and the one with "the greatest impact on the culture and consciousness of the nation."[24] O'Connor cautions readers that the impact of the WPA was so great that many people tend to label any or all art projects of the 1930s as "WPA." Of course all the art projects did not fall under the WPA; most people, however, do not have any idea of the genesis of the federal art projects, which reached throughout the nation. The debate from Congress and the public over the financial allocation for the art projects also helped to make the WPA memorable.

The WPA established in July 1935 the Division of Professional and Service Projects. Within the Division of Professional and Service Projects was Federal Project Number I. Federal Project Number I included activities devoted to literature, theatre, art, and music. Established in August, the four projects began functioning in October when the funds became available. Nikolai Sokoloff served as the national director of the Federal Music Project.

Under Jacob Baker (1935–1936), the WPA had as its primary objective work-relief. The WPA helped to abolish "the dole" for the unskilled, the blue collar, and the white collar workers—including the artists. The participants worked to earn their stipends.

Ellen Sullivan Woodward had joined the FERA in 1933. When Baker left the WPA in July 1936, Woodward took over the control of Federal Project Number I and remained in charge through December 1938. Woodward was responsible for overseeing the restructuring Federal One to meet the modified needs and goals of the WPA.

Each state had its own WPA director and its own staff to administer the WPA/FAP. The WPA/FAP was a relief program. As was the case with TRAP, in the early years of the relief program, 90 percent of the artists came from the relief rolls; later, the percentage dropped to 75 percent.[25]

The main purpose of the FAP that fell under the jurisdiction of the Works Progress Administration (WPA) was initially to provide relief for unemployed artists by supplying jobs for them and providing art for the public. The programs were tax-supported; institutions that were partially tax-supported could apply for receiving the work that the WPA artists completed.

The WPA/FAP was a successful program with great influence.

At its peak in 1936, it [WPA/FPA] provided work for more than 5,000 artists from relief rolls. Over the eight years of its existence, its employees produced 2,566 murals, more than 100,00 easel paintings, about 17,700 sculptures, and nearly 300,000 fine prints. The project also developed an audience by establishing more than 100 community art centers and galleries in regions where art was generally unknown. The total federal investment was about $35 million. It was the first major attempt at U.S. government patronage of the visual arts.[26]

The manual of operation for the Federal Art Project had four areas of artistic activity: the creation of art, art education, art as related to community service, and both technical and archeological research. Artists were free to select their own subject matter, to work in their own studios, and to submit one product—depending on size and the developer's normal work rate—every month or two. If the work seemed to be the best effort of the artist, the work was automatically accepted. The average wage was $95 a month.

WPA monies funded Federal Project Number I, which functioned from 1935–1939. There was much controversy surrounding Federal Project Number I; this was particularly evident in New York City, where symbols of Communism seemed apparent in many works.

President Roosevelt moved the WPA to the Federal Works Agency in July of 1939 and changed the name of the Federal Works Agency to the Federal Works Administration.

VIII. The Art Program of the
Federal Works Administration: 1939–1942

The Art Program of the Federal Works Administration lasted from September 1939 until March 1942. World War II brought about a change in goals for the nation.

Congress abolished the Federal Project Number I in September 1939. It cut off appropriations for the Federal Theatre Project, for which Hallie Flanagan had served as national director from 1935 to 1939. The other three projects—music, literature, and art—had the requirement that 25 percent of the funding for them must come from state or local sponsors. In addition, the new rulings required the immediate termination of employment of any employee who had worked there for more than eighteen months. These actions worked against the relief aspects of the programs.

IX. The First and Second Graphic Sections
of the War Services Division

The Art Program became the Graphic Section of the War Services Division in March 1942. The artists and facilities had an important new goal: to further the war effort. World War II was bringing about changes in the art products within the nation.

There were two different time periods for the Graphic Sections of the War Services Division. The First Graphic Section of the War Services Division had as its time period March 1942 until October 1942.

The Second Graphic Section of the War Services Division functioned from October 1942 until April 1943. On December 4, 1942, President Franklin Delano Roosevelt signed an order giving the Graphic Section of the War Services Division "its honorable discharge as soon as possible within the physical year."[27]

The Second Graphic Section of the War Services Division "ceased to function and by July 1, 1943, they were completely liquidated."[28]

World War II would change significantly both the goals of the federal government and the world.

Notes

INTRODUCTION

1. Robert S. McElvaine, *Down and Out in the Great Depression* (Chapel Hill: University of North Carolina Press, 1983), 20.

2. Roger Biles. *The South and the New Deal* (Lexington: University of Kentucky Press, 1994), 120.

3. *Farm Journal*, December 1931, 15.

4. Oliver Perry Chitwood, Frank Lawrence Owsley, and H. C. Nixon, *The United States from Colony to World Power* (New York: D. Van Nostrand, 1953), 765.

5. Time-Life Editors, *This Fabulous Century: 1930–1940*, Vol. IV. New York: Time-Life Books, 1969).

6. Chitwood Owsley and Nixon, *The United States from Colony to World Power*, 765.

7. Peter Jennings and Todd Brewster, *The Century* (New York: Doubleday, 1998), 154.

8. Time-Life Editors, *This Fabulous Century*, Vol. IV, 23.

9. Milton Meltzer, *Violins and Shovels* (New York: Delacorte Press, 1976), 2–3.

10. Francis V. O'Connor, *Federal Art Patronage: 1933 to 1943: An Exhibition. April 6 to May 13, 1966, University of Maryland Art Gallery, J. Millard Tawes Fine Arts Center, College Park, Maryland*, copyright Dr. Francis V. O'Connor, 1966, catalog designed by Ralph Freeny, 6.

11. Meltzer, *Violins and Shovels*, 2–3.

12. George Biddle, "An Art Renascence under Federal Patronage," *Scribner's Magazine*, June 1934, 428.

13. O'Connor, *Federal Art Patronage*, 8.

14. Biddle, "An Art Renascence under Federal Patronage," 428.

15. O'Connor, *Federal Art Patronage*, 8.

16. Biddle, "An Art Renascence under Federal Patronage," 428.

17. O'Connor, *Federal Art Patronage*, 6.

18. Biddle, "An Art Renascence under Federal Patronage," 429.

19. Biddle, "An Art Renascence under Federal Patronage," 430.

20. Biddle, "An Art Renascence under Federal Patronage," 430.

ALEXANDER CITY

1. Peter Hastings Falk, *Who's Who in American Art*, Vol. I (Guilford, CT: Sound View Press, 1985), 189.

2. "Epping, Franc (Dorothy)," Ancestry. com.

3. Karal Ann Marling, *Wall-to-Wall America* (Minneapolis: University of Minnesota Press, 1982), 4.

4. "Alabama," *Compton's Pictured Encyclopedia* (Chicago: F. E. Compton, 1948), 98g–98j, 99.

5. William Warren Rogers, Robert David Ward, Leah Rawls Atkins, and Wayne Flynt, *Alabama: The History of a Deep Southern State* (Tuscaloosa: University of Alabama Press, 1994), 9.

6. "Alexander City," http:wikipedia.org/wiki/Alexander_City.http://en.wikipedia.org/wiki/Alexander_City,_Alabama-cite_note-2.

7. "Alabama," *Compton's Pictured Encyclopedia*, 98g–98j, 99.

8. "Main Street," http://www.mainstreetalabama.org/alexander-city/.

9. Charles R. Shaw, "Welcome Home," http://www.alexandercityonline.com/index.html.

10. Sandra S. Wilson, Abstractor, "City Cemetery (It was once called "Laurel Park Cemetery."): Charles T. Porch." *Tallapoosa County Archives*, 1994.

11. Alexander City Library staff, "Alexander

City Library Retires Two Public Servants," *Alabama Currents,* January-February 2013, 9.

12. "Adelia M. Russell Library," http://www.amrlibrary.net/index.php/en/2013-03-05-22-24-15.

13. "Adelia M. Russell Library," http://www.alexandercityonline.com/amrl-history.html.

14. Falk, *Who's Who in American Art,* Vol. I, 189.

15. Falk, *Who's Who in American Art,* Vol. I, xxiii; additional information from her nephew Michael Shermer, *Skeptic Magazine.*

16. Ralph Mayer, *A Dictionary of Art Terms and Techniques* (New York: Thomas Y. Crowell, 1969), 351.

17. Mayer, *A Dictionary of Art Terms and Techniques,* 325–327.

18. Mayer, *A Dictionary of Art Terms and Techniques,* 392.

19. Mayer, *A Dictionary of Art Terms and Techniques,* 301.

20. Mayer, *A Dictionary of Art Terms and Techniques,* 79.

21. "Policies and Procedures," *Berea College Catalog* (online catalog, no pagination), http://catalog.berea.edu/current/Catalog/Policies-and-Procedures.

22. "Mission: Berea College," http://www.berea.edu/about/files/2012/08/GreatCommitments.pdf.

23. *Berkshire Eagle,* Pittsfield, Massachusetts, April 16, 1943.

24. Glenn B. Opitz, *Mantle Fielding's Dictionary of American Painters, Sculptors, and Engravers* (Poughkeepsie: Apollo, 1986), 262.

25. Falk, *Who's Who in American Art,* Vol. I, 189.

26. "Epping, Franc (Dorothy)," Ancestry.com.

ATMORE

1. Falk, *Who's Who in American Art,* Vol. I, 236.

2. Penny Dunford, *A Biographical Dictionary of Women Artists in Europe and America Since 1850* (New York: Harvester Wheatsheaf, 1990), 112–113.

3. Marling, *Wall-to-Wall America,* 146.

4. Hugh C. Bailey, "Alabama and Alabama Maps," *Merit Students Encyclopedia, A Volume* (London: P.F.), 274–279.

5. "Escambia County Alabama: History," http://www.archives.state.al.us/counties/escambia.html.

6. Blogger Jen, "Marble Towns Blog: Charles Pawson Atmore [1834–1900]—Cave Hill Cemetery," October 28, 2012, http://marbletowns.com/?s=atmor&search=Go.

7. Photograph by Jimmy S. Emerson of marker in Atmore, Alabama.

8. Blogger Jen, "Marble Towns Blog: Charles Pawson Atmore [1834–1900]—Cave Hill Cemetery."

9. Gombach Group, "Louis A. Simon, Architect [1867–1958]," http://www.livingplaces.com/people/louis-a-simon.html.

10. Evan Terry Associates, *Pocket Guide to the ADA: Americans with Disabilities Act Accessibility Guidelines for Buildings and Facilities* (Hoboken: John Wiley, 2007).

11. Dunford, *A Biographical Dictionary of Women Artists in Europe and America Since 1850,* 112–113.

12. "Anne Wilson Goldthwaite: The Johnson Collection, LLC (Spartanburg, South Carolina)," http://thejohnsoncollection.org/anne-wilson-goldthwaite.

13. Phyllis Peet, "Goldthwaite, Anne (1869–1944)," in Jules Heller and Nancy G. Heller, *North American Women Artists of the Twentieth Century: A Biographical Dictionary* (New York: Garland, 1995), 224.

14. Penny Dunford states in *A Biographical Dictionary of Women Artists in Europe and America Since 1850* that "an uncle [not an aunt] persuaded her to train as a professional artist, a course of action he was prepared to pay for" (113).

15. Falk, *Who's Who in American Art,* Vol. I., 236.

16. Falk, *Who's Who in American Art,* Vol. I., 418.

17. "Anne Wilson Goldthwaite: The Johnson Collection, LLC (Spartanburg, South Carolina)," http://thejohnsoncollection.org/anne-wilson-goldthwaite.

18. Margaret Barlow, *Women Artists* (Hong Kong: Hugh Lauter Levin Associates, 1999), 121–122.

19. "Anne Wilson Goldthwaite: The Johnson Collection, LLC (Spartanburg, South Carolina)," http://thejohnsoncollection.org/anne-wilson-goldthwaite.

20. Falk, *Who's Who in American Art,* Vol. I, 566.

21. FilmMakers Magazine, "Stanley Kubrick Biography," http://www.filmmakers.com/artists/Kubrick/biography.

22. "Anne Wilson Goldthwaite: The Johnson Collection, LLC (Spartanburg, South Carolina)," http://thejohnsoncollection.org/anne-wilson-goldthwaite.

23. Martin Birnbaum, *Jacovleff and Other Artists* (New York: P. A. Struck, 1946), 225–226.

24. Falk, *Who's Who in American Art,* Vol. I., xx–xxx, 236. Opitz, *Mantle Fielding's Dic-*

tionary of American Painters, Sculptors, and Engravers, 333.

25. "Anne Wilson Goldthwaite," http://www.findagrave.com.

26. "Captain Richard W. Goldthwaite," http://www.findagrave.com.

27. "Lucy Boyd *Armistead* Goldthwaite," http://www.findagrave.com.

28. Jeanette M. Smith, "Yellow Calla Lilies." *JAMA* 310, No. 17 (November 6, 2013), 1774–1775.

BAY MINETTE

1. Falk, *Who's Who in American Art,* Vol. I, 365.

2. "Joel W. Solomon Federal Building and United States Courthouse," http://en.wikipedia.org/wiki/Joel_W._Solomon_Federal_Building_and_United_States_Courthouse#cite_note-GSA-3.

3. Marling, *Wall-to-Wall America,* 4; "The Allegory of Chattanooga: Mural Study Acquired by Historical Society of the U.S. District Court," http://www.examiner.com/article/the-allegory-of-chattanooga-mural-study-acquired-by-hist orical-society-of-the-u-s-district-court.

4. "An Unveiling," *Court Historical Society Newsletter: Eastern District of Tennessee*, March 2010, 1–2.

5. Baldwin County Administration, "Various Historical Compilations about Baldwin County, Alabama," http://www.co.baldwin.al.us/PageView.asp?edit_id=156, www.baldwincountyal.gov.

6. Alabama Department of Archives and History, "Alabama Moments in American History: New Deal Art in Alabama Post Offices and Federal Buildings," http://www.alabamamoments.alabama.gov/sec49det.html; Marling, *Wall-to-Wall America,* 205–206.

7. Alabama Historical Commission, "Alabama Register of Landmarks and Heritage Nomination Form: U.S. Post Office in Bay Minette," September 11, 1985, 1–3.

8. Alabama Historical Commission, "Alabama Register of Landmarks and Heritage Nomination Form: U.S. Post Office in Bay Minette," September 11, 1985, 3.

9. Alabama Historical Commission, "Alabama Register of Landmarks and Heritage Nomination Form: U.S. Post Office in Bay Minette," September 11, 1985, 6–8.

10. Alabama Historical Commission, "Alabama Register of Landmarks and Heritage Nomination Form: U.S. Post Office in Bay Minette," September 11, 1985, 1–8.

11. Alabama Department of Archives and History, "New Deal Art in Alabama Post Offices and Federal Buildings," http://www.alabamamoments.alabama.gov/sec49det.html.

12. "Hilton Leech," *AskArt: The Artists' Bluebook,* http://www.askart.com/askart/artist.aspx?artist=117671.

13. Falk, *Who's Who in American Art,* Vol. I, 188.

14. "Joseph Hilton Leech (1906–1969)," http://www.findagrave.com.

15. Robert E. Perkins, *The First Fifty Years—Ringling School of Art and Design, 1931–1981* (Florida Graphic Arts, 1982), 10.

16. "Joseph Hilton Leech," http://www.findagrave.com.

17. "Florida Memory," http://www.floridamemory.com/items/show/246380.

18. A. M. Nagler, "John Ringling," *Merit Students Encyclopedia, Volume 16* (New York: Crowell-Collier Educational Corporation, 1969), 55.

19. "Hilton Leech," *AskArt: The Artists' Bluebook,* http://www.askart.com/askart/artist.aspx?artist=117671.

20. "An Unveiling," *Court Historical Society Newsletter: Eastern District of Tennessee*, March 2010, 1–2.

21. Hilton Leech and Emily Holmes, *The Joys of Watercolor* (New York: Van Nostrand Reinhold, 1973).

22. Leech and Holmes, *The Joys of Watercolor,* 47.

23. "Hilton Leech," *AskArt: The Artists' Bluebook,* http://www.askart.com/askart/artist.aspx?artist=117671.

24. "Laurel Park Historic District," http://laurelparkhistoricdistrict.com/sarasota-districts/.

BREWTON

1. Courtesy Jimmy Emerson and the National Archives.

2. Lydia Grimes, *Brewton and East Brewton* (Mount Pleasant, SC: Arcadia, 2011), 7.

3. "Brewton," http://www.city-data.com/city/Brewton-Alabama.html#ixzz38lCMgeyx; Claire M. Wilson, "Encyclopedia of Alabama: Brewton," http://www.encyclopediaofalabama.org/face/Article.jsp?id=h-2507.

4. "Brewton," http://www.city-data.com/city/Brewton-Alabama.html#ixzz38lCMgeyx; Claire M. Wilson, "Encyclopedia of Alabama: Brewton," http://www.encyclopediaofalabama.org/face/Article.jsp?id=h-2507.

5. Chamber of Commerce, "Greater Brewton Area Chamber of Commerce: August 23, 2014," http://www.brewtonchamber.com/.

6. Claire M. Wilson, "Encyclopedia of Alabama: Brewton," http://www.encyclopediaofalabama.org/face/Article.jsp?id=h-2507.

7. Letter from Dallan C. Wordekemper to Jimmy S. Emerson, January 9, 2006.

8. Section of Fine Arts, Public Buildings Administration, Federal Works Agency, "Mural Painting by John Von Wicht: *Logging*." From the files of Jimmy S. Emerson.

9. Section of Fine Arts, Public Buildings Administration, Federal Works Agency, "Mural Painting by John Von Wicht: *Logging*." From the files of Jimmy S. Emerson.

10. Bailey, "Alabama and Alabama Maps," *Merit Students Encyclopedia*, 274–279; "Escambia County Alabama: History." http://www.archives.state.al.us/counties/escambia.html.

11. "Brewton, Alabama," http://www.brewton.org/; "Brewton," http://www.city-data.com/city/Brewton-Alabama.html#ixzz38lCMgeyx; Chamber of Commerce, "Greater Brewton Area Chamber of Commerce: August 23, 2014," http://www.brewtonchamber.com/; "Brewton Tourism Guide," http://www.villageprofile.com/alabama/brewton/tourism.htm.

12. Jimmy S. Emerson, co-author of *New Deal Art in Alabama*.

13. Falk, *Who's Who in American Art*, Vol. I, 650.

14. Lauren A. Zelaya, comp., "Caldwell Gallery: John G. F. Von Wicht," http://www.caldwellgallery.com/bios/vonwichtbio.html, 1.

15. Mayer, *A Dictionary of Art Terms and Techniques*, 1–2.

16. "John von Wicht," http://www.annexgalleries.com/artists/biography/2457/Wicht/John, 2.

17. Zelaya, comp., "Caldwell Gallery: John G. F. Von Wicht," http://www.caldwellgallery.com/bios/vonwichtbio.html, 1–2.

18. "John von Wicht," http://www.annexgalleries.com/artists/biography/2457/Wicht/John, 2.

19. Falk, *Who's Who in American Art*, Vol. I, 650.

20. Zelaya, comp., "Caldwell Gallery: John G. F. Von Wicht," http://www.caldwellgallery.com/bios/vonwichtbio.html, 1–4.

21. "Summary of the John Von Wicht papers, 1950–1970," Archives of American Art: Smithsonian Institution, http://www.aaa.si.edu/collections/john-von-wicht-papers-9269.

22. Falk, *Who's Who in American Art*, Vol. I, 650.

CARROLLTON

1. Purser Studio, "Stuart Purser's Biography," http://www.purserstudio.com/sBio.html.

2. "Carrollton, Alabama," http://www.city-data.com/city/Carrollton-Alabama.html.

3. Alabama Historical Association, "Pickens County Courthouse," http://www.civilwaralbum.com/misc14/2010/carrolton2lg.jpg.

4. "New Deal Art in Alabama Post Offices and Federal Buildings: Carrollton," http://www.alabamamoments.alabama.gov/sec49det.html.

5. Katie Hines, "History in Pickens: The Farmer, the Politician, the Artist and the Cow," *Dateline Pickens: Pickens' Weekly Webzine*, September 12, 2003, October 11, 2003, http://www.datelinepickens.com/historyinpickens/mural.shtml.

6. "John Hollis Bankhead (1842–1920)," *Concise Dictionary of American Biography* (New York: Scribner's, 1977), 48.

7. Rogers, Ward, Atkins, and Flynt, *Alabama: The History of a Deep South State*, 489.

8. "William Brockman Bankhead (1874–1940)," *Concise Dictionary of American Biography* (New York: Scribner's, 1977), 48.

9. Katie Hines, "The Farmer, the Politician, the Artist and the Cow," *Dateline Pickens: Pickens' Weekly Webzine*, October 11, 2003, http://www.datelinepickens.com/historyinpickens/mural.shtml.

10. Purser Studio, "Biography: Stuart Purser," http://www.purserstudio.com/sBio.html.

11. Falk, *Who's Who in American Art,* Vol. I, 365.

12. "Post Office Mural *How Happy Was the Occasion*: Clarksville, Arkansas," http://livingnewdeal.berkeley.edu/projects/post-office-mural-happy-occasion-clarksville-ar/.

13. Purser Studio, "Biography: Stuart Purser," http://www.purserstudio.com/sBio.html.

14. Falk, *Who's Who in American Art*, Vol. I, 365.

15. Purser Studio, "Biography: Stuart Purser," http://www.purserstudio.com/sBio.html.

16. Worldcat.org, "Purser, Stuart," http://www.worldcat.org/search?qt=worldcat_org_all&q=purser%2C+stuart.

17. Purser Studio, "Biography: Stuart Purser," http://www.purserstudio.com/sBio.html.

18. Worldcat.org, "Purser, Stuart," http://www.worldcat.org/search?qt=worldcat_org_all&q=purser%2C+stuart.

19. Stuart Purser, *The Drawing Handbook*, http://www.ebay.com/itm/The-Drawing-Handbook-/360982827937?pt=US_Nonfiction_Book&hash=item540c40d3a1.

20. Purser Studio, "Biography: Stuart Purser," http://www.purserstudio.com/sBio.html.

21. Worldcat.org, "Purser, Stuart," http://www.worldcat.org/search?qt=worldcat_org_all&q=purser%2C+stuart.

22. Purser Studio, "Biography: Stuart Purser," http://www.purserstudio.com/sBio.html.

ENTERPRISE

1. Coffee County (Alabama) Heritage Book Committee, *The Heritage of Coffee County, Alabama* (Clanton, AL: Heritage, 2002), Vol. 16, 4–5.

2. "Alabama: The Heart of the New Industrial South," *Compton's Pictured Encyclopedia and Fact-Index* (Chicago: F.E. Compton, 1948), Vol. I, 98.

3. "Boll Weevil," *Encyclopaedia Britannica, Encyclopaedia Britannica Online Academic Edition*, Encyclopædia Britannica Inc., 2014, Web, 07 Aug. 2014, http://0-www.britannica.com.marie.converse.edu/EBchecked/topic/72178/boll-weevil.

4. "Art Trails in Alabama Public Art: Continuing the Trail," *Alabama Arts* XXI, no. 2, 32–33.

5. Futility Closet, "A Virtue of Necessity," http://www.futilitycloset.com/2011/07/30/a-virtue-of-necessity.

6. "Enterprise, Alabama: Boll Weevil Monument," http://www.roadsideamerica.com/tip/19.

7. "Post: This Belongs in a Museum," http://thisbelongsinamuseum.com/post/55184490477/in-enterprise-alabama-one-will-find-a-walmart.

8. Sue Bridwell Beckham, *Depression Post Office Murals and Southern Culture: A Gentle Reconstruction* (Baton Rouge: Louisiana State University Press, 1989), 289.

9. Mayor Kenneth Boswell, "Enterprise, Alabama," http://www.enterpriseal.gov/.

10. Boswell, "Enterprise, Alabama," http://www.enterpriseal.gov/.

11. "Enterprise Public Library: General Information," http://www.enterpriselibrary.org/Default.asp?ID=480.

12. Lee Eudon Holland, Laurie A. Pallazolo, and Danny Kanat, *Boiled Peanuts and Buckeyes: A Memoir-Novel* (Northville, MI: Ferne Press, 2006), vi.

13. Holland, Pallazolo, and Kanat, *Boiled Peanuts and Buckeyes*, v.

14. Holland, Pallazolo, and Kanat, *Boiled Peanuts and Buckeyes*, vi.

15. Holland, Pallazolo, and Kanat, *Boiled Peanuts and Buckeyes*, back cover.

16. Beckham, *Depression Post Office Murals and Southern Culture*, 289–289.

17. Futility Closet, "A Virtue of Necessity," http://www.futilitycloset.com/2011/07/30/a-virtue-of-necessity.

18. Holland, Pallazolo, and Kanat, *Boiled Peanuts and Buckeyes*, vii.

19. Beckham, *Depression Post Office Murals and Southern Culture*, 289–293.

20. Jennifer Medina, "Paul T. Arlt, Artist and Cartoonist, 91, Dies," *New York Times,* September 26, 2005, http://www.nytimes.com/2005/09/26/nyregion/26arlt.html?_r=0; *Who's Who in American Art* by Peter Hastings Falk, however, gives Paul Arlt's birthplace as Arlington Virginia. Falk, "Paul Theodore Arlt," *Who's Who in American Art*, Vol. I, 18.

21. Medina, "Paul T. Arlt, Artist and Cartoonist, 91, Dies."

22. Joe Holley, "Longtime Washington Artist, Political Cartoonist Paul Arlt Dies," *Washington Post,* Friday, September 23, 2005, http://www.washingtonpost.com/wp-dyn/content/article/2005/09/22/AR2005092202047.html.

23. "Exhibition Artists: Paul Arlt," Smithsonian Institution Traveling Exhibition Service, NASA/ART, 1. Files of Jimmy S. Emerson.

24. Medina, "Paul T. Arlt, Artist and Cartoonist, 91, Dies."

25. Holley, "Longtime Washington Artist, Political Cartoonist Paul Arlt Dies"; "Paul T. Arlt, Artist and Cartoonist, 91, Dies."

26. "Rollins University Alumnae Connections: In Memoriam," http://www.hollins.edu/alumnae/archive_2007.htm.

27. The DC Voter, *League of Women Voters of the District of Columbia* 77, no. 6 (June 2001), http://www.dcwatch.com/lwvdc/lwv0106.htm.

28. "Municipal Arts Society of New York City," http://www.mas.org/summitnyc/speakers/ronay-menschel/.

29. "Frank H.T. Rhodes Exemplary Alumni Service Award," http://ezramagazine.cornell.edu/Update/July13/EU.FHTR.awards.html.

30. *An Exhibition of Art from the Marine Corps Museum: 75 Years of Marine Corps Aviation—A Tribute* (exhibit brochure; distribution is unlimited). http://www.marines.mil/Portals/59/Publications/75%20Years%20of%20Marine%20Corps%20Aviation%20-%20A%20Tribute%20%20PCN%2019000416100_1.pdf.

31. Falk, "Paul Theodore Arlt," *Who's Who in American Art*, Vol. I, 18.

EUTAW

1. Patricia Hoskins Morton, "Greene County," http://www.encyclopediaofalabama.org/face/Article.jsp?id=h-1329.

2. Oliver Perry Chitwood, Frank Lawrence Owsley, and H. C. Nixon, *The United States from Colony to World Power* (New York: D. Van Nostrand, 1949), 121.

3. Natalie D. Saba, "Nathanael Greene (1742–1786)," *New Georgia Encyclopedia*, 11 August 2013, Web, 9 August 2014.

4. Claire Wilson, "Eutaw," http://www.encyclopediaofalabama.org/face/Article.jsp?id=h-2501.

5. Michael Kammen, *Robert Gwathmey: The Life and Art of a Passionate Observer* (Chapel Hill: University of North Carolina, 1999), 29.

6. "Speaking of Pictures: This Is Mural America for Rural Americans," *Life,* December 4, 1939, 12.

7. Kammen, *Robert Gwathmey*, 29.

8. Charles K. Piehl, "The Eutaw Mural and Southern Art of Robert Gwathmey," *The Alabama Review*, April 1992, 108.

9. Alabama Moments from American History, "New Deal Art in Alabama Post Offices and Federal Buildings: Eutaw," http://www.alabamamoments.alabama.gov/sec49det.html.

10. Kammen, *Robert Gwathmey*, 30.

11. Kammen, *Robert Gwathmey*, 28.

12. Piehl, "The Eutaw Mural and Southern Art of Robert Gwathmey," 130.

13. Piehl, "The Eutaw Mural and Southern Art of Robert Gwathmey," 130.

14. Piehl, "The Eutaw Mural and Southern Art of Robert Gwathmey," 131.

15. Piehl, "The Eutaw Mural and Southern Art of Robert Gwathmey," 131.

16. Anita Price Davis. *North Carolina During the Great Depression* (Jefferson, NC: McFarland, 2003), 223–241.

17. Kammen, *Robert Gwathmey: The Life and Art of a Passionate Observer*, 4.

18. Arts Connected, "ArtsNet Minnesota: Identity: Robert Gwathmey," ArtsNet Minnesota: Identity: Robert Gwathmey, Arts Net Minnesota, n.d., Web, 05 May 2013.

19. "Biography for Robert Gwathmey," *Archives of AskART*, http://www.askart.com/AskART/artists/biography.aspx?artist=23904.

20. Kammen, *Robert Gwathmey: The Life and Art of a Passionate Observer*, 13.

21. Lauren A. Zelaya, "Robert Gwathmey (1903–1988)," http://www.caldwellgallery.com/bios/gwathmey_biography.html.

22. Falk, *Who's Who in American Art*, Vol. I, 253.

23. Kammen, *Robert Gwathmey: The Life and Art of a Passionate Observer*, 28–30.

24. Kammen, *Robert Gwathmey: The Life and Art of a Passionate Observer*, 19.

25. Fred A. Bernstein, "Charles Gwathmey, Architect Loyal to Aesthetics of High Modernism, Dies at 71," *New York Times*, August 9, 2009, http://www.nytimes.com/2009/08/05/arts/design/05gwathmey.html?scp=2&_r=0.

26. Zelaya, "Robert Gwathmey (1903–1988)."

27. Piehl, "The Eutaw Mural and the Southern Art of Robert Gwathmey," 114–115.

28. Piehl, "The Eutaw Mural and the Southern Art of Robert Gwathmey," 118, 130.

29. "Robert Gwathmey," http:en.wikipedia.org/wiki/Robert_Gwathmey.

30. "Robert Gwathmey," http:en.wikipedia.org/wiki/Robert_Gwathmey.

31. Harold Feinstein, photog., "Up-date on the Photo League Negatives: Rosalie Gwathmey Shares Her Work at a Photo League Meeting, 1947," http://haroldfeinstein.com/up-date-on-the-photo-league-negatives/.

32. Erika Duncan, "ENCOUNTERS; 'I Just Quit,' Rosalie Gwathmey Said. And She Walked Away," *New York Times*, September 4, 1994, http://www.nytimes.com/1994/09/04/nyregion/encounters-i-just-quit-rosalie-gwathmey-said-and-she-walked-away.html.

33. Erika Duncan, "ENCOUNTERS; 'I Just Quit,' Rosalie Gwathmey Said. And She Walked Away."

34. "Rosalie Gwathmey: Photographed Blacks in 1940s," Obituary: February 25, 2001, http://articles.latimes.com/2001/feb/25/local/me-30234.

35. Margarett Loke, "Rosalie Gwathmey, 92, a Photographer of Southern Black Life," *New York Times*, February 16, 2001, http://www.nytimes.com/2001/02/16/arts/rosalie-gwathmey-92-a-photographer-of-southern-black-life.html?module=Search&mabReward=relbias%3Aw.

FAIRFIELD

1. Some articles refer to the artist and wife of Frank Hartley Anderson as Mary; others refer to her as Martha. Her grave marker uses Martha Fort Anderson. We will use the names interchangeably as per the source.

2. Hugh C. Bailey, "Alabama," *Merit Students Encyclopedia, Volume 1*, 276–279.

3. Christopher Maloney, "Fairfield," *Encyclopedia of Alabama*, http://www.encyclopediaofalabama.org/face/Article.jsp?id=h-3142.

4. "City Data for Fairfield, Alabama," http://www.city-data.com/city/Fairfield-Alabama.html.

5. Bailey, "Alabama," 276–279.

6. Beckham, *Depression Post Office Murals and Southern Culture*, 314.

7. "Artists & Their Work in *The Birmingham Scene* Exhibition," *The Birmingham Historical Society Newsletter*, November 2011, 1–2.

8. "New Deal Art During the Great Depression," http://www.wpamurals.com/.

9. "New Deal Art in Alabama Post Offices

and Federal Buildings," http://www.alabama moments.alabama.gov/sec49det.html.

10. "Frank Hartley Anderson (1890–1947)," *Imprinting the South: Works on Paper from the Collection of Lynn Barstis Williams and Stephen J. Goldfarb*, http://www.tfaoi.com/aa/9aa/9aa 236.htm.

11. "New Deal Art in Alabama Post Offices and Federal Buildings," http://www.alabama moments.alabama.gov/sec49det.html.

12. Marling, *Wall-to-Wall America*, 172–174.

13. Marling, *Wall-to-Wall America*, 174.

14. "New Deal Art in Alabama Post Offices and Federal Buildings," http://www.alabama moments.alabama.gov/sec49det.html.

15. "The New Deal in Jefferson County: An Alphabet Soup," http://www.bponline.org/re sources/exhibits/new_deal/murals/Fairfield/ga ll.

16. Falk, *Who's Who in American Art*, Vol. I, 14.

17. "Frank Hartley Anderson," http://www. bhamwiki.com/w/Frank_Hartley_Anderson.

18. Falk, *Who's Who in American Art*, Vol. I, 14.

19. "Frank Hartley Anderson," http://www. bhamwiki.com/w/Frank_Hartley_Anderson.

20. Beckham, *Depression Post Office Murals and Southern Culture*, 83.

21. Edward Rowan to Frank Hartley Anderson, January 16, 1936, in Jackson, Mississippi, file, as cited by Beckham, *Depression Post Office Murals and Southern Culture*, 83.

22. William H. Gandy to Edward Rowan, June 14, 1938, June 19, 1938, and June 27, 1938, all in Jackson, Mississippi, file, as cited by Beckham, *Depression Post Office Murals and Southern Culture*, 84.

23. Beckham, *Depression Post Office Murals and Southern Culture*, 85.

24. "Frank Hartley Anderson," http://www. bhamwiki.com/w/Frank_Hartley_Anderson.

25. "Artists & Their Work in *The Birmingham Scene* Exhibition," *The Birmingham Historical Society Newsletter*, November 2011, 1–2.

26. Information courtesy Ron Glaze, current owner of the Fort home.

FORT PAYNE

1. Albert Burton Moore, *History of Alabama* (Tuscaloosa: Alabama Book Store, 1951), 32–33.

2. Moore, *History of Alabama*, 32–33.

3. Dale Cox, "Fort Payne, Alabama." http:// www.exploresouthernhistory.com/fortpayne. html.

4. "Decline of the Hosiery Industry," http:// blog.al.com/huntsville-times-business/2011/04/ the_decline_of_the_hosiery_ind.html.

5. Information from Jimmy S. Emerson.

6. James Ray Kuykendall, and Elizabeth S. Howard, "Reminiscing About DeKalb's Special People ... the Post Office Mural," *The DeKalb Advertiser*, June 5, 2003, 8–9.

7. Kuykendall and Howard, "Reminiscing About DeKalb's Special People," 8–9.

8. Kuykendall and Howard, "Reminiscing About DeKalb's Special People," 8–9.

9. Kuykendall and Howard, "Reminiscing About DeKalb's Special People," 8–9.

10. Beckham, *Depression Post Office Murals and Southern Culture*, 120–121.

11. Kukykendall and Howard, "Reminiscing About DeKalb's Special People," 8; "The Living New Deal: States and Cities: Alabama," http:// livingnewdeal.berkeley.edu/projects/old-post-office-hunt-hall-mural-harvest-fort-payne-mural-fort-payne-al/.

12. "Change of View: Fabric Designer, Harwood Steiger," http://madpatterdesign.blog spot.com/search?q=steiger.

13. "Harwood Steiger (1900–1980)," *Ask-ART: Worldwide Edition*. Information provided by Covington Fine Arts Gallery, Inc., http:// askart.com/AskART/artists/biography/aspx?ar tist=100147.

14. "Massachusetts, Town and Vital Records, 1620–1988," http://search.ancestry.com.

15. Cynthia deVillemaretta, "Fabric Designer, Harwood Steiger," http://madpatterde sign.blogspot.com/2013/02/fabric-designer-harwood-steiger.html.

16. "Tubac: Santa Cruz County, Arizona," http://visittubac.com/; "Southern Arizona's Colony & The First European Settlement in Arizona: Tubac: Founded 1752," http://www.tub acarizona.com/.

17. Elizabeth R. Brownell, *They Lived in Tubac* (Tucson: Westernlore Press, 1986), 172.

18. Brownell, *They Lived in Tubac*, 172.

19. Brownell, *They Lived in Tubac*, 184.

20. Brownell. *They Lived in Tubac*, 197.

21. Brownell. *They Lived in Tubac*, 172.

22. "Discovering Harwood Steiger," http:// gotvintageshops.blogspot.com/2014/02/vin tage-fabrics-steiger.html.

23. "Harwood Steiger (1900–1980)," *Ask-ART: Worldwide Edition*. Information provided by Covington Fine Arts Gallery, Inc., http:// askart.com/AskART/artists/biography/aspx?ar tist=100147.

24. Shaw Kinsley, *Images of America: TUBAC* (Charleston, SC: Arcadia, 2009), 78.

GUNTERSVILLE

1. "Yours Truly: December 21, 2006," http://yourstrulyforever.blogspot.com/2006/12/some-more-family-history.html.

2. Frank Roylance, "A Family Tree's American Tale," John Gunter Family Tree," http://articles.baltimoresun.com/2001-03-11/topic/0103100129_1_john-gunter-augustus-cherokee.

3. Economic Development Council, "Marshall County," http://www.marshallteam.org/community-profiles/city-of-guntersville.html.

4. Elizabeth Ann Brown, *National Register of Historic Places Registration Form: Guntersville Post Office Building*, July 7, 2010.

5. *Advertiser Democrat*, November 29, 1933, as cited by Brown, *National Register of Historic Places Registration Form*.

6. Brown, *National Register of Historic Places Registration Form*.

7. Robin Conn, "Cornerstone of the Guntersville Post Office," http://photos.al.com/huntsville-times/2010/09/guntersville_post_office_3.html.

8. Brown, *National Register of Historic Places Registration Form*.

9. Brown, *National Register of Historic Places Registration Form*.

10. "Colonial Revival Style: 1880–1960," http://www.portal.state.pa.us/portal/server.pt/community/late_19th_early_20th_century_revival_period/2390/colonial_revival_style/294769.

11. "Postoffice Dedication to Be Monday; Public Will Be Given Opportunity to Inspect Entire $115,000 Building," *The Guntersville Gleam*, May 29, 1941, 1, 3.

12. Alabama Historical Commission, Preservation Report, U.S. Post Office, Guntersville, Marshall County: *Indians Receiving Gifts from the Spanish*, November-December 2010.

13. Beckham, *Depression Post Office Murals and Southern Culture*, 314.

14. "WPA Murals," http://wpamurals.org/florida.html.

15. Brown, *National Register of Historic Places Registration Form*.

16. Beckham, *Depression Post Office Murals and Southern Culture*, 305.

17. "Art Deco," *Encyclopædia Britannica*, retrieved from http://www.britannica.com/EBchecked/topic/36505/Art-Deco.

18. "Post Office Murals: Miami Beach, Florida," http://livingnewdeal.berkeley.edu/artists/charles-russell-hardman/. (See more on Jesup in Gloria Jahoda's *The Trail of Tears: The Story of the American Indian Removals 1813–1855* [New York: Holt, Rinehart and Winston, 1975].)

19. Beckham, *Depression Post Office Murals and Southern Culture*, 75–76.

20. "Post Office Murals: Miami Beach, Florida," http://livingnewdeal.berkeley.edu/artists/charles-russell-hardman/. (See more on Jesup in Gloria Jahoda's *The Trail of Tears: The Story of the American Indian Removals 1813–1855* [New York: Holt, Rinehart and Winston, 1975].)

21. "Postoffice Dedication to Be Monday; Public Will Be Given Opportunity to Inspect Entire $115,000 Building," *The Guntersville Gleam*, May 29, 1941, 1, 3; "PO Mural Shows First White Men to Come Here," *Time*, December 10, 1947.

22. Falk, *Who's Who in American Art*, Vol. I, 262.

23. "Charles Russell Hardman," http://www.findagrave.com.

HALEYVILLE

1. "Haleyville City: A Community of Excellence," http://www.haleyvillechamber.org/pages/history.html.

2. "City of Haleyville, Alabama," http://www.nacolg.com/Community_Planning/Documents/HaleyvilleComprehensivePlan_5-16-08.pdf.

3. "Cumberland Plateau," *Encyclopaedia Britannica, Encyclopaedia Britannica Online Academic Edition*, Encyclopædia Britannica, 2014, Web. 26 Aug. 2014.

4. Frank Ahnert, "Cumberland Plateau," *Merit Students Encyclopedia* (Springfield, OH: Crowell-Collier Educational Corporation, 1969), Vol. 5, 379.

5. "The History of 911 Emergency Calls," http://inventors.about.com/library/inventors/bl911.htm.

6. Hollis Holbrook to Edward Rowan on March 29, 1940, as quoted by Beckham, *Depression Post Office Murals and Southern Culture*, 144.

7. Holbrook to Rowan, March 29, 1940, Beckham, *Depression Post Office Murals and Southern Culture*, 144.

8. "William B. Bankhead National Forest," http://www.stateparks.com/william_b_bankhead_national_forest_in_alabama.html.

9. Alabama Department of Archives and History, "New Deal Art in Alabama Post Offices and Federal Buildings: Haleyville," http://www.alabamamoments.alabama.gov/sec49det.html.

10. Beckham, *Depression Post Office Murals and Southern Culture*, 146.

11. Hollis Holbrook to Edward Rowan on September 4, 1940, as quoted by Beckham,

Depression Post Office Murals and Southern Culture, 146.

12. "Mural Completed at Post Office," Clipping from September 26, 1940, sent by Hollis Holbrook to Edward Rowan, as quoted by Beckham, *Depression Post Office Murals and Southern Culture*, 146.

13. Marlene Park and Gerald E. Markowitz, *Democratic Vistas: Post Offices and Public Art in the New Deal* (Philadelphia: Temple University Press, 1984), 63.

14. Haleyville Chamber of Commerce, "Haleyville City: A Community of Excellence," http://www.haleyvillechamber.org/pages/history.html.

15. Falk, *Who's Who in American Art*, Vol. I, 262.

16. Meghan Navarro, "Indians at the Post Office: Native Themes in New Deal-Era Murals," http://npm.si.edu/indiansatthepostoffice/mural16.html/.

17. "New Deal/WPA Art Project," http://www.wpamurals.com/.

18. C.W. Short and R. Stanley-Brown, *Public Buildings: Architecture Under the Public Works Administration: 1933 to 1939* (Washington, D.C.: U.S. Government Printing Office, 1939), 338.

19. Park and Markowitz, *Democratic Vistas*, 70.

20. Navarro, "Indians at the Post Office: Native Themes in New Deal-Era Murals."

21. "Controversial Post Office Mural to Be Restored," *Natick Bulletin & Tab (Massachusetts)*, September 9, 2007. (See more at http://www.postalreporternews.net/category/murals/#sthash.MV4wig4j.dpuf.

22. Edward Rowan to Hollis Holbrook, University of Florida, School of Architecture, September 26, 1939.

Hartselle

1. "History of Hartselle." http://www.hartsellechamber.com/.

2. "Depot Days Festival Rolls into Hartselle September 20." *49 County News*, August 27, 2014.

3. "History of Hartselle," http://www.hartsellechamber.com/.

4. "History of Hartselle," http://www.hartsellechamber.com/.

5. "Depot Days Festival Rolls into Hartselle September 20." *49 County News*, August 27, 2014.

6. "Hartselle, Alabama," *Rand McNally World Atlas*, 46.

7. "Hartselle, Alabama," http://en.wikipedia.org/wiki/Hartselle,_Alabama.

8. "Latitude 34 North," http://www.lat34

north.com/historicmarkersal/MarkerDefinition.cfm.

9. "Hartselle, Alabama," http://en.wikipedia.org/wiki/Hartselle,_Alabama.

10. Milt Dolinger, "How CSX Got Its Name," *Trains*, May 1, 2006. (Online at http://trn.trains.com/sitecore/content/Home/Railroad%20Reference/Freight%20Railroads/2006/05/How%20CSX%20got%20its%20name.aspx?sc_lang=en.)

11. "Siding," *Webster's New Unabridged Dictionary* (New York: Dorset & Baber, 1979), 1686.

12. "Alabama Railfan," http://www.alabamarailfan.com/railfanning.php?location=cullman.

13. Mayer, *A Dictionary of Art Terms and Techniques*, 322.

14. Letter from Lee R. Warthen to Postmaster of the Hartselle Post Office, May 20, 1941. Courtesy Kathryn Smith, granddaughter of Lee R. Warthen.

15. Park and Markowitz, *Democratic Vistas*, 85.

16. "Harry S. Truman Federal Building, Washington, DC," http://www.gsa.gov/portal/ext/html/site/hb/category/25431/actionParameter/exploreByBuilding/buildingId/700.

17. Mayer, *A Dictionary of Art Terms and Techniques*, 322–323.

18. Park and Markowitz. *Democratic Vistas*, 85.

19. "Lee Roland Warthen," http://www.findagrave.com.

20. Information courtesy Kathi Lee Smith.

21. "Ferol Sibley Warthen; Kathi Smith," *Provincetown Art Guide*, http://provincetownartguide.com/2008/article3.htm.

22. "Ferol Sibley Warthen and the Provincetown Print," March 19, 2010, http://anurbancottage.blogspot/2010/03/ferol-sibley-warthen-and-provincetown-print; Falk, *Who's Who in American Art*, Vol. I, 660.

23. Taos and Santa Fe Painters, "Taos Painters: Bror Julius Olsson Nordfeldt," http://www.bjonordfeldtpaintings.com/.

24. "Ferol Sibley Warthen; Kathi Smith," *Provincetown Art Guide*, http://provincetownartguide.com/2008/article3.htm.

25. "Ferol Sibley Warthen and the Provincetown Print," March 19, 2010.

http://anurbancottage.blogspot.com/2010/03/ferol-sibley-warthen-and-provincetown-print; Falk, *Who's Who in American Art*, Vol. I, 660.

26. Kathryn Lee Smith, "Contemporary White Line Prints," http://www.kathrynleesmithwhitelineprints.com/resume.htm.

27. "Kathryn Lee Smith," *Provincetown Art Registry*, http://www.provincetownartistregistry.com/S/smith_kathi.html.

28. "Lee Roland Warthen," http://www.ask art.com/AskART/artists/search/Search_Grid. aspx?searchtype=BOOKS&artist=108382.

HUNTSVILLE

1. "About Huntsville," http://www.hunts villeal.gov/about/index.php.
2. Rogers, Ward, Atkins, and Flynt, *Alabama*, 63–66.
3. "About Huntsville," http://www.hunts villeal.gov/about/index.php.
4. "Best Cities: It's All About Jobs," http://www.kiplinger.com/article/business/T012-C000-S002-best-cities-it-s-all-about-jobs. html.
5. National Trust for Historic Preservation, "America's Dozen Distinctive Destinations for 2010," http://www.preservationnation.org/mag azine/2010/march-april/2010_ddd.html.
6. Chitwood, Owsley, and Nixon. *The United States from Colony to World Power*, 783.
7. "About Huntsville," http://www.hunts villeal.gov/news/Huntsville_Community_In formation.pdf.
8. Beckham, *Depression Post Office Murals and Southern Culture*, 300–301.
9. "U.S. Post Office and Courthouse, Huntsville, AL," http://www.gsa.gov/portal/ext/html/ site/hb/category/25431/actionParameter/ex ploreByBuilding/buildingId/668.
10. There are differences in the given date of construction of the U.S. Post Office and Courthouse in Huntsville, Alabama, according to sources that the writer consulted. For instance, "U.S. Post Office and Courthouse, Huntsville, AL" gives the date as 1936. (http://www.gsa.gov/portal/ext/html/site/hb/cate gory/25431/actionParameter/exploreByBuild ing/buildingId/668). The article "Focus: United States Court House and Post Office, Huntsville, Alabama" gives the date as 1932 (http://image1. nps.gov:9001/StyleServer/calcrgn?cat=NRHP& item=Text/81000129.djvu&style=nps/FOCUS-DJview.xsl&wid=640&hei=480&oif=jpeg&pro ps=item(SUMMARY,COPYRIGHT),cat(Name) &page=0).
11. Francis D. K. Ching, *Architecture, Form, Space and Order* (Hoboken, NJ: John Wiley, 2012), 130.
12. Ching, *Architecture, Form, Space and Order*, 268.
13. "U.S. Post Office and Courthouse, Huntsville, AL," http://www.gsa.gov/portal/ext/html/ site/hb/category/25431/actionParameter/ex ploreByBuilding/buildingId/668.
14. "Louis A. Simon," http://www.living places.com/people/louis-a-simon.html.

15. "U.S. Post Office and Courthouse, Huntsville, AL," http://www.gsa.gov/portal/ext/html/ site/hb/category/25431/actionParameter/ex ploreByBuilding/buildingId/668.
16. National Park Service, "Focus: United States Court House and Post Office, Huntsville, Alabama," http://image1.nps.gov:9001/Style Server/calcrgn?cat=NRHP&item=Text/810001 29.djvu&style=nps/FOCUS-DJview.xsl&wid= 640&hei=480&oif=jpeg&props=item(SUM MARY,COPYRIGHT),cat(Name)&page=0.
17. "U.S. Post Office and Courthouse, Huntsville, AL," http://www.gsa.gov/portal/ext/html/ site/hb/category/25431/actionParameter/ex ploreByBuilding/buildingId/668.
18. Alabama Department of Archives and History, "New Deal Art in Alabama Post Offices and Federal Buildings: Huntsville, Alabama," http://www.alabamamoments.alabama. gov/sec49det.html.
19. Alabama Department of Archives and History, "New Deal Art in Alabama Post Offices and Federal Buildings: Huntsville, Alabama," http://www.alabamamoments.alabama. gov/sec49det.html.
20. Lonn Taylor, "Xavier Gonzalez: Muralist in the Big Bend," *Cenizo Journal* 2, no. 3 (Third Quarter 2010), 10.
21. Falk, *Who's Who in American Art*, Vol. I, 237.
22. "Xavier Gonzalez (1918–1993)," http:// www.daviddike.com/artists/181-gonzalez-xav ier.html.
23. Taylor, "Xavier Gonzalez," 11.
24. Taylor, "Xavier Gonzalez," 11.
25. Beckham, *Depression Post Office Murals and Southern Culture*, 303.
26. Beckham, *Depression Post Office Murals and Southern Culture*, 301.
27. Taylor, "Xavier Gonzalez," 11.
28. Kate Bruce, "Ethel Edwards," *KnowLA Encyclopedia of Louisiana*, David Johnson, ed. Louisiana Endowment for the Humanities, 2010–. Article published September 12, 2012. http://www.knowla.org/entry/1245/.
29. Edith Edwards Gonzalez obituary, *New Orleans Times-Picayune*, January 24, 1999.
30. "Xavier Gonzalez (1918–1993)," http:// www.daviddike.com/artists/181-gonzalez-xav ier.html.

LUVERNE

1. "Friendliest City in the South," http:// www.luverne.org/history.asp.
2. "ePODUNK Home Towns Index," http:// www.epodunk.com/top10/home_towns/towns. html.

3. "Crenshaw County Profile," http://www.luverne.org/profile.asp.

4. "About Luverne, Alabama," https://www.facebook.com/pages/Luverne-Alabama/108638815826702#.

5. "Profile for Luverne, Alabama, AL," http://www.epodunk.com/cgi-bin/genInfo.php?locIndex=12051.

6. "City of Luverne: Educational Attainment," http://www.luverne.org/profile.asp.

7. "Festival and Event Calendar," http://alabama.travel/upcoming-events/search?q=Luverne.

8. "The Alabama Properties Listed on the National Register of Historic Places," http://www.preserveala.org/pdfs/TAX_CREDIT/New_Folder/List_NR_Properties_n_AL.pdf.

9. "Harry S. Truman Federal Building, Washington, DC," http://www.gsa.gov/portal/ext/html/site/hb/category/25431/actionParameter/exploreByBuilding/buildingId/700.

10. "Harry S. Truman Federal Building, Washington, DC."

11. "New Deal Art in Alabama Post Offices and Federal Buildings," http://www.alabamamoments.state.al.us/sec49det.html.

12. "Texas Cotton Gin Museum," http://www.cottonginmuseum.org/museum.htm.

13. Askart.com erroneously, according to relative Sarah Getz, lists *Arthur Kimmig Getz's* name as *Arthur Kimmel Getz.* http://www.askart.com/askart/artist.aspx?artist=69724.

14. "Arthur Getz," http://en.wikipedia.org/wiki/Arthur_Getz.

15. Jim Noles. "An Unlikely Canvas." *Alabama Heritage* 75 (Winter 2005), 42–43.

16. "Arthur Getz, 82, Magazine Illustrator," *New York Times*, January 22, 1996, http://www.nytimes.com/1996/01/22/arts/arthur-getz-82-magazine-illustrator.html?module=Search&mabReward=relbias%3Ar.

17. "Arthur Getz," http://en.wikipedia.org/wiki/Arthur_Getz.

18. Noles, "An Unlikely Canvas," 44.

19. "New Deal Art in Alabama Post Offices and Federal Buildings," http://www.alabamamoments.alabama.gov/sec49det.html.

20. "Arthur Getz," http://en.wikipedia.org/wiki/Arthur_Getz.

21. "Getz: *The New Yorker* Covers," http://www.getzart.com/nycovers.htm.

MONROEVILLE

1. "Monroeville, Alabama," http://www.city-data.com/cityw/Monroeville-AL.html.

2. Monroeville/Monroe County Chamber of Commerce, *Monroeville Walking Tour.* A copy of the brochure is at http://www.monroecountyal.com/Walking%20tours2.htm.

3. *Harvesting* by Arthur Leroy Bairnsfather in *Monroeville Walking Tour.* http://www.ruralswalabama.org/attractions/harvesting-mural-at-monroeville-alabama-post-office/.

4. Chamber of Commerce, *Monroeville/Monroe County* (brochure), http://www.monroecountyal.com/literary-heritage.htm.

5. "Academy Awards Database: *To Kill a Mockingbird*," http://awardsdatabase.oscars.org/ampas_awards/DisplayMain.jsp?curTime=1403323106459.

6. Anita Price Davis, *MAX Notes: Harper Lee's* To Kill a Mockingbird (Piscataway, NJ: Research and Education Association, 1994), 1–4.

7. Chamber of Commerce, *Monroeville/Monroe County* (brochure) http://www.monroecountyal.com/literary-heritage.htm.

8. Monroeville/Monroe County Chamber of Commerce, "Monroeville Walking Tour Brochure." A copy of the brochure is online at http://www.monroecountyal.com/Walking%20tours2.htm.

9. George Thomas Jones, "Will the Real Mural Artist Please Stand Up," *Monroe Journal*, May 29, 2003.

10. Monroeville/Monroe County Chamber of Commerce, "Monroeville Walking Tour Brochure." A copy of the brochure is online at http://www.monroecountyal.com/Walking%20tours2.htm.

11. "Arthur L. Bairnsfather Will Paint Murals for Display in the Lobby of Post Office," *The Burlington Times-News,* Wednesday, July 12, 1939.

12. Courtesy Teresa Mansfield, manager, Community Affairs, Federal Building, Burlington, North Carolina.

13. Audrey Middleton Whitehurst, *Taste, Talent, and Tradition: Art and the New Deal in North Carolina*, unpublished thesis, School of Art, East Carolina University, August 1977, 187.

14. Ancestry.com, *Social Security Death Index* [database online]. Original data, Social Security Administration, *Social Security Death Index, Master File,* Social Security Administration.

15. "Loveliest," *Time* 31, no. 20 (May 16, 1938), 41.

16. www.monroecountyal.com/Walking%20tours2.html.

17. "New Deal Art in Alabama Post Offices and Federal Buildings," http://www.alabamamoments.alabama.gov/sec49det.html.

18. Contract WAlph-602 as cited by Whitehurst, *Taste, Talent, and Tradition,* 85.

19. Davis, *New Deal Art in North Carolina*, 45.

20. Davis, *New Deal Art in North Carolina*, 45.

21. Davis, *New Deal Art in North Carolina*, 45.

22. "United States Post Office: Burlington, North Carolina," http://en.wikipedia.org/wiki/United_States_Post_Office_(Burlington,_North_Carolina)#cite_note-nris–1.

23. Ancestry.com, *Social Security Death Index* [database online]. Original data, Social Security Administration, *Social Security Death Index, Master File*, Social Security Administration.

24. Falk, *Who's Who in American Art*, Vol. I, 28.

25. Davis, *New Deal Art in North Carolina*, 47.

MONTEVALLO

1. "Welcome to Historic Montevallo," http://www.hmdb.org/marker.asp?marker=37178.

2. "Early Days In and Around Montevallo," http://www.rootsweb.ancestry.com/~alshelby/Montevallo.html.

3. "Early Days In and Around Montevallo," http://www.rootsweb.ancestry.com/~alshelby/Montevallo.html.

4. "Montevallo, Alabama," http://www.city-data.com/city/Montevallo-Alabama.html.

5. "Welcome to Historic Montevallo," http://www.hmdb.org/marker.asp?marker=37178.

6. "Welcome to Historic Montevallo," http://www.hmdb.org/marker.asp?marker=37178.

7. "City of Montevallo: University of Montevallo," http://montevallo.homestead.com/universityofmontevallo.html.

8. Clark Hultquist and Carey Heatherly, *Images of America: Montevallo* (Mt. Pleasant, SC, 2011), 22.

9. "New Deal Art in Alabama Post Offices and Federal Buildings," http://www.alabamamoments.state.al.us/sec49det.html.

10. "New Deal Art in Alabama Post Offices and Federal Buildings," http://www.alabamamoments.state.al.us/sec49det.html.

11. "New Deal Art in Alabama Post Offices and Federal Buildings," http://www.alabamamoments.state.al.us/sec49det.html.

12. Letter to Section of Fine Arts, Public Buildings Administration, Federal Works Agency from William Sherrod McCall. Files of Jimmy S. Emerson.

13. William Sherrod McCall, *Early Settlers Weighing Cotton*: Mural Panel for Post Office, Montevallo, Alabama." Files of Jimmy S. Emerson.

14. William Sherrod McCall, *Early Settlers Weighing Cotton*: Mural Panel for Post Office, Montevallo, Alabama." Files of Jimmy S. Emerson.

15. Section of Fine Arts, "Mural Painting by William McCall," Files of Jimmy S. Emerson.

16. Letter to Section of Fine Arts, Public Buildings Administration, Federal Works Agency. Files of Jimmy S. Emerson.

17. Letter to Section of Fine Arts, Public Buildings Administration, Federal Works Agency. Files of Jimmy S. Emerson.

18. "Murals, Murals Artists," *Birmingham Historical Society Newsletter*, November 2010, 2.

19. "William Sherrod McCall," http://www.findagrave.com/cgi-bin/fg.cgi?page=pv&GRid=84374842&PIpi=55146060.

20. "Murals, Murals Artists," *Birmingham Historical Society Newsletter*, November 2010, 2.

ONEONTA

1. "Oneonta: A Small Town with Big Ideas," http://www.cityofoneonta.us/visitors/about-oneonta.html.

2. Blount County Historic Marker as photographed by Jimmy Emerson and shared at https://www.flickr.com/photos/auvet/30813141114/in/photolist-a2PSdD-5Ghxkq-a2PSdH-5Ghxkm.

3. "Oneonta: A Small Town with Big Ideas," http://www.cityofoneonta.us/visitors/about-oneonta.html.

4. "Oneonta: A Small Town with Big Ideas," http://www.cityofoneonta.us/visitors/about-oneonta.html.

5. "The Covered Bridge Trail in Blount County," http://co.blount.al.us/documents/Covered+Bridge+Trail.pdf.

6. Blount-Oneonta Chamber of Commerce, "Blount County Covered Bridge Festival," http://bocc.publishpath.com/covered-bridge-festival.

7. "Oneonta: A Small Town with Big Ideas," http://www.cityofoneonta.us/visitors/about-oneonta.html; Jimmy S. Emerson.

8. Alabama Historical Commission, "Alabama Register Property Information: 1995," http://preserveala.org/ARdigital/Blount/AL.BlountCounty.OneontaPostOffice.pdf.

9. "Oneonta," http://livingnewdeal.berkeley.edu/projects/old-post-office-mural-oneonta-al/.

10. Although the Berkeley website notes that

Browne had painted directly on the wall, "New Deal/WPA Art in Oneonta, Alabama" observed that Aldis Birdseye Browne, II, used oil on canvas for his mural.

11. Although "New Deal/WPA Art in Oneonta, Alabama" notes that Browne used oil on canvas for the mural, "Oneonta" (http://living newdeal.berkeley.edu/projects/old-post-office-mural-oneonta-al/) noted that Browne had painted directly on the wall.

12. Eddie Wayne Shell, *Evolution of the Alabama Agroecosystem: Always Keeping Up, but Never Catching Up* (Montgomery, AL: New-South Books, 2013), 4.

13. "Aldis Birdseye Browne, II," http://www.askart.com/AskART/artists/biography.aspx?artist=101498.

14. Opitz, *Mantle Fielding's Dictionary of American Painters, Sculptors, and Engravers*, 110.

15. "United States Coast Guard Academy: Hamilton Hall," http://www.cga.edu/campus2.aspx?id=504.

16. "Aldis Birdseye Browne, II," http://www.askart.com/AskART/artists/biography.aspx?artist=101498.

17. "Artist Records Coast Guard's Iceberg Patrol," *Life* (Vol. 8, no. 1, January 1, 1940), 30–31.

18. "Aldis Birdseye Browne, II," http://www.askart.com/AskART/artists/biography.aspx?artist=101498.

Opp

1. "Opp, Alabama," http://en.wikipedia.org/wiki/Opp,_Alabama.

2. "Mobile, Alabama," http://en.wikipedia.org/wiki/Mobile,_Alabama.

3. "Alabama's Highest and Lowest Elevations," http://www.classbrain.com/artstate/publish/AL_highest_lowest_elevation.shtml.

4. James P. Kaetz, "Opp." http://www.encyclopediaofalabama.org/face/Article.jsp?id=h-3160.

5. "City of Opp," http://www.cityofopp.com/Content/Default/1/28/0/about/our-history.html.

6. Rogers, Ward, Atkins, and Flynt, *Alabama*, 72.

7. "Opp, Alabama," http://en.wikipedia.org/wiki/Opp,_Alabama.

8. "Louisville and National Railroad," http://en.wikipedia.org/wiki/Louisville_and_Nashville_Railroad.

9. "Alabama and Florida Railway Company," http://hawkinsrails.net/shortlines/af/af.htm.

10. "Louisville and National Railroad," http://en.wikipedia.org/wiki/Louisville_and_Nashville_Railroad.

11. "Opp, Alabama," http://en.wikipedia.org/wiki/Opp,_Alabama.

12. "City of Opp: Rattlesnake Rodeo," http://www.cityofopp.com/Content/Default/7/7/0/rattlesnake-rodeo/rattlesnake-rodeo.html.

13. Center for Biological Diversity, "Outlawing Rattlesnake Rodeos," http://www.biologicaldiversity.org/campaigns/outlawing_rattlesnake_roundups/index.html.

14. Center for Biological Diversity, "Outlawing Rattlesnake Rodeos," http://www.biologicaldiversity.org/campaigns/outlawing_rattlesnake_roundups/index.html.

15. The Courthouse Lover, Cornerstone of Opp, Alabama, Post Office, as seen on Flickr.

16. "Alabama Moments in American History: Opp, Alabama," http://www.alabamamoments.alabama.gov/sec49det.html.

17. Mayer, *A Dictionary of Art Terms and Techniques*, 326.

18. Karen I. Peterson Henricks, "New Deal Art in Alabama Post Offices and Federal Buildings: Opp, Alabama." http://www.alabamamoments.alabama.gov/sec49det.html.

19. Information from Jimmy Emerson, Post Mark Collectors Club (PMCC) photo page.

20. Falk, *Who's Who in American Art*, Vol. I, 392.

21. William Weathersby, "Wandering Artist Relates Story of Colorful Career," *Times-Picayune* (New Orleans), June 27, 1937, 34.

22. "U.S. Army Engineer Base Yard," http://www.history.army.mil/html/artphoto/pripos/finalstages.html.

23. "Wind Talkers: Navajo Code Talkers in WWII—AMPHIBIOUS ASSAULT on SAIPAN," https://www.awesomestories.com/asset/view/AMPHIBIOUS-ASSAULT-on-SAIPAN-Wind-Talkers-Navajo-Code-Talkers-in-WWII, 9.

24. "Hans Mangelsdorf," http://www.askart.com/askart/m/hans_mangelsdorf/hans_mangelsdorf.aspx.

25. Falk, *Who's Who in American Art*, Vol. I, 392.

Ozark

1. "Ozark, Alabama," http://en.wikipedia.org/wiki/Ozark,_Alabama.

2. United States Census Bureau, "Census of Population and Housing."

3. United States Census Bureau, "Annual Estimates of the Resident Population: April 1, 2010 to July 1, 2013."

4. "Ozark, Alabama," http://en.wikipedia.org/wiki/Ozark,_Alabama.

5. "Community Data: Ozark and Dale County," http://ozarkalchamber.com/home/CommunityData.aspx.

6. "Muscogee," http://en.wikipedia.org/wiki/Muscogee.

7. "Ozark: The Heart of Dale County," http://www.villageprofile.com/alabama/ozark/history.html.

8. Photo of Ozark Post Office, 1936. Photographer Jimmy S. Emerson. Used with permission of the United States Postal Service. All rights reserved.

9. "FDR Library's List of New Deal Projects," http://viewshare.org/views/kcarter/fdr-library-list-of-new-deal-projects-part-1/.

10. "Dale County Sheriff's Office," http://daleso.com/contact.

11. Alabama Department of Archives and History, "New Deal Art in Alabama Post Offices and Federal Buildings," http://www.alabamamoments.state.al.us/sec49det.html.

12. "Galleries: John Kelly Fitzpatrick," http://www.encyclopediaofalabama.org/face/Galleries.jsp?id=e-104.

13. "New Deal Art in Alabama Post Offices and Federal Buildings," *Alabama Art: Art Trails in Alabama Public Arts* XXI, No. 2, 42.

14. James L. Noles, *Hearts of Dixie: Fifty Alabamians and the State They Called Home* (Birmingham, AL: Will Publishing, 2004), 65.

15. Johnson Collection, "John Kelly Fitzpatrick," http://thejohnsoncollection.org/john-kelly-fitzpatrick/.

16. Noles. *Hearts of Dixie* (Birmingham, AL: Will, 2004), page 66–67.

17. Johnson Collection, "John Kelly Fitzpatrick," http://thejohnsoncollection.org/john-kelly-fitzpatrick/.

18. Johnson Collection, "John Kelly Fitzpatrick," http://thejohnsoncollection.org/john-kelly-fitzpatrick/.

19. Johnson Collection, "John Kelly Fitzpatrick," http://thejohnsoncollection.org/john-kelly-fitzpatrick/.

20. Johnson Collection, "John Kelly Fitzpatrick," http://thejohnsoncollection.org/john-kelly-fitzpatrick/.

21. Johnson Collection, "John Kelly Fitzpatrick," http://thejohnsoncollection.org/john-kelly-fitzpatrick/.

22. Noles. *Hearts of Dixie*, 67.

23. "John Kelly Fitzpatrick: Wetumpka City Cemetery," http://www.findagrave.com.

24. Noles, *Hearts of Dixie*, 67.

Phenix City

1. "City of Phenix, Alabama: History," http://www.phenixcityal.us/Default.asp?ID=5&pg=History

2. "Phenix City," *Encyclopedia of Alabama*, http://www.encyclopediaofalabama.org/face/Article.jsp?id=h-2133.

3. John Lyles, *Images of America: Phenix City* (Charleston, SC: Arcadia, 2010), 113–114.

4. Jimmy S. Emerson, "Caption for Photograph of the Russell County Courthouse in Phenix City, Alabama," https://www.flickr.com/photos/auvet/3174824861/in/photolist-Heiem-6DAhTk-5QxNPF-bcFH2Z-HehmD.

5. "Phenix City," *Encyclopedia of Alabama*, http://www.encyclopediaofalabama.org/face/Article.jsp?id=h-2133.

6. Jordan McAlister, "1938 Phenix City Post Office," https://www.flickr.com/search/?q=phenix%20city%20post%20office%20alabama.

7. James Agee and Walker Evans, *Cotton Tenants* (Brooklyn: Melville House, 2013), 30.

8. Alabama Department of Archives and History, "New Deal Art in Alabama Post Offices and Federal Buildings," http://www.alabamamoments.state.al.us/sec49det.html.

9. Margaret Lynne Ausfeld, "John Kelly Fitzpatrick," *Encyclopedia of Alabama*, http://www.encyclopediaofalabama.org/face/Article.jsp?id=h-1155.

10. Noles, *Hearts of Dixie: Fifty Alabamians and the State They Called Home* (Birmingham, AL: Will, 2004), 66.

11. Ausfeld, "John Kelly Fitzpatrick."

12. Ausfeld, "John Kelly Fitzpatrick."

13. Noles, *Hearts of Dixie*, 67.

14. Noles, *Hearts of Dixie*.

Russellville

1. Patricia Hoskins Morton, "Franklin County," *Encyclopedia of Alabama*, http://eoatest.auburn.edu/drupal/article/h-1338#sthash.

2. "Franklin County: Our History," http://www.franklincountyal.org/our-history.html.

3. "Franklin County," *Encyclopedia of Alabama*, http://www.encyclopediaofalabama.org/face/Article.jsp?id=h-1338.

4. Morton, "Franklin County."

5. Dr. J. M. Clark to Hon. W. B. Bankhead, August 19, 1937, Russellville, Alabama, file, RG 121, NA, as quoted in Beckham, *Depression Post Office Murals and Southern Culture*, 280.

6. "New Deal Art in Alabama Post Offices and Federal Buildings: Russellville," http://www.alabamamoments.alabama.gov/sec49det.html.

7. Dr. J. M. Clark to Hon. W. B. Bankhead, August 19, 1937, Russellville, Alabama, file, RG 121, NA as quoted in Beckham, *Depression Post*

Office Murals and Southern Culture: A Gentle Reconstruction, 280.

8. Beckham, *Depression Post Office Murals and Southern Culture: A Gentle Reconstruction* (Baton Rouge: Louisiana State Press, 1989), 281.

9. Barry C. Cowan, "Conrad Albrizio," *Know LA: Encyclopedia of Louisiana*, http://www.knowla.org/entry/583/.

10. Edward Bruce and Forbes Watson, *Art in Federal Buildings. Volume I: Mural Designs, 1934–1936* (Washington, D.C.: Art in Federal Buildings Incorporated, 1936), 291.

11. Barry C. Cowan, "Conrad Albrizio," *Know LA: Encyclopedia of Louisiana*, http://www.knowla.org/entry/583/.

12. "Painting," *Compton's Pictured Encyclopedia and Fact-Index, Volume 11* (Chicago: F. E. Compton, 1948), 23–24.

13. Edward Bruce and Forbes Watson, *Art in Federal Building. Volume I: Mural Designs, 1934–1936* (Washington, D.C.: Art in Federal Buildings Incorporated, 1936), 291.

14. Barry C. Cowan, "Conrad Albrizio," *Know LA: Encyclopedia of Louisiana*, http://www.knowla.org/entry/583/.

15. Falk, *Who's Who in American Art*, Vol. I, 8.

16. Barry C. Cowan, "Conrad Albrizio," *Know LA: Encyclopedia of Louisiana*, http://www.knowla.org/entry/583/.

17. Falk, *Who's Who in American Art*, Vol. I, 8.

18. Mayer, *A Dictionary of Art Terms and Techniques*, 164.

19. Barry C. Cowan, "Conrad Albrizio," *Know LA: Encyclopedia of Louisiana*, http://www.knowla.org/entry/583/.

20. "Jeff," *Good Reads.com*, https://www.goodreads.com/topic/show/1090983-the-union-passenger-terminal-mural#comment_form.

SCOTTSBORO

1. "Scottsboro, Alabama," http://www.citytowninfo.com/places/alabama/Scottsboro.

2. "Scottsboro, Alabama," http://en.wikipedia.org/wiki/Scottsboro,_Alabama#Early_history.

3. John Robert Kennamer, Sr., *History of Jackson County Alabama* (Scottsboro: Jackson County Historical Association, 1935), 1–5. Reprinted 1993.

4. Josephine Lindsay Bass, July 26, 1996, condensation of John Robert Kennamer, Sr., *History of Jackson County Alabama*, 4–5.

5. Dan T. Carter, *Scottsboro: A Tragedy of the American South* (Baton Rouge: Louisiana State University Press, 1969), 11.

6. "Scottsboro, Alabama," http://www.citytowninfo.com/places/alabama/Scottsboro.

7. Kennamer, *History of Jackson County Alabama*, 1–5.

8. "Welcome to Scottsboro—Someplace Special," http://www.cityofscottsboro.com/.

9. Carter, *Scottsboro*, xiii–xxvii.

10. "Unclaimed Baggage Center," http://www.unclaimedbaggage.com/about/.

11. Gombach Group, "Louis A. Simon, Architect [1867–1958]," http://www.livingplaces.com/people/louis-a-simon.html.

12. "Save the Post Office," http://www.savethepostoffice.com/about.

13. Quote from Constance Ortmayer in "Post Office Reliefs: Scottsboro, Alabama," http://www.alabamamoments.state.al.us/sec49det.html.

14. Quote from Treasury Section of Fine Arts in "Post Office Reliefs: Scottsboro, Alabama," http://www.alabamamoments.state.al.us/sec49det.html.

15. "Constance Ortmayer (1902–1988): Renowned Artisan and Professor of Sculpture," http://lib.rollins.edu/olin/oldsite/archives/golden/Ortmayer.htm.

16. Opitz, *Mantle Fielding's Dictionary of American Painters, Sculptors, and Engravers*, 684–685.

17. Jeff Starck, "Cincinnati Music Center Coin Designer Has Varied Career," *Coin World*, March 29, 2010, 58.

18. Rollins College, "Faculty File 45-E for Constance Ortmayer." Courtesy Rollins College.

19. Files of Jimmy S. Emerson.

20. Rollins College, "Faculty File 45-E for Constance Ortmayer." Courtesy Rollins College.

21. Starck, "Cincinnati Music Center Coin Designer Has Varied Career," 58–80.

22. Dennis Henbeveld, "1936 Cincinnati Music Center Half Dollar," http://news.coinup date.com/cincinnati-music-center-half-dollar-4465/.

23. Henbeveld, "1936 Cincinnati Music Center Half Dollar."

24. Starck, "Cincinnati Music Center Coin Designer Has Varied Career," 56.

25. Opitz, *Mantle Fielding's Dictionary of American Painters, Sculptors, and Engravers*, 684–685.

TUSCUMBIA

1. Students of the University of North Alabama Computer Science and Information Systems Department, "Tuscumbia: History," http://cityoftuscumbia.org/?page_id=16.

2. Linda Thornton, "Tuscumbia, Alabama:

History," http://www.encyclopediaofalabama. org/.

3. Gombach Group, "Louis A. Simon, Architect [1867–1958]," http://www.livingplaces. com/people/louis-a-simon.html.

4. Brian A. McMillen, email to Anita Price Davis, May 12, 2014, 9:22 a.m.

5. McMillen, email.

6. Falk, *Who's Who in American Art*, Vol. I, 411.

7. McMillen, email, 9:53 a.m.

8. McMillen, email, 9:22 a.m.

9. McMillen, email, 9:22 a.m.

10. Nancy McGillicuddy, "Professor Finds Father's Lost Art in National Museum," *Pieces of Eight*, April 17, 2006, 1, 5. (The article is also available online at http://www.ecu.edu/cs-ad min/news/poe/406/foundart.cfm.)

11. McGillicuddy, "Professor Finds Father's Lost Art in National Museum."

Tuskegee

1. "Tuskegee, Alabama," *Encyclopedia of Alabama*, http://www.encyclopediaofalabama. org/face/Article.jsp?id=h-2051.

2. Information from Scenic South Card Company, Bessemer, Alabama 35020.

3. Booker Taliaferro Washington, biography.com, retrieved 7:10, Nov. 2, 2014, http:// www.biography.com/people/booker-t-washing ton-9524663.

4. Rogers, Ward, Atkins, and Flynt, *Alabama*, 330.

5. Susan M. Reverby, *Examining Tuskegee: The Infamous Syphilis Study and Its Legacy* (Chapel Hill: University of North Carolina Press, 2009), end pages.

6. William J. Clinton, "President William J. Clinton's Remarks," *Tuskegee's Truths Rethinking the Tuskegee Syphilis Study*, Susan M. Reverby, ed., 574–77 (Chapel Hill: University of North Carolina Press, 2000), and as cited in Reverby, *Examining Tuskegee*, 225, 347.

7. Commemorative Air Force, "Red Tail Squadron," http://www.redtail.org/.

8. "Tuskegee," http://www.encyclopediaof alabama.org/face/Article.jsp?id=h-2051.

9. City of Tuskegee, "Welcome to Tuskegee, Alabama," http://www.tuskegeealabama. gov/.

10. Dyann Robinson, www.tuskegeerep. com, email to Anita Price Davis, November 3, 2014.

11. Falk, *Who's Who in American Art*, Vol. I, 188.

12. Margaret Lynne Ausfeld, "Anne Wilson Goldthwaite," *Eight Southern Women* (Green ville, SC: Greenville County Museum of Art, 1986), 12.

13. Ausfeld, "Anne Wilson Goldthwaite," 14.

14. Martin Birnbaum, *Jacovleff and Other Artists; Alexandre Jacovleff, William Blake and other illustrators of Dante, Thomas Rowlandson, Aubrey Beardsley, Marcus Behmer, Arthur Rackham, Hermann Struck, Anne Goldthwaite* (New York: P.A. Struck, 1946), 226.

15. Ausfeld, "Anne Wilson Goldthwaite," 14.

Appendix

1. Florence Loeb Kellogg, "Art Becomes Public Works," http://newdeal.feri.org/survey/ 34279.htm.

2. Biddle, "An Art Renascence under Federal Patronage," 428.

3. Biddle, "An Art Renascence under Federal Patronage," 430.

4. "History of the New Deal Projects," http://www.wpamurals.com/history.html.

5. O'Connor, *Federal Art Patronage*, 12, copyright Dr. Francis V. O'Connor, 1966.

6. Jerry Adler, "1934: The Art of the New Deal an Exhibition of Depression-Era Paintings by Federally-Funded Artists Provides a Hopeful View of Life During Economic Travails," *Smithsonian Magazine*, June 2009, http://www. smithsonianmag.com/arts-culture/1934-the-art-of-the-new-deal-132242698/.

7. "History of the New Deal Projects." http://www.wpamurals.com/history.html.

8. O'Connor, *Federal Art Patronage*, 12–13.

9. "Post Office Murals," http://uca.edu/post officemurals/.

10. "History of the New Deal Art Projects," http://www.wpamurals.com/history.html.

11. "Post Office Murals," http://uca.edu/post officemurals/.

12. Barbara Melosh, *Engendering Culture: Manhood and Womanhood in New Deal Public Art and Theatre* (Washington, D.C.: Smithsonian Press, 1991), 222.

13. Park and Markowitz, *Democratic Vistas*, 8.

14. "Post Office Murals," http://uca.edu/post officemurals/.

15. "Post Office Murals," http://uca.edu/post officemurals/.

16. "History of the New Deal Projects," http://www.wpamurals.com/history.html.

17. O'Connor, *Federal Art Patronage*, 20.

18. "48 States Competition," http://www. wpamurals.com/48states.htm.

19. O'Connor, *Federal Art Patronage*, 6.

20. O'Connor, *Federal Art Patronage*, 26.

21. "History of the New Deal Projects," http://www.wpamurals.com/history.html.

22. O'Connor, *Federal Art Patronage*, 26–27.

23. "History of the New Deal Projects," http://www.wpamurals.com/history.html.

24. O'Connor, *Federal Art Patronage*, 26–27.

25. "History of the New Deal Projects," http://www.wpamurals.com/history.html.

26. Editors of Encyclopedia Britannica, "WPA Federal Art Project," http://www.britannica.com/EBchecked/topic/649339/WPA-Federal-Art-Project.

27. O'Connor, *Federal Art Patronage*, 28.

28. O'Connor, *Federal Art Patronage*, 28.

Bibliography

PRINT MATERIALS

Advertiser Democrat, November 29, 1933, as cited by Brown, Elizabeth Ann. *National Register of Historic Places Registration Form: Guntersville Post Office Building.* July 7, 2010.

Agee, James, and Walker Evans. *Cotton Tenants*. Brooklyn: Melville House, 2013.

Alabama Historical Commission. Preservation Report. U.S. Post Office, Guntersville, Marshall County: *Indians Receiving Gifts from the Spanish*. November-December 2010.

Alexander City Library Staff. "Alexander City Library Retires Two Public Servants." *Alabama Currents,* January-February 2013.

"Arthur Getz, 82, Magazine Illustrator." *New York Times*, January 22, 1996.

"Artist Records Coast Guard's Iceberg Patrol." *Life* 8, no. 1 (January 1, 1940), 30–31.

"Artists & Their Work in *The Birmingham Scene* Exhibition." *The Birmingham Historical Society Newsletter* (November 2011), 1–2.

Ausfeld, Margaret Lynne. "Anne Wilson Goldthwaite." *Eight Southern Women*. Greenville, SC: Greenville County Museum of Art, 1986.

Bailey, Hugh C. "Alabama." *Merit Students Encyclopedia, Volume 1.* New York: Crowell-Collier Educational Corporation, 1969.

Barlow, Margaret. *Women Artists*. Hong Kong: Hugh Lauter Levin Associates, 1999.

Bass, Josephine Lindsay. July 26, 1996, condensation of Kennamer, John Robert, Sr. *History of Jackson County Alabama*. Scottsboro: Jackson County Historical Association, 1935.

Beckham, Sue Bridwell. *Depression Post Office Murals and Southern Culture: A Gentle Reconstruction.* Baton Rouge: Louisiana State University Press, 1989.

Berkshire Eagle. Pittsfield, Massachusetts, April 16, 1943.

Biddle, George. "An Art Renascence Under Federal Patronage." *Scribner's Magazine,* June 1934.

Biles, Roger. *The South and the New Deal.* Lexington: University of Kentucky Press, 1994.

Birnbaum, Martin. *Jacovleff and Other Artists; Alexandre Jacovleff, William Blake and Other Illustrators of Dante, Thomas Rowlandson, Aubrey Beardsley, Marcus Behmer, Arthur Rackham, Hermann Struck, Anne Goldthwaite.* New York: P.A. Struck, 1946.

Brown, Elizabeth Ann. *National Register of Historic Places Registration Form: Guntersville Post Office Building.* July 7, 2010.

Brownell, Elizabeth R. *They Lived in Tubac.* Tucson: Westernlore Press, 1986.

Bruce, Edward, and Forbes Watson. *Art in Federal Buildings. Volume I: Mural Designs, 1934–1936.* Washington, D.C.: Art in Federal Buildings Incorporated, 1936.

Bruce, Kate. "Ethel Edwards." *KnowLA Encyclopedia of Louisiana,* edited by David C.W. Short and R. Stanley-Brown. *Public Buildings: Architecture Under the Public Works Administration: 1933 to 1939.* Washington, D.C.: U.S. Government Printing Office, 1939, page 338.

Carter, Dan T. *Scottsboro: A Tragedy of the American South.* Baton Rouge: Louisiana State University Press, 1969.

Chitwood, Oliver Perry, Frank Lawrence Owsley, and H. C. Nixon. *The United States from Colony to World Power.* New York: D. Van Nostrand, 1953.

Clarke, Georgine. "Art Trails in Alabama Public Art: Continuing the Trail." *Alabama Arts* XXI, no. 2, 32–33.

Clinton, William J. "President William J. Clinton's Remarks." *Tuskegee's Truths Rethinking the Tuskegee Syphilis Study,* edited by Susan M. Reverby, 574–77. Chapel Hill: University of North Carolina Press, 2000, and as cited in Reverby, Susan M. *Examining Tuskegee: The Infamous Syphilis Study and Its Legacy.* Chapel Hill: University of North Carolina Press, 2009.

Coffee County Heritage Book Committee. *The Heritage of Coffee County, Alabama.* Clanton, AL: Heritage, 2002.

Concise Dictionary of American Biography. New York: Scribner's, 1977.

"Controversial Post Office Mural to Be Restored." *Natick Bulletin & Tab* (Massachusetts).

Davis, Anita Price. *North Carolina During the Great Depression.* Jefferson, NC: McFarland, 2003.

"Depot Days Festival Rolls into Hartselle September 20." *49 County News.* August 27, 2014.

Dolinger, Milt. "How CSX Got Its Name." *Trains,* May 1, 2006.

Dunford, Penny. *A Biographical Dictionary of Women Artists in Europe and America Since 1850.* New York: Harvester Wheatsheaf, 1990.

Evan Terry Associates. *Pocket Guide to the ADA: Americans with Disabilities Act Accessibility Guidelines for Buildings and Facilities.* Hoboken, NJ: John Wiley, 2007.

"Exhibition Artists: Paul Arlt." Smithsonian Institution Traveling Exhibition Service, NASA/ART. Files of Jimmy S. Emerson.

Falk, Peter Hastings. *Who's Who in American Art,* Volume I. Guilford, CT: Sound View Press, 1985.

Farm Journal. December 1931.

Grimes, Lydia. *Brewton and East Brewton.* Mount Pleasant, SC: Arcadia, 2011.

"Hartselle, Alabama." *Rand McNally World Atlas.* Chicago: Rand McNally, 1968.

Holland, Lee Eudon, Laurie A. Pallazolo, and Danny Kanat. *Boiled Peanuts and Buckeyes: A Memoir-Novel.* Northville, MI: Ferne Press, 2006.

Hultquist, Clark, and Carey Heatherly. *Images of America: Montevallo.* Mt. Pleasant, SC: Arcadia, 2011.

Jahoda, Gloria. *The Trail of Tears: The Story of the American Indian Removals 1813–1855.* New York: Holt, Rinehart and Winston, 1975.

Jennings, Peter, and Todd Brewster. *The Century.* New York: Doubleday, 1998.

"John Hollis Bankhead (1842–1920)." *Concise Dictionary of American Biography.* New York: Scribner's, 1977.

Kammen, Michael. *Robert Gwathmey: The Life and Art of a Passionate Observer.* Chapel Hill: University of North Carolina, 1999.

Kennamer, John Robert, Sr. *History of Jackson County Alabama.* Scottsboro: Jackson County Historical Association, 1935 (reprinted 1993).

Key, Jay B. "John Hollis Bankhead (July 8, 1872–June 12, 1846)." *Dictionary of American Biography.* New York: Scribner's, 1974.

Kinsley, Shaw. *Images of America: TUBAC.* Charleston, SC: Arcadia, 2009.

Kuykendall, James Ray, and Elizabeth S. Howard. "Reminiscing About DeKalb's Special People ... the Post Office Mural." *The DeKalb Advertiser,* June 5, 2003.

Letter from Dallan C. Wordekemper to Jimmy S. Emerson, January 9, 2006.

Letter from Lee R. Warthen to Postmaster of the Hartselle Post Office, May 20, 1941. Courtesy Kathryn Smith, granddaughter of Lee R. Warthen.

Letter to Section of Fine Arts, Public Buildings Administration, Federal Works Agency from William Sherrod McCall. Files of Jimmy S. Emerson.

Lyles, John. *Images of America: Phenix City.* Charleston, SC: Arcadia, 2010.

Marling, Karal Ann. *Wall-to-Wall America.* Minneapolis: University of Minnesota Press, 1982.

Mayer, Ralph. *A Dictionary of Art Terms and Techniques.* New York: Thomas Y. Crowell, 1969.

McCall, William Sherrod. *"Early Settlers Weighing Cotton*: Mural Panel for Post Office, Montevallo, Alabama." Files of Jimmy S. Emerson.

McElvaine, Robert S. *Down and Out in the Great Depression.* Chapel Hill: University of North Carolina Press, 1983.

Melosh, Barbara. *Engendering Culture: Manhood and Womanhood in New Deal Public Art and Theatre.* Washington, D.C.: Smithsonian Press, 1991.

Meltzer, Milton. *Violins and Shovels.* New York: Delacorte Press, 1976.

Moore, Albert Burton. *History of Alabama.* Tuscaloosa: Alabama Book Store, 1951.

"Murals, Murals Artists." *Birmingham Historical Society Newsletter,* November 2010, 2.

"New Deal Art in Alabama Post Offices and Federal Buildings." *Alabama Art: Art Trails in Alabama Public Arts* XXI, no. 2.

Noles, James L., Jr. *Hearts of Dixie: Fifty Alabamians and the State They Called Home.* Birmingham: Will Publishing, 2004.

Noles, Jim. "An Unlikely Canvas." *Alabama Heritage,* 75 (Winter 2005), 42–43.

Opitz, Glenn B. *Mantle Fielding's Dictionary of American Painters, Sculptors, and Engravers.* Poughkeepsie: Apollo Book, 1986.

"Painting." *Compton's Pictured Encyclopedia and Fact-Index, Volume 11.* Chicago: F.E. Compton, 1948.

Park, Marlene, and Gerald E. Markowitz. *Democratic Vistas: Post Offices and Public Art in the New Deal.* Philadelphia: Temple University Press, 1984.

Peet, Phyllis. "Goldthwaite, Anne (1869–1944)." *North American Women Artists of the Twentieth Century: A Biographical Dictionary,* edited by Jules Heller and Nancy G. Heller. New York: Garland, 1995.

Piehl, Charles K. "The Eutaw Mural and Southern Art of Robert Gwathmey." *The Alabama Review,* April 1992.

"PO Mural Shows First White Men to Come Here." *Time,* December 10, 1947.

"Postoffice Dedication to Be Monday; Public Will Be Given Opportunity to Inspect Entire $115,000 Building." *The Guntersville Gleam.* May 29, 1941, 1, 3.

Purser, Stuart. *The Drawing Handbook.* Worcester, MA: Davis Publications, 1976.

Rand McNally World Atlas. Chicago: Rand McNally, 1968.

Reverby, Susan M. *Examining Tuskegee: The Infamous Syphilis Study and Its Legacy.* Chapel Hill: University of North Carolina Press, 2009, page 225.

Rogers, William Warren, Robert David Ward, Leah Rawls Atkins, and Wayne Flynt. *Alabama: The History of a Deep Southern State.* Tuscaloosa: University of Alabama Press, 1994.

Rollins College. "Faculty File 45-E for Constance Ortmayer." Courtesy Rollins College.

Rowan, Edward (Assistant Chief, Section of Fine Arts) to Hollis Holbrook, University of Florida, School of Architecture, September 26, 1939.

Section of Fine Arts. "Mural Painting by William McCall." Files of Jimmy S. Emerson.

Shell, Eddie Wayne. *Evolution of the Alabama Agroecosystem: Always Keeping Up, but Never Catching Up.* Montgomery: NewSouth Books, 2013.
"Siding." *Webster's New Unabridged Dictionary.* New York: Dorset & Baber, 1979.
Smith, Jeanette M. *Yellow Calla Lilies. JAMA.* 310, no. 17, November 6, 2013, 1774–1775.
"Speaking of Pictures: This Is Mural America for Rural Americans." *Life,* December 4, 1939.
Starck, Jeff. "Cincinnati Music Center Coin Designer Has Varied Career." *Coin World,* March 29, 2010.
Taylor, Lonn. "Xavier Gonzalez: Muralist in the Big Bend." *Cenizo Journal* 2, no. 3 (Third Quarter 2010), 10–11.
Time-Life Editors. *This Fabulous Century: 1930–1940,* Volume IV. New York: Time-Life Books, 1969.
United States Census Bureau. "Annual Estimates of the Resident Population: April 1, 2010 to July 1, 2013."
Weathersby, William. "Wandering Artist Relates Story of Colorful Career." *Times-Picayune* (New Orleans), June 27, 1937.
Wilson, Sandra S., abstractor. "City Cemetery (It was once called "Laurel Park Cemetery."): "Charles T. Porch Center." *Tallapoosa County Archives,* 1994.

Web Sites

"About Huntsville." http://www.huntsvilleal.gov/about/index.php.
"About Huntsville." http://www.huntsvilleal.gov/news/Huntsville_Community_Information.pdf.
"About Luverne, Alabama." https://www.facebook.com/pages/Luverne-Alabama/108638815826702#.
"Adelia M. Russell Library." http://www.alexandercityonline.com/amrl-history.html.
"Adelia M. Russell Library." http://www.amrlibrary.net/index.php/en/2013-03-05-22-24-15.
Adler, Jerry. "1934: The Art of the New Deal an Exhibition of Depression-Era Paintings by Federally-Funded Artists Provides a Hopeful View of Life During Economic Travails." *Smithsonian Magazine,* June 2009. http://www.smithsonianmag.com/arts-culture/1934-the-art-of-the-new-deal-132242698/.
Ahnert, Frank. "Cumberland Plateau." *Merit Students Encyclopedia,* Vol. 5 (Springfield, OH: Crowell-Collier Educational Corporation), 1969.
"Alabama: The Heart of the New Industrial South." *Compton's Pictured Encyclopedia and Fact-Index,* Vol. I (Chicago: F. E. Compton), 1948.
"Alabama and Florida Railway Company." http://www.allenrailroad.com/shortline trader/Alabama_&_Florida_Railway_Co.htm.
Alabama Department of Archives and History. "New Deal Art in Alabama Post Offices and Federal Buildings." http://www.alabamamoments.state.al.us/sec49det.html.
Alabama Historical Association. "Pickens County Courthouse." http://www.civilwaralbum.com/ miscl4/2010/carrolton2lg.jpg.
Alabama Historical Commission. "Alabama Register Property Information: 1995." http://preserveala.org/ARdigital/Blount/AL.BlountCounty.OneontaPostOffice.pdf.
Alabama Moments from American History. "New Deal Art in Alabama Post Offices and Federal Buildings: Eutaw." http://www.alabamamoments.alabama.gov/sec49 det.html.
"Alabama Railfan." http://www.alabamarailfan.com/railfanning.php?location=cullman.
"Alabama's Highest and Lowest Elevations." http://www.classbrain.com/artstate/pub lish/AL_highest_lowest_elevation.shtml.
"Aldis Birdseye Browne, II." http://www.askart.com/AskART/artists/biography.aspx?artist=101498.
"Alexander City." http:wikipedia.org/wiki/Alexander_City.

"Anne Wilson Goldthwaite." http://www.findagrave.com.

"Anne Wilson Goldthwaite: Johnson Collection, LLC." http://thejohnsoncollection.org/anne-wilson-goldthwaite.

"Art Deco." In *Encyclopedia Britannica*. Retrieved from http://www.britannica.com/EBchecked/topic/36505/Art-Deco.

"Arthur Getz." http://en.wikipedia.org/wiki/Arthur_Getz.

Arts Connected. "ArtsNet Minnesota: Identity: Robert Gwathmey." ArtsNet Minnesota: Identity: Robert Gwathmey. Arts Net Minnesota, n.d. Web. 5 May 2013.

Ausfeld, Margaret Lynne. "John Kelly Fitzpatrick." *Encyclopedia of Alabama*. http://www.encyclopediaofalabama.org/face/Article.jsp?id=h-1155.

Bernstein, Fred A. "Charles Gwathmey, Architect Loyal to Aesthetics of High Modernism, Dies at 71." http://www.nytimes.com/2009/08/05/arts/design/05gwathmey.html?scp=2&_r=0.

"Best Cities: It's All About Jobs." http://www.kiplinger.com/article/business/T012-C000-S002-best-cities-it-s-all-about-jobs.html.

"Biography for Robert Gwathmey." *Archives of AskART*, http://www.askart.com/AskART/artists/biography.aspx?artist=23904.

Blogger Jen. "Marble Towns Blog: Charles Pawson Atmore [1834–1900]—Cave Hill Cemetery." October 28, 2012. http://marbletowns.com/?s=atmor&search=Go.

Blount County Historic Marker. Photographed by Jimmy Emerson. https://www.flickr.com/photos/auvet/3081314114/in/photolist-a2PSdD-5Ghxkq-a2PSdH-5Ghxkm.

Blount-Oneonta Chamber of Commerce. "Blount County Covered Bridge Festival." http://bocc.publishpath.com/covered-bridge-festival.

"Boll Weevil." *Encyclopedia Britannica. Encyclopedia Britannica Online Academic Edition.* Encyclopedia Britannica, 2014. Web. 7 Aug. 2014. http://0-www.britannica.com.marie.converse.edu/EBchecked/topic/72178/boll-weevil.

Booker Taliaferro Washington. Biography.com. Retrieved 07:10, Nov. 2, 2014, from http://www.biography.com/people/booker-t-washington-9524663.

Boswell, Mayor Kenneth. "Enterprise, Alabama." http://www.enterpriseal.gov/.

"Brewton." http://www.city-data.com/city/Brewton-Alabama.html#ixzz38lCMgeyx.

"Brewton, Alabama." http://www.brewton.org/.

"Brewton Tourism Guide." http://www.villageprofile.com/alabama/brewton/tourism.htm.

"Captain Richard W. Goldthwaite." http://www.findagrave.com.

"Carrollton, Alabama." http://www.city-data.com/city/Carrollton-Alabama.html.

Center for Biological Diversity. "Outlawing Rattlesnake Rodeos." http://www.biological diversity.org/campaigns/outlawing_rattlesnake_roundups/index.html.

Chamber of Commerce. "Greater Brewton Area: August 23, 2014." http://www.brewton-chamber.com/.

"Change of View: Fabric Designer, Harwood Steiger." http://madpatterdesign.blogspot.com/2013/02/fabric-designer-harwood-steiger.html.

"Charles Russell Hardman." http://www.findagrave.com.

"City Data for Fairfield, Alabama." http://www.city-data.com/city/Fairfield-Alabama.html.

"City of Haleyville, Alabama." http://www.nacolg.com/Community_Planning/Documents/HaleyvilleComprehensivePlan_5-16-08.pdf.

"City of Luverne: Educational Attainment." http://www.luverne.org/profile.asp.

"City of Montevallo: University of Montevallo." http://montevallo.homestead.com/universityofmontevallo.html.

"City of Opp." http://www.cityofopp.com/Content/Default/1/28/0/about/our-history.html.

"City of Opp: Rattlesnake Rodeo." http://www.cityofopp.com/Content/Default/7/7/0/rattlesnake-rodeo/rattlesnake-rodeo.html.

"City of Phenix, Alabama: History." http://www.phenixcityal.us/Default.asp?ID=5&pg=History.

City of Tuskegee. "Welcome to Tuskegee, Alabama." http://www.tuskegeealabama.gov/.
"Colonial Revival Style: 1880–1960." http://www.portal.state.pa.us/portal/server.pt/com
munity/late_19th_early_20th_century_ revival_period/2390/colonial_revival_
style/294769.
Commemorative Air Force. "Red Tail Squadron." http://www.redtail.org/.
"Community Data: Ozark and Dale County." http://ozarkalchamber.com/home/Com
munityData.aspx.
Conn, Robin. "Cornerstone of the Guntersville Post Office." http://photos.al.com/hunts
ville-times/2010/09/guntersville_post_office_3.html.
"Constance Ortmayer (1902–1988): Renowned Artisan and Professor of Sculpture."
http://lib.rollins.edu/olin/oldsite/archives/golden/Ortmayer.htm.
The Courthouse Lover. Cornerstone of Opp, Alabama, Post Office, as seen on Flickr.
"The Covered Bridge Trail in Blount County." http://co.blount.al.us/documents/Cov
ered+Bridge+Trail.pdf.
Cowan, Barry C. "Conrad Albrizio." *Know LA: Encyclopedia of Louisiana.* http://www.
knowla.org/entry/583/.
Cox, Dale. "Fort Payne, Alabama." http://www.exploresouthernhistory.com/fortpayne.
html.
"Crenshaw County Profile." http://www.luverne.org/profile.asp.
"Cumberland Plateau." *Encyclopedia Britannica. Encyclopedia Britannica Online Academic Edition.* Encyclopedia Britannica, 2014. Web. 26 Aug. 2014.
"Dale County Sheriff's Office." http://daleso.com/contact.
The DC Voter. *League of Women Voters of the District of Columbia.* Volume 77, Number
6, June 2001. http://www.dcwatch.com/lwvdc/lwv0106.htm.
"Decline of the Hosiery Industry." http://blog.al.com/huntsville-times-business/2011/
04/the_decline_of_the_hosiery_ind.html.
deVillemaretta, Cynthia. "Fabric Designer, Harwood Steiger." http://madpatterdesign.
blogspot.com/search?q=steiger.
"Discovering Harwood Steiger." http://gotvintageshops.blogspot.com/2014/02/vintage-
fabrics-steiger.html.
Duncan, Erika. "ENCOUNTERS; 'I Just Quit,' Rosalie Gwathmey Said. And She Walked
Away." http://www.nytimes.com/1994/09/04/nyregion/encounters-i-just-quit-ros
alie-gwathmey-said-and-she-walked-away.html.
"Early Days In and Around Montevallo." http://www.rootsweb.ancestry.com/~alshelby/
Montevallo.html.
Editors of Encyclopedia Britannica. "WPA Federal Art Project." http://www.britannica.
com/EBchecked/topic/649339/WPA-Federal-Art-Project.
Emerson, Jimmy S. "Caption for Photograph of the Russell County Courthouse in
Phenix City, Alabama." https://www.flickr.com/photos/auvet/3174824861/in/pho
tolist-Heiem-6DAhTk-5QxNPF-bcFH2Z-HehmD.
"Enterprise, Alabama: Boll Weevil Monument." http://www.roadsideamerica.com/tip/19.
"Enterprise Public Library: General Information." http://www.enterpriselibrary.org/
Default.asp?ID=480.
"ePODUNK Home Towns Index." http://www.epodunk.com/top10/home_towns/towns.
html.
"Epping, Franc (Dorothy)." Ancestry.com.
"Escambia County Alabama: History." http://www.archives.state.al.us/counties/escam
bia.html.
*An Exhibition of Art from the Marine Corps Museum: 75 Years of Marine Corps Avia-
tion—A Tribute* (exhibit brochure; distribution is unlimited). http://www.marines.
mil/Portals/59/Publications/75%20Years%20of%20Marine%20Corps%20Aviation
%20-%20A%20Tribute%20%20PCN%2019000416100_1.pdf.

"FDR Library's List of New Deal Projects." http://viewshare.org/views/kcarter/fdr-librarys-list-of-new-deal-projects-part–1/.

"Ferol Sibley Warthen and the Provincetown Print." March 19, 2010. http://anurbancottage.blogspot/2010/03/ferol-sibley-warthen-and-provincetown-print.

"Ferol Sibley Warthen; Kathi Smith." *Provincetown Art Guide*, http://provincetownartguide.com/2008/article3.htm.

"Festival and Event Calendar." http://alabama.travel/upcoming-events/search?q=Luverne.

FilmMakers Magazine. "Stanley Kubrick Biography." http://www.filmmakers.com/artists/Kubrick/biography Gombach Group.

"48 States Competition." http://www.wpamurals.com/48states.htm.

"Frank H.T. Rhodes Exemplary Alumni Service Award." http://ezramagazine.cornell.edu/Update/July13/EU.FHTR.awards.html.

"Frank Hartley Anderson." http://www.bhamwiki.com/w/Frank_Hartley_Anderson.

"Frank Hartley Anderson (1890–1947)." *Imprinting the South: Works on Paper from the Collection of Lynn Barstis Williams and Stephen J. Goldfarb*. http://www.tfaoi.com/aa/9aa/9aa236.htm.

"Franklin County." *Encyclopedia of Alabama*, http://www.encyclopediaofalabama.org/face/Article.jsp?id=h-1338.

"Franklin County: Our History." http://www.franklincountyal.org/our-history.html.

"Friendliest City in the South." http://www.luverne.org/history.asp.

Futility Closet. "A Virtue of Necessity." http://www.futilitycloset.com/2011/07/30/a-virtue-of-necessity.

"Galleries: John Kelly Fitzpatrick." http://www.encyclopediaofalabama.org/face/Galleries.jsp?id=e-104.

"Getz: *The New Yorker* Covers." http://www.getzart.com/nycovers.htm.

Haleyville Chamber of Commerce. "Haleyville City: A Community of Excellence." http://www.haleyvillechamber.org/pages/history.html.

"Haleyville City: A Community of Excellence." http://www.haleyvillechamber.org/pages/history.html.

"Hans Mangelsdorf." http://www.askart.com/askart/m/hans_mangelsdorf/hans_mangelsdorf.aspx.

Harold Feinstein, photog. "Up-date on the Photo League Negatives: Rosalie Gwathmey Shares Her Work at a Photo League Meeting, 1947." http://haroldfeinstein.com/up-date-on-the-photo-league-negatives/.

Harris, Mark. *Kelly Fitzpatrick Memorial Gallery*. 408 South Main Sreet, Wetumpka, Alabama.

"Harry S. Truman Federal Building, Washington, DC." http://www.gsa.gov/portal/ext/html/site/hb/category/25431/actionParameter/exploreByBuilding/buildingId/700.

"Hartselle, Alabama." http://en.wikipedia.org/wiki/Hartselle,_Alabama.

"Harwood Steiger (1900–1980)." *AskART: Worldwide Edition*. Information provided by Covington Fine Arts Gallery, Inc., http://askart.com/AskART/artists/biography/aspx?artist=100147.

"History of Hartselle." http://www.hartsellechamber.com/.

"The History of 911 Emergency Calls." http://inventors.about.com/library/inventors/bl911.htm.

Henbeveld, Dennis. "1936 Cincinnati Music Center Half Dollar." http://news.coinupdate.com/cincinnati-music-center-half-dollar-4465/.

Henricks, Karen I. Peterson. "New Deal Art in Alabama Post Offices and Federal Buildings: Opp, Alabama." http://www.alabamamoments.alabama.gov/sec49det.html.

Hines, Katie. "History in Pickens: The Farmer, the Politician, the Artist and the Cow." *Dateline Pickens: Pickens' Weekly Webzine*. September 12, 2003, October 11, 2003. http://www.datelinepickens.com/historyinpickens/mural.shtml.

"History of the New Deal Art Projects." http://www.wpamurals.com/history.html.
Holley, Joe. "Longtime Washington Artist, Political Cartoonist Paul Arlt Dies." *Washington Post,* Friday, September 23, 2005. http://www.washingtonpost.com/wp-dyn/content/article/2005/09/22/AR2005092202047.html.
"Jeff." *Good Reads.com.* https://www.goodreads.com/topic/show/1090983-the-union-passenger-terminal-mural#comment_form.
"John Kelly Fitzpatrick: Wetumpka City Cemetery." http://www.findagrave.com.
"John von Wicht." http://www.annexgalleries.com/artists/biography/2457/Wicht/John.
Johnson Collection. "John Kelly Fitzpatrick." http://thejohnsoncollection.org/john-kelly-fitzpatrick/.
Kaetz, James P. "Opp." http://www.encyclopediaofalabama.org/face/Article.jsp?id=h-3160.
"Kathryn Lee Smith." *Provincetown Art Registry,* http://www.provincetownartistregistry.com/S/smith_kathi.html.
Kellogg, Florence Loeb. "Art Becomes Public Works." *Survey Graphic,* 23, no. 6 (June 1934), p. 279. http://newdeal.feri.org/survey/34279.htm.
"Latitude 34 North." http://www.lat34north.com/historicmarkersal/MarkerDefinition.cfm.
"Lee Roland Warthen." http://www.askart.com/AskART/artists/search/Search_Grid.aspx?searchtype=BOOKS&artist=108382.
"Lee Roland Warthen." http://www.findagrave.com.
Loke, Margarett. "Rosalie Gwathmey, 92, a Photographer of Southern Black Life." http://www.nytimes.com/2001/02/16/arts/rosalie-gwathmey-92-a-photographer-of-southern-black-life.html.
"Louis A. Simon, Architect [1867–1958]." Gombach Group. http://www.livingplaces.com/people/louis-a-simon.html.
Louisiana Endowment for the Humanities, 2010– . Article published September 12, 2012. http://www.knowla.org/entry/1245/.
"Louisville and National Railroad." http://en.wikipedia.org/wiki/Louisville_and_Nashville_Railroad.
"Lucy Boyd *Armistead* Goldthwaite." http://www.findagrave.com.
"Main Street." http://www.mainstreetalabama.org/alexander-city/.
Maloney, Christopher. "Fairfield." *Encyclopedia of Alabama.* http://www.encyclopediaofalabama.org/face/Article.jsp?id=h-3142.
"Massachusetts, Town and Vital Records, 1620–1988—AncestryLibrary.com." http://search.ancestry.com.
McAlister, Jordan. "1938 Phenix City Post Office." https://www.flickr.com/search/?q=phenix%20city%20post%20office%20alabama.
Medina, Jennifer. "Paul T. Arlt, Artist and Cartoonist, 91, Dies." *New York Times,* September 26, 2005. http://www.nytimes.com/2005/09/26/nyregion/26arlt.html?_r=0.
"Mission: Berea College." http://www.berea.edu/about/files/2012/08/GreatCommitments.pdf.
"Mobile, Alabama." http://en.wikipedia.org/wiki/Mobile,_Alabama.
"Montevallo, Alabama." http://www.city-data.com/city/Montevallo-Alabama.html.
Morton, Patricia Hoskins. "Franklin County." *Encyclopedia of Alabama.* http://eoatest.auburn.edu/drupal/article/h-1338#sthash.
Morton, Patricia Hoskins. "Greene County." http://www.encyclopediaofalabama.org/face/Article.jsp?id=h-1329.
"Municipal Arts Society of New York City." http://www.mas.org/summitnyc/speakers/ronay-menschel/.
"Muscogee." http://en.wikipedia.org/wiki/Muscogee.
National Park Service. "Focus: United States Court House and Post Office, Huntsville, Alabama." http://image1.nps.gov:9001/StyleServer/calcrgn?cat=NRHP&item=Text/

81000129.djvu&style=nps/FOCUS-DJview.xsl&wid=640&hei=480&oif=jpeg& props=item(SUMMARY,COPYRIGHT),cat(Name)&page=0.

National Trust for Historic Preservation. "America's Dozen Distinctive Destinations for 2010." http://www.preservationdirectory.com/PreservationBlogs/ArticleDetail.aspx ?id=405&catid=12.

Navarro, Meghan. "Indians at the Post Office: Native Themes in New Deal-Era Murals." http://npm.si.edu/indiansatthepostoffice/mural16.html\.

"New Deal Art During the Great Depression." http://www.wpamurals.com/.

"New Deal Art in Alabama Post Offices and Federal Buildings." http://www.alabamamo ments.alabama.gov/sec49det.html.

"The New Deal in Jefferson County: An Alphabet Soup." http://www.bponline.org/ resources/exhibits/new_deal/murals/Fairfield/gall.

O'Connor, Francis V. *Federal Art Patronage: 1933 to 1943: An Exhibition. April 6 to May 13, 1966, University of Maryland Art Gallery, J. Millard Tawes Fine Arts Center, College Park, Maryland.* Copyright by Dr. Francis V. O'Connor, 1966. Catalog designed by Ralph Freeny. https://openlibrary.org/works/OL4429683W/Federal_art_patron age_1933_to_1943.

"Oneonta." http://livingnewdeal.berkeley.edu/projects/old-post-office-mural-oneonta-al/.

"Oneonta: A Small Town with Big Ideas." http://www.cityofoneonta.us/visitors/about-oneonta.html.

"Oneonta, Alabama." http://www.city-data.com/city/Oneonta-Alabama.html.

"Opp, Alabama." http://en.wikipedia.org/wiki/Opp,_Alabama.

"Ozark, Alabama." http://en.wikipedia.org/wiki/Ozark,_Alabama.

"Ozark: The Heart of Dale County." http://www.villageprofile.com/alabama/ozark/his tory.html.

"Phenix City." *Encyclopedia of Alabama*, http://www.encyclopediaofalabama.org/face/ Article.jsp?id=h-2133.

"Policies and Procedures." *Berea College Catalog.* (Online catalog, with no pagination). http://catalog.berea.edu/current/Catalog/Policies-and-Procedures.

"Post: This Belongs in a Museum." http://thisbelongsinamuseum.com/post/551844904 77/in-enterprise-alabama-one-will-find-a-wal-mart.

"Post Office Mural *How Happy Was the Occasion*: Clarksville, Arkansas." http://living newdeal.berkeley.edu/projects/post-office-mural-happy-occasion-clarksville-ar/.

"Post Office Murals." http://uca.edu/postofficemurals/.

"Post Office Murals: Miami Beach, Florida." http://livingnewdeal.berkeley.edu/artists/ charles-russell-hardman/.

"Profile for Luverne, Alabama, AL." http://www.epodunk.com/cgi-bin/genInfo.php?loc Index=12051.

Purser Studio. "Biography: Stuart Purser." http://www.purserstudio.com/sBio.html.

Raynor, Patricia. "New Deal Post Office Murals." *Articles from EnRoute* 6, no. 4 (October–December 1997). http://www.wpamurals.com/OffWall.pdf.

"Robert Gwathmey." http://en.wikipedia.org/wiki/Robert_Gwathmey.

"Rollins University Alumnae Connections." http://www.rollins.edu/alumnae/archive_ 2007.htm.

"Rosalie Gwathmey: Photographed Blacks in 1940s." Obituary: February 25, 2001. http:// articles.latimes.com/2001/feb/25/local/me-30234.

Roylance, Frank. "A Family Tree's American Tale." John Gunter Family Tree." http://articles. baltimoresun.com/2001-03-11/topic/0103100129_1_john-gunter-augustus-chero kee.

Saba, Natalie D. "Nathanael Greene (1742–1786)." *New Georgia Encyclopedia*, 11 August 2013. Web. 9 August 2014.

"Save the Post Office." http://www.savethepostoffice.com/about.

"Scottsboro, Alabama." http://en.wikipedia.org/wiki/Scottsboro,_Alabama#Early_history.

"Scottsboro, Alabama." http://www.citytowninfo.com/places/alabama/Scottsboro.

Section of Fine Arts, Public Buildings Administration, Federal Works Agency. "Mural Painting by John Von Wicht: *Logging*." http://www.caldwellgallery.com/bios/von wichtbio.html.

Shaw, Charles R. "Welcome Home." http://www.alexandercityonline.com/index.html.

Smith, Kathryn Lee Smith. "Contemporary White Line Prints." http://www.kathrynlee smithwhitelineprints.com/resume.htm.

"Southern Arizona's Colony & The First European Settlement in Arizona: Tubac: Founded 1752." http://www.tubacarizona.com/.

"Summary of the John Von Wicht papers, 1950–1970." Archives of American Art, Smithsonian Institution. http://www.aaa.si.edu/collections/john-von-wicht-papers-9269.

Taos and Santa Fe Painters. "Taos Painters: Bror Julius Olsson Nordfeldt." http://www.bjonordfeldtpaintings.com/.

"Texas Cotton Gin Museum." http://www.cottonginmuseum.org/museum.htm.

"Tubac: Santa Cruz County, Arizona." http://visittubac.com/.

"Tuskegee." http://www.encyclopediaofalabama.org/face/Article.jsp?id=h-2051.

"Unclaimed Baggage Center." http://www.unclaimedbaggage.com/about/.

"U.S. Army Engineer Base Yard." http://www.history.army.mil/html/artphoto/pripos/finalstages.html.

"United States Coast Guard Academy: Hamilton Hall." http://www.cga.edu/campus2.aspx?id=504.

"U.S. Post Office and Courthouse, Huntsville, AL." http://www.gsa.gov/portal/ext/html/site/hb/category/25431/actionParameter/exploreByBuilding/buildingId/668.

"Welcome to Historic Montevallo." http://www.hmdb.org/marker.asp?marker=37178.

"Welcome to Scottsboro—Someplace Special." http://www.cityofscottsboro.com/.

"William B. Bankhead National Forest." http://www.stateparks.com/william_b_bankhead_national_forest_in_alabama.html.

"William Sherrod McCall." http://www.findagrave.com.

Wilson, Claire M. "*Encyclopedia of Alabama: Brewton*." http://www.encyclopediaofalabama.org/face/Article.jsp?id=h-2507

Wilson, Claire. "*Encyclopedia of Alabama: Eutaw*." http://www.encyclopediaofalabama.org/face/Article.jsp?id=h-2507.

"Wind Talkers: Navajo Code Talkers in WWII—AMPHIBIOUS ASSAULT on SAIPAN." https://www.awesomestories.com/asset/view/AMPHIBIOUS-ASSAULT-on-SAIPAN-Wind-Talkers-Navajo-Code-Talkers-in-WWII.

"WPA Murals." http://wpamurals.org/florida.html.

"Xavier Gonzalez (1918–1993)." http://www.daviddike.com/artists/181-gonzalez-xavier.html.

"Yours Truly: December 21, 2006." http://yourstrulyforever.blogspot.com/2006/12/some-more-family-history.html.

Zelaya, Lauren A. "Caldwell Gallery: John G. F. Von Wicht," https://www.caldwellgallery.com/bios/vonwichtbio.html.

Zelaya, Lauren A. "Robert Gwathmey (1903–1988)." http://www.caldwellgallery.com/bios/gwathmey_biography.html.

Index

www.ingramcontent.com/pod-product-compliance
Lightning Source LLC
Chambersburg PA
CBHW072134170526
45158CB00004BA/1363